JamesBaldwinReview

Volume Six

In Memoriam

Professor Cheryl Wall (1948–2020) will be hugely missed by *James Baldwin Review*. A Board of Governors Zora Neale Hurston Professor of English at Rutgers University, and author of works including *Women of the Harlem Renaissance* (Indiana University Press, 1995) and *Worrying the Line: Black Women Writers, Lineage, and Literary Tradition* (University of North Carolina Press, 2005), Cheryl Wall was an astute Baldwin scholar. She was also a generous reader and a wise consultant editor, who always brought positive energy with her, along with sage advice.

We invite colleagues and friends to send brief recollections about Professor Wall's life and work, which we will publish in *JBR*. Please send your contributions to *JBR*'s Managing Editor, Justin A. Joyce: joyceja@newschool.edu.

James Baldwin Review

Volume Six

Contents

Introduction

Feature Essay

Essays

Graduate Student Essay Award Winner

Graduate Student Essays

⌐JamesBaldwinReview

James Baldwin Review (*JBR*) is an annual journal that brings together a wide array of peer-reviewed critical and creative non-fiction on the life, writings, and legacy of James Baldwin. In addition to these cutting-edge contributions, each issue contains a review of recent Baldwin scholarship and an award-winning graduate student essay. *James Baldwin Review* publishes essays that invigorate scholarship on James Baldwin; catalyze explorations of the literary, political, and cultural influence of Baldwin's writing and political activism; and deepen our understanding and appreciation of this complex and luminary figure.

It is the aim of *James Baldwin Review* to provide a vibrant and multidisciplinary forum for the international community of Baldwin scholars, students, and enthusiasts.

Editors

Douglas Field, *University of Manchester*
Justin A. Joyce, *The New School*
Dwight A. McBride, *The New School*

Editorial Assistant

Ryan Kendall, *Emory University*

Associate Editors

Houston A. Baker, *Vanderbilt University*
Herb Boyd, *City College of New York*
Matt Brim, *College of Staten Island, CUNY*
Robert Corber, *Trinity College*
Morris Dickstein, *CUNY Graduate Center*
Eddie S. Glaude, *Princeton University*
Clarence E. Hardy III, *Yale University*
Randall Kenan, *University of North Carolina*

D. Quentin Miller, *Suffolk University*
Leah Mirakhor, *Yale University*
Brian Norman, *Simmons University*
Ed Pavlić, *University of Georgia*
Hortense Spillers, *Vanderbilt University*
Eleanor W. Traylor, *Howard University*
Mikko Tuhkanen, *Texas A&M University*
Magdalena J. Zaborowska, *University of Michigan*

Contributing Editors

Victor Anderson, *Vanderbilt University*
Rich Blint, *The New School*
Rashida Braggs, *Williams College*
Margo Natalie Crawford, *University of Pennsylvania*
Michele Elam, *Stanford University*
Roderick Ferguson, *Yale University*
Jacqueline Goldsby, *Yale University*
Martin Halliwell, *University of Leicester*
Nigel Hatton, *University of California, Merced*
Carol E. Henderson, *Emory University*

Davis Houck, *Florida State University*
Jenny James, *Pacific Lutheran University*
E. Patrick Johnson, *Northwestern University*
Sylvester Johnson, *Virginia Tech*
Cora Kaplan, *University of Southampton*
John Keene, *Rutgers University*
William Maxwell, *Washington University in St. Louis*
Joshua L. Miller, *University of Michigan*
Koritha Mitchell, *The Ohio State University*
Aleksander Motturi, *Clandestino Festival*

Copyright © 2020, James Baldwin Review
ISSN 2056-9203 (Print) ISSN 2056-9211 (Online)
ISBN 978 1 5261 5397 5

Published by Manchester University Press and the University of Manchester Library

Manchester University Press, Altrincham Street, Manchester, M1 7JA, UK
Tel: +44 (0)161 275 2310
Email: mup@manchester.ac.uk
Web address: www.manchesteruniversitypress.co.uk

University of Manchester Library, Oxford Road, Manchester, M13 9PP, UK
Tel: +44 (0)161 275 3751
Web address: www.library.manchester.ac.uk

James Baldwin Review is a collaborative venture made possible by support from
The New School and The University of Manchester.

Subscriptions

JBR is an Open Access journal, freely available at: www.manchesteropenhive.com/jbr

Articles

The editors encourage the submission of cross disciplinary articles on the life, writings, and
legacy of James Baldwin. Possible contributors are welcome to discuss an article proposal
or outline with the Managing Editor (joyceja@newschool.edu) before committing to a full
submission.

Articles should be a minimum of 5,000 words and not exceed 10,000 words, including notes.
Submissions should be made via email to the Managing Editor, Justin A. Joyce (joyceja@
newschool.edu).

The publisher has no responsibility for the persistence or accuracy of URLs for any external
or third-party internet websites referred to in this journal, and does not guarantee that any
content on such websites is, or will remain, accurate or appropriate.

Every effort has been made to obtain permission to reproduce copyright material, and the
publisher will be pleased to be informed of any errors and omissions for correction in the
electronic edition.

Typeset by Sunrise Setting Ltd, Brixham

Manchester University Press

The University of Manchester

INTRODUCTION

To Minimize the Bill That They Must Pay

Justin A. Joyce   The New School

Abstract

Recounting the failures of the United States to adequately address the COVID-19 pandemic, reflecting on the parade of mendacity that has encapsulated the 45th presidency, and interpreting Baldwin's call to be responsible to our children, Justin A. Joyce introduces the sixth volume of *James Baldwin Review*.

Keywords: James Baldwin, COVID-19, impeachment, Donald Trump, *Little Man, Little Man*

> Every day of your lives is practice in becoming the person you want to be. No instantaneous miracle is suddenly going to occur and make you brave and courageous and true. And every day that you sit back silent, refusing to use your power, terrible things are being done in our name.
> Audre Lorde, Oberlin College Commencement, 1989[1]

> No society can smash the social contract and be exempt from the consequences, and the consequences are chaos for everybody in the society.
> James Baldwin, interview with Julius Lester, 1984[2]

At the time of this writing, the global death toll from COVID-19 has surpassed 200,000. I shudder to think how many will have died by the time you read this. In the U.S. alone, the number of confirmed cases has been doubling every three days.[3] Current case counts worldwide have surpassed three million. Seven weeks ago, the suburban Detroit elementary school my children attend was closed for two weeks. At that time, school was rumored to be resuming again after a month of "social distancing." This initial estimate has been revised and extended a few times; we are experiencing week seven now, with the current "stay at home" order expected to extend another two weeks. I'm terrified that won't be nearly long enough.

James Baldwin Review, Volume 6, 2020, © The Authors. Published by Manchester University Press and The University of Manchester Library
http://dx.doi.org/10.7227/JBR.6.1

At the end of March, Detroit achieved the grisly accolade of being discussed on the 24-hour news cycle as a new epicenter for the spread of COVID-19. In nearly the same breath, with only a slight pivot to Camera Two to signal the change, the well-groomed anchor informed me as well that the United States now leads the world in confirmed cases. A few hours later, Michigan's governor, Gretchen Whitmer, revealed that our schools may well remain shuttered for the rest of the school year. The pace at which the situation is changing seems unrelentingly accelerated. During April, the number of cases in Michigan alone surged from 7,615 on 31 March to an astounding 41,379 by 1 May, and this surge has occurred despite the yawning lack of adequate testing equipment.[4] As tests become available, these numbers will surely spike further. Not weeks, not days, but hours pass and the whole situation has again changed. In the three weeks that have passed as I've drafted and tinkered with this introduction, Michigan's governor has, quite wisely, extended the "stay at home" order and canceled the remaining school year.

Homeschooling, then, will continue apace until further notice. Between us, my spouse and I have earned six degrees, four of them in the liberal arts. I'm not worried about whether or not we can finish up third grade here at home. We have a robust library and amiable pupils who are able and earnest readers. Perhaps, like Baldwin, who was self-educated through his voracious reading at the New York Public Library, they too will fashion their own unique education from among the shelves. Having worked remotely for most of my professional life, I'm not worried about schedules or "work/life balance." Business on top, pajamas on the bottom, the work from home uniform of the spring of 2020—we've got that covered too. We've also very reliable WiFi, so I'm sure we will figure out how to Skype or Zoom some virtual participation among classmates. The school district and its skeleton staff of underpaid and underappreciated are scrambling to present ever more online learning, though at the elementary level at least all that they are learning appears to be how to be online. How long we will be sequestered in our home, however, is a far more open question.

That we were spectacularly unprepared for this, you already know. As Juliette Kayyem, a former Department of Homeland Security official, put it in *The Atlantic* that same week schools were initially closed in Michigan, "A crisis finds a nation as it is, not as its citizen wish it to be."[5] That the United States is currently being misled and mismanaged, this too you already know. That an election is just around the corner, we all know. I'm painfully aware as I write this in May of 2020 that it won't be released as part of the sixth volume of *James Baldwin Review* until October. By the time you read this, our situation is bound to have gotten more dire. I know this as surely as I know that no one among us wanted to be facing such a crisis with our purportedly united states competing with each other for desperately needed supplies to make up for a deficient federal response. What I cannot know now is how bad it will be, how many more will perish as the impatient among us chafe at "social distancing" and figure that "flattening the curve" is someone else's responsibility. Will market concerns trump concern for our health? Will common sense prevail over market sense? In the eerily Faustian bargain we now face, will we have chosen mass casualties, or mass unemployment? Will tens—perhaps hundreds—of thousands of deaths finally be enough to spur my neighbors and fellow citizens to vote on the right side of history?

I wish I knew. Not just the macabre stats I allude to above, but also—and more crucially—I wish I knew how to convince my fellow Americans of a relatively simple fact: installing a liar to head your government is a bad idea. It is bad for business; bad for diplomacy; it is bad, in the most elemental way, for your health.

How many more will die before those who fashion themselves Republicans, conservatives, or "Red State" loyalists are forced to recognize, as does Frida Ghitis, writing for *The Atlantic*, that "the timeline of the pandemic is a story of Trumpian misinformation. Trump's alternative reality has grown familiar, but this time the consequences are deadly."[6] Unfortunately, the echo chamber that comprises our current media landscape leaves little room for hope in this arena. I'll not belabor here a Luddite's cry to abandon social media, but will remind readers instead that in the original Greek myth, when her voice was restricted by the vengeful Juno to only being able to parrot back what others spoke, the nymph Echo literally wasted away. Speaking nothing other than someone else's parting thoughts, not unlike the trolling anonymity of Facebook or the in-your-face, all caps screaming of a twisted Trump tweet, Echo hid in a cave, her body evaporating until only her voice remained.

Before we go any further, I want you to know that I've been putting this off for months now. Since at least August 2019 I've been collecting bits of news, pulling quotes, and generally stewing about how I am to frame the 2020 volume of *James Baldwin Review*. It is my honor and privilege to pen the editorial introduction to our journal, but the yoke has weighed more heavily this time than most. Chiefly because I've been unable to find an anchor. The news, as it is, spins so fast it's been hard to stop the rotation long enough to see the picture clearly. To see, that is, in the arc of history longer than the next hour, which moment is going to hold, to last. Which political misstep, which gaffe on the campaign trial, which vote would truly begin to make something like Brexit not simply a thorny theoretical, but instead a real logistical nightmare in the lives and economies of our interconnected worlds; which miscarriage of the America system of checks and balances, to not put too fine a point on it, would still matter when this issue is released in the fall of 2020? These were the issues I started thinking about when I began planning this introduction. As 2019 came to a close and the hard winter of 2020 began, I became resigned to the mundanity of Trump's mendacity. His appalling lack of veracity no longer surprised me. What surprised me, instead, was the lack of an outcry.

The things not seen as evidence in the impeachment of the 45th President of the United States are enormously revealing: from the flagrant defiance of the Emoluments Clause from the very first day of his ascendency to the presidency to explicit collusion with foreign powers in the disruption of the American electoral system; from repeated attacks on the very notion of a free press, not to mention the blatant, egregious disregard for truth; from seemingly obtuse notions about "alternative facts" to an elected official whose lies are so numerous as to keep a press core busy attempting to "fact check" a dizzying maze of conspiracies and fabrications.

What these stunning omissions in the record of high crimes and misdemeanors systematically perpetrated against the American people and our system of government reveal, most of all, is precisely the terror that ensues when sycophants and yes men and yes women hold fast to craven convictions. Convinced that their jobs as elected representatives mattered more than the day-to-day welfare of their electors; convinced that their perverse religious notions about controlling others' bodies and proscribing reproductive choice mattered enough to allow a known philanderer to claim the mantle of the religious right; convinced that packing courts with conservative justices—no matter their qualifications, or, as the case might have it, their numerous disqualifications—mattered more than the system of checks and balances they quite literally swore an oath to uphold; convinced, perhaps most of all, that fattening their wallets and padding the balance sheets of the corporations that lobbied on their behalf trumped any other consideration, with a steadfastness that might be admired as courageous were it not so basely motivated, a parade of elected officials marched us all steadily toward this moment.

What these lacunae in the impeachment record reveal most of all is that none of this was an accident. The outbreak of a novel coronavirus may well have been an act of God or Mother Nature, but the spectacular failures of this nation's federal government to address in any substantive way other than distrust and misdirection the very existential threat facing us was the direct result of the actions, plans, and investments made over the last several decades, exponentially accelerated over the last three years of this so wildly inept presidency. That a people would let their elected representatives vote in such a sycophantic kangaroo court as was convened by the United States Senate in February wasn't just appalling, it was downright alarming. I therefore resigned myself to raising the hue and cry.

The problem with the hue and cry, though, is that it requires, grammatically, a direct object. The voice and the trumpet, that is, are raised in pursuit of some *one*. Early English statutes reveal that the hue and cry was designed as a way of sharing liability. If one came across a crime and didn't raise the hue, one was liable for that crime; similarly, if you refused to enter into pursuit upon hearing the hue and cry, then you were held liable. The rub here, is twofold: firstly, as our epigraph from Audre Lorde suggests, when we allow our representatives to be derelict in their duties, we are all liable for the damage they do in our name. Secondly, as any good Foucauldian can tell you, power is not that simple. Even were there *only one* culpable party in this, a resounding *j'accuse!* rolling from sea to shining sea might not be enough.

When the Emperor has no clothes, we expect the court to play along. But the version of the story I heard included a little boy, the child's wisdom that often saves us all, who pointed out the folly of the naked man. Most versions of this fable end here, with a fairly apparent moral: when a ruse as transparent as invisible clothing is so baldly denied, only an innocent child—one not yet corrupted by self-interest—is courageous enough to speak the truth. This, surely, is the moral that is traditionally endorsed by the tale. It has mostly survived as a children's fable, after all. It was always my assumption that at this point the people rose up and deposed that fool. The naked, raving Emperor was removed once the people saw him clearly. Wasn't he?

The version of the story that comes to us from Hans Christian Andersen, how-ever, contains some ominous final lines, lines worth pausing over, for he has woven another lesson into the Emperor's magical robe.[7] The final paragraph is, in my reading, both the most sinister and most pertinent:

> "But he has nothing on!" said the whole people at length. That touched the Emperor, for it seemed to him that they were right; but he thought within himself, "I must go through with the procession." And so he held himself a little higher, and the chamber-lains held on tighter than ever, and carried the train which did not exist at all.[8]

Knowing full well the fabric was a sham, the Emperor and his retinue continue the ruse. In this final moment of the fable, the existence of the fabric has ceased to be relevant at all, the procession is all that matters.

When the procession trumps everything else, as Baldwin suggests in our sec-ond epigraph, surely our social contract—that implicit agreement wherein the importance of truth and the rule of law are sacred—is smashed and we cannot avoid the consequences. What if it's not just the Emperor and his court that play along, but all the gullible citizenry? And if that's not bad enough, what about those who aren't gullible, but instead are knowingly, cynically enabling his unchecked mendacity for their own gain? The parade of pretense in the tale of the Emperor and his clothes is merely that, a parade. A march down the street, a celebration of sorts to mark the event of his majesty's insecurities and narcissism.

But what if the march, instead, was to a press conference? What if the Emperor, as it were, stood behind the podium preparing his subjects for a great trial? What if, in the final postulation that I dearly wish were only hypothetical, he stood there ranting, lying not just about his clothes, but about everything else? Lying about the availability of tests?[9] Lying about the timelines for a vaccination or a cure? Turning daily televised coronavirus "updates" into miniature campaign rallies? Rallies that appear designed specifically to ease economic worries and get the stock market back on track? Suggesting outlandish and dangerously irresponsible things like injecting bleach as a cure?[10] Updates purporting to address a scientific matter and a clinical crisis with an incoherent word salad devoid of scientific grounding of any sort, trading instead on a mixture of xenophobic, racist dog whistles that sow further the seeds of distrust? Addresses that amount to nothing more than another round of gaslighting, producing only more cognitive dissonance? What if the parade and the misinformation at the podium continue even then?

Finding ourselves at this terrifying juncture, I take solace in the fact that one of the cures, as it were, for gaslighting and the cognitive dissonance it provokes is to establish a baseline. It helps pull us away from the clamor of competing narratives when we corroborate some key aspects of a lived reality. To act, in short, as a wit-ness to one's time and place, to stand bravely before the weight of history and declare, "It happened like this," is to counteract piece by piece, witness by witness, moment by moment, and life by life the torrent of occlusion and misdirection that is currently being sold as a "decentralized" approach to the pandemic by the

United States government. By raising, if not the hue and cry then at least your own voice to cry foul—as the child in our fable has—is to insist that the continued pretense of an unclothed emperor is a danger to us all. Such witnessing is surely the only way to prevent the parade from marching us to our doom.

James Baldwin Review's sixth volume begins with our "Feature Essay" by Nicholas Buccola, "The Great Debate: James Baldwin, William F. Buckley, Jr., and the Civil Rights Revolution." In "The Great Debate," Buccola introduces readers to the story at the heart of his new book, *The Fire Is upon Us: James Baldwin, William F. Buckley Jr., and the Debate over Race in America* (Princeton University Press, 2019). The Harlem-raised James Baldwin and the privileged William F. Buckley, Jr. could not have been more different, Buccola notes, but they both rose to the height of American intellectual life during the civil rights movement. By the time they met in February 1965 to debate at the Cambridge Union, the stage was set for a clash between what Buccola terms "Baldwin's call for a moral revolution in race relations against Buckley's unabashed elitism and implicit commitment to white supremacy." Buccola's engagement with the lives of these men on opposite ends of the political spectrum is a compelling lead-in to the analyses that follow, most of which deal more narrowly with the specifics of Baldwin's life, works, and legacies. That these specificities have a history, a heritage, a lineage that links today's troubles to yesterday's debates is the Baldwinian historical lesson write large, and Buccola's focus on the two influential figures and their juxtaposition on the debate stage is a ready primer in this curriculum.

Nadia Alahmed's essay, "'The Shape of the Wrath to Come': James Baldwin's Radicalism and the Evolution of his Thought on Israel," begins our formal essay section with another lesson in Baldwin's history, this time of the arc of his thoughts on the Israeli state. Tracing the evolution of Baldwin's discourse on Arab–Israeli conflict as connected to his own evolution as a Black thinker, activist, and author, Alahmed explores Baldwin's relationship with some of the major radical Black movements and organizations of the twentieth century to argue that "Baldwin's transformation from a supporter of the Zionist project of nation-building to an advocate of Palestinian rights and national aspirations reveals much about the ideological transformations of the larger Black liberation movement." Marquita R. Smith's essay, "'Birthing a New World: Black Women as Surrogates of Liberation in James Baldwin's *If Beale Street Could Talk*," continues our examination of the contours of political thought and activism that found expression in Baldwin's writing. By exploring representations of Black women as caregivers in *Beale Street*, Smith argues that "Black women's care work in the face of social death [is] an example of how Black women act as surrogates for Black liberation." Monica Pearl's essay, "*Chagrin d'amour*: Intimacy, Shame, and the Closet in *Giovanni's Room*," brings us from history and politics to literature and sexuality, with an exploration of Baldwin's second novel. For Pearl, as for many other critics before her, *Giovanni's Room* is a text "riven with shame" that navigates the uneven terrain of a non-normative love affair. Pearl's reexamination of the closet, a conceit she sees as both "literal enclosure and metaphorical description," presents a fresh reading of this novel, as

Pearl offers up unique insights into the protagonist's oscillating flirtations with desire, disgust, and disclosure.

JBR volume 6 presents an expanded graduate student essay section from previous volumes, part of a renewed commitment to our editorial mandate to foster diverse conversations around James Baldwin. This volume's Graduate Student Essay Award winner, Emily Na, starts the section with a fascinating examination of Baldwin's life as a cook and epicure, noting how food and food cultures have impacted his writing with her marvelous essay, "Baldwin's Kitchen: Food and Identity in His Life and Fiction." Nicholas Binford's contribution, "The Warrior and the Poet: On James Baldwin and the Many Roles in Revolution," prods us to greater care in our word choice, noting the unthinking ease with which many label Baldwin as a revolutionary to argue "that thoughtlessly calling James Baldwin revolutionary obscures and erases the non-revolutionary strategies and approaches he employed in his contributions to the civil rights movement and to race relations as a whole." Our expanded graduate student section concludes with Miller Wilbourn's essay, "Baptism by History: Reading James Baldwin's Existential Hindsight in *Go Tell It on the Mountain*." Bringing key existentialist thinkers to an examination of the existentialist strains in Baldwin's prose, Wilbourn also brings to bear some impressive archival work in his examination of the textual and developmental history of *Go Tell It*.

Our "Dispatch" for volume 6 is a personal account about film, filmmaking, and friendship in a career of working with and on Baldwin from none other than acclaimed filmmaker Karen Thorsen, whose magisterial documentary *James Baldwin: The Price of the Ticket* (1990) continues to inspire with the moving recollections and remembrances Thorsen collected. Her contribution to the study and appreciation of Baldwin cannot be overstated; *James Baldwin Review* is therefore honored to share with our readers the beginning of her own remembrance of how that film came into being. Her essay, "The Disorder of Life: James Baldwin on My Shoulder," represents but the first part of her remembrance; Part Two will follow in our next volume, due out in the fall of 2021.

Volume 6's bibliographic essay comes to us from Joseph Vogel, whose review article charts the general direction of scholarship in Baldwin studies between the years 2016 and 2017. His judicious and nuanced survey of the field identifies notable features including the "political turn" connecting Baldwin's social insights from the past to the present; renewed interest in the Baldwin archive; and continued interest in situating Baldwin in national, regional, and geographical contexts as well as issues of gender and sexuality. Vogel's bibliographic entry is followed by a review from D. Quentin Miller of a remarkable, interdisciplinary symposium that brought scholars together to consider anew the works and relationships between Baldwin and his "spiritual father," the painter Beauford Delaney, over three days at the University of Tennessee on 19–21 February 2020 at an event entitled, "In a Speculative Light: The Arts of James Baldwin and Beauford Delaney."

Our 2020 volume finishes with two submissions "From the Field": two collected conference panels, one from 2018 and one from 2019. Stemming from a roundtable that followed a screening of Raoul Peck's *I Am Not Your Negro* (2017) in Zurich in February 2018, co-authors Jovita dos Santos Pinto, Noémi Michel, Patricia Purtschert, Paola Bacchetta, and Vanessa Naef present here a collective essay wandering between the audio-visual and textual matter of the film and Baldwin's essay "Stranger in the Village," which was also adapted into a film-essay directed by Pierre Koralnik, staging Baldwin in the Swiss village of Leukerbad. "Rebranding James Baldwin and His Queer Others" was a session held at the annual meeting of the American Studies Association in November 2019 in Honolulu, Hawaii. The conference papers gathered here—by Magdalena J. Zaborowska, Nicholas F. Radel, Nigel Hatton, and Ernest L. Gibson III—show how Baldwin's writings and life story participate in dialogues with other authors and artists who probe issues of identity and identification, as well as with other types of texts and non-American stories, boldly addressing theoretical and political perspectives different from his own.

Theoretical and political perspectives different than Baldwin's own is a tempting way to refer to the seeming distance between the concerns of the 1960s, or even the mid-1980s, and our worries today amid a global pandemic. As we look to the life, works, and legacies of James Baldwin for solace, inspiration, and compassionate humanity as our aid in these crises, we come to see him, not unlike this volume's cover, primarily as a kind of ur-witness. The cover for volume 6 comes to us from pioneering Atlanta-based artist Dr. Fahamu Pecou, whose portrait of Baldwin, *Eleri (Witness)*, evokes Baldwin's understanding of himself as primarily an observer, a commentator. The diffused light and the angelic glow rendered masterfully by Pecou's brushstrokes, juxtaposed with the clerical garb, suggest as well Baldwin's somewhat recent reception as a prophet, a seer of sorts upon whom we can depend for comfort, for guidance, and for instruction in a perilous time.

In a 1984 interview with Julius Lester, Baldwin was asked about his self-designation of this role as "witness," and his response is instructive: "I am a witness. In the church in which I was raised you were supposed to bear witness to the truth. Now, later on, you wonder what in the world the truth is, but you do know what a lie is."[11] This remark has, understandably, been quoted numerous times as a testament to Baldwin's own sense of artistic imperative, his understanding of his duty and role as a literary artist. What's often left out, however, is that the comment comes amid Baldwin's repudiation of being overly ideological, notwithstanding his own political activism. In other words, Baldwin claims the role of witness directly after he refuses the moniker of "spokesman." Picking up on this, Lester prods Baldwin further about the difference between a spokesman and a witness. Baldwin's answer has something to do with the difference between speaking for others— spokesman—and trying to make clear the state of things as they are. As he puts it, his aim is "to interpret and make clear."[12] And still Lester presses him, wondering about the confidence Baldwin seems to have about his role as witness, wondering "if it's possible for writers now, black or white, to have that confidence."[13] As the whole of this interview has been framed by the difference between Lester and Baldwin, writers whose careers began roughly fifteen years apart, Lester poses his next question as one of generational difference: "I wonder if the world hasn't changed between the time you started and the time we started?"[14] Again, Baldwin's response is instructive, and worth quoting at length:

> Well, it may have. In one way or another, one is very much a prisoner of his time. But I know what I've seen and what I've seen makes me know I have to say, *I know*. I won't say I believe, because I know that we can be better than we are. That's the sum total of my wisdom in all these years. We can also be infinitely worse, but I know that the world we live in now is not necessarily the best world we can make. I can't be entirely wrong. There's two things we have to do—love each other and raise our children.[15]

As in so many other instances in his interviews and writings, when pushed to the wall, rhetorically, Baldwin claims the children. He claims our collective responsibility to them in his searing jeremiad concerning mid-twentieth-century race relations, *The Fire Next Time*: "For the sake of one's children, in order to minimize the bill that *they* must pay, one must be careful not to take refuge in any delusion..."[16] Nearer the end of his life, intense eyes ablaze with sorrowful worry over the state of the country in the aftermath of the civil rights era, he refuses the notion of despair in Thorsen's *The Price of the Ticket*—"I'm not in despair, I'm enraged"— and pivots again to our responsibilities: "You can't tell the children that there's no hope."[17] The children Baldwin evokes as a last rhetorical resort aren't simply metaphorical. They are, instead, children whose lives he knew and cherished. Nieces and nephews like those just born to his sisters when he embarked on the collaborative venture with the Turkish painter Yoran Cazac that would result in *Little Man, Little Man: A Story of Childhood* (1976).

Billed as a "children's book for adults" on the original dustjacket, *Little Man, Little Man* has received scant attention. Panned or ignored upon release, the book quickly went out of print. It is not a standard children's book, that's for certain, for *Little Man* is devoid of the clear moral or aphoristic fable that motivates so much of the genre. It's rerelease in 2018 allows us a new opportunity to explore and experience it, to wrestle with the very adult themes within as presented through Cazac's impressionistic watercolors and the narrative perspective of a young Black child in Harlem, TJ.

As he bounces his red ball and encounters the characters in his life and on his street—for a young Black boy from Harlem, they are nearly synonymous—we glean a number of things about TJ and his companions in this limited world. We learn that there is power in music and dance to enliven and unite, even amid poverty, addiction, and dereliction. We learn that something is off with Ms. Lee. She gets sad sometimes, TJ notes, and "she walk like she don't know where she going."[18] TJ and the slightly older WT are enraptured by her beauty, but the evasive yet insightful Blinky is more guarded in her assessment. We suspect Ms. Lee's walk, where "her eyes is red sometime and she smell strong, like smoke, and sweet, like she been eating peppermint candy, and sometime she smell like licorice" can be attributed to her addictions, her actions on the roof that her husband, Mr. Man, warns against.[19]

As TJ's ball comes crashing down on him near the close of the book, accompanied by a glass bottle from the same roof that shatters and leaves WT cut and bleeding, we learn most of all that we cannot abdicate our responsibility to our children. In as much as anything is clear in this impressionistic book, it is clear to this reader that Ms. Lee is responsible for the bottle falling, responsible, then, albeit obliquely for the cut on WT's foot. As she bandages his foot in the basement apartment, it's equally clear that what TJ, WT, and Blinky need most from the adults in the room, more than medical care perhaps, is assurance. Assurance that some adult among them is responsible, not just for them, but responsible to them. As Ms. Lee takes WT's tear-stained head in her hands and plaintively reassures him, all she can muster is "Little Man, Little Man," emblazoned across the page in brilliant rainbow letters.[20] But it is enough, for in these words she provides WT and his friends assurance that no matter the mess, no matter the proximate or immediate cause of the conundrum or crisis, more mature heads will prevail to ensure that tomorrow will arrive with an able hand on the tiller.

"Everything now, we must assume, is in our hands; we have no right to assume otherwise."[21] Baldwin, of course, was right about this when he penned it in 1963. It is no less true today. It is entirely in our hands to educate the children, to better equip them for their futures than we have for their present. It is in our hands to hold accountable our representatives for their crimes, be they of commission, omission, or accessory. It is in our hands to bear witness to their failures. It is in our hands to demand change, for it will be our hands that cast the votes. It is, finally, in our hands to minimize the bill our children will pay for the delusions we have thus far allowed to parade in our name.

What has changed between Baldwin's 1963 and the time of this writing, perhaps, is our recognition of how interconnected we have become. Our globalized flows of supply and demand, our just-in-time logistics chains, have proven this most spectacularly when they have faltered. When the myriad of shopping and delivery services with which many of us supply and structure our lives are overcome by unprecedented and unanticipated demand, like a run on a bank, panicked without dependable leaders or even reliable facts, we assuage our fears with shopping, with provisioning for the apocalypse, and suddenly all the toilet paper is gone. So too are the bottles of hand sanitizer and the soap gone. Empty are the spaces on the shelves that used to hold a dizzying array of cleaning products. Fresh meat and produce are scarce, and with the restaurants closed by state order to all but take-away, a nation of plenty worries about how long the virus can live on cardboard and Styrofoam containers. Because it is all in our hands, please remember to wash them.

Grosse Pointe Park, MI, 1 May 2020

Notes

1   Audre Lorde, commencement address, Oberlin College, 29 May 1989, in *I Am Your Sister: Collected and Unpublished Writings of Audre Lorde*, ed. Rudolph Byrd, Johnnetta Betsch Cole, and Beverly Guy-Sheftall (New York, Oxford University Press, 2009), p. 216.

2   James Baldwin, "James Baldwin: Reflections of a Maverick" (1984), interview with Julius Lester, in *James Baldwin: The Last Interview and Other Conversations* (New York, Melville House, 2014), pp. 35–53 (p. 44).

3 Derek Thompson, "All the Coronavirus Statistics are Flawed," *The Atlantic*, 26 March 2020, www.theatlantic.com/ideas/archive/2020/03/fog-pandemic/608764/ (accessed 10 June 2020).

4 Daily counts and statistics are available via www.michigan.gov/coronavirus.

5 Juliette Kayyem, "The U.S. Isn't Ready For What's About to Happen," *The Atlantic*, 8 March 2020, www.theatlantic.com/ideas/archive/2020/03/us-isnt-ready-whats-about-happen/607636/ (accessed 10 June 2020).

6 Frida Ghitis, "The Political Genius of Donald Trump," *The Atlantic*, 31 March 2020, www.theatlantic.com/ideas/archive/2020/03/trump-genius/609142/ (accessed 10 June 2020).

7 I am indebted to Dwight A. McBride, whose commencement address to The Graduate School at Northwestern University in 2017 brought this ominous ending of the tale to my attention. I have adapted his remarks from that occasion in this essay.

8 Hans Christian Andersen, "The Emperor's New Clothes," in Charles W. Eliot (ed.), *The Harvard Classics: Folk-Lore and Fable* (New York, P. F. Collier & Son, 1937), p. 238.

9 Seven weeks after President Trump erroneously announced that "anyone who wants a test gets a test," the New York Times reported on 28 April that less than 2 percent of the U.S. has been tested. See reporting by Jack Healey, Manny Fernandez, and Peter Baker, "Reopening Plans Across U.S. Are Creating Confusing Patchwork," *The New York Times*, 27 April, 2020, www.nytimes.com/2020/04/27/us/coronavirus-governors-states-reopening.html (accessed 10 June 2020).

10 On 23 April 2020 President Trump suggested that injecting or drinking bleach and other disinfectants might be a cure. See Jane C. Timm, "'It's irresponsible and it's dangerous': Experts Rip Trump's Idea of Injecting Disinfectant to Treat COVID-19," NBC News, 23 April 2020, www.nbcnews.com/politics/donald-trump/it-s-irresponsible-it-s-dangerous-experts-rip-trump-s-n1191246 (accessed 10 June 2020).

11 Baldwin, "Reflections of a Maverick," p. 44.

12 *Ibid.*

13 *Ibid.*, p. 45.

14 *Ibid.*

15 *Ibid.*

16 James Baldwin, *The Fire Next Time* (New York, Dell, 1963), p. 139.

17 James Baldwin, quoted in *The Price of the Ticket* (dir. Karen Thorsen, 1990).

18 James Baldwin and Yoran Cazac, *Little Man, Little Man: A Story of Childhood* (1976), ed. Nicholas Boggs and Jennifer DeVere Brody (Durham, NC, Duke University Press, 2018), p. 34.

19 *Ibid.*

20 *Ibid.*, p. 91.

21 Baldwin, *The Fire Next Time*, p. 141.

Works Cited

Andersen, Hans Christian, "The Emperor's New Clothes," in Charles W. Eliot (ed.), *The Harvard Classics: Folk-Lore and Fable* (New York, P. F. Collier & Son , 1937), pp. 234–8.

Baldwin, James, "James Baldwin: Reflections of a Maverick" (1984), interview with Julius Lester, in *James Baldwin: The Last Interview and Other Conversations* (New York, Melville House, 2014), pp. 35–53.

_____ *The Fire Next Time* (New York, Dell, 1963).

Baldwin, James, and Yoran Cazac, *Little Man, Little Man: A Story of Childhood* (1976), ed. Nicholas Boggs and Jennifer DeVere Brody (Durham, NC, Duke University Press, 2018).

Ghitis, Frida, "The Political Genius of Donald Trump," *The Atlantic*, 31 March 2020, www.theatlantic.com/ideas/archive/2020/03/trump-genius/609142/ (accessed 10 June 2020).

Healey, Jack, Manny Fernandez, and Peter Baker, "Reopening Plans Across U.S. Are Creating Confusing Patchwork," *The New York Times*, 27 April 2020, www.nytimes.com/2020/04/27/us/coronavirus-governors-states-reopening.html (accessed 10 June 2020).

Kayyem, Juliette, "The U.S. Isn't Ready For What's About to Happen," *The Atlantic*, 8 March 2020, www.theatlantic.com/ideas/archive/2020/03/us-isnt-ready-whats-about-happen/607636/ (accessed 10 June 2020).

Lorde, Audre, "Commencement Address, Oberlin College, May 29, 1989," in *I Am Your Sister: Collected and Unpublished Writings of Audre Lorde*, ed. Rudolph Byrd, Johnnetta Betsch Cole, and Beverly Guy-Sheftall (New York, Oxford University Press, 2009), pp. 213–18.

Thompson, Derek, "All the Coronavirus Statistics are Flawed," *The Atlantic*, 26 March 2020, www.theatlantic.com/ideas/archive/2020/03/fog-pandemic/608764/ (accessed 10 June 2020).

Timm, Jane C. "'It's irresponsible and it's dangerous': Experts Rip Trump's Idea of Injecting Disinfectant to Treat COVID-19," *NBC News*, 23 April 2020, www.nbcnews.com/politics/donald-trump/it-s-irresponsible-it-s-dangerous-experts-rip-trump-s-n1191246 (accessed 10 June 2020).

Contributor's Biography

Justin A. Joyce is one of the founding editors of *James Baldwin Review*, the journal's current managing editor, and Research Director at the New School. His work on James Baldwin has appeared in *James Baldwin Review*, *A Historical Guide to James Baldwin* (Oxford University Press, 2009) and *James Baldwin in Context* (Cambridge University Press, 2019). He has co-edited *A Melvin Dixon Critical Reader* (University Press of Mississippi, 2006), *Racial Blackness and the Discontinuity of Western Modernity* (University of Illinois Press, 2014), and the Lambda Literary Award-winning study *The Delectable Negro: Human Consumption and Homoeroticism in U.S. Slave Culture* (NYU Press, 2014). An interdisciplinary scholar of American literature, film, and popular culture, his writing on the Western genre has appeared in *Western American Literature*, *Pacific Northwest Quarterly*, *Great Plains Quarterly*, an edited collection on the HBO series *Deadwood* (Bloomsbury, 2013), and is the subject of his first monograph, *Gunslinging Justice: The American Culture of Gun Violence in Westerns and the Law* (Manchester University Press, 2018).

FEATURE ESSAY

The Great Debate: James Baldwin, William F. Buckley, Jr., and the Civil Rights Revolution

Nicholas Buccola   Linfield University

Abstract

Born in New York City only fifteen months apart, the Harlem-raised James Baldwin and the privileged William F. Buckley, Jr. could not have been more different, but they both rose to the height of American intellectual life during the civil rights movement. By the time they met in February 1965 to debate race and the American Dream at the Cambridge Union, Buckley—a founding father of the American conservative movement—was determined to sound the alarm about a man he considered an "eloquent menace." For his part, Baldwin viewed Buckley as a deluded reactionary whose popularity revealed the sickness of the American soul. The stage was set for an epic confrontation that pitted Baldwin's call for a moral revolution in race relations against Buckley's unabashed elitism and implicit commitment to white supremacy. In this article I introduce readers to the story at the heart of my new book about Baldwin and Buckley, *The Fire Is Upon Us*.

Keywords: James Baldwin, William F. Buckley, Jr., the American Dream, Cambridge Debate

The following essay is based on remarks delivered by the author at Columbia University on Tuesday, 26 November 2019.

On the evening of 18 February 1965, the Cambridge Union—the world's oldest and most prestigious debating society—was abuzz with excitement. More than 700 students and guests of the Union packed into the debating hall, which was modeled after the British House of Commons. Attendees filled every spot on the benches and in the galleries and still more sat in the aisles and on floors throughout the space. More than 500 additional people crammed into other rooms on the Union premises, to which the proceedings would be broadcast by the B.B.C. on closed circuit televisions.

James Baldwin Review, Volume 6, 2020, © The Authors. Published by Manchester University Press and The University of Manchester Library
http://dx.doi.org/10.7227/JBR.6.2

Why were all of these people packed into the 150-year-old debating society that night? The primary reason they were there was to see James Baldwin, the world-famous writer who was aptly described by Malcolm X as "*the* poet of the civil rights revolution."[1] By this, Malcolm meant that Baldwin was the leading writer associated with the movement that was—at that very moment—in the midst of transforming the country. In his novels, plays, essays, and speeches, Baldwin plumbed the depths of the human soul and strived to give his readers a sense of what it might be like to view the world through the eyes of others. In order to make sense of the struggle for civil rights and the backlash against it, Baldwin insisted, we must come to terms with fundamental questions about identity, morality, and power.

Baldwin's presence alone might have been enough to pack the Union that night, but attendees were also intrigued by the prospect of seeing Baldwin participate in a debate. The motion before the House that night was "The American Dream is at the expense of the American Negro," and Union officials had arranged for Baldwin to square off with an opponent tailor-made for the role: William F. Buckley, Jr. The mostly British audience was not as familiar with Buckley, but rumor had it that he was a founding father of the American conservative movement, a skilled debater, and one of the country's leading opponents of civil rights. The stage was set for an intellectual prizefight for the ages.

On the same night Baldwin and Buckley would square off in Cambridge, a group of civil rights protesters gathered at their church in Marion, Alabama, just outside of Selma. These protesters were among the thousands of Americans who had mobilized in an effort to secure voting rights in the South. On 18 February, the activists in Marion had planned to march from their church to the jail where one of their leaders was incarcerated for civil rights agitation. They knew that Alabama law enforcement officers would not allow them to complete their march that night, so they formulated a plan to kneel and pray when they were confronted by police, after which they would return to their church. Upon kneeling to pray, though, the activists were assaulted by the police—who also attacked journalists there to cover the march—and one of their number, a 26-year-old church deacon named Jimmie Lee Jackson, was mortally wounded by officers.

The fact that the epic Baldwin–Buckley debate occurred on the same night as the Marion protest captures what my new book, *The Fire Is Upon Us*, is about.[2] The debate itself constitutes two climactic chapters in the story, but the book is about far more than what happened on that fateful night in February. Baldwin (b. 1924) and Buckley (b. 1925) were almost exact contemporaries and *The Fire Is Upon Us* weaves the stories of their lives against the backdrop of the rise of the civil rights and conservative movements they did so much, respectively, to shape. Baldwin and Buckley turn out to be the perfect vehicles to tell the story of the struggle to achieve racial justice in the United States. As the civil rights and conservative movements rose, Baldwin and Buckley were at the eye of the storm, and their prolific writings—both published works and unpublished correspondence—give us a glimpse into their minds on practically every day of this dramatic history. The story is enriched by the fact that both Baldwin and Buckley lived active and interesting lives; this is not a story of two men at their respective typewriters. Instead, it is a story filled with their dramatic encounters with a wide array of characters who dominated the political and cultural landscape, including the Kennedy brothers, Martin Luther King, Jr., Malcolm X, Lorraine Hansberry, George Wallace, Barry Goldwater, Medgar Evers, Elijah Muhammad, and the leaders of extremist groups such as the White Citizens' Council and the John Birch Society. Through their writings, we are there with them as they think through the major events of the era, including the Montgomery bus boycott, massive resistance to school desegregation, the Little Rock crisis, the rise of the Nation of Islam, the sit-in protests, the Freedom Rides, the Battle at Ole Miss, the rise of the John Birch Society, the election of John F. Kennedy, the Birmingham campaign, the March on Washington, the passage of the Civil Rights Act of 1964, the Johnson–Goldwater campaign, and the assassinations of Medgar Evers, John F. Kennedy, Malcolm X, and Martin Luther King, Jr. In sum, this is an epic story of the clash of two of the most important movements of the twentieth century, told by way of two of the champions of each movement. *The Fire Is Upon Us* tells a story worth telling for its own sake, but it is also a story that is as urgent as ever. Today, I would like to give you a sense of that story and why I think it is so relevant to our times.

The Ghetto and the Mansion: Baldwin and Buckley Growing Up

James Baldwin and William F. Buckley, Jr. were born in the same city only fifteen months apart from each other, but they may as well have been born on different planets. Baldwin describes his childhood in the Harlem of the 1920s and 1930s as one marked by claustrophobia, domination, and despair. In order to capture a sense of the sort of claustrophobia he felt inside his family's home he asks his readers to imagine what it might feel like to sleep in a bed occupied by up to six of your siblings. Life on "the Avenue" in Harlem was also marked by a sense of claustrophobia because the world told Baldwin in no uncertain terms that he had better not venture out beyond the borders of "the ghetto." Within that space, Baldwin said that his life was dominated by "the millions of details of every day that communicated to him that he was a worthless human being."[3] Some of these experiences of domination could be linked to a human face—the police officers, the landlords, the shopkeepers, and so on—but he also described the feeling of being dominated by the faceless, deeply cruel structures of power that limited the freedom and opportunity of himself and his neighbors. Baldwin said that in this context the defining fact of the lives of his parents was that they struggled to keep their children alive.

It is not surprising that this context led Baldwin's stepfather, David, to be consumed by despair. From his son's perspective, David had come to believe what the white world said about him and this led him to hate himself and treat all of those around him with great cruelty. David would eventually succumb to this despair and die in a mental institution in 1943. As a young man, Baldwin set out to avoid the fate of his father. The "lever" or the "handle" he would hold onto in order to avoid falling into the pit of despair was language.[4] Through words—through reading, writing, and preaching in Harlem's storefront churches—Baldwin would make sense of his experience and think through how he might find freedom and fulfillment in the world.

It is difficult to imagine a childhood more different from Baldwin's than the one lived by William F. Buckley, Jr. Buckley was born to immense wealth and privilege. His mother came from "old money" in New Orleans and his Texan father was awash in "new money" as a result of his real estate and oil investments. With this wealth, Buckley's parents acquired a 47-acre estate in Sharon, Connecticut, and provided their ten children with lives filled with servants, in-home tutors, world travel, and other luxuries that are the stuff of dreams for most people. While Baldwin identified claustrophobia as a defining feature of his childhood, Buckley identified seemingly limitless space as a defining feature of his. Whether it be exploring the many rooms of his family's mansion or frolicking in the grounds of one of his family's estates, Buckley felt a great sense of freedom and opportunity to do just about anything under the sun.

With their immense wealth, Buckley's parents provided their children with a robust education right there in the family home. The children studied every conceivable subject with the goal, in the words of one of Buckley's sisters, of making them "absolutely perfect in every way."[5] Most importantly, the Buckley children were taught a distinctive worldview. One pillar of that worldview was a conservative brand of Catholicism and the other pillar was a political doctrine the family called "individualism," a catch-all term meant to capture their hostility to any form of "collectivism," such as communism, socialism, and the New Deal policies of Franklin Delano Roosevelt. The Buckley children were also taught to be suspicious of democracy. Some people are fit *to rule*, the children were taught, and others were fit *to be ruled*. This belief in hierarchy was thoroughly racialized in the Buckley household, where the children were taught to believe in a philosophy of white supremacy that was infused with a sense of *noblesse oblige*. White people are superior, they were taught, but this superiority came with a sense of obligation to take care of their inferiors, especially those who were loyal.

Disturbing the Peace: Buckley and Baldwin Arrive on the Intellectual Scene

Buckley did not set out to *become* his father, but he did set as his mission in life to use his gifts as a writer and speaker to defend his father's worldview. Buckley set out to do that first at Millbrook Prep School, then during a brief stint in the U.S. Army, and finally as an undergraduate at Yale, where he was a formal debater and editor-in-chief—or chairman—of the *Yale Daily News*. In his public speeches and editorials, Buckley expressed his conservative views on international, national, and campus politics. Most provocatively, Buckley editorialized against the views of Yale professors, who he thought brought a liberal bias into their classrooms. Soon after graduating from Yale, Buckley published a book-length indictment of his alma mater. In *God and Man at Yale* (1951), Buckley called for an end to the

"superstition" of academic freedom by way of alumni and boards of trustees exert-
ing power over the faculty whom universities hired and fired and what was being
taught.[6] If that wasn't controversial enough, Buckley devoted his second book,
McCarthy and His Enemies (1954), co-authored with his brother-in-law L. Brent
Bozell, to defending Senator Joseph McCarthy, who was spearheading the latest
"Red scare." Buckley conceded that McCarthy was an imperfect instrument in the
anticommunist fight, but he insisted that his cause was just. McCarthy was engaged
in the all-important work of enforcing a "public orthodoxy," which, for Buckley,
most definitely did not include toleration of communism.[7]

While Buckley was making waves on the American scene with his calls for
greater orthodoxy on college campuses and in the society writ large, Baldwin was
establishing himself as an estimable literary provocateur. In his literary criticism,
fiction, and essays, he was setting out to determine what it meant to be "an honest
man and a good writer."[8] By 1948, Baldwin was so fed up with American racism
that he decided he must leave the country for Paris in order to survive. Baldwin
also realized that leaving the United States would be necessary in order for him to
write about the country. In 1953, Baldwin published *Go Tell It on the Mountain*, an
autobiographical novel about a family attempting to survive the American racial
nightmare and find meaning in their lives and relationships. A few years later,
Baldwin completed his second novel, *Giovanni's Room*, which was the story of a
love affair between a wayward white American, David, and an Italian bartender
named Giovanni. Many of the same people who worked with Baldwin on *Go Tell
It* refused to work with him on *Giovanni's Room* because of the fact that the second
novel told the story of a gay love affair.

Baldwin insisted that these skeptics were missing the point. There was little
doubt that *Go Tell It* and *Giovanni's Room* contained deep insights into the roots of
racism and homophobia, but these books were not—at their core—*about* race and
sex. Instead, Baldwin said these novels and most of the nonfiction writing he was
doing in this period were focused on something deeper. That something was "the
question of identity." Who do we take ourselves to be and how does our conception of identity lead us to treat other people? As Baldwin reflected on these questions through his characters and his nonfiction subjects, he concluded that we are
usually in a state of identity crisis because we lack the courage to come to terms
with who we really are. We avoid this confrontation with our true selves because
we are scared. Our fear leads us to delude ourselves and wrap ourselves in false
identities that we think might make us feel safe. Alas, this strategy only deepens
our trouble as we get caught in a web of "social paranoia"—we rely on status to
make ourselves feel superior to others, but we are always haunted by the fact that
someone, somewhere has reason to feel superior to us.

"The Claims of Civilization": Buckley Confronts Black Liberation

In the mid-1950s, Buckley played a crucial role in the creation of the conservative
movement in the United States by founding *National Review* magazine. Buckley

recognized that magazines such as *The Nation* and *The New Republic* had played crucial roles in the creation and flourishing of the progressive movement in the first half of the twentieth century and he was hopeful that *National Review* might play a similar role for the American right in the second half of the century. His hope was that the magazine could serve as a vehicle to build a coalition of libertarians and traditionalists who disagreed on a number of issues but were united in their disdain for communism and liberalism. Buckley hoped to play the role of "editor of conservatism," deciding which intellectuals and politicians would be part of the new conservative movement and who would be left out in the ideological wilds.[9] And so he did.

Buckley played an outsized role in the shaping of the conservative movement, and given the timing of *National Review*'s founding—with the build-up occurring in 1954 and the launch occurring in late 1955—his role was especially important in shaping how the American right would respond to the civil rights movement. In 1954, the Supreme Court handed down its landmark *Brown* v. *Board* school desegregation decision, which was met with an intense white backlash from segregationist elites as well as white supremacist terrorist organizations such as the Ku Klux Klan and the White Citizens' Councils. The following year witnessed the lynching of Emmett Till, the arrest of Rosa Parks, the rise to national prominence of a 26-year-old Baptist minister named Martin Luther King, Jr., and the Montgomery bus boycott. In the face of this changing landscape, Buckley made a fateful decision that has reverberations down to us today. *National Review*, which would establish itself in short order as the most important conservative journal of opinion in the country, was deeply opposed to any federal intervention to challenge segregation, was consistently skeptical of King and other nonviolent protesters, was explicitly opposed to any meaningful civil rights legislation (including the Civil Rights Act of 1964 and the Voting Rights Act of 1965), and was supportive of numerous segregationist politicians, organizations, and policies. Buckley and his colleagues sometimes disagreed at the margins about how Black liberation ought to be resisted, but they were in near-uniform agreement that it must be resisted in one way or another.

Ten years after the founding of *National Review*, Buckley said that his goal for the magazine on the question of civil rights had been for it to be "extremely articulate" and "non-racist," but not "attempting a dogmatic racial egalitarianism either."[10] Buckley relied on a stable of segregationist writers—including James Jackson Kilpatrick, Richard Weaver, Anthony Harrigan, Forrest Davis, and Sam M. Jones—to rationalize resistance to Black liberation in the pages of the magazine. Weaver, a Southerner who taught rhetoric at the University of Chicago, provided a philosophical defense of everything Buckley's mother ever taught him about race. Yes, Weaver conceded, the "regime of the South" was premised on racial hierarchy, but it was a benevolent hierarchy that provided all people—high and low—with a sense of their place and a sense of their obligations to each other.[11] Figures like Jones and Davis celebrated the "statesmen" in the South who were interposing themselves between the federal law and the segregationist way of life. Jones went so far as to call the Buckley family friend Strom Thurmond "a latter-day Patrick Henry" in the pages of *National Review*. And Kilpatrick was really Buckley's "go-to-guy" on race and civil rights. Wherever the hottest battle was in the war over racial equality—from Little Rock in 1957 to the debate over the Voting Rights Act in 1965—Buckley relied on Kilpatrick to offer *National Review*'s signature response, which was usually a mixture of Weaver-like "traditionalism" and quasi-sophisticated jurisprudential defenses of "states' rights" ideology.

Buckley mostly relied on this stable of writers to offer "nonracist" but not dogmatically racially egalitarian arguments against civil rights, but he also made his own thinking clear in a series of pieces on the subject, most infamously in a 1957 essay called "Why the South Must Prevail."[12] The proximate cause for the piece was the debate over the Civil Rights Act of 1957, a piece of legislation that was principally concerned with securing Black voting rights in the South. It is a piece of legislation we seldom talk about anymore because it was hollowed out of just about any meaning by Southern segregationists like Thurmond and their allies. One of the primary ways the legislation was effectively stripped was through the inclusion of a clause that said any claims of civil rights violations under the Act would be considered by juries, not by federal judges. Thurmond and his allies knew full well that no Southern jury would ever convict any official of violating the rights of an African American. The clause was, in effect, an endorsement of jury nullification: juries would be empowered to interpose themselves between the federal law and Southern officials who flagrantly violated it.

Buckley wrote "Why the South Must Prevail" in order to defend this jury nullification clause. In his defense, he rehashed many of the arguments that had been made by his stable of segregationist writers, but he also provided an explanation of what he took to be the heart of the matter. The white South, Buckley concluded, was entitled to do whatever it deemed necessary to resist Black liberation because it was, "for the time being, the advanced race." As the "advanced race," it had one duty that was superior to all others: it must act to protect "civilization" from those who would destroy it. Buckley explicitly rejected the idea that the matter ought to be resolved by way of consulting the "catalogue of the rights of American citizens, born Equal." Damn your "rights," Buckley seemed to be saying, "civilization" trumps all.[13]

In the next issue of *National Review*, associate editor L. Brent Bozell took Buckley to task for "Why the South Must Prevail." Bozell, it should be noted, was no friend of civil rights. He was deeply opposed to the *Brown v. Board* school desegregation decision and he was supportive of "massive resistance" to it. But Bozell was also a lawyer and he called Buckley out for being so quick to disregard the rule of law. We conservatives, Bozell argued, are supposed to care about the rule of law and there was a law at stake in this instance: the Fifteenth Amendment, which protects the right to vote. Buckley might not like the Civil Rights Act of 1957, Bozell concluded, but he should care enough about the Constitution to oppose any attempt to undermine it through jury nullification.[14]

Buckley's response to Bozell—in the same issue in which he was criticized—is telling. In addition to rehashing many of the arguments he made previously, Buckley wrote two things that are especially noteworthy. First, he cast doubt on whether the Fifteenth Amendment—as a "Civil War Amendment"—really had the same legitimacy as the rest of the Constitution. These amendments, he said, were viewed by much of the South as "inorganic accretions" on the original document that were "grafted" on by "victors-at-war."[15] One has to wonder, then, where this leaves the legitimacy of the Thirteenth Amendment, which abolished slavery. Buckley did not say, but his logic points in a troubling direction. Second, Buckley suggested that the South might free itself from the charge of racism not by enfranchising Black people, but rather by disenfranchising more white people. Perhaps the South ought to adopt more "color-blind" policies of disenfranchisement that would have the effect of keeping many Black people from voting but would also have the effect of keeping uneducated whites from the polls.[16]

What Had These Eyes Seen Lately? Baldwin as a Witness to Black Liberation

Right at the very moment when Buckley and his colleagues were working out the finer points of how civil rights ought to be resisted, Baldwin was staring into the eyes of a 15-year-old boy, who was the first African-American student to attend a previously all-white school in Charlotte, North Carolina. Baldwin wanted to know what the world looked like through this young man's eyes, which "not only spoke, but registered volumes."[17] What had this boy's eyes seen lately? He had seen a barricade of white students assembled to keep him out of school. He had seen classmates intent on physically assaulting him. He had seen the twisted faces of peers hurling insults his way. He had seen his parents threatened with physical violence and economic ruin because they dared apply for the school integration program. Baldwin wanted to know what it was like for this young man to confront "what must surely have been the worst moment of his day—the morning, when he opened his eyes and realized that it was all to be gone through again."[18]

Baldwin was also curious about what the world looked like through the eyes of this young man's mother. As the oldest of nine siblings, Baldwin often felt himself to be in a quasi-parental role and he was intrigued—and haunted—by what the world looked like through the eyes of a parent at the margins of society. This young man's mother was one of only a few dozen Black parents—in a city with 50,000 Black people—who even dared apply for this school integration program. Baldwin wanted to know what gave her the courage and the audacity to take this step. As one thinks about Baldwin's engagement with this mother, one cannot help but recall Baldwin's powerful reflections on his father's funeral in Harlem in 1943. In that moment, which he described so vividly in "Notes of a Native Son," Baldwin found himself looking around the church at the Black parents, wondering how they confronted "the impossibility": "how to prepare the child for the day when the child would be despised and how to *create* for the child—by what means?—a stronger antidote to this poison than one had found for oneself."[19] Baldwin concluded that this was just what this mother was trying to do: to provide her son with a quality education, which she hoped might be an antidote to the poison of white supremacy.[20]

After speaking with this young man and his mother, Baldwin made his way to the young man's school so he could speak with the white principal. Baldwin found the young principal to be a "gentle" and even "honorable" human being, but he was also struck by the fact that the man was still trapped in the delusion of white supremacy. He did not seem to have any hatred in his heart for the young man, but he was unable—really—to appreciate his full humanity. As Baldwin went back and forth with the principal, he found himself far less interested in what the man thought of *Brown* v. *Board* or the local school integration program. Instead, Baldwin found himself wanting to try to get a sense of what the world looked like through his eyes. "I should think that the trouble in this situation," Baldwin said to the principal, "is that it's very hard for *you* to face a child and treat him unjustly because of something for which he is no more responsible than—than *you* are."[21] Baldwin said that with these words, the principal's "eyes came to life" and they were filled with "anguish" and "bewilderment." This, Baldwin concluded, was "the impossibility which he faced every day."[22] Baldwin's use of "the impossibility"—the phrase he had used when he reflected on what confronted those Harlem parents in 1943—is remarkable. There was something about the situation before those parents and the situation before this principal that seemed beyond the capacity of human beings to overcome. And yet one must persist. One is reminded of the ideas Baldwin used to conclude "Notes of a Native Son": "injustice is a commonplace" and is likely to remain so, but "one must never, in one's own life, accept these injustices as commonplace but must fight them with all one's strength."[23]

The Clash Before the Clash: Baldwin and Buckley at the Eye of the Storm

In the early 1960s, Baldwin and Buckley were firmly entrenched on the American intellectual and political scene. In addition to *National Review*, Buckley began publishing a syndicated newspaper column thrice weekly, appearing as a guest on radio and television programs as a conservative talking head, and touring the country to lecture and debate any liberal or radical who came into his path. Baldwin, for his part, was a fixture in the New York intellectual community and his works were appearing in increasingly high-profile publications such as the *New York Times* and *Esquire*. But Baldwin's biggest splash came in late 1962, when he published a 20,000-word essay called "Letter from a Region in My Mind" in *The New Yorker*. The essay proved to be a literary event of the highest order and it shot Baldwin's already rising star to international fame. In early 1963, the essay would be published along with one other piece as the book *The Fire Next Time*, which was on the bestseller charts for 41 weeks. He embarked on a lecture tour on behalf of civil rights organizations, and by mid-1963, he was second only to King as "the face" associated with the movement.

In the years leading up to their Cambridge debate, Baldwin and Buckley were engaged in both implicit and explicit intellectual combat. In late 1962, for example, Baldwin appeared opposite Buckley's go-to writer on civil rights, James Jackson

Kilpatrick, in a televised debate on segregation. This encounter occurred just after "the Battle at Ole Miss," when segregationist mobs killed and injured people in an attempt to keep a Black Air Force veteran named James Meredith from enrolling in the University of Mississippi. When face-to-face with Kilpatrick, Baldwin accused him of bearing far more responsibility for such violence than those who actually perpetrated it. Many of the people in these racist mobs, he insisted, were caught in webs of delusion they did not really understand. Kilpatrick and his allies, Baldwin declared, were responsible for weaving these webs and they did so for one reason and one reason only: they were concerned with conserving their own power.

Baldwin said Kilpatrick and his ilk were guilty of two betrayals. First, he was betraying those whites who had been seduced by the idea of white supremacy. Kilpatrick had convinced them to construct identities that completely undermined their moral lives. Second, Baldwin accused Kilpatrick of betraying Western civilization. Kilpatrick had claimed during the course of their conversation that his devotion to white supremacy and apartheid were rooted in his desire to conserve Western civilization, something he believed white people were best positioned to do. But in fact, Baldwin insisted, Kilpatrick was undermining everything that was good in Western civilization. Kilpatrick was claiming to care about the Judeo-Christian tradition, but how could he square his positions with the idea that each human being was created in the image of God? Kilpatrick claimed to care about the Constitution of the United States, but what had he done lately to secure the "blessings of liberty" or the "equal protection of the laws" for his fellow citizens?[24]

It was also in these years that Baldwin found himself occasionally doing battle with those closer to him politically. In mid-1963, for example, Baldwin, Lorraine Hansberry, and several other artists, intellectuals, and activists met with Attorney General Robert F. Kennedy in order to push the administration to take more decisive action on civil rights. In these exchanges, Baldwin and Hansberry called on the Kennedy brothers to declare the civil rights struggle to be a *moral* one and to communicate to the country that anyone willing to spit on a Black child walking to school was also spitting on the President and the Constitution of the United States. Baldwin's clash with Kennedy was a dramatic manifestation of his misgivings about the role of many "white liberals" in the civil rights struggle. Although many liberals had some of the right attitudes about race matters, they failed all too often to demonstrate the sort of moral commitment necessary to bring about justice.

While Baldwin was squaring off in person and in print with Kilpatrick and others who were impeding the liberation of the country, Buckley was keeping a close eye on Baldwin and doing all he could to warn the country to resist the ideas of this "eloquent menace" and everything he represented. In addition to criticizing Baldwin's ideas, Buckley opposed many of the civil rights actions Baldwin supported, including the Birmingham campaign and the March on Washington. In these years, we see Buckley's racial politics adapting to new circumstances. As he lost many battles—over the Civil Rights Act of 1964, for example—he realized that the key to conservative ascendancy would be to harness the "political energy" of "the white backlash" to Black liberation.[25] This slightly more subtle racial politics scrapped outright defenses of segregation and white supremacy in favor of more targeted attacks on policies that even moderates believed were a step too far, such as busing to achieve greater racial balance in schools and fair housing laws that might integrate the suburbs.[26]

The Clash at Cambridge

Thanks to the ingenuity and persistence of a British publicist with Corgi Books, Bill Kolins, and a small group of undergraduates, the Baldwin–Buckley clash at Cambridge was arranged for 18 February 1965. As the civil rights movement reached its apex, Baldwin had reached the peak of his literary fame and Buckley had established himself as the chief polemicist of the American right. On the night in question, the motion before the House was: "The American Dream is at the expense of the American Negro." Two student debaters—one on each side—spoke, before Baldwin was invited to address the House. It was Baldwin's first time participating in formal debate and he delivered a speech unlike anything the students had ever heard. Rather than delivering a traditional Union speech, which is some combination of intellectual exercise and jocular performance art, Baldwin—forever the preacher—delivered a sermon about the perils of white supremacy for both "the subjugated" and "the subjugators." For the subjugated, the doctrine of white supremacy leads to "the millions of details of every day" that communicate to you that your life does not quite matter as much as the lives of others, and you are haunted by the fact that you cannot feel much confidence that the lives of the next generation will be better than your own. For the subjugators—the would-be beneficiaries of white supremacy—the picture is no more promising. Many people who imagine themselves to be white are in thrall to the delusion that their value and role in the world is inextricably bound to the color of their skin. The "moral lives" of these people, Baldwin told the students, have been "destroyed by the plague called color."

After Baldwin delivered his speech, he received a standing ovation, a very rare thing in the Union, and Buckley was called to speak. Buckley said he recognized that it was not going to be "his night," but he refused to concede much of anything to Baldwin's side. Baldwin, he warned the elite British students, was hellbent on overthrowing Western civilization and he was offering them a philosophy of despair that was dangerous to those he claimed to want to help. Buckley called on Baldwin to stop complaining and start using his platform to encourage "the Negro community" to take advantage of the opportunities that already existed. After Buckley sat down and a few students delivered short speeches on each side, the members of the Union voted. Baldwin's side was triumphant by a vote of 544 to 164.[27]

The Aftermath

The day after his triumph in Cambridge, Baldwin heard about the violence in Marion, Alabama, that would lead to the death of Jimmie Lee Jackson. Two days after that, he received word that his friend Malcolm X had been assassinated. And two weeks further on, the U.S. would witness "Bloody Sunday," a vicious attack on civil rights marchers fighting for voting rights in Alabama. Meanwhile, Buckley was busy explaining away his loss in Cambridge as an "orgy of anti-Americanism," rather than a meaningful exchange of ideas. Buckley would say later that he had never lost a debate by such a wide margin, but it was the debate about which he had the most pride because he refused to "give them one goddam inch."[28] A few weeks later, Buckley would get his chance to avenge his defeat at Baldwin's hands. One of the kings of American television, David Susskind, invited Baldwin and Buckley onto his show, *Open End*, to engage each other once more. When they did, Buckley got the better of Baldwin by getting under his skin in a way that led Baldwin ("to my eternal dishonor," he would say later) to "tune out." The *Open End* exchange led Baldwin to conclude that Buckley was a bully who was unwilling to listen and, if he had it to do all over again, he would have hit Buckley over the head with his coffee cup.[29] This joke contained a deadly serious point at its core. In Cambridge, Baldwin had said that what "concerns me most" is that we will become so unwilling to listen to each other that the very authority of reasoned discourse will break down. Where reason ends, war begins.[30]

Just a few days after their *Open End* encounter, Buckley would launch a third-party bid for the mayoralty of New York. His bid was never serious in electoral terms, but it could not have been more serious in ideological terms. In one of the great ironies of American political history, Buckley—one of the most *elitist* figures on the scene—ran a *populist* campaign that was fueled by racial resentment at every turn. In the end, what was most interesting about Buckley's bid was not how many votes he received, but rather *who* cast their vote in his favor. Buckley did not receive support from upper-crust elites like himself. Instead, he received the support of working-class whites from New York's outer boroughs.

Buckley's mayoral campaign brings into relief the enduring relevance of this story. Throughout the 1950s and 1960s, Buckley worked hard to promote an intellectually serious conservative case against civil rights. Although he lost many battles in this period, his political instincts helped the right win an ideological war that would contribute to conservative ascendancy in the decades that followed. Racial resentment was an invaluable political resource and Buckley encouraged conservatives to take advantage of it at every turn. The consequences of the politics of racial resentment are felt in the millions of details of every day that communicate to so many of our fellows that their lives do not matter quite as much.

The story of Buckley's role in the promotion of the politics of racial resentment is worth telling in itself, but telling it through the lens of Baldwin is all the more powerful. Baldwin's point of view is unlike any other in American political thought. He helps us see—from the inside—what the world might look through the eyes of those at the margins and he displays an almost superhuman empathy for those caught in the grip of delusions like white supremacy. Baldwin was, at his core, an existential detective, who masterfully used his fictional characters and the subjects of his nonfiction writing to help us make sense of fundamental questions of identity and how we ought to live. Through Baldwin's eyes, we are able to see that the price of power for Buckley and the American right has been a deal with devil of white supremacy. By the end of this story, Baldwin is there to ask Buckley: was it worth it? You may have acquired power, but you have sacrificed the dignity of so many—including yourself—in the process.

But Baldwin's role in this story amounts to more than simply a powerful lens through which to think about Buckley and the rise of the American right. Baldwin also provides us with the beginnings of an answer to the question: what are we to do? In the face of the human conundrum at the root of our trouble—that nexus of identity, morality, and power I described earlier—Baldwin prescribed love. The sort of love Baldwin prescribed, though, was not much like love as it is usually understood. His was not an understanding of love that was sentimental, infantile, or necessarily comforting. Instead, Baldwin insisted that "love is a battle, love is a war. Love is a growing up."[31] Baldwin called on all of us to love ourselves enough to engage in ruthless inspection of our own identities. And he also called on us to love one another enough to be willing to confront each other about the delusions under which we live. When we are willing to do this, Baldwin concluded, we do "what lovers do, which is to reveal the beloved to himself, and with that revelation, make freedom real."[32]

Notes

1   As quoted in Magdalena J. Zaborowska, *James Baldwin's Turkish Decade: The Erotics of Exile* (Durham, NC, Duke University Press, 2008), p. 260.
2   Nicholas Buccola, *The Fire Is Upon Us* (Princeton, NJ, Princeton University Press, 2019).
3   Transcript of the Baldwin–Buckley debate at the Cambridge Union, 18 February 1965, in Buccola, *Fire*, p. 381.
4   James Baldwin, "The Fire Next Time," in *Collected Essays*, ed. Toni Morrison (New York, Library of America, 1998), p. 299.
5   Priscilla L. Buckley and William F. Buckley Jr., *WFB: An Appreciation* (privately published, 1959).
6   William F. Buckley, Jr., *God and Man at Yale* (1951) (Washington, D.C., Regenery Publishing, 2001), p. 123.
7   The concept of public orthodoxy is explained in Buccola, *Fire*, p. 63.
8   James Baldwin, "Autobiographical Notes," in Morrison (ed.), *Collected Essays*, p. 9.
9   Susan Currie Sivek, "Editing Conservatism: How *National Review* Magazine Framed and Mobilized a Political Movement," *Mass Communication and Society*, 11:3 (2008), pp. 247–74.
10 As quoted in Buccola, *Fire*, p. 83.
11 Richard M. Weaver, "The Regime of the South," *National Review*, 14 March 1959, pp. 587–9.
12 William F. Buckley, Jr., "Why the South Must Prevail," *National Review*, 24 August 1957, pp. 148–9.
13 *Ibid.*
14 L. Brent Bozell, "The Open Question," *National Review*, 7 September 1957, p. 209.
15 William F. Buckley, Jr., "A Clarification," *National Review*, 7 September 1957, p. 199.

16 *Ibid.*

17 James Baldwin, "A Fly in Buttermilk," in Morrison (ed.), *Collected Essays*, p. 188.

18 *Ibid.*

19 James Baldwin, "Notes of a Native Son," in Morrison (ed.), *Collected Essays*, p. 78.

20 *Ibid.*, p. 192.

21 Baldwin, "A Fly in Buttermilk," p. 195.

22 *Ibid.*, pp. 195–6.

23 Baldwin, "Notes of a Native Son," p. 84.

24 I discuss Baldwin's encounter with Kilpatrick at greater length in "Don't Do It, Jimmy: James Baldwin and the Duty to Confront Racism," *The Common Reader*, 23 September 2019, https://commonreader.wustl.edu/c/dont-do-it-jimmy/ (accessed 15 June 2020).

25 William F. Buckley, Jr., "The Mess in Mississippi," *National Review*, 23 October 1962, p. 305.

26 See extensive discussion of the shifting racial politics of *National Review* in Buccola, *Fire*, pp. 220–3.

27 All citations from the Cambridge debate are from the transcript included as an Appendix to Buccola, *Fire*.

28 Garry Wills, "Buckley, Buckley, Bow Wow Wow," *Esquire*, January 1968, http://classic.esquire.com/article/1968/1/1/buckley-buckley-bow-wow-wow (accessed 12 June 2020).

29 C. Robert Jennings, "A Warning for Mr. Charlie," *Los Angeles Times West Magazine*, 7 July 1968, pp. 18–23.

30 Buccola, *Fire*, p. 385.

31 James Baldwin, "In Search of a Majority," in Morrison (ed.), *Collected Essays*, p. 220.

32 James Baldwin, "The Creative Process," in Morrison (ed.), *Collected Essays*, p. 672.

Works Cited

Baldwin, James, "Autobiographical Notes" (1949), in *Collected Essays*, ed. Toni Morrison (New York, Library of America, 1998), pp. 5–10.

_____ "The Creative Process" (1962), in *Collected Essays*, ed. Toni Morrison (New York, Library of America, 1998), pp. 669–72.

_____ "The Fire Next Time" (1963), in *Collected Essays*, ed. Toni Morrison (New York, Library of America, 1998), pp. 291–348.

_____ "A Fly in Buttermilk" (1954), in *Collected Essays*, ed. Toni Morrison (New York, Library of America, 1998), pp. 187–96.

_____ "In Search of a Majority" (1954), in *Collected Essays*, ed. Toni Morrison (New York, Library of America, 1998), pp. 215–21.

_____ "Notes of a Native Son" (1949), in *Collected Essays*, ed. Toni Morrison (New York, Library of America, 1998), pp. 63–84.

Bozell, L. Brent, "The Open Question," *National Review*, 7 September 1957, p. 209.

Buccola, Nicholas, "Don't Do It, Jimmy: James Baldwin and the Duty to Confront Racism," *The Common Reader*, 23 September 2019, https://commonreader.wustl.edu/c/dont-do-it-jimmy/ (accessed 15 June 2020).

_____ *The Fire Is Upon Us: James Baldwin, William F. Buckley Jr., and the Debate over Race in America* (Princeton, NJ, Princeton University Press, 2019).

Buckley, Priscilla L., and William F. Buckley Jr., *WFB: An Appreciation* (privately published, 1959).

Buckley, Jr., William F., "A Clarification," *National Review*, 7 September 1957, p. 199.

_____ *God and Man at Yale* (1951) (Washington, D.C., Regenery Publishing, 2001).

_____ "The Mess in Mississippi," *National Review*, 23 October 1962, p. 305.

_____ "Why the South Must Prevail," *National Review*, 24 August 1957, pp. 148–9.

Jennings, C. Robert, "A Warning for Mr. Charlie," *Los Angeles Times West Magazine*, 7 July 1968, pp. 18–23.

Sivek, Susan Currie, "Editing Conservatism: How *National Review* Magazine Framed and Mobilized a Political Movement," *Mass Communication and Society*, 11:3 (2008), pp. 247–74.

Weaver, Richard M., "The Regime of the South," *National Review*, 14 March 1959, pp. 587–9.

Wills, Garry, "Buckley, Buckley, Bow Wow Wow," *Esquire*, January 1968, http://classic.esquire.com/article/1968/1/1/buckley-buckley-bow-wow-wow (accessed 12 June 2020).

Zaborowska, Magdalena J., *James Baldwin's Turkish Decade: The Erotics of Exile* (Durham, NC, Duke University Press, 2008).

Contributor's Biography

Nicholas Buccola is a writer, lecturer, and teacher who specializes in American political thought. He is the author of *The Fire Is Upon Us: James Baldwin, William F. Buckley Jr., and the Debate over Race in America* (Princeton University Press, 2019) and *The Political Thought of Frederick Douglass: In Pursuit of American Liberty* (NYU Press, 2012). He is the editor of *The Essential Douglass: Writings and Speeches* (Hackett, 2016) and *Abraham Lincoln and Liberal Democracy* (University Press of Kansas, 2016). His essays have appeared in scholarly journals including *The Review of Politics and American Political Thought* as well as popular outlets such as the *New York Times*, *Salon*, the *Baltimore Sun*, and *Dissent*. He is the Elizabeth and Morris Glicksman Chair in Political Science at Linfield University in McMinnville, Oregon.

ESSAY

"The Shape of the Wrath to Come": James Baldwin's Radicalism and the Evolution of His Thought on Israel

Nadia Alahmed   Dickinson College

Abstract

This article traces the evolution of James Baldwin's discourse on the Arab–Israeli conflict as connected to his own evolution as a Black thinker, activist, and author. It creates a nuanced trajectory of the transformation of Baldwin's thought on the Arab–Israeli conflict and Black and Jewish relations in the U.S. This trajectory is created through the lens of Baldwin's relationship with some of the major radical Black movements and organizations of the twentieth century: Malcolm X, Elijah Muhammad and the Nation of Islam, and, finally, the Black Power movement, especially the Black Panther Party. Using Baldwin as an example, the article displays the Arab–Israeli conflict as a terrain Black radicals used to articulate their visions of the nature of Black oppression in the U.S., strategies of resistance, the meaning of Black liberation, and articulations of Black identity. It argues that the study of Baldwin's transformation from a supporter of the Zionist project of nation-building to an advocate of Palestinian rights and national aspirations reveals much about the ideological transformations of the larger Black liberation movement.

Keywords: James Baldwin, Palestine, Israel, Black radicalism, Malcolm X, Elijah Muhammad, Nation of Islam, Black Power

> I think black people have always felt this about America, and Americans, and have always seen, spinning above the thoughtless American head, the shape of the wrath to come.
>
> James Baldwin, *No Name in the Street*[1]

As the state of Israel was established in 1948, James Baldwin felt the urge to flee America. Although he ended up in Paris, in *No Name In the Street* (1972) he reveals that this was actually an accident; he had "seriously considered" going to

James Baldwin Review, Volume 6, 2020, © The Authors. Published by Manchester University Press and The University of Manchester Library
http://dx.doi.org/10.7227/JBR.6.3

Israel and working on a kibbutz.[2] Considering Israel as his possible destination for this self-imposed exile suggests that, like many other Black intellectuals—such as Paul Robeson, W. E. B. Du Bois, Bayard Rustin, and Stokely Carmichael (later Kwame Ture)—Baldwin viewed the newly established Jewish republic quite favorably. The history of connections between Black and Jewish intellectuals is defined by leftist organizations and ideologies like the Communist Party and various Marxist and socialist organizations. Baldwin was sympathetic to many of them. He was also close with the Jewish intelligentsia of New York City, specifically Saul Levitas of *The New Leader*, Randall Jarrell of *The Nation*, and Cohen and Robert Warshow of *Commentary*. He was introduced to these editors and intellectuals by Eugene Worth in December of 1943.[3] These connections proved crucial for the young Baldwin's nascent career as a writer and a New York intellectual.

It is not surprising that like the Black intellectuals mentioned above, Baldwin viewed Israel in a positive light. At this point in 1948 the writer saw Israel as a sanctuary, and his view was somewhat idealistic. However, by the early 1970s, at the peak of the Black Power movement, he would come to view the state as a neo-colonial project put in place to support Western, specifically American, imperial interests in the Middle East, and would subject Israel to caustic criticism.

This article traces the nuanced trajectory of the evolution of Baldwin's thought on the Palestinian conflict in order to trace the contours of this transformation and the forces behind it. I highlight the connections between his changing discourse on the conflict and his development as a writer, intellectual, and activist as a whole. I will show how Baldwin's positioning of the American Jewish diaspora within the system of U.S. racial stratification affected the way he thought and wrote about the conflict. Lastly, I foreground Baldwin's relationship and proximity to Black Power figures and ideologies as forces that brought about the transformation of his views on Palestine and Israel as well as the significance of Palestinian liberation for a global Black struggle for freedom.

The dynamics of Black and Jewish relationships are directly related, if not defined, by the nature of Black discourse on Palestine and the political climate in the region. When the state of Israel was created in 1948, the event was celebrated by Black intellectuals as the victory of an oppressed people after an arduous struggle for sovereignty and self-determination. In the context of the devastating aftermath of the Holocaust and this victory, Baldwin wrote about a powerful sense of identification with the American Jewish diaspora: "At this point, the Negro identifies himself almost wholly with the Jew. The more devout Negro considers that he *is* a Jew, in bondage to a hard taskmaster and waiting for a Moses to lead him out of Egypt."[4] Even though he does not directly mention the Holocaust, he speaks of a prolonged and intimate connection based on a shared history of oppression. At this point, Baldwin framed Israel as founded by oppressed, displaced people, who had reclaimed their ancient home. Black Zionism, its history and implications are beyond the scope of this article. However, 1948 can be justly viewed as a peak of the ideology that was created by Black nationalists like Martin Delany and Edward Blyden in the nineteenth century and later reinforced by Marcus Garvey and many other Black nationalists and intellectuals alike.[5]

Baldwin had a long and complex relationship with the Jewish community through-out his life. He went to school with a large Jewish student population and had a lot of close connections and friendships in the Jewish intellectual circles of New York City and the Jewish left. These connections, and, of course, his prominence and recognition as a writer, intellectual, and public figure, prompted the Israeli government to issue him an official invitation in 1961. In "Letters from a Journey," Baldwin wrote about his experience in Israel, his understanding of its nature as related to its past and present, racism, and liberation. He arrived in Israel in October and his first impressions were defined by the pleasant nature of Israeli hospitality. His tone is sunny, full of optimism and excitement: "The visit seems, so far, to have been a great success: Israel and I seem to like each other."[6] Nevertheless, even in the first entry about his visit, he is hyper-aware of the significance of this trip. He also cannot avoid questioning the realities of the newly established Jewish republic:

> This is not going to be easy; and yet, since this trip is clearly my prologue to Africa, it has become very important to me to assess what Israel makes me feel. In a curious way, since it does function as a homeland, however beleaguered, you can't walk five minutes without finding yourself at a border, can't talk to anyone for five minutes without being reminded first of the mandate (British) then the war—and of course the entire Arab situation, outside this country, and, above all, within.[7]

Baldwin's trip to Africa was going to be a tremendously important landmark. At that point, he felt ambivalent about the Negritude movement and the meaning and implications of Africa for Black Americans, but he was also aware of the magnitude of his trip there and its potential for him as an intellectual, a Black American, and a human being. Israel as a gateway to Africa placed additional pressure on his visit, which is discussed further in his writing.

The view of Israel Baldwin expresses is not one-dimensional from the start. On the one hand, he recognizes the Zionist ideal of the state as a Jewish homeland. On the other hand, he is acutely aware of the borders and spatial stratifications of the state. He struggles to negotiate the colonial past and Western domination over the land by the British Empire with the new sense of freedom created by Israeli national mythology. Above all, he cannot ignore the instances of the mistreatment of Palestinians and Arab Israelis.

Despite this uneasy awareness of these difficulties, Baldwin is hesitant to express direct criticism. He appears to strive to understand both sides of the conflict and, at this stage, approaches the matter carefully:

> I cannot blame them for feeling dispossessed; and in a literal way, they have been. Furthermore, the Jews, who are surrounded by forty million hostile Muslims, are forced to control the very movements of Arabs within the state of Israel. One cannot blame the Jews for this necessity; one cannot blame the Arabs for resenting it. *I* would—indeed, in my own situation in America, I do, and it has cost me—costs me—a great and continuing effort not to hate the people who are responsible for the societal effort to limit and diminish me.[8]

Here, Baldwin resonates with Zionist rhetoric again, describing Israel as vulnerable, "surrounded" by "hostile Muslims." He justifies surveillance practices and control over "Arabs"; "Palestinians" as a people were erased by the Zionist discourse and would not become a part of Baldwin's vocabulary until the 1970s. Nevertheless, he begins a very important line of thought here: drawing parallels between Palestinian and Black experience, comparing his experience as a Black man in America to the oppression of Palestinians. During the Black Power era this vision would culminate in a profound and deep sense of identification with Palestinians.

Baldwin recognizes another crucial flaw of the state of Israel, in a way more significant than its treatment of "Arabs," as he points out the unequal social stratifications among the Jewish population itself:

> In spite of the fact that the nation of Israel cannot afford, and is far too intelligent, to encourage any form of social discrimination, the fact remains that there is a tremendous gap between a Jew from Russia or France or England or Australia and a Jew but lately arrived from the desert.[9]

What Baldwin is alluding to here is the racial stratification in Israel that privileges Jews of Western origin over Jews who immigrated to Israel from Africa and other Middle Eastern countries. This social stratification was not dissimilar to the one in the U.S., which Baldwin immediately recognized and which triggered his original suspicion.

This criticism addresses a complicated and vulnerable aspect of Israel and its national mythology: unequal racial stratification among the Jewish population of the country. It collapses the Zionist ideal of homeland, dignity, and self-determination for the Jews that Baldwin sought to affirm earlier. In a way, he echoes the ideals of equality and self-determination as propagated by Zionist ideology, calling Israel "intelligent," a wisdom stemming from centuries of oppression and antisemitism. Nevertheless, he is not afraid to point out that Arab, African Jews "arrived from the desert"—Jews who possibly looked like him—did not find self-determination, equality, or a true homeland in the fulfilled Zionist dream.

As Baldwin's reflection progresses, his ambivalence toward Israel grows. While expressing admiration of Jews and their accomplishment embodied in the founding of Israel, he writes of another significant point of contention in the country, the imperial implications of its history: "One cannot but respect the energy and the courage of this handful of people; but one can't but suspect that a vast amount of political cynicism, on the part of the English and the Americans, went into the creation of this state."[10] He points to the role of Western neocolonial powers embodied by the U.S. and U.K., which were defining forces that guaranteed and fulfilled the Zionist dream, from the Balfour Declaration during the British mandate, which promised the creation of the Jewish homeland, to the unconditional political and economic support of Israel on behalf of the U.S. The "political cynicism" of these powers is Baldwin's reminder that they had a very specific political calculus and self-interest in supporting Israel before and after its creation, factors that did not align with Zionist ideas of Jewish empowerment. Baldwin would continue to speak about the impact of Western imperialism on Israel in his writing into the 1970s.

Baldwin's "Letters from a Journey" reflects a multifaceted struggle and a crisis in which he finds himself. He attempts to mollify his disenchantment but reinforces the main reason why it is impossible for him to maintain a positive attitude toward Israel, specifically its oppression of Palestinians: "Or perhaps I would not feel this way if I were not helplessly and painfully—most, painfully—ambivalent concerning the status of the Arabs here."[11] This is the coda of his visit.

The effect of his visit was devastating for Baldwin. His earlier idealistic approach to Israel was shattered by the country's realities and the parallels between the Black and Palestinian experiences he witnessed and described in his writing. Years before Black Power figures articulated their platform of support of Palestinians, rooted in the powerful resonance between the nature of their oppressions, Baldwin based his changing views on his firsthand experience.

The magnitude of the effect of his visit is hard to overestimate, as he poses complex and extremely difficult questions for himself and the world: "'What is a Jew?' is also, for me, to ask myself 'What is a Black man?' and what, in the name of heaven, is an American Negro? I have a gloomy feeling that I won't find any answers in Africa, only more questions."[12] Baldwin echoes a parallel between Jewish and Black experience, here expressed in the essay, "The Harlem Ghetto." His ambivalence about the definitions of the Jewish and Black diaspora and their experiences after his visit to Israel points to a serious identity crisis.

In *James Baldwin's Turkish Decade* Magdalena Zaborowska quotes Baldwin's letter to his editor that speaks to his experience of Israel after the fact in more explicit terms: "When I was in Israel it was as though I was in the middle of *The Fire Next Time*. I didn't dare to go from Israel to Africa, so I went to Turkey, just across the road."[13] The choice to use *The Fire Next Time* (1963) as a metaphor to describe his experience is telling. At that point in his career, the essay exemplified a series of painful epiphanies about racial relationships in the U.S., the importance of Black Islam, and some of the most complicated and urgent questions he had to ask himself and his readers. As mentioned above, Zionism was an important model for Black nationalists.[14] And while Baldwin was in no way a follower of this ideology, the influence of Afro-Zionism on how Black people viewed Israel was profound. His disenchantment with Israel hinted at how devastating a disenchantment in Africa might be. "Letters from a Journey" contains some of the most important questions about identity, diaspora, race, state violence, and homeland. All of these questions are informed, if not defined, by Baldwin's painful awareness of the Palestinian condition.

In *A Rap on Race* (1971) and later in *No Name in the Street* (1972)—both published during the peak of the Black Power movement and Baldwin's growing connections with its leaders—Baldwin displayed caustic criticism of Israel, using language much stronger than in "Letters from a Journey." It is important to acknowledge that several global movements impacted the shift in Baldwin's attitude: anticolonial movements on the African continent, the Third World movement (that made Palestinian liberation a significant aspect of global liberation), and, more locally, the anti-imperialist implications of the anti-Vietnam War movement the author participated in actively. However, as this article argues, Black Power and its predecessors and influencers like Nation of Islam and Malcolm X impacted his rhetoric on Israel.

Baldwin's firsthand experience of the Nation of Islam and its leader Elijah Muhammad, as well as his debate with Malcolm X, were noteworthy landmarks in the development of his political thought. Black Power, the major ideological force that impacted Baldwin's view on Palestine and Israel, borrowed many ideological and structural characteristics from the Nation of Islam and was essentially inspired by the teachings of Malcolm X. Most significantly, Malcolm X and the Nation of Islam were some of the first voices to support Palestinians in a systematic and vocal fashion, as evident in the N.O.I. newsletter, "Muhammad Speaks."[15]

Baldwin received a unique insight into the inner workings of the Nation of Islam and the organization's leader, Elijah Muhammad, due to a somewhat unexpected dinner invitation. He provided a detailed account of this meeting in *The Fire Next Time*. The tone of the essay is somewhat cautious. Baldwin appears to be humbled by the presence of the leaders of one of the biggest and oldest twentieth-century Black organizations. Even though Baldwin had denounced the ideologies of Black religion since he had left the Pentecostal Church, he was cognizant of the political and ideological significance of Black Islamic faith:

> God had come a long way from the desert—but then so had Allah, though in a very different direction. God, going North, and rising on the wings of power, had become white, and Allah, out of power, and on the dark side of heaven, had become—for all practical purposes anyway—Black.[16]

Baldwin is creating a powerful dichotomy here, conflating racial and religious identities. He recognizes that the Western, or white, imaginary and portrayal of God has been used to subjugate Blacks and to differentiate between Black and white Americans. This is a significant departure from the discourse of "The Harlem Ghetto," which is saturated in Judeo-Christian mythology, and toward an alignment between Jewish and Black experience and history. Baldwin's cognizance of the significance of Black Islam as a source of alternative racial identity and empowerment also creates a hierarchy of oppression predicated on religion. In this hierarchy, Judeo-Christian mythology is aligned with whiteness, and Blackness with Islam. Baldwin would continue this line of thought, aligning Judeo-Christian traditions with whiteness, later in his writing. This discourse is important because, as discussed earlier in this article, how Baldwin saw the Jewish diaspora in the U.S. within the system of white supremacy was directly related to how he envisioned the conflict between Palestinians and Israel.

It is also notable that Baldwin introduces Israel into the discussion of his meeting with the N.O.I. leader: "When Malcolm X … points out that the cry for 'violence' was not raised, for example, when the Israelis fought to regain Israel, and indeed, is raised only when Black men indicate that they will fight for their rights, he is speaking the truth."[17] Baldwin subscribes to the Zionist idea that the land that came to be known as Israel in 1948 was "regained" and not stolen. However, he points out the hypocrisy of America celebrating Jewish insurgency while condemning the militant approaches of Malcolm X and the Nation of Islam. This is the continuation of the rhetoric begun with his musings on Black Islam. Instead of presenting Jews as victims of a prolonged history of oppression in resonance with Black experience, Israeli Jews are presented as protégés of the U.S., its racism, and its imperialism. This is the first mention of Israel in Baldwin's writing since his trip there, and it is obvious that his criticism of the state is burgeoning and becoming sharper in the context of his recognition of the importance of the Nation of Islam on ideological and practical levels. He praises the organization for its efforts in the rehabilitation of Black community members, emphasizing that their success is unprecedented.[18]

The Fire Next Time was published the same year Baldwin debated Malcolm X. And even though at that point it is clear that their visions of the Black freedom struggle were contradictory, nine years later in *No Name in the Street* Baldwin would call Malcolm X a "genuine revolutionary."[19] Some of Baldwin's most critical statements on Israel appear in the same book. The mechanisms of this correlation can be traced through Baldwin's further engagement with Black radicalism, and, specifically, the Black Power movement.

As "Black Power," the slogan, politics, and ideology, were taking over the Black political stage, in 1966 Baldwin penned "A Report from the Occupied Territory."[20] He had a complicated relationship with Black nationalist ideology, which was a significant Black Power tenet. Nevertheless, it didn't stop him from using Black nationalist language in his article, framing Harlem as a Black, "occupied" land. Moreover, the concepts, patterns, and ideas he describes in the article are in strong resonance with Palestinian history and experience. Even more significantly, they echo his own experiences of the treatment of Palestinians living in Israel he had witnessed during his visit:

> The police are afraid of everything in Harlem and they are especially afraid of the roofs, which they consider to be guerrilla outposts. This means that the citizens of Harlem who, as we have seen, can come to grief at any hour on the streets, and who are not safe at their windows, are forbidden the very air. They are safe only in their houses—or were, until the city passed the No Knock, Stop and Frisk laws, which permit a policeman to enter one's home without knocking and to stop anyone on the streets, at will, at any hour, and search him.[21]

From referring to the roofs as "guerrilla outposts" and residents of Harlem as "citizens," to the title describing the neighborhood as an "occupied territory," the parallels with Palestine are significant. For one, Baldwin uses a Black nationalist trope, the idea that Harlem is a country within the United States "occupied" by the hostile police. The image of the Palestinian guerrilla fighters had captured the imagination of radicals all over the world when Baldwin was writing the essay.

Timothy Seidel discusses the significance of Baldwin's piece in "Occupied Territory is Occupied Territory":

> Though written almost 50 years ago, Baldwin's observations continue to resonate with the experiences of marginalized and dispossessed communities today, indicating historical trends across geographical experiences … Whether it is the construction of walls, militarization of borders, the confiscation of land, or the brutalization and incarceration of bodies, activists and academics are identifying commonalities across experiences that transcend national boundaries and identities. The situation in Palestine has played an increasingly significant role in mobilizing transnational solidarities that cross such boundaries.[22]

Rhetorically, Baldwin made Harlem a powerful microcosm of oppression. Seidel believes that Baldwin created a compelling discourse and framework for transnational solidarity: "Baldwin's claim that 'occupied territory is occupied territory' has not diminished in terms of the contentious politics and transnational solidarities that continue to carry that claim."[23] Seidel's article credits Baldwin not only with his contributions to the discourse of racism, but to a transnational tradition of solidarity. And while in the context of African-American politics, Du Bois and especially Black Power figures are traditionally associated with this achievement, Seidel's article foregrounds Baldwin's work in this sphere. A work that preceded and anticipated Black Power's articulations of Third World solidarity and its implications for Black liberation, "Report from the Occupied Territory" was published the same year the Black Panther Party was founded by Bobby Seale and Huey Newton in Oakland. Black Power began to gain real momentum, transforming Baldwin's discourse on American politics, as well as the way that he wrote and understood the position of the Jewish diaspora within the racial hierarchy in the U.S.

The year 1967 marked a dramatic transformation in Black discourse on the Arab–Israeli conflict. The major landmark in this transformation can be traced to the Student Nonviolent Coordinating Committee's (S.N.C.C.) publication of a pro-Palestinian article in its newsletter in the aftermath of the 1967 war, which established the unequivocal military dominance of the Jewish republic. Many historians, including Clayborne Carson, saw this moment as a point when a majority of Jews who supported the civil rights struggle left the movement and thus propelled the growing popularity of Black Power and its separatist agenda.[24]

Years later Stokely Carmichael, chairman of the S.N.C.C. at the time of the 1967 publication, mused about the incident. He believed that the backlash against the organization's publication in particular, and his own support of the Palestinian cause in general, created a lot of hostility toward him. He recalled his strong ties to the Jewish community and culture and refused the accusations of antisemitism. Instead he created a complex narrative of how he became familiar with and invested in the Palestinian cause. He cited the Nation of Islam, Malcolm X, and, above all, Ethel Minor as the main causes of his interest in Arab–Israeli conflict. Minor was the one who encouraged the publication of the newsletter. However, this was not an isolated instance of the S.N.C.C.'s interest in Palestine and Israel. Carmichael claimed that by the time he had become chairman, the S.N.C.C. caucus would read "a book a month" on Palestine as well as Zionism.[25] Carmichael concludes his narrative about the history of his own support for the Palestinian cause with a passionate statement: "So I can tell the world: I am not now, have never been, nor can ever be anti-Semitic or anti-Judaic. However, I am, and will be unto death, anti-Zionist."[26] Carmichael was instrumental in introducing and popularizing Palestinian liberation as an integral part of Black struggle waged by Black Power. Baldwin's relationship with the S.N.C.C. and later the Black Panther Party, as well as the pro-Palestinian newsletter, must be cited as contributing forces that changed his discourse on Palestine.

The year 1967 also marked Baldwin's publication of "Negroes Are Anti-Semitic Because They're Anti-White" in the *New York Times* magazine. In the essay, Baldwin explored the relationship between race and gentrification and how it affected Jewish racial positionality within the U.S. racial order. Keith Feldman connects this phenomenon directly to the Middle Eastern political climate:

> [The essay] maps the relationship between racism and ghettoization at a time of heightened tension in Israel-Palestine. If in 1948 Baldwin saw Jews living in the midst of Harlem ghetto, by 1967, Baldwin suggests that anti-Semitism emerged because not only had American Jews become assimilated into a national ideology of exclusion, predicated on race ... they had embraced a spatially stratified whiteness.[27]

Feldman argues that Baldwin saw Jewish withdrawal from the houses and streets of Harlem as a point of integration into a mainstream American national narrative, and, essentially, whiteness. He also echoes Carson's stance on the effect that the S.N.C.C.'s pro-Palestinian newsletter had on Black and Jewish relationships during the civil rights movement. It would be inaccurate to claim that the Jewish community embraced Israel wholeheartedly and did not display any of the concerns voiced by the newsletter. Nevertheless, an astounding majority of Jewish S.N.C.C. members perceived the newsletter as hostile and the organization lost almost all of its Jewish membership in the aftermath of the incident.

Once again, a strong resonance between Black and Jewish relationships and Black politics on Palestine resurfaced and was reflected in Baldwin's writing. It would be an overstatement to claim that the S.N.C.C. newsletter was the only catalyst for the cleavage in Black and Jewish relationships. The overall shift to embrace the Third World ideology by several groups and outlets at this time implied a critical stance toward Israel.

The Black Power movement was defined by opposition to the policies, ideas, and ideals of the civil rights movement and its leaders. It was one of the major reasons why the relationship between Black Power and James Baldwin was tumultuous at its early stages. But Baldwin was antagonized by the movement not only because he was perceived as a poster child of the civil rights movement and white liberalism. The hostility was also fueled by the blatant homophobia of the Black

Power leaders. Douglas Field discusses the nature of Baldwin's relationship with the movement, and its leaders, their contours, and their transformations in "Looking for Jimmy Baldwin: Sex, Privacy, and Black Nationalist Fervor." He points out that once Baldwin joined the civil rights struggle, he became a member of both the Congress of Racial Equality and the S.N.C.C., which were major direct-action organizations of the movement.[28] The latter organization is important for this discussion because of the S.N.C.C.'s (in)famous 1967 newsletter, mentioned above.

According to Field, Baldwin constantly came under harsh criticism from Black Power figures like Eldridge Cleaver and was accused of political ineffectiveness. This criticism not only came from a place of disapproval for the civil rights movement and its tactics, but was, above all, a result of homophobia. In Cleaver's eyes, Baldwin's homosexuality prevented him from being a powerful speaker or defender of Black freedom. The movement appeared to launch a campaign against the writer and even published a hateful homophobic cartoon meant to undermine his sexual prowess and thus his authority as a leader.[29]

Despite these acts of hostility on behalf of the Black Panthers and Cleaver, Baldwin grew interested in the revolutionary youth of the movement, and specifically Stokely Carmichael. He expressed admiration for the S.N.C.C. chairman and began to challenge the myth that Black Power preached hatred and violence. According to Baldwin, Carmichael's ideology originally held no hate and only developed a more blatant, militant tone out of necessity. Along with other Black Panther icons such as Bobby Seale, Huey Newton, and Eldridge Cleaver, each of whom Baldwin would later come into close relationships with, Carmichael was responsible for integrating Palestinian solidarity deeper within the fabric of the ideology of his organization and Black Power discourse as a whole.

As the popularity of the Black Panther Party burgeoned, Baldwin became more and more curious about them and their potential for improving the lives and freeing the minds of Black people. He befriended one of the founders of the Black Panthers, Bobby Seale, and later hosted a fundraiser for Huey Newton to raise money for his legal fees while he was in jail. He spoke of Newton with extreme admiration and reverence, praising his "bright dignity," and describing his imprisonment as a microcosm of Black oppression. Baldwin went on to praise the Black Panther Party for its ability to define and address the needs of the Black community directly, citing the multitude of Black Panther community programs.[30] His argument had a powerful resonance with the point he made in writing about the Nation of Islam, praising it for effective social programs and direct positive impact on the everyday lives of Black people.

It is curious that besides these efforts, Baldwin was in direct ideological alignment with Newton on the basis of socialism: "Huey believes, and I do, too, in the necessity of establishing a form of socialism in this country—what Bobby Seale would probably call a 'Yankee Doodle type' socialism. This means an indigenous socialism, formed by, and responding to, the real needs of the American people."[31] Baldwin had flirted with leftist ideas and organizations since before his rise to literary stardom. Douglas Field has provided a comprehensive history of the writer's connections to them, from his membership of the Young People's Socialist League, to his self-identification as a Trotskyite, to his relationships with the leftist editors, activists, and intellectuals in New York.[32] It was thus natural that various strains of Marxist and socialist ideologies shared by him and Black Panthers became a common ground on which to identify with Newton and his ideals and political goals.

Newton was also instrumental in embedding the Palestinian cause in the fabric of Black Power's vision of liberation. In 1974 he traveled to Beirut and met with Yassir Arafat, the leader of the Palestine Liberation Organization, and visited Palestinian refugee camps. In the aftermath of his travels, he wrote "Position Paper on the Middle East," with a complex analysis of the conflict in the context of Arab politics and supporting Palestinian human rights.[33] Along with Carmichael and Amiri Baraka, Newton became important for Baldwin as a new generation and new age of Black liberation. Following Newton's career and embracing him in the way Baldwin did would have been impossible without at least considering his politics and the significance of Palestine.

In *No Name in the Street*, Baldwin not only celebrated Black radicals like Newton, Carmichael, and Malcolm X, but he also rethought several other stances on Black politics. Originally overtly critical of armed violence as a means of resistance, Baldwin came to understand its place. Field highlights Baldwin's admission to having to rely on his armed friends and associates for protection, for example.[34] Baldwin writes about the place of violence in Black psychology in *No Name in the Street* in a way that substantially contradicts his earlier philosophy: "It is not necessary for a Black man to hate a white man, or to have any particular feelings about him at all, in order to realize that he must kill him."[35] This view cannot be divorced from his immersion in the ideology of Black Power generally, and his close relationship with the Black Panthers specifically. The contrast between his view of violence during his civil rights era and after Black Power took center stage in Black politics is indeed striking. Scholarship commonly discusses Baldwin's literary and intellectual accomplishments, as well as his direct involvement in the Black struggle, in the context of the civil rights movement. The ideas expressed in *No Name in the Street* suggest instead an understanding of the importance of a militant approach, Third World politics, socialism, pan-Africanism, and the profound positive ideological, political, and practical effect of the Black Panther Party. These all define Baldwin as a powerful voice of Black liberation, a voice that has not been given enough attention until recently.

Aside from Baldwin's relationships with Black Panther leaders like Newton, Seale, Cleaver, and Carmichael, Baldwin became close to Amiri Baraka. Baraka founded the first Black Arts organization, the Black Arts Repertory Theater and School, in 1965, and, like many Black Arts figures, he was also a Black Power leader and founded the Congress of Afrikan People. In the introduction to a collection of documents and speeches from the conference organized by the Congress of Afrikan People, Baraka wrote: "There will be Congresses until we meet in Congress as one people, whether in Harlem or Johannesburg, whether resisting the oppression of Israelis or Quakers, one people, one flag, one leadership, one identity, purpose and direction."[36] Baraka remained a vocal supporter of the Palestinians throughout his life, dedicating both writing and activism toward the cause. Along with the Black Panther Party, Baraka created and solidified the Black and Palestinian solidarity movement during the Black Power era. This movement created and propagated an ideology that drew parallels and highlighted connections between South African apartheid and Israel, articulating Black and Palestinian oppression through a colonial framework, an ideology that would find its way into the mind and writing of James Baldwin.

Scholarship exploring Black Power's relationship with the Jewish diaspora in the U.S. and the history and forces behind the movement's embrace of the Palestinian cause is relatively new. Eric Sundquist outlines the history of shifting attitudes toward Zionism and Israel in *Strangers in the Land* (2005). He explores the forces that contributed to the alignment between Black Power and the tactics and cause of the Palestine Liberation Organization and connects the changing landscapes of Black/Jewish relationships and rhetoric of liberation to the conflict. He reveals how powerful the influence of Jewish experience and history had been for how Black people envisioned their own oppression, drawing notable parallels between the Holocaust and Black experience, and how dramatically this discourse changed after the 1967 war:

> Alignment with Arab anti-Zionism or the ideology and tactics of the Palestine Liberation Organization (PLO) by definition committed Black Power to a rejectionist stance toward Israel in which resentment of Jews abroad became entangled with resentment of Jews at home and in which the lessons of Holocaust were put to very different use.[37]

Sundquist's argument resonates with the one articulated by Keith Feldman, who explores the impact of Middle Eastern politics on Black–Jewish relationships, especially after the Six Day War. Feldman's *A Shadow Over Palestine* (2015) explores the significance of the ethno-racial relationships between Blacks and Jews in the U.S. in the context of Black politics on Palestine and Israel. Alex Lubin's map of Black and Palestinian solidarity is larger than that of the aforementioned authors, and spans the entire Middle East, as reflected in *Geographies of Liberation* (2014). Nevertheless, he highlights Palestine as an especially significant location for Black liberation: "Palestine was a generative site for Black American diasporic political imaginaries that confronted the dehumanizing politics of race within Europe and United States."[38] These authors, however, pay very little attention to Baldwin and his role in the shaping of Black discourse on Palestine.

A Rap on Race was published at the peak of the Black Power era. It demonstrates Baldwin's changing stance on the issues of race, racism, and liberation in a way that strongly resonates with those articulated and solidified by Black Power. The book documents the writer's conversations with anthropologist Margaret Mead, covering a variety of subjects, tied together by the thread of race and racial relationships in America. Aside from the book, a recording of Baldwin and Mead's conversation was released the same year. As Feldman points out in the introduction to *A Shadow Over Palestine*, the section on Palestine and Israel was completely removed from the recording. I do not intend to explain this erasure; rather, I seek to highlight Baldwin's remarks on Palestine and Israel and place them within the larger context of his political discourse.

Baldwin makes one of his most uncompromising statements on Israel in his dialogue with Mead: "However bitter this may sound, no matter how bitter I may sound, that I have been, in America, the Arab at the hands of the Jews."[39] This statement transcends his earlier sentiments that read like sympathy toward "Arab" oppression. Instead, the writer articulates his experience as a Black man in America *through* the Palestinian experience in Israel. This belief is in direct contradiction with the sentiment and view expressed in 1948 in "The Harlem Ghetto", which drew identical alliance with the Jews in America. Even though the discussion of Palestine and Israel is brief, Mead's reaction—emotionally condemning Baldwin's statement—and the fact that this piece was eliminated from the recording speak volumes about the impact it made.

Along with his views on Black Power, Malcolm X, the implications of capitalism for justice and liberation, and the Third World movement, *No Name in the Street* also marked Baldwin's changing stance on Palestine. Reflecting on his place in the world as an American and a Black man, Baldwin found himself thinking about his place in Palestine and Israel: "And if I had fled, to Israel, a state created for the purpose of protecting Western interests, I would have been in yet a tighter bind: on which side of Jerusalem would I have decided to live?"[40] Envisioning Israel as a neo-colonial force is something Baldwin expressed on multiple occasions. However, questioning whether he had a place in the Jewish republic is something that was not explored in his earlier essays. Jerusalem was a dividing line between Israel and the Occupied Palestinian Territories as Baldwin was writing this in 1972. By positioning Israel as a part of the colonial project of which he saw himself to be a victim, Baldwin denied himself a place in the country, in a way seeking a place for himself among the Palestinians. This was a big transformation for someone who considered Israel as a potential place of sanctuary and refuge in 1948, when the state was established. Baldwin's question was larger than seeking a place between Palestine and Israel, however. He saw Israel as a Western invention and a symbol of the West, a symbol of the colonial and imperial status quo. Palestine thus became its antithesis, representing the colonized peoples of the Third World. Israel was initially considered a symbol of the victory of the oppressed, as envisioned by many Black intellectuals, including Baldwin himself. They saw it as a people originating in the Middle East triumphing against Western aggression and the horror of the Holocaust. Baldwin challenged this geography with a bitter doubt about being welcomed in Israel.

In the concluding pages of *No Name in the Street*, Baldwin speaks about the relationship between Black and Third World struggles:

> And, of course, any real commitment to Black freedom in this country would have the effect of reordering all our priorities, and altering all our commitments, so that, for

horrendous example, we would be supporting Black freedom fighters in South Africa and Angola, and would not be allied with Portugal, would be closer to Cuba than we are to Spain, would be supporting the Arab nations instead of Israel, and would never have felt compelled to follow the French into Southeast Asia.[41]

This statement represents an ideology that was tremendously important for the Black Power movement and swayed Baldwin in that direction in the same fashion it swayed him to take an interest in Black nationalism and to come to understand the significance of violence for Black liberation. Aside from emphasizing the importance of embracing Third World struggles in order to achieve true liberation in the U.S., Baldwin specifically addressed the conflict between the Palestinians and Israel. He highlighted the issue as one of the central locations of world radicalism and other locations directly related to the Black liberation struggle.

Seven years after *No Name in the Street*, in 1979 Baldwin published an article in the *Nation*, "Open Letter to the Born Again." The article is the most extensive discussion of Palestine in Baldwin's writing. An aspect of his philosophy that has not yet been discussed here is the importance of theology and his Christian upbringing as a framework for formulating his vision. And even though Baldwin realized that Christianity was not his pulpit early on, it would be a mistake to dismiss the impact that religious iconography and mythology made on his writing and his vision of Palestine and Israel. His early writing is saturated with references to the Judeo-Christian tradition, and even though these examples do not express any kind of religious fervor, this framework must be taken into consideration. In fact, it resurfaces in "Open Letter" in the concept of "born again" and in the phraseology of the discourse.

The article was prompted by the scandal that emerged after Andrew Young was stripped of his position as the U.S. ambassador to the United Nations as punishment for a brief meeting with the P.L.O. representative Zehdi Terezi. The prominent civil rights leader and politician was the first Black man to hold this high post. He was asked to resign by President Jimmy Carter, a decision met with outrage from the Black community. Indeed, the incident sent ripples throughout the Black leadership, and made them question their stance on Palestine and Israel. For example, in the aftermath of this incident, a group of Martin Luther King, Jr.'s Southern Christian Leadership organization members, led by Revd. Joseph Lowery, traveled to Lebanon to meet with Yassir Arafat and visit the Palestinian refugee camps.[42]

Baldwin approached the issue with a degree of expertise and a firsthand experience of the region and its politics unavailable to many other Black intellectuals. From the opening lines of the article Baldwin demonstrates that he was not only familiar, but was also well informed about the conflict and its history:

Jews and Palestinians know of broken promises. From the time of the Balfour Declaration (during World War I), Palestine was under five British mandates, and England promised the land back and forth to the Arabs or the Jews, depending on which horse seemed to be in the lead. The Zionists—as distinguished from the people known as

Jews—using, as someone put it, the "available political machinery," i.e., colonialism, e.g., the British Empire—promised the British that, if the territory were given to them, the British Empire would be safe forever.[43]

Introducing the issue in terms of the colonial framework not only implied a powerful criticism of the Zionist project, but also strongly resonated with the ideological approach to the issue designed and voiced by Black Power leaders. The fact that Baldwin framed it as a colonial issue defied the Zionist approach and made it a matter of economic and political convenience for neocolonial powers rather than serving justice to an oppressed people. It is also significant that Baldwin drew a distinction between Jews and Zionists, dismantling another aspect of Zionist ideology that has claimed to speak for the interests of Jews worldwide. He continues this line of thought when he states: "But absolutely no one cared about the Jews, and it is worth observing that non-Jewish Zionists are very frequently anti-Semitic."[44]

Many Black Power leaders like Stokely Carmichael, Huey Newton, and Eldridge Cleaver expressed criticism of the neocolonial nature of Israel. Not many, however, explicitly addressed the high price the Palestinians had to pay so that the dream of the Jewish republic could be fulfilled:

> But the state of Israel was not created for the salvation of the Jews; it was created for the salvation of the Western interests. This is what is becoming clear (I must say that it was always clear to me). The Palestinians have been paying for the British colonial policy of "divide and rule" and for Europe's guilty Christian conscience for more than thirty years.[45]

Here Baldwin complicates the conflict between Palestine and Israel and expresses the fact that economic and political interests behind the establishment of the state of Israel were also ideological and framed by the Judeo-Christian tradition.

Lastly, the article makes an almost unprecedented political intervention when Baldwin emphasizes the significance of Palestinian agency, speaking about their importance for the peace process: "Finally: there is absolutely—repeat: *absolutely*—no hope of establishing peace in what Europe so arrogantly calls the Middle East (how in the world would Europe know? having so dismally failed to find a passage to India) without dealing with the Palestinians."[46] This point of view was unpopular as far as mainstream U.S. discourse on the conflict was concerned. It emphasized the importance of Andrew Young's decision to meet Zehdi Terezi. Terezi served as the first Palestinian ambassador to the United Nations from 1974 until 1991 and would provide a necessary insight for a dialog that was embedded in the concept of a peace process. Baldwin understood this very well and criticized President Carter and the people who pressed for Young's dismissal for their arrogance and lack of insight.

The article was a powerful letter of support advocating for the importance of Young's role in the Middle East process. More importantly, the article's ideological framework had strong resonance with the discourse formulated by the Black Power movement, framing Black conditions in the U.S. and Palestinian conditions in Israel through the lens of colonial and postcolonial theory. Oppression rooted in the colonial past and present was the bedrock on which Black Power formulated a sense of solidarity with the Palestinians. Baldwin adopted this discourse, inspired by his proximity to the movement and its leaders.

Baldwin's own writing and thinking on Palestine extended into the last years of his life. In his 1985 open letter to the South African anti-apartheid and human rights activist Desmond Tutu, he writes about his ambivalence:

> I may be ambivalent concerning the physical purposes of the state of Israel, but American Jews are, in the main, indistinguishable from American white Christians: and I would not like to be an Arab in Jerusalem. And, Israel is, also, an ally of South Africa—which Western nation, indeed, is not? (And it is worth pointing out that the ANC [African National Congress] is as homeless as the PLO, for the same reasons.)[47]

Here he continues a few lines of thought demonstrated in his writing about the position of the Jewish diaspora in America within the racial system in the U.S. He sees Jews as an integral part of the white and Christian system which also makes them a part of the system of white supremacy. He repeatedly uses Jerusalem as a microcosm of Palestinian oppression, echoing his argument in *No Name in the Street* discussed above. Further, echoing the rhetoric of many Black Power figures, Baldwin highlights Israel's role in South African apartheid. In several of his writings in the 1970s, he criticizes the Jewish republic for its support of Western nations and their neocolonial projects in the Middle East and Africa, which also resonates with his argument in the letter. Finally, Baldwin echoes the ideology created by Black Power that drew powerful parallels between Palestinian and global Black liberation struggles, when he compares the P.L.O. and the A.N.C. In his discussion of race and power and the place of Israel within the system of white supremacy, Baldwin evokes arguments that were made by Black Power figures like Hoyt Fuller, Amiri Baraka, and Stokely Carmichael, figures who envisioned Palestinians as a people of color, if not an African people. The impact that U.S. involvement in Palestine had on ethno-racial politics in the country deserves sustained discussion.[48]

As discussed above, racial and ethnic tensions between Black and Jewish communities in the U.S. reached their peak in the twentieth century due to changes in racial stratification and the integration of the Jews into American mainstream society and whiteness. James Baldwin is one of the foremost Black authors to have written about this matter. Discussion of the issue goes back to the beginning of his career, with his 1948 essay "The Harlem Ghetto." In this piece, he targeted Jewish landlords in Harlem and accused the community of perpetuating Black dispossession. In *Black Power and Palestine: Transnational Countries of Color* Michael Fischbach provides a comprehensive context of the history of Black and Jewish tensions in the mid-twentieth century, highlighting Baldwin's writing on the matter and citing "The Harlem Ghetto" and "Negroes Are Anti-Semitic Because They're

Anti-White." Fischbach reveals that Baldwin echoed Black writers and intellectuals like Kenneth Clark, Harold Cruise, and even Amiri Baraka in their attacks on Jewish participation in Black oppression and rejection of the parallels between racism and antisemitism.[49] The nature of the aforementioned writers' sentiments toward the Jewish community is beyond the scope of this article. But presenting Baldwin's writing on the issue as a matter of unjustified hostility and the prejudice of antisemitism would be too simplistic and unfair.

Baldwin rejected the idea that Black and Jewish tensions are rooted in a supposed implicit bias against the Jews; instead, he said that these are a result of the complex conflicts rooted in Black and white relationships in America, positioning Jews as an integral part of the white supremacist system. Baldwin understood that the Jews were not a homogeneous community. While he was suspicious of the Jewish community in Harlem and their sometimes unfair practices toward its inhabitants, his connections to a leftist Jewish scene and decades-long friendships with Jewish editors were instrumental in his career.

There is a tradition of Black politics that embraces the Palestinian cause in times of political resurgence that dates back to the Black Power movement. The Black feminist movement that followed the Black Power era was marked by the amazing pro-Palestinian activism and writing of June Jordan, and the activism of Alice Walker and Angela Davis. Not dissimilar to the incident with Andrew Young's firing from his post with the U.N., Davis was disinvited from joining the Birmingham Civil Rights institute. Just like the incident in 1978 that prompted Baldwin to write "Open Letter to the Born Again," this event caused a major uproar among the Black community and led to an article by Michelle Alexander in the *New York Times*. Davis's book *Freedom is a Constant Struggle: Ferguson, Palestine, and the Foundations of a Movement* (2016) is a powerful testament that explains the ideological, political, and historical past and present of Black and Palestinian struggles. Focusing on the prison-industrial complex, Davis explains how U.S. and Israeli surveillance practices and state violence define the Palestinian and Black experience of oppression, and thus how a truly unified struggle can bring about both people's true freedom.

Palestine was not only a metaphorical, ideological terrain through which Baldwin and other Black intellectuals, leaders, and radicals articulated their visions of Black liberation. Besides Baldwin, Malcolm X, Jesse Jackson, and Martin Luther King, Jr. all visited Palestine.[50] The effect of these journeys is beyond the scope of this article, but this detailed study of Baldwin's visit and the impact it had on his discourse on freedom and justice presents a compelling case for further studies of this kind.

Notes

1 James Baldwin, *No Name in the Street* (New York, Dial Press, 1972), p. 172.
2 *Ibid.*, p. 39.
3 Douglas Field, "James Baldwin's Life on the Left: A Portrait of the Artist a Young New York Intellectual," *ELH*, 78:4 (2011), p. 837.

4 James Baldwin, "The Harlem Ghetto," in *Collected Essays*, ed. Toni Morrison (New York, Library of America, 1998), p. 49.

5 Benyamin Neuberger, "Early African Nationalism, Judaism and Zionism: Edward Wilmot Blyden," *Jewish Social Studies*, 47:2 (1985), pp. 151–6.

6 James Baldwin, "Letters from a Journey," in Herbert Hill (ed.), *Soon, One Morning: New Writing By American Negroes, 1940–1962* (New York, Alfred Knopf, 1968), p. 38.

7 *Ibid.*, p. 39.

8 *Ibid.*, p. 41.

9 *Ibid.*

10 *Ibid.*

11 *Ibid.*

12 *Ibid.*, p. 42.

13 Magdalena Zaborowska, *Baldwin's Turkish Decade: Erotics of Exile* (Durham, NC, Duke University Press, 2009), p. 28.

14 Zionism and its implications have evolved since its inception in 1897 by Theodor Herzl. At its nascent stage its goal was the establishment of Israel. After 1948, and until the present day, Zionism has implied the protection and development of the Jewish republic. Despite its ideological and epistemological connections to Judaism, Zionism must not be conflated with Jewish identity. For a detailed analysis of the relationship between Zionism and Judaism, see Gil Hochberg, *In Spite of Partition: Jews, Arabs, and the Limits of Separatist Imagination* (Princeton, NJ, Princeton University Press, 2007).

15 Melanie McAlister, *Epic Encounters: Culture, Media, & US Interests in the Middle East Since 1945* (Los Angeles and Berkeley, University of California Press, 2005), p. 94.

16 James Baldwin, *The Fire Next Time* (New York, Dial Press, 1963), p. 46.

17 *Ibid.*, p. 58.

18 *Ibid.*, pp. 50–1.

19 Baldwin, *No Name in the Street*, p. 178.

20 The article was dedicated to the aftermath of an incident that was later referred to as the case of the Harlem Six. Six residents of Harlem, Wallace Baker, Daniel Hamm, William Craig, Ronald Felder, Walter Thomas, and Robert Rice, were wrongfully accused of the murder of Margit Sugar and Frank Sugar. For more on Harlem Six, see Arnold H. Lubasch, "Ruling to Throw Out Conviction In 'Harlem Six' Case Reversed," *New York Times*, 8 February 1974, p. 38.

21 James Baldwin, "A Report from the Occupied Territory," in Morrison (ed.), *Collected Essays*, p. 784.

22 Timothy Seidel, "'Occupied Territory is Occupied Territory': James Baldwin, Palestine and the Possibilities of Transnational Solidarity," *Third World Quarterly*, 37:9 (2016), pp. 1644–60, www.tandfonline.com/doi/full/10.1080/01436597.2016.1178063 (accessed 4 June 2020).

23 *Ibid.*

24 Clayborne Carson, "Blacks and Jews in the Civil Rights Movement," in John H. Bracey and Maurianne Adams (eds.), *Strangers & Neighbors: Relations Between Blacks and Jews in the United States* (Amherst, MA, University of Massachusetts Press, 1999), p. 584.

25 Stokely Carmichael, *Ready for Revolution: The Life and Struggles of Stokely Carmichael* (New York, Scribner, 2003), pp. 557–61.

26 *Ibid.*, p. 563.

27 Keith Feldman, "Representing Permanent War: Black Power's Palestine and the End(s) of Civil Rights," in Manning Marable and Hisham Aidi (eds.), *Black Routes to Islam* (London, Palgrave Macmillan, 2009), p. 85.

28 Douglas Field, "Looking for Jimmy Baldwin: Sex, Privacy, and Black Nationalist Fervor," *Callaloo*, 27:2 (2004), p. 460.

29 *Ibid.*, p. 463.

30 Baldwin, *No Name in the Street*, pp. 174–5.

31 *Ibid.*, p. 174.

32 Field, "James Baldwin's Life on the Left".

33 Alex Lubin, *Geographies of Liberation: The Making of an Afro-Arab Political Imaginary* (Chapel Hill, NC, University of North Carolina Press, 2014), p. 127.

34 Quoted in Field, "Looking for Jimmy Baldwin," p. 466.

35 *Ibid.*, p. 468.

36 Amiri Baraka (ed.), *African Congress: A Documentary of the First Modern Pan-African Congress* (New York, Morrow, 1972), p. xix.

37 Eric Sundquist, *Strangers in the Land: Blacks, Jews, Post-Holocaust America* (Cambridge, MA, Harvard University Press, 2005), p. 312.

38 Lubin, *Geographies of Liberation*, p. 19.

39 James Baldwin and Margaret Mead, *A Rap on Race* (Philadelphia, J.B. Lippincott, 1971), p. 132.

40 Baldwin, *No Name in the Street*, p. 42.

41 *Ibid.*, p. 178.

42 Ronald W. Waters, "The Black Initiatives in the Middle East," *Journal of Palestine Studies*, 10:2 (1981), pp. 2–9.

43 James Baldwin, "Open Letter to the Born Again," in Morrison (ed.), *Collected Essays*, p. 787.

44 *Ibid.*, p. 785.

45 *Ibid.*, p. 786.

46 *Ibid.*

47 James Baldwin, "An Open Letter to Desmond Tutu," qtd. in Leah Mirakhor, "The Hoodie and the Hijab: Arabness, Blackness, and the Figure of Terror," *Los Angeles Review of Books*, 6 June 2015, https://lareviewofbooks.org/article/the-hoodie-and-the-hijab-arabness-Blackness-and-the-figure-of-terror-james-baldwin/ (accessed 4 June 2020).

48 A notable example of such scholarship is Keith Feldman, *A Shadow Over Palestine: The Imperial Life of Race in America* (Minneapolis, MN, University of Minnesota Press, 2015).

49 Michael Fischbach, *Black Power and Palestine: Transnational Countries of Color* (Stanford, CA, Stanford University Press, 2019), pp. 73–6.

50 *Ibid.*, pp. 32–4.

Works Cited

Baldwin, James, *Fire Next Time* (New York, Dial Press, 1963).

_____ "The Harlem Ghetto" (1948), in *Collected Essays*, ed. Toni Morrison (New York, Library of America, 1998), pp. 42–53.

_____ "Letters from a Journey" (1963), in Herbert Hill (ed.), *Soon, One Morning: New Writing By American Negroes, 1940–1962* (New York, Alfred Knopf, 1968), pp. 39–47.

_____ *No Name in the Street* (New York, Dial Press, 1972).

_____ "Open Letter to the Born Again" (1979), in *Collected Essays*, ed. Toni Morrison (New York, Library of America, 1998), pp. 784–7.

_____ "A Report from the Occupied Territory" (1966), in *Collected Essays*, ed. Toni Morrison (New York, Library of America, 1998), pp. 728–38.

Baldwin, James, and Margaret Mead, *A Rap on Race* (Philadelphia, J.B. Lippincott, 1971).

Baraka, Amiri (ed.), *African Congress: A Documentary of the First Modern Pan-African Congress* (New York, Morrow, 1972).

Carmichael, Stokely, *Ready for Revolution: The Life and Struggles of Stokely Carmichael* (New York, Scribner, 2003).

Carson, Clayborne, "Blacks and Jews in the Civil Rights Movement," in John H. Bracey and Maurianne Adams (eds.), *Strangers & Neighbors: Relations Between Blacks and Jews in the United States* (Amherst, MA, University of Massachusetts Press, 1999), pp. 574–89.

Davis, Angela, *Freedom is a Constant Struggle: Ferguson, Palestine, and the Foundations of a Movement* (Chicago, Haymarket Books, 2016).

Feldman, Keith, *A Shadow Over Palestine: The Imperial Life of Race in America* (Minneapolis, MN, University of Minnesota Press, 2015).

_____ "Representing Permanent War: Black Power's Palestine and the End(s) of Civil Rights," in Manning Marable and Hisham Aidi (eds.), *Black Routes to Islam* (London, Palgrave Macmillan, 2009), pp. 79–98.

Field, Douglas, "James Baldwin's Life on the Left: A Portrait of the Artist a Young New York Intellectual," *ELH*, 78:4 (2011), pp. 833–62.

_____ "Looking for Jimmy Baldwin: Sex, Privacy, and Black Nationalist Fervor," *Callaloo*, 27:2 (2004), pp. 457–80.

Fischbach, Michael, *Black Power and Palestine: Transnational Countries of Color* (Stanford, CA, Stanford University Press, 2019).

Hochberg, Gil, *In Spite of Partition: Jews, Arabs, and the Limits of Separatist Imagination* (Princeton, NJ, Princeton University Press, 2007).

Lubasch, Arnold H., "Ruling to Throw Out Conviction In 'Harlem Six' Case Reversed," *New York Times*, 8 February 1974, p. 38.

Lubin, Alex, *Geographies of Liberation: The Making of an Afro-Arab Political Imaginary* (Chapel Hill, NC, University of North Carolina Press, 2014).

McAlister, Melanie, *Epic Encounters: Culture, Media, & US Interests in the Middle East Since 1945* (Los Angeles and Berkeley, University of California Press, 2005).

Mirakhor, Leah, "The Hoodie and the Hijab: Arabness, Blackness, and the Figure of Terror," *Los Angeles Review of Books*, 6 June 2015, https://lareviewofbooks.org/article/the-hoodie-and-the-hijab-arabness-Blackness-and-the-figure-of-terror-james-baldwin/ (accessed 4 June 2020).

Neuberger, Benyamin, "Early African Nationalism, Judaism and Zionism: Edward Wilmot Blyden," *Jewish Social Studies*, 47:2 (1985), pp. 151–6.

Seidel, Timothy, "'Occupied Territory is Occupied Territory': James Baldwin, Palestine and the Possibilities of Transnational Solidarity," *Third World Quarterly*, 37:9 (2016), pp. 1644–60, www.tandfonline.com/doi/full/10.1080/01436597.2016.1178063 (accessed 4 June 2020).

Sundquist, Eric, *Strangers in the Land: Blacks, Jews, post-Holocaust America* (Cambridge, MA, Harvard University Press, 2005).

Waters, Ronald W., "The Black Initiatives in the Middle East," *Journal of Palestine Studies*, 10:2 (1981), pp. 2–14.

Zaborowska, Magdalena, *Baldwin's Turkish Decade: Erotics of Exile* (Durham, NC, Duke University Press, 2009).

Contributor's Biography

Nadia Alahmed is an assistant professor of Africana Studies at Dickinson College. Her research interests include Black radical thought and politics, Black internationalism, Black Islam, critical hip-hop studies and historical, political, and cultural connections between Black America and the Middle East. She is currently working on her first book exploring parallels and interactions between Black and Palestinian social justice and liberation movements, from the Black Power movement until the present day.

ESSAY

Birthing a New World: Black Women as Surrogates of Liberation in James Baldwin's *If Beale Street Could Talk*

Marquita R. Smith   Rowan University

Abstract

This essay analyzes how James Baldwin's late novel *If Beale Street Could Talk* represents Black women's care work in the face of social death as an example of how Black women act as surrogates for Black liberation giving birth to a new world and possibilities of freedom for Black (male) people. Within the politics of Black nationalism, Black women were affective workers playing a vital role in the (re)creation of heteronormative family structures that formed the basis of Black liberation cohered by a belief in the power of patriarchy to make way for communal freedom. This essay demonstrates how *Beale Street*'s imagining of freedom centers not on what Black women do to support themselves or each other, but on the needs of the community at large, with embodied sacrifice as a presumed condition of such liberation.

Keywords: incarceration, affect, embodiment, intimacy, liberation

> An old world is dying, and a new one, kicking in the belly of its mother, time, announces that it is ready to be born. This birth will not be easy, and many of us are doomed to discover that we are exceedingly clumsy midwives. No matter, so long as we accept that our responsibility is to the newborn: the acceptance of responsibility contains the key to the necessarily evolving skill.
> James Baldwin, *No Name in the Street*[1]

> And the baby kicks again. Time.
> James Baldwin, *If Beale Street Could Talk*[2]

In *No Name in the Street* (1972) James Baldwin analogizes the act of childbirth to the liberatory and revolutionary processes a society must undertake to make way for a new way of living and being. Grounded in the corporeality of reproduction, this language figures sociopolitical change in a familiar and familial format: that of

James Baldwin Review, Volume 6, 2020, © The Authors. Published by Manchester University Press and The University of Manchester Library
http://dx.doi.org/10.7227/JBR.6.4

the birthing mother. Published two years later, Baldwin's *If Beale Street Could Talk* (1974) imagines this possibility of freedom as emerging from the labor of Black women, particularly in support of the incarcerated Black man. The Black women of the novel enact and embody the power of life in the face of death, demonstrating the myriad ways Black women's bodies are a critical part of the Black nationalist desire for liberation that was prevalent during the 1970s post-civil rights moment. The imperatives of Black nationalism relied upon standardized arrangements of kinship centralized in the heteropatriarchal nuclear family, with women as caregivers and mothers. Within this framework, Black women were affective workers playing a vital role in the reproduction of heteronormative family structures that formed the basis of Black liberation cohered, ultimately, by a belief in the power of patriarchy to make way for communal freedom. As Aliyyah Abdur-Rahman notes, "black nationalists sought to seize state power as it pervaded the lives of black people and to develop in its place logics and (communal) infrastructures that were racially affirming and preserving."[3]

This essay analyzes *Beale Street*'s representation of Black women's care work intended to preserve the recognition of individual and collective lives in the face of social death as an example of how Black women act as surrogates for Black liberation, giving birth to a new world and possibilities of freedom, particularly for Black men as representatives of a wider Black community. This imagining of freedom centers not on what Black women do to support themselves or each other, but on the needs of the community at large vis-à-vis Black men, with embodied sacrifice as a presumed condition of such liberation.

In the wake of the civil rights movement, Baldwin engaged with the Black nationalist movement to address issues of hypercriminalization and incarceration. Much of his later work, including publications such as "An Open Letter to My Sister, Miss Angela Davis" (1971) and *One Day When I Was Lost* (1972), demonstrates his nuanced and prophetic response to the post-civil rights backlash in American society. The time period called for radical change through Black nationalist ideals in the face of what many considered to be complacency after attaining formal civil rights equality.[4] Baldwin's post-civil rights era writing focused on incarceration as a matter of social justice and, according to Leeming, he saw the incarcerated as "those who were deprived of their birthright in the unfeeling and unseeing prison that was racism in America."[5] For Baldwin, both material and metaphorical prisons and prisoners were important subjects for critical reflection as his writing detailed the affective aspects of confinement that often attended everyday life.

Beale Street illuminates the various ways in which the ongoing crisis of incarceration disrupts the intimate sphere of African American life and the implications this has for a people's liberation. Reading the novel in the contemporary moment continues be relevant as racial prison demographics have remained largely unchanged for African Americans since 1974.[6] Indeed, Baldwin's insight into post-civil rights society takes on new import within the contemporary context of mass incarceration. Despite Baldwin's highly lauded literary reputation, studies of *Beale Street* have been limited to a handful of texts by scholars such as Nathaniel Mills, Trudier Harris, Lynn Orilla Scott, and D. Quentin Miller. This essay explores *Beale Street* as a meditation on how the "criminal power" of incarceration encroaches upon the Black intimate sphere, particularly as it is represented through Black interiority and the Black female body.[7] The novel, I argue, highlights the myriad ways Black women's bodies become sites of struggle and a somewhat limited liberation under the conditions of carcerality.

The relation between law and bodies requires an attentive turn to the body as both a site and source of affective, political significance. As Saidiya Hartman explicates, Black men and women have been subject to the violent power of law yet excluded from its protection.[8] This is something that Baldwin intimately understood as, according to Miller, Baldwin's eight days in a Parisian prison in December 1949 "clarified for him the reality of the law's power over lives like his."[9] Motivated to speak out in support of the imprisoned activist and scholar Angela Davis, Baldwin boldly declared in his 1971 open letter that Americans "appear to measure their safety in chains and corpses."[10] In other words, the confined Black body provides the image of safety that comforts the minds of Americans. Baldwin understood carceral displays of power to be driven by racist and xenophobic anxiety, with dire consequences for Black populations. This is a crisis that takes comfort in the use of imprisonment as a salve for American society's unresolved ills.

Though contemporary assessments of Black nationalism point to its failure to account for diverse structures of kinship and sexual orientations, I want to maintain an attentiveness to the importance of Black Power politics during the post-civil rights moment. Such an understanding of Blackness as political extends beyond the nation-specific goals of the civil rights movement to reach toward a more global sense of Black liberation that envisioned Black life otherwise and elsewhere. Given the hardships of life in the United States for African Americans, envisioning such a life was also a way to build a sense of racial pride that was not based on assimilation. Black nationalism sought to articulate a shared heritage among people of African descent to encourage fighting for a common goal of freedom. This nationalism beyond borders is something Baldwin attempts to represent in *Beale Street*, though it is limited in its ability to actually flourish. When Sharon Rivers attempts to connect with Victoria Rogers in Puerto Rico on the basis of a shared African history, she fails because of the gulf between what Victoria feels and how Sharon is beginning to understand her own place in the diaspora. In the contemporary moment, as in the novel, the dream of diasporic unity has yet to be fully realized.

Baldwin's Black Power fiction engaged such issues in literary form. In his critique of protest fiction, "Everybody's Protest Novel" (1949), he points out the ontological cage that confines both the oppressed and the oppressor in novels written from either perspective. He understands this metaphysical enclosure as an impediment to the oppressed being able to truly imagine life otherwise, despite the claims made by and about the existence of protest fiction. As Marlon B. Ross observes, Baldwin criticizes the reinforcing of oppressive principles in such fiction and instead "wants to explode those categories, offering not a protest but rather a critique that disables the categories from retaining their oppressive power."[11] This is not an easy task, but literature offers a means of potentially unmaking these categories with nuanced characterization that avoids the "failures" of the protest novel to recognize and represent the (Black) human being in "his beauty, dread, power"—in all that makes up Black subjectivity.[12] This is the framework from which I analyze *Beale Street* as Baldwin's anti-protest novel that exemplifies an affectively rich understanding of what I call "carceral feeling," or the affective relations to and beyond the carceral space of the prison. In *Beale Street*, Baldwin approaches the sociopolitical issues of anti-Black violence and policing in ways that emphasize rather than reject the fullness of life as a way of imagining a new world of possibility in the face of immense struggle.

The resistant acts of love by the Rivers family demonstrate the significance of the affective realm to the novel's representation of struggle and the possibility of freedom. Baldwin's notion of love, as Douglas Field reminds us, is not about sentimentality but is "explicitly active and political."[13] Field describes this as Baldwin's "new humanist religion of love, where redemption is found in one another."[14] Baldwin's belief in love as a political practice, not mere feeling, aligns with my reading of love as an affect with transformative power for those who give and receive it. Theorists of affect describe it as potential for a "body's capacity to affect and to be affected."[15] In other words, what we sense, know, and believe about the world produces our visceral, visible, and legible responses. This power can be wielded destructively or to build relations. From the novel's outset, Baldwin invites empathetic identification, as Tish turns to the reader asking, "can you imagine what anybody on this bus would say to me if they knew, from my mouth, that I love somebody in jail? ... What would *you* say?"[16] The question reveals Baldwin's artistic didacticism to be centered on love, of self and others, as motivation for action. He argues elsewhere that "relatively conscious whites and the relatively conscious blacks ... must, like lovers, insist on, or create, the consciousness of the others" to "end the racial nightmare, and achieve our country, and change this history of the world."[17] For Baldwin, the mission was to love because "lovers recognize the need of human beings for 'each other.'"[18] Attending to affect in *Beale Street* means thinking carefully about the author's aesthetic choice to represent Fonny's wrongful incarceration in a manner that shows how it shapes the interior lives of both the Hunt and Rivers families.

It is not enough simply to point to this Black Power representation; we must also attend to the how of the narrative perspective of a young, pregnant Black woman. *Beale Street* is a story of injustice that finds hope in the love of a young Black couple, and Tish embodies this hope through her pregnancy. The metaphorical use of the unborn child as an indicator of Fonny's fate also highlights the significance of the intimate sphere as the site of struggle and resistance against confinement. As Tish articulates, "I understand that the growth of the baby is connected with his determination to be free. ... The baby wants out. Fonny wants out. And we are going to make it: in time."[19] The baby must be born and, therefore, Fonny must be freed. The baby serves as the exigency for freeing Fonny and further binds the characters to one another. Sharon's words of encouragement for

Tish culturally legitimate the baby and affirm the kinship tie between the Rivers family and Fonny. Sharon often reminds Tish, "He needs that baby," stressing to her, "you ain't really alone in that bed."[20] The child, a symbol of love and inno-cence, signifies a possible future in which racial oppression ceases to exist and the criminal power of law is overcome. As a mother, Tish is tasked with ushering in this new life with all of its radical power, and she remains steadfast in her belief in Fonny, who also relies on her to bring forth his freedom.

In *Beale Street* the role of mother extends beyond its biologically based and socially naturalized definition. Mrs. Hunt, Fonny's mother, is a woman unable and unwilling to accept her son's reality. After she refuses to help him, or to accept his unborn child, her husband Frank sadly muses, "I thought she loved him—like I guess I thought, one time, she loved me."[21] Baldwin's scathing representation of Mrs. Hunt as a religious woman without the ability to love demonstrates what Field identifies as a rewriting of Christian identity through which salvation and redemption comes "not through God, but through a love that is founded on the sharing of pain."[22] Field reads Baldwin's religious sensibility in the novel as a sug-gestion that "love can only be attained through acceptance of the body as well as the spirit."[23] In her refusal to accept Tish's pregnancy, Mrs. Hunt also rejects Baldwin's vision of a future without racial oppression. Sharon counters the maternal failures of Mrs. Hunt by taking on the task of traveling to Puerto Rico in an attempt to convince an important witness to testify to Fonny's innocence. Sharon's desire to care for Tish and to act on Fonny's behalf demonstrates the material and emo-tional work that will hopefully produce substantive change in the lives of future generations, and further suggests that the family, through both quotidian and extraordinary acts of love, will be the force for revolutionary transformation.

Black nationalism gives important context to this reproductive representation of Black women giving birth to liberation. As Abdur-Rahman states, "black nation-alists believed that the creation of black families and reproduction of black chil-dren would both prevent genocide and restore patriarchal legitimacy to black manhood."[24] The Rivers family in particular is the "site of personal and political resistance to racist values and actions."[25] The characters of *Beale Street* are aligned by their mission to save the Black male artist, Fonny, for his and the unborn child's sake. As Trudier Harris suggests, the reader is encouraged to "identify with Fonny's plight *as male*" and the narrative voice rests upon a "subservience" that is "grounded in femininity."[26] *Beale Street* is a clear example of Baldwin's critical engagement with the Black radical movement. Nathaniel Mills offers a convincing reading of the novel as a response to Eldridge Cleaver's *Soul on Ice* and, more generally, a "disidentification" from Black nationalism. He argues that Baldwin used *Beale Street* as a means of theorizing Black revolution and the radical potential of Black art in a way that revises "black nationalism's separatist, heteropatriarchal, and masculinist tendencies while appropriating its revolutionary militancy, and it is thus not evidence of Baldwin's meek submission to the late-1960s radical turn in the black movement but of his creative and idiosyncratic participation in that turn."[27] The novel reveals the extent to which Black nationalist ideals of family are reproducible only with limited conceptions of gender and sexuality. Abdur-Rahman argues that though Baldwin attended to and represented issues of womanhood, he was preoccupied overall with "defining and expanding constructions of masculin- ity so that black men, gay men, and men who were artists could claim manhood as the initial step to defining themselves and to gaining social recognition and civic entitlements."[28] In many ways, this is in keeping with what Abdur-Rahman identifies as "black nationalist imperatives that centralize black masculinity in African American cultural renovation and political resistance."[29] Indeed, Baldwin's characterization of Tish follows this line, revealing how, despite Black women's laboring for liberation, such work only gains recognition according to a logic that registers its support of patriarchy.

The heteropatriarchal vision of liberation struggle in *Beale Street* presents an interesting case of Baldwin's dissemblance of representation, akin to what Mae G. Henderson deftly analyzes in her reading of *Giovanni's Room*. Henderson assesses that novel as the author's exploration of gender and sexuality in the absence of Blackness. Henderson reads this narrative framing as an authorial choice that allows Baldwin to explore the "complexities of gender, national, and sexual iden- tity, uncomplicated by the issue of racialized blackness."[30] I view a similar bifurca- tion of issues in *Beale Street* as Baldwin adopts the Black feminine narrative voice of Tish to create space for his contextualized social commentary on matters of gender, race, and imprisonment from the relative safe haven of normalized het- erosexuality. The intersections of race and gender, gender and liberation, and lib- eration and race can each be mapped as discrete categories in the text. In his desire to address the concerns of the post-civil rights moment, Baldwin uses the micro- cosm of the heteropatriarchal family to interrogate the troubling consequences of incarceration. The Rivers family is an idealized version of the Black family that, when faced with extreme hardship, draws itself even closer together in its resis- tance to oppression. Tish comes to understand the power of familial love during the conversation in which she reveals her pregnancy to her mother, Sharon. Fear- ful of what lies ahead for her nascent family, Tish needs both encouragement and help. Her mother tells her not to be ashamed of her out-of-wedlock pregnancy, saying, "when we was first brought here, the white man he didn't give us no preachers to say words over us before we had our babies. And you and Fonny be together right now, married or not, wasn't for that same damn white man."[31] As Melinda Plastas and Eve Allegra Raimon point out, the naming of whiteness as a source of oppression supports the view that the Rivers "derive strength from the Black Power movement."[32] More specifically, the emphasis on protecting the unborn male child is critical to understanding how Baldwin makes use of preg- nancy in both the literal and metaphorical sense. Because the Black Power frame- work envisions the heteropatriarchal, reproductive family as the means through which revolution will come, Tish's commitment to Fonny and the care of her baby fulfills the Black nationalist mandate of motherhood.

Black women's laboring for liberation is also embodied by other acts of care on Fonny's behalf. Outside of Tish's regular visits, strategies for working toward

Fonny's release are part of daily discussions in the Rivers household, particularly on the part of the women. In representing the work of liberation in this way, Baldwin complicates a significant part of the heteropatriarchal rhetoric of Black nationalism. Though Joseph, Tish's father, asks questions and occasionally offers his thoughts, the women of the family are regularly called upon to do the practical tasks of working toward Fonny's freedom. This characterization of Tish, Sharon, and Ernestine carefully resists the stereotype of women being overly sentimental in times of stress, without unnecessarily or uncritically advancing the myth of strong Black womanhood. However, this too can be read as women, regardless of their specific kinship tie, being placed in the role of mother/caretaker for men/children, as the men are portrayed as suffering from the emotional and symbolic burden of having an imprisoned son. The fathers are victims of a constraining masculinity, one that leaves them "no time for crying," and Frank tragically so.[33] In *Beale Street*, the women's affective work maintains order and seeks to restore stability within a ruptured familial structure.

Baldwin's desire to construct an ideal empowered Black family relies on the perpetuation of heteropatriarchy, yet this incongruity helps to clarify, perhaps unintentionally, a critical feature of the novel's gender politics. Despite their practicality in working to support Fonny, the Rivers women are careful to avoid overtly undermining the patriarchal leadership of the household. Rather than showing patriarchy as the solution, the women's work subverts the assumption of patriarchal ideals. A prime example is the toast scene that unfolds when Tish's pregnancy is announced to her family. Drinking as a social and emotional release is an important enactment of masculinity that is seemingly reserved for the novel's men in response to disillusionment. Sharon is clear in her insistence that her husband Joseph pour the first drink of comfort by saying, "You the man of the house."[34] The bottle of French brandy is the last one from "her days as a singer, her days with the drummer," a reminder of her life before marriage and motherhood.[35] This act, initiated and made possible by Sharon, undermines her performance of subservience by reminding readers of her expression of independence and pursuit of her desires as a young woman, while honoring her daughter's transition into a new life phase. In the end, after Joseph pours the drinks, Sharon is the one who declares it sacrament and commands the family to drink. Within the context of her affective and physical laboring to see to her family's wellbeing, this act underscores the work of womanhood that is often rendered invisible within masculinist frameworks of imagined power and agency.

Both Frank and Joseph are looked to as heads of their households, but both are emasculated by state power. Over drinks at a bar, the two of them discuss their feelings of failure. Frank confides in Joseph, "I don't know what I should have done. I ain't a woman. And there's some things only a woman can do with a child."[36] While this exchange does, in some ways, work toward an understanding of "homosocial intimacy and love both outside and inside prison walls" as an "antidote to male-on-male brutality," it also reveals how assumptions of care and childrearing are unequally allocated.[37] Joseph tells Frank, "these are our children and we got to set them free," but Frank feels that he has failed to be the kind of parent his son needs because he is not a woman.[38] If, as Plastas and Raimon suggest, Fonny's release from jail "rests on the ability of men to constitute new forms of manhood and togetherness," the novel's gender politics help clarify its ambiguous ending.[39] While useful for creating stronger homosocial intimacy, the new forms of manhood and togetherness modeled by the fathers of *Beale Street*, I suggest, ultimately fail to do the work of freeing Fonny because the conditions of carcerality necessitate collaboration for resistance that goes beyond the dictates of heteropatriarchy. The political practice of love is not, cannot be solely the province of femininity. Frank's suicide just as Ernestine shares the news that she has procured enough money for Fonny's bail highlights how the actions of women in response to the hardships they face are critical to sustaining the lives of those reliant upon them. Frank's lack of hope in his own masculine power to bring change largely because of gender forestalls his ability to recognize the material effort of the women working for Fonny's liberation.

Baldwin draws on the actions of Tish's broader intimate network to highlight the work of pursuing Fonny's freedom. The extent of communal care is underscored during the disastrous meeting between the Hunt and Rivers families. After the meeting, Tish is especially observant of the role her mother and sister, Ernestine, play in Fonny's care and in her own:

> I knew they were sending me to bed so that they could sit up for a while, without me, without the men, without anybody, to look squarely in the face the fact that Fonny's family didn't give a shit about him and were not going to do a thing to help him. We were his family now, the only family he had: and now everything was up to us.[40]

Baldwin's emphasis on the women performing this strategizing work "without the men" is indicative of the gendered nature of care. Such notions of care emphasize and support a heteropatriarchal familial structure that reproduces itself, and concern for Tish's wellbeing is often expressed in reference to her pregnancy. Those who care for her see her wellbeing as tied to the health of the baby, and to Fonny's emotional state. Indeed, Tish also sees her subjectivity as subsumed to the needs of Fonny as she comes to realize that "dealing with the reality of men leaves a woman very little time, or need, for imagination."[41] In other words, the duty of care for others takes priority over self-interest or the luxury of reflection for Black women in the work of liberation.

Despite Tish's assertion about the lack of women's space for imagination, her narrative voice enables a reading that sees power modeled outside of patriarchal channels of authority, particularly in the character of Ernestine. Tish is in a place of vulnerability in which her sense of agency is limited, but she most clearly recognizes this when comparing her demeanor to that of Ernestine. She says of herself, "I look as though I just can't make it, she looks like can't nothing stop her."[42] Ernestine is a model of power that is realistic and attainable. Tish credits her sister's strength to looking into the mirror during their childhood, a repetitive act that she believes led to Ernestine knowing who she is or "who she damn well isn't."[43] Tish's youth combined with her pregnant body reveal her vulnerability in ways that cannot be hidden. Yet the publicness of pregnancy invites others to care for her in ways that demonstrate the reach and power of the intimate sphere to strengthen and encourage. As Baldwin shared in correspondence to a friend, *Beale Street* is "partly about the price that we all have to pay and the ways in which we help each other to survive."[44] Because she cannot bear it alone, Tish relies on the strength of others to help her through. It is precisely because of the support of her intimate network that she comes to realize the measure of her embodied strength and agency to, as Mills asserts, "organize and give life to sociopolitical change."[45]

Bodies in *Beale Street* are framed in various ways: as sites of vulnerability, of presumed criminality, and of sacred pleasure. Bodies act and are acted upon. Both Fonny and Tish experience the sensation of their bodies being outside of their own control. Tish, as she does with Ernestine, sees a confidence in Fonny that she struggles to find in herself, yet she recognizes the penalty for such self-assuredness: "The same passion which saved Fonny got him into trouble, and put him in jail. … he had found his center, his own center, inside him: and it showed. He wasn't anybody's nigger. And that's a crime, in this fucking free country."[46] Tish's biting sarcasm about paradoxical freedom in the United States turns the indictment of criminality back on the state, reminding us that racism is the nation's crime. Baldwinian in its critical scope, this narrative tone takes aim at the broader relationship between race and autonomy in American culture. In this culture, self-possessed Black men are seen as criminally threatening.

Baldwin further elucidates the implicit assumptions about the entanglement of race, autonomy, and gender in the scene of Fonny's confrontation with the police officer who will later accuse him of raping a Puerto Rican woman. In that fateful encounter, Tish makes a conscious decision to guard Fonny's body with her own, making her subject to the dangerous power of a police officer:

> I was sure that the cop intended to kill Fonny; but he could not kill Fonny if I could keep my body between Fonny and this cop; and with all my strength, with all my love, my prayers, and armed with the knowledge that Fonny was not, after all, going to knock *me* to the ground, I held the back of my head against Fonny's chest, held both his wrists between my two hands, and looked up into the face of this cop.[47]

This scene of bodily protection, retold near the novel's conclusion, forecasts Tish's continual protection of Fonny. The risk Tish takes, believing that the cop will not harm her to get to Fonny, comes immediately after she is sexually assaulted in a public market. Shielding Fonny's body with her own, Tish connects the harassment from the young man to the sexualized threat posed by the officer, noting how his eyes "flicked over [her] in exactly the same way the boy's eyes had."[48] This scene reiterates the everyday risks Black women face at the intersection of race and gender. In this moment, Tish's intervention on Fonny's behalf does prevent further escalation; however, this act returns to haunt the couple when the same officer works to charge Fonny with sexual assault, reminding us of the cost of claiming access to rights when confronting state power.

Despite the bodily separation imposed by incarceration, Tish continues to use her body as a safeguard for Fonny. The carceral environment is one driven by spectacles of shame for both the confined and the free. Shame, in all its visibility and palpability, is one obstacle Tish must work to overcome as she fights to keep Fonny from the depths of despondency and complete isolation. She concludes that she and other women of color whose loved ones are also in jail should not be ashamed. Instead, she says, "The people responsible for these jails should be ashamed."[49] Tish's observation of women of diverse ethnic backgrounds and ages within this space underscores the gendered and classed state of care under carcerality.[50] She notes that the "poor are always crossing the Sahara" while the "vultures"—lawyers and bondsmen—circle around them, waiting for their death.[51] These parasitic, predatory figures are shameless in their manipulation of the women who populate the visitation space. However, Tish remains steadfast in her efforts to minimize the harm Fonny faces despite being exposed to those who seek to exploit her while she is in a position of presumed vulnerability.

In the context of incarceration, both small and grand acts of kindness or care take on greater significance as acts of politicized affective labor. Tish's despondency over having to view Fonny through a glass partition provides a clear example of one way that intimacy is now mediated and diminished by their inability to touch one another. Her wish that no one else experience this pain reminds us that this is not just a story about Tish and Fonny—countless others have had or will have such an experience. In the space of the prison visit, the prisoner and visitor are both held under the control of the space as bodies to be acted upon, as objects subject to carceral power. During their visits, Tish and Fonny take advantage of their capacity to act by mimicking the touch of intimacy—"I kissed the glass. He kissed the glass"— and relying upon their sight of one another as an expression of intimacy.[52] Harris gets to this point when she notes that eye contact "is the *saving* power that sustains [Fonny and Tish] as they talk to each other at the Tombs through telephones separated by a glass partition. They see in each other's eyes what they cannot give by touching; they commune, they comfort."[53]

Intimacy, narrowly defined, relies upon physical touch and emotional connectedness. Though Miller reads their gestures to each other within prison as inadequate substitutes for sexual intimacy, I see such gestures as enactments of love that extend an understanding of intimacy into what Lauren Berlant characterizes as an "emancipating [kind] of love."[54] In other words, in the absence of the ability to act upon the need for touch, vision—the ability to see and be seen—protects both Fonny and Tish from spiritual evisceration at the hands of the carceral state. In this sense, Tish and Fonny are able to grant each other the kind of recognition that is life affirming and critical to their survival within and beyond the prison. In the carceral space, one's most private, intimate moments are made public, and looking through the partition glass signifies being exposed to the taxing power of the carceral environment. This presents the constant threat of destruction for both the imprisoned and the visitor, who represent caged vulnerability as the glass amplifies their exposure to the criminal power of the state.

Visits, though often taxing on the visitor emotionally, physically, and financially, are critical to the emotional wellbeing to the imprisoned. Miller notes that though their positive relationship helps preserve them within the alienating space of the prison, Fonny and Tish's "attempt at connection is tainted by the very structure of the prison which exists to separate and compartmentalize bodies."[55] In confronting such alienation, Tish strives to reconcile the daily visits to see Fonny with her material reality. She must work to earn money for Fonny's support, but the necessity of work often comes into conflict with the need for intimacy for both Tish and Fonny that is met through visitation. Tish carefully contemplates the risks of not visiting:

> It seems to me that if I quit my job, I'll be making the six o'clock visit forever. I explain this to Fonny, and he says he understands, and in fact, he does. But understanding doesn't help him at six o'clock. No matter what you understand, you can't help waiting: for your name to be called, to be taken from your cell and led downstairs. If you have visitors, or even if you have only one visitor, but that visitor is constant, it means that someone outside cares about you. … if no one comes to see you, you are in very bad trouble. And trouble, in here, means danger.[56]

Tish knows that a choice between immediate survival and future freedom are at odds in this situation. The threat of isolation, and the dangerous despondency that can grow out of it, looms large. The care Fonny requires while incarcerated, in many ways, conscripts Tish's life in service of his own. Yet Tish recognizes that intimacy matters for wellbeing, and without it, one is at risk of losing a sense of humanity.

At the novel's end, Baldwin underscores the power of women's work to bring about change when Tish goes into labor with her eyes fixed solely upon her "mother's eyes."[57] The narrative alignment of the news of Fonny's possible, if only temporary, freedom arriving just as Tish goes into labor suggests an embodied connection between the physical, material, and affective labor of the Rivers women. Through childbirth, the metaphorical promise of the child as representative of a future free of oppression is entering fulfillment. In this reading, the vignette of Fonny happily working on his sculpture as the baby cries "like it means to wake the dead" signals a new, unknown future where freedom may become more than a possibility.[58] The 2018 film adaptation of the novel mostly holds fast to Baldwin's voice and tone, but its ending transforms the author's closing vision from one that rests in the ambiguous possibility of the new world's arrival into an ending that constricts that hope by revealing Fonny to be still imprisoned as his son grows up.

When Baldwin completed the novel he wrote to his brother David, declaring it "the strangest novel I've ever written."[59] Perhaps it was strange to imagine such a sociopolitical change as truly possible. In the epilogue to *No Name in the Street*, Baldwin suggests that "an old world is dying, and a new one, kicking in the belly of its mother, time, announces that it is ready to be born."[60] The contemporary moment demonstrates that the old world Baldwin sought to bury in 1972 did not go quietly into the night. Instead, the legacy of the old world lives on in the current state of mass incarceration in the United States, demonstrating the lasting acuity of Hortense Spillers's description of *Beale Street* as one of Baldwin's "penetrating, occasionally scary investigations into a familial politics of intimacy."[61] Attending to the representation of birth as revolutionary in *Beale Street* enables recognition of how Black women's political practice of love can mount meaningful resistance to the challenges imposed by carcerality, even when it means offering most or all of oneself.

Notes

1 James Baldwin, *No Name in the Street* (1972), in *Collected Essays*, ed. Toni Morrison (New York, Library of America, 1998), p. 475.
2 James Baldwin, *If Beale Street Could Talk* (1974) (New York, Vintage, 2006), p. 186.
3 Aliyyah I. Abdur-Rahman, *Against the Closet: Black Political Longing and the Erotics of Race* (Durham, NC, Duke University Press, 2012), p. 99.
4 As Nathaniel Mills argues, "Baldwin's shift in this period can be attributed to [Eldridge] Cleaver particularly and to the homophobic, heteropatriarchal rhetoric of black nationalism more generally." Though Baldwin never responded directly to Cleaver's scathingly homophobic/heterosexist attack in *Soul on Ice*, Baldwin's post-civil rights movement writing offers nuanced engagement with Black nationalism and insight into both the problems and solutions of his contemporaneous moment. See Nathaniel Mills, "Cleaver/Baldwin Revisited: Naturalism and the Gendering of Black Revolution," *Studies in American Naturalism*, 7:1 (2012), p. 51.
5 David Leeming, *James Baldwin: A Biography* (1994) (New York, Arcade Publishing, 2015), p. 323.
6 Though contemporary assessments of mass incarceration detail increased imprisonment rates across the population, in 1974 African American men made up nearly 35 percent of all men who had ever been incarcerated in the United States. At that time, African Americans represented only 11.1 percent of the U.S. population. See Thomas P. Bonzcar, "Prevalence of Imprisonment in the U.S. Population, 1974–2001," *US Bureau of Justice Statistics* (Rockville, MD: Bureau of Justice Statistics, 2003).
7 D. Quentin Miller, *A Criminal Power: James Baldwin and the Law* (Columbus, OH, Ohio State University Press, 2012), p. 9.
8 Saidiya Hartman, *Scenes of Subjection: Terror, Slavery, and Self-making in Nineteenth-Century America* (New York, Oxford University Press, 1997), pp. 98–9.
9 D. Quentin Miller, "Separate and Unequal in Paris: *Notes of a Native Son* and the Law," in Cora Kaplan and Bill Schwarz (eds.), *James Baldwin: America and Beyond* (Ann Arbor, MI, University of Michigan Press, 2011), p. 160.
10 James Baldwin, "An Open Letter to My Sister, Miss Angela Davis," *New York Review of Books*, 19 November 1970, www.nybooks.com/articles/1971/01/07/an-open-letter-to-my-sister-miss-angela-davis/ (accessed 5 June 2020).
11 Marlon B. Ross, "White Fantasies of Desire: Baldwin and the Racial Identities of Sexuality," in Dwight A. McBride (ed.), *James Baldwin Now* (New York, New York University Press, 1999), p. 36.
12 James Baldwin, "Everybody's Protest Novel," in Morrison (ed.), *Collected Essays*, p. 18.

13 Douglas Field, *All Those Strangers: The Art and Lives of James Baldwin* (New York, Oxford University Press, 2015), p. 96.

14 *Ibid.*, pp. 106–7.

15 Gregory J. Siegworth and Melissa Gregg, "An Inventory of Shimmers," in Melissa Gregg and Gregory J. Siegworth (eds.), *The Affect Theory Reader* (Durham, NC, Duke University Press, 2010), p. 2.

16 Baldwin, *Beale Street*, p. 8.

17 James Baldwin, *The Fire Next Time* (1963) (New York, Vintage International, 1993), p. 105.

18 Qtd. in Leeming, *James Baldwin*, p. 321.

19 Baldwin, *Beale Street*, p. 162.

20 *Ibid.*, pp. 33, 112.

21 *Ibid.*, p. 125.

22 Field, *All Those Strangers*, p. 96.

23 *Ibid.*, p. 107.

24 Abdur-Rahman, *Against the Closet*, pp. 99–100.

25 Lynn Orilla Scott, *James Baldwin's Later Fiction: Witness to the Journey* (East Lansing, MI, Michigan State University Press, 2002), p. 63.

26 Trudier Harris, *Black Women in the Fiction of James Baldwin* (Knoxville, TN, University of Tennessee Press, 1985), p. 156.

27 Mills, "Cleaver/Baldwin Revisited," p. 52.

28 Abdur-Rahman, *Against the Closet*, p. 100.

29 *Ibid.*, p. 126.

30 Mae G. Henderson, "James Baldwin: Expatriation, Homosexual Panic, and Man's Estate," *Callaloo*, 23:1 (2000), p. 313.

31 Baldwin, *Beale Street*, p. 33.

32 Melinda Plastas and Eve Allegra Raimon, "Brutality and Brotherhood: James Baldwin and Prison Sexuality," *African American Review*, 46:4 (2013), p. 689.

33 Baldwin, *Beale Street*, p. 190.

34 *Ibid.*, p. 43.

35 *Ibid.*

36 *Ibid.*, p. 125.

37 Plastas and Raimon, "Brutality and Brotherhood," p. 690.

38 Baldwin, *Beale Street*, p. 126.

39 Plastas and Raimon, "Brutality and Brotherhood," p. 690.

40 Baldwin, *Beale Street*, p. 74.

41 *Ibid.*, p. 59.

42 *Ibid.*, p. 46.

43 *Ibid.*, p. 47.

44 Qtd. in Leeming, *James Baldwin*, p. 323.

45 Mills, "Cleaver/Baldwin Revisited," p. 68.

46 Baldwin, *Beale Street*, p. 37.

47 *Ibid.*, p. 137.

48 *Ibid.*

49 *Ibid.*, p. 7.

50 Brian Norman suggests that "Baldwin sets in motion a desire for the reunification of an African American family, and he also instigates a parallel desire for a cross-ethnic community of women." Though outside the scope of this essay, this scene in particular holds potentially important implications for cross-ethnic solidarity within the context of the

penal system. See Brian Norman, "James Baldwin's Confrontation with US Imperialism in *If Beale Street Could Talk*," *MELUS*, 32:1 (2007), p. 123.
51 Baldwin, *Beale Street*, p. 7.
52 *Ibid.*, p. 111.
53 Trudier Harris, "The Eye as Weapon in *If Beale Street Could Talk*," *MELUS*, 5:3 (1978), p. 62.
54 Miller, *A Criminal Power*, p. 143; Lauren Berlant, "Intimacy: A Special Issue," *Critical Inquiry*, 24:2 (1998), p. 281.
55 Miller, *A Criminal Power*, p. 143.
56 Baldwin, *Beale Street*, pp. 157–8.
57 *Ibid.*, p. 197.
58 *Ibid.*
59 Qtd. in Leeming, *James Baldwin*, p. 321.
60 Baldwin, *No Name in the Street*, p. 475.
61 Hortense Spillers, "Afterword," in Cora Kaplan and Bill Schwarz (eds.), *James Baldwin: America and Beyond* (Ann Arbor, MI, University of Michigan Press, 2011), pp. 243–4.

Works Cited

Abdur-Rahman, Aliyyah I., *Against the Closet: Black Political Longing and the Erotics of Race* (Durham, NC, Duke University Press, 2012).
Baldwin, James, "Everybody's Protest Novel" (1949), in *Collected Essays*, ed. Toni Morrison (New York, Library of America, 1998), pp. 11–18.
_____ *The Fire Next Time* (1963) (New York, Vintage International, 1993).
_____ *If Beale Street Could Talk* (1974) (New York, Vintage, 2006).
_____ *No Name in the Street* (1972), in *Collected Essays*, ed. Toni Morrison (New York, Library of America, 1998), pp. 353–475.
_____ "An Open Letter to My Sister, Miss Angela Davis," *New York Review of Books*, 19 November 1970, www.nybooks.com/articles/1971/01/07/an-open-letter-to-my-sister-miss-angela-davis/ (accessed 5 June 2020).
Berlant, Lauren, "Intimacy: A Special Issue," *Critical Inquiry*, 24:2 (1998), pp. 281–8.
Bonzcar, Thomas P., "Prevalence of Imprisonment in the U.S. Population, 1974–2001," *US Bureau of Justice Statistics* (Rockville, MD: Bureau of Justice Statistics, 2003).
Field, Douglas, *All Those Strangers: The Art and Lives of James Baldwin* (New York, Oxford University Press, 2015)
Harris, Trudier, *Black Women in the Fiction of James Baldwin* (Knoxville, TN, University of Tennessee Press, 1985)
_____ "The Eye as Weapon in *If Beale Street Could Talk*," *MELUS*, 5:3 (1978), pp. 54–66.
Hartman, Saidiya, *Scenes of Subjection: Terror, Slavery, and Self-making in Nineteenth-Century America* (New York, Oxford University Press, 1997).
Henderson, Mae G., "James Baldwin: Expatriation, Homosexual Panic, and Man's Estate," *Callaloo*, 23:1 (2000), pp. 313–27.
Leeming, David, *James Baldwin: A Biography* (1994) (New York, Arcade Publishing, 2015).
Miller, D. Quentin, *A Criminal Power: James Baldwin and the Law* (Columbus, OH, Ohio State University Press, 2012).
_____ "Separate and Unequal in Paris: *Notes of a Native Son* and the Law," in Cora Kaplan and Bill Schwarz (eds.), *James Baldwin: America and Beyond* (Ann Arbor, MI, University of Michigan Press, 2011), pp. 159–72.

Mills, Nathaniel, "Cleaver/Baldwin Revisited: Naturalism and the Gendering of Black Revolution," *Studies in American Naturalism*, 7:1 (2012), pp. 50–79.

Norman, Brian, "James Baldwin's Confrontation with US Imperialism in *If Beale Street Could Talk*," *MELUS*, 32:1 (2007), pp. 119–38.

Plastas, Melinda, and Eve Allegra Raimon, "Brutality and Brotherhood: James Baldwin and Prison Sexuality," *African American Review*, 46:4 (2013), pp. 687–99.

Ross, Marlon B., "White Fantasies of Desire: Baldwin and the Racial Identities of Sexuality," in Dwight A. McBride (ed.), *James Baldwin Now* (New York, New York University Press, 1999), pp. 13–55.

Scott, Lynn Orilla, *James Baldwin's Later Fiction: Witness to the Journey* (East Lansing, MI, Michigan State University Press, 2002).

Siegworth, Gregory J., and Melissa Gregg, "An Inventory of Shimmers," in Melissa Gregg and Gregory J. Siegworth (eds.), *The Affect Theory Reader* (Durham, NC, Duke University Press, 2010), pp. 1–25.

Spillers, Hortense, "Afterword," in Cora Kaplan and Bill Schwarz (eds.), *James Baldwin: America and Beyond* (Ann Arbor, MI, University of Michigan Press, 2011), pp. 241–6.

Contributor's Biography

Marquita R. Smith is Assistant Professor of English at Rowan University. Her research and teaching interests include African American literature and culture, hip-hop studies, gender and sexuality, and critical race studies. Her critical writings on the intersection of sexuality, race, and gender in African American and Black diasporic literature and culture have been published in forums such as *Postcolonial Text* (2013), *Popular Music and Society* (2014, 2019), *The Routledge Research Companion to Popular Music and Gender* (2017), *Popular Music and the Politics of Hope: Queer and Feminist Interventions* (2019), *The Puritan Magazine* (2017), and *The Black Scholar* (2018). Her current book project, *Through the Glass: Contemporary African American Literature and Carceral Feeling*, examines the affective presence of incarceration in contemporary African American literature. In 2018 she was awarded a Career Enhancement Fellowship by the Woodrow Wilson National Fellowship Foundation.

ESSAY

Chagrin d'amour: Intimacy, Shame, and the Closet in James Baldwin's *Giovanni's Room*

Monica B. Pearl   University of Manchester

Abstract

This essay's close interrogation of James Baldwin's 1956 novel *Giovanni's Room* allows us to see one aspect of how sexual shame functions: it shows how shame exposes anxiety not only about the feminizing force of homosexuality, but about how being the object of the gaze is feminizing—and therefore shameful. It also shows that the paradigm of the closet is not the metaphor of privacy and enclosure on one hand and openness and liberation on the other that it is commonly thought to be, but instead is a site of illusory control over whether one is available to be seen and therefore humiliated by being feminized. Further, the essay reveals the paradox of denial, where one must first know the thing that is at the same time being disavowed or denied. The narrative requirements of fictions such as *Giovanni's Room* demonstrate this, as it requires that the narrator both know, in order to narrate, and not know something at the same time.

Keywords: Eve Kosofsky Sedgwick, Silvan Tompkins, queer literature, gay literature, effeminacy, masculinity, Freud

James Baldwin's novel *Giovanni's Room*, published in 1956, is in American letters an unusually early, frank, fictional depiction of homosexuality between men. Its frankness does not, however, mitigate how riven it is with shame. Disgust and shame are its principal attitudes toward the homosexuality that gives the novel its plot. Judith Butler tells us that the term "queer" "has operated as one linguistic practice whose purpose has been the shaming of the subject it names or, rather, the producing of a subject *through* the shaming interpellation."[1] "Queer" is not the epithet in operation in *Giovanni's Room*; however, the risk of being seen to be queer—in the landscape of this book it is effeminacy that is at stake, and the term used to interpellate that effeminacy is "fairy"—is anathema. One can avoid it through vigilance and denial, a paradox of exigencies. The novel describes and

James Baldwin Review, Volume 6, 2020, © The Authors. Published by Manchester University Press and
The University of Manchester Library
http://dx.doi.org/10.7227/JBR.6.5

enacts a crucial and disturbing lesson about what might feel and look like para-doxical intertwined connections between desire and shame. While this seems especially applicable to homosexuals, and even more so to homosexuals in the United States and Europe in the 1950s, in fact this is a collocation, this essay argues, that is operative for everyone.

If shame is an anxiety over "visibility and spectacle," as Eve Kosofsky Sedgwick suggests, or, as Silvan Tomkins puts it, an "ambivalence about looking and being looked at," then the antidote to shame is control over how and whether one is seen.[2] It is a practice that David, the novel's protagonist and narrator, deploys in his attempts to convince himself of his heterosexuality: he confirms that there are queers who are a far worse kind of queer than he might be; indeed, in his thinking, maybe the only kind. If other men—the "fairies"—are *really* queer, this thinking goes, then he cannot be. He despises them and describes them—effeminate men who cannot hide or dis-guise, or resist, their desire for men—with utter disgust and dismissiveness. For exam-ple, Guillaume, the owner of the bar where Giovanni works, is referred to many times as "such a disgusting old fairy," and the conclusion is that "he should be ashamed."[3]

Giovanni's Room begins at its denouement. David has escaped to a house in the South of France to avoid, but also to wait out, the execution of his erstwhile lover, Giovanni, in Paris. He is extremely unhappy, enduring a terrible night, "a drink in my hand … a bottle at my elbow," anticipating "the most terrible morning of my life."[4] In his dark night of the soul, David admits to himself that he treats people "lightly" and that he is "too various to be trusted": "If this were not so I would not be alone in this house tonight. Hella would not be on the high seas. And Giovanni would not be about to perish, sometime between this night and this morning, on the guillotine."[5] Hella is his fiancée and one of the women to whom David attaches himself as one way to persuade himself that he wants women, not men; his ratio-nale for becoming engaged to Hella is that he "thought she would be fun to have fun with … that was all it meant to me."[6]

Upon receiving a letter that informs him that Hella is coming back to Paris from Spain—where she has gone to decide if she wants to marry David—he is desperate to confirm his sexual preference for women, as he has been living for a long time in her absence with Giovanni. He "felt elated," he narrates, "yet, as I walked down Raspail toward the cafes of Montparnasse, I could not fail to remember that Hella and I had walked here, Giovanni and I had walked here."[7] And although it seems for a moment that he might be equally torn between Hella and Giovanni in his reflections and affection, "with each step, the face that glowed insistently before me was not her face, but his."[8] Suddenly, he thinks, "I wanted to find a girl, any girl at all."[9] Many have suggested that *Giovanni's Room* is a portrait of bisexuality because David is sexually involved with both men and women, but David's sex with women is always desperate, and always a way of disavowing his desire for men. Upon Hel-la's return from Spain, David describes their physical intimacy in this way: "I kept kissing her and holding her, trying to find my way in her again, as though she were a familiar, darkened room in which I fumbled to find the light … I hoped to burn out, through Hella, my image of Giovanni and the reality of his touch."[10]

In this search for "any girl at all" David encounters a former acquaintance, Sue, who immediately becomes his target for conquest. With her he experiences what is thematic in the novel: ambivalence—an ambivalence that is evident not only in the content of his thoughts but in the syntax of his expression. He encounters Sue and recognizes her desirability—she has "the quality ... of the girls who are selected each year to be Miss Rheingold"—yet "she was not pretty."[11] He is "both dismayed and relieved to see her."[12] Here we have in the prose a concomitant to the ambivalence conveyed in the novel, and this is something that is already a mark of Baldwin's style: a capacity to contain multitudes within accounts of feelings—that no feeling or affect is ever one thing, it contains gradations and it also often contains the paradox of opposites. These paradoxes and contradictions are the template for the core contradiction in the novel: David's denial and desire—he wants Giovanni, and other men, but cannot bear the implications of his desires, and so he must quash them, often syntactically, of which more below. This creates an impossible amalgamation: that he must know and feel something at the same time that he must deny it, and therefore not know it and not feel it.

With Sue, David denies his relationship with Giovanni. "No," he replies to Sue's question about his living arrangements, he does not live alone in "the maid's room ... very cheap ... out at the end of Paris, near the zoo"; he does not even mention Giovanni by name, but describes "this French kid I know, he lives with his mistress, but they fight a lot and it's really *his* room so sometimes, when his mistress throws him out, he bunks with me for a couple of days."[13] It seems he is able to get Sue to express the very heartbreak he is experiencing in forcing himself to flee from Giovanni, but transposed onto this fabricated couple—Giovanni and an invented mistress—when she sighs in response "Ah! ... *Chagrin d'amour!*"[14] This is a small example of something David does in a larger sense elsewhere in the novel with men; that is, he projects onto them his own anxieties and feelings so that they are enacting a noxious affect in order that he then does not have to. He knows that by seducing Sue to rid himself of thoughts of Giovanni and reinstate his heterosexuality, he "was doing something very cruel";[15] and in fact he cannot banish thoughts of Giovanni: every single moment with Sue makes him think of him. The waiter's surly subservience: "I thought of Giovanni and of how many times in an evening the phrase, *Oui monsieur* fell from his lips."[16] And even when he "tried not to think," he nevertheless attempts to make a moral bargain that exalts his homosexual desire over this debased enactment of heterosexual performance; he compares what he is doing with Sue with what he has done with Giovanni: "I was thinking that what I did with Giovanni could not possibly be more immoral than what I was about to do with Sue."[17]

With a woman—a woman he is with for the most instrumental of purposes: "I ... approached Sue as if she were a job of work"—he has compassion for Giovanni, and, also, a recollection of their intimacy: "With this fleeting thought there came another, equally fleeting: a new sense of Giovanni, his private life and pain, and all that moved like a flood in him when we lay together at night."[18] He attempts to fabricate intimacy with Sue, but as soon as he is back in her room, and takes her in his arms, he thinks of Giovanni "for some reason": "For some reason I was terribly aware that it was after seven in the evening, that soon the sun would have disappeared from the river, that all the Paris night was about to begin, and that Giovanni was now at work."[19] During sex with Sue he has further oppositional thoughts, this time on a theme that is among the main preoccupations of the novel: inside/outside, entrapment/freedom; in worrying over whether Sue has "done anything to prevent herself from becoming pregnant," he is able to see the irony of his "being trapped in that way—in the very act ... of trying to escape."[20] He is enacting here the persistent syntactical viscera of the novel, his knowing exactly what he is doing even while he is pursuing his denial of it. His "realizations" are constant: "I realized that I was doing something awful to her"; "I realized that my fears had been excessive and groundless and, in effect, a lie: it had nothing to do with my body. Sue was not Hella and she did not lessen my terror of what would happen when Hella came."[21] "At the same time," his narration continues, "I realized that my performance with Sue was succeeding even too well."[22] The novel is full of this kind of simultaneous knowing and not knowing. David's assignation with Sue is successful insofar as he accomplishes the task of engaging in a heterosexual union despite his longing for Giovanni; it also is meant to underwrite his masculinity in an equation that the narrative cannot let go of.

It is not a peculiarity of Baldwin's or of his protagonist to equate masculinity, or—in the parlance of the novel—manliness, with heterosexuality, and therefore femininity with homosexuality. This was a conception of the 1950s and one that persists—that homosexuality is a failure of masculinity and is evidenced in acute effeminacy.[23] The novel makes these delineations, and the attendant disgust with any failure of masculinity, very clear. When David first walks to Montparnasse looking for female company, he rejects "a couple of girls," who he decides are "French whores," who anyway "were not very attractive"; he tells himself, vehemently, "I could do better than *that*."[24] His syntax here is identical to when he reveals his disdain for gay men, with its final pronoun spat out. Of the effeminate homosexuals he encounters in the bar where he is about to meet and fall in love with Giovanni, David thinks: "I always found it difficult to believe that they ever went to bed with anybody for a man who wanted a woman would certainly have rather had a real one and a man who wanted a man would certainly not want one of *them*."[25]

Though this misogynist dismissal is not exceptional in Baldwin's books, here it takes the form of disgust for men who are too much like women: this is the substance of David's loathing. It is not enough to refer to them derogatorily as women—and as mad women: *les folles*—but he further compares them to animals: "There were, of course, *les folles*, always dressed in the most improbable combinations, screaming like parrots the details of their latest love-affairs" and "they looked like a peacock garden and sounded like a barnyard."[26] David's language exposes the extremity of his horror when the equation of effeminate men with animals takes this turn to "utter grotesqueness"; of a young man "who came out at night wearing makeup and earrings and with his heavy blond hair piled high" and who "sometimes ... actually wore a skirt and high heels," David remarks: "People said he was very nice but I confess that his utter grotesqueness made me uneasy, perhaps in the same way that the sight of monkeys eating their own excrement turns some people's stomachs."[27] The misogyny here is not incidental, for it is precisely the effeminacy of homosexuality that so disgusts him.

David's concern about his "manhood" first arises the morning after a sexual encounter with his boyhood friend Joey. "I was suddenly afraid," he recalls. "The power and the promise and the mystery of that body made me suddenly afraid," he repeats. He and Joey have sex after they kiss "as it were, by accident," a night of—in the paradoxical way that is the undercurrent of the novel—"astounding intolerable pain" out of which "came joy."[28] It is worth quoting the whole passage of his post-coital terror, for the repetitions—the refrain of being "suddenly afraid," for example, is stated three times—are telling:

> I was suddenly afraid. Perhaps it was because he looked so innocent lying there, with such perfect trust; perhaps it was because he was so much smaller than me; my own body suddenly seemed gross and crushing and the desire which was rising in me seemed monstrous. But, above all, I was suddenly afraid. It was borne in on me: *But Joey is a boy*, I saw suddenly the power in his thighs, in his arms, and in his loosely curled fists. The power and the promise and the mystery of that body made me suddenly afraid. That body suddenly seemed the black opening of a cavern in which I would be tortured till madness came, in which I would lose my manhood.[29]

Slightly later in the novel we learn of some of the circumstances of his childhood which we might understand as the basis of these terrible anxieties about masculinity. For example, David overhears an argument his father has with his aunt, with whom he is raising David following the death of David's mother. David's aunt accuses his father of dereliction: "Do you really think it's a good idea for David to see you staggering home drunk all the time? And don't fool yourself ... that he doesn't know where you're coming from, don't think he doesn't know about your women!"[30] To which David's father replies: "all I want is for David is that he grow up to be a man. And when I say a man, Ellen, I don't mean a Sunday school teacher."[31]

So by the time David is measuring his heterosexuality not only against his own masculinity but against the imputed effeminacy of homosexuals, we are well mired in complicated notions of manhood: all that being a white man at a certain moment in American history includes, and the weight it has to carry. Late in the novel, when David's father is writing letters to David exhorting him to return home, we discover that his nickname for David is "Butch": "'*Dear Butch,*' my father said, '*aren't you ever coming home?*'"[32] We see the efforts of interpellation at work here: be the name I call you. In fact, the question he imagines his father is not asking is "*Is it a woman, David? Bring her on home. I don't care who she is. Bring her on home and I'll help you get set up.*"[33] David believes his father "could not risk the question because he could not have endured the answer in the negative."[34]

In the paragraph after the astonishment or disgust he imagines his father might feel if he knew that the reason David stayed in Paris was the "negative" of a woman, he cruises a sailor—and admires his masculinity: "I was staring at him … he wore his masculinity as unequivocally as he wore his skin."[35] Even Jacques, the friend who first introduces David to Giovanni—though inadvertently, as he is trying to get David, and subsequently Giovanni, for himself—recognizes that it is the presentation of masculinity that is at issue for David: "'I am not suggesting that you jeopardize, even for a moment, that'—he paused—'*immaculate* manhood which is your pride and joy.'"[36] David's ultimate fantasy of "light and safety" is one in which his "manhood [is] unquestioned."[37]

This arduous effort of scaffolding his masculinity is built on the foundation of disavowing his homosexuality. This in turn is built on vilifying femininity in men—of doing to other men precisely what the sailor in this scene is doing to David: "We came abreast and … he gave me a look contemptuously lewd and knowing; just such a look as he might have given to [a] nymphomaniac or trollop who was trying to make him believe she was a lady."[38] David feels his "face flame" and worriedly wonders "what he had seen in me to elicit such instantaneous contempt," imagining it had something to do with his "walk or the way I held my hands," or, even though "he had not heard" it, "my voice."[39] And while his worrying suggests that he does not know why the sailor is looking at him with contempt, he also "knew that what the sailor had seen in my unguarded eyes was envy and desire."[40] His worst worry—that he is the effeminate, desiring man—is realized here in this complicated amalgam of his desire for the sailor and the contempt for his femininity he imagines the sailor must therefore have for him.

It is, of course, paradoxical that David not only refuses his homosexuality through disgust with homosexuals—those he designates far further gone than himself—but that he also knows he is doing it. He recognizes the parallel of what he sees in Jacques and what the sailor has seen in him: "my reaction [to Jacques] and the sailor's had been the same."[41] In the most profound scorn that he can express, his contempt for homosexuals is that they are not men, not real men, not manly enough. What he envies in the sailor is his masculinity, at least partially evinced by the sailor's projected contempt for David.

Paradox is a signal theme and feature of *Giovanni's Room*. Often it takes the form of denial. Exhaustively, David tries to hide and deny his homosexuality from others and from himself. As a young man, this takes the form of whistling at girls who he knows do not believe him or believe in his interest in them. In a youthful prefiguring of his adult assignation with Sue:

> I think we had been lying around the beach, swimming a little and watching the near-naked girls pass, whistling at them, and laughing. I am sure that if any of the girls we whistled at that day had shown any signs of responding the ocean would not have been deep enough to drown our shame and terror.[42]

It is at this point in the novel that David recollects his youthful affair with his best friend, Joey, one night of "[g]reat thirsty heat, and trembling, and tenderness so painful I thought my heart would burst."[43] And although it "seemed, then, that a lifetime would not be long enough for me to act with Joey the act of love ... that lifetime was short."[44] Immediately David commences the distancing that he is invested in believing will protect him from "proof of some horrifying taint in me."[45] In the morning, "the sweat on my back grew cold. I was ashamed. The very bed, in its sweet disorder, testified to vileness."[46] This recollection comes early in the novel and exposes already the paradox, contradiction, and shame that are thematic; and it is tied to his lament for the loss of Giovanni: "I began, perhaps, to be lonely that summer and began, that summer, the flight which has brought me to this darkening window," where he waits out Giovanni's execution.[47]

Although one way to disavow homosexuality as an identity or predilection is to foreclose the wider wish to sleep with men by deciding that it is just this one man whom one wants—David has fallen for Giovanni but does not care for men generally—David nevertheless reveals the ways that his desire is wider and more indiscriminate than that, and always more than he feels comfortable with. He discloses that he does not admit to Giovanni that he has been with men before—and to us, the reader, he confides the story of only one, Joey—but he nevertheless cryptically reveals several other moments of desire. One is an actual sexual encounter when he was in the army "which involved a fairy who was later court-martialed out."[48] As is his desperate wont, it is the other who is the fairy and the other who is punished.

Yet he admits that being with Giovanni was not about wanting only Giovanni: "Giovanni had awakened an itch, had released a gnaw in me."[49] In this regard there are two revealing moments of happiness in the novel, and both are stories of walking in the open air with the man who is his lover. Both are quashed almost as soon as they are indulged. He narrates a story of pleasure with Giovanni, of openness, guilelessness, and happiness:

> I realized it one afternoon, when I was taking him to work via the boulevard Montparnasse. We had bought a kilo of cherries and we were eating them as we walked along. We were both insufferably childish and high-spirited that afternoon and the spectacle we presented, two grown men, jostling each other on the wide sidewalk, and aiming the cherry-pips, as though they were spitballs, into each other's faces, must have been outrageous. And I realized that such childishness was fantastic at my age and the happiness out of which it sprang yet more so; for that moment I really loved Giovanni, who had never seemed more beautiful than he was that afternoon. And, watching his face, I realized that it meant much to me that I could make his face so bright. I saw that I might be willing to give a great deal not to lose that power. And I felt myself flow toward him, as a river rushes when the ice breaks up.[50]

David indulges an uncharacteristic ebullience in this passage, yet it marks a rupture: the intimacy he and Giovanni share in the confines of their room has now leaked out onto the street. It recalls a nearly identical moment with Joey, the easy camaraderie and intimacy of walking down the street together: "We were walking along and Joey was making dirty wisecracks and we were laughing. Odd to remember, for the first time in so long, how good I felt that night, how fond of Joey."[51]

The aperture created by this openness, however, exposes David's desires not just for the particular other he is walking with, but for men more generally; in the perambulation episode with Giovanni he refers to his homosexuality, to this wide-ranging desire, as a "beast":

> Yet, at that very moment, there passed between us on the pavement another boy, a stranger, and I invested him at once with Giovanni's beauty and what I felt for Giovanni I also felt for him. Giovanni saw this and saw my face and it made him laugh the more. I blushed and he kept laughing and then the boulevard, the light, the sound of his laughter turned into a scene from a nightmare. I kept looking at the trees, the light falling through the leaves. I felt sorrow and shame and panic and great bitterness. At the same time—it was part of my turmoil and also outside it—I felt the muscles of my neck tighten with the effort I was making not to turn my head and watch that boy diminish down the bright avenue. The beast which Giovanni had awakened in me would never go to sleep again; but one day I would not be with Giovanni any more. And would I then, like all the others, find myself turning and following all kinds of boys down God knows what dark avenues, into what dark places?[52]

"The beast" is his homosexuality, for now he is not only delighting in being with Giovanni but he is cruising other boys. Even in the past it was not just the one other: after Joey is abandoned, we learn obliquely that "there were a number of those, all drunken, all sordid."[53] In all these encounters, the other must always be not only the gay one, the fairy, but the one who is punished. Of his encounter in the army, David confesses that the "panic his punishment caused in me was as close as I ever came to facing in myself the terrors I sometimes saw clouding another man's eyes."[54]

This candid moment on the street with Giovanni is threatening because it suggests that David's desire and happiness are not momentary lapses with one man—he likes *men*. And—this is important—he also sees that Giovanni observes this in him. Giovanni notices it and laughs at him: "Giovanni saw this and saw my face and it made him laugh the more."[55] It is the moment of humiliation. David is at his happiest, behaving like a child, and that is when he is helpless: his desires show something true about him that he cannot conceal. For a moment he has stopped being paranoid, stopped being vigilant. And that exposes him. His desire is seen by Giovanni. This is the paradox of intimacy: vulnerability has to be not only known to oneself, but witnessed by another. And one has to live with that person having seen one be vulnerable. The paradox is that this is also the structure of the dynamic of shame.

In his initial encounter with Joey we see that David imagines Joey's body as "the black opening of a cavern."[56] Later on that page, within the same reverie, he again mentions a cavern: "A cavern opened in my mind, black, full of rumor, suggestion, of half-heard, half-forgotten, half-understood stories, full of dirty words."[57] Here is the first instance when David enters a room for its homosexual pleasures and then flees it out of the shame that he experiences there. These rooms are spaces that he continually leaves, only to find—or indeed to construct—others wherever he has

managed to escape to. The routes and the destinations are not thoughtful but desperate. "My flight may, indeed, have begun that summer [of his encounter with
Joey]—which does not tell me where to find the germ of the dilemma which resolved
itself, that summer, into flight."[58] And again when he imagines what is in store for
him: "I thought I saw my future in that cavern. I was afraid. I could have cried, cried
for shame and terror, cried for not understanding how this could have happened to
me, how this could have happened *in* me."[59] Given the themes in this novel of homosexuality and its disavowals, it is easy to think of this cavern as a closet.

In *Giovanni's Room* the closets are both literal enclosures and metaphorical
descriptions; they take shape in the world and also in David's own mind: "when
one begins to search for the crucial, the definitive moment, the moment which
changed all others, one finds oneself pressing, in great pain, through a maze of
false signals and abruptly locking doors."[60] "Of course," he comments knowingly,
"it is somewhere before me, locked in that reflection I am watching in the window
as the night comes down outside. It is trapped in the room with me, always has
been, and always will be."[61] Colm Tóibín tells us that the

> idea of concealment and disclosure is central to *Giovanni's Room*, as the narrator
> moves from being or seeming straight to being or seeming homosexual to being or
> seeming both, all the time both prepared and unprepared to reveal himself or his
> confusion by a look, a stare, a moment of pure recognition.[62]

Giovanni's Room announces its preoccupation with enclosed spaces that we might
read as closets from the outset: the "room" of the title. And throughout, the novel is
riven with references to small spaces—that room and myriad other enclosures.
Giovanni throws this knowledge at David when he exclaims: "the world is full of
rooms—big rooms, little rooms, round rooms, square ones, rooms high up, rooms
low down—all kinds of rooms!"[63] Even at the very beginning of the novel David
anticipates a negotiation over a small space, an enclosure, a compartment on the
train: "At each stop, recruits in their baggy brown uniforms and colored hats will
open the compartment door to ask *Complet*?"[64] This is immediately attached to a
question of sexuality and David's insufficiently heterosexual enactment of it. He is
projecting all of this, imagining himself the next morning after Giovanni's execution on the train back to Paris, when he continues his imagined story: "There will
be a girl sitting opposite me who will wonder why I haven't been flirting with her."[65]

A colloquial term, the closet has come to be understood as the metaphorical
space in which one might hide to protect one's secrets, and from which one might
step out when one is ready for those secrets to become known. Although the closet
and the emergence from it has become a metaphor for many secrets and disclo-
sures, the closet and its apertures are still primarily a homosexual discourse.
"Vibrantly resonant as the image of the closet is for many modern oppressions,"
Eve Kosofsky Sedgwick tells us, "it is indicative for homophobia in a way it cannot
be for other oppressions."[66] And while the closet is a trope that usually refers to a
mechanism for hiding one's privately acknowledged homosexuality from other

people, it does not always work this way. The metaphor allows that one can be in the closet even to oneself.

David often behaves as though he does not know he harbors desires for men. But at the same time he always knows. For example, he lies to Giovanni that he "had never slept with a boy before";[67] about this he comments that the lie emerged out of a wishful conclusion: "I had decided that I never would again."[68] Here is where he shows that he knows he has gone to Europe in order to flee that very knowledge; he knows he has lied, at the same time that he lies, and he knows he has attempted to escape, even though the escape demands that he not know it:

> There is something fantastic in the spectacle I now present to myself of having run so far, so hard, across the ocean even, only to find myself brought up short once more before the bulldog in my own backyard—the yard, in the meantime, having grown smaller and the bulldog bigger.[69]

He has fled one closet in order to find another. He says it with precise self-aware-ness several pages later: "I think now that if I had had any intimation that the self I was going to find would turn out to be only the same self from which I had spent so much time in flight, I would have stayed at home."[70] This is one of the primary paradoxes of the novel: that in order to hide something from oneself one has first to know it. It happens again when David first accompanies Giovanni to his room:

> We passed the vestibule and the elevator into a short, dark corridor which led to his room. The room was small ... He locked the door behind us, and then for a moment, in the gloom, we simply stared at each other—with dismay, with relief, and breathing hard. I was trembling. I thought, if I do not open the door at once and get out of here, I am lost. But I knew I could not open the door, I knew it was too late.[71]

The closet is both an obvious and a limited metaphor for what is happening in this novel, not least because it not only suggests but seems to require the possibility of escape and for that escape to equal liberation. As Marlon B. Ross suggests, the metaphor of the closet, particularly in Western white usage, insists on exactly this "evolutionary" logic of "progress."[72] Although *Giovanni's Room* is riven with rooms and dark crevices that can be read as closets, these small quarters and their thresh-olds offer only more anguish, and not actual control but anxiety over control. The closet is exposed as itself paradoxical, on several levels: it is a putative place in which one can keep secret one's private self, yet it is also a place of utmost pleasure and intimacy; it is the place without which one is not safe. But because it contains pleasure as well as privacy, it can never stay safe, or private, for long.

Both *Giovanni's Room* and the closet have been designated as "raceless," "Bald-win's so-called raceless novel," because, exceptionally for Baldwin, it contains no obviously Black characters, and the closet, as a discursive paradigm, according to Ross and others, does not take race sufficiently into account.[73] It may therefore seem as though, even for Baldwin, homosexuality has to exist outside of the discourse of race. However, there is reason to read *Giovanni's Room* as neverthe-less concerned with race and racial difference, not least in the ways that David's lovers are denoted as "dark." As Kathryn Bond Stockton observes, "Giovanni's darkness (as was Joey's darkness) is also a metaphorical blackness."[74] She notes that in this formulation, with David described from the beginning as blond, in *Giovanni's Room*, "Baldwin shows a white man thinking obsessively about a dark man, from whom he is now strikingly severed."[75]

Further, even though *Giovanni's Room* was only Baldwin's second novel, it is, if not impossible, then a challenge to read anything of Baldwin's as "raceless," given his preeminence as the great spokesperson on matters of race during his lifetime.[76] Finally, even though the closet metaphor suggests "sexual identity as a threshold experience in which one side of the door harbors deprivation and dispossession, while the other side reveals the potential for psychosexual fulfillment, and cultural belonging," that is decidedly not what the closet is doing here in the novel.[77] Here the closet does not present the possibility of, in Ross's words, a "progress narra-tive," which, he argues, places it into a certain white Western conception of libera-tion ideology; on the contrary, my argument exposes the closet as not a threshold of liberation after all, but, instead, as a trope that allows for an investment in the illusion of control over how one is known or seen. Here I am reading closets into the enclosures and apertures of the novel as a way of understanding the protago-nist's evasion of homosexuality—and therefore his evasion of shame. Because the closet metaphors in this novel, as elsewhere, promise control but never deliver it, these evasions do not work.

In *Giovanni's Room* we see such paradoxes and contradictions not only on the level of plot but on the level also, and even especially, of syntax and structure, and of narration. In this syntactical exertion of control is legible the battle between safety and privacy on the one hand, and indulgence and capitulation to pleasure on the other. For example, David says of Giovanni: "I was guilty and irritated and full of love and pain," and a page later: "I wanted to kick him and I wanted to take him in my arms."[78] Similarly, the following two sentiments are expressed separated only by a semicolon: "His touch could never fail to make me feel desire; yet his hot sweet breath also made me want to vomit."[79] These syntactical parallels—"I wanted … I wanted…"—convey the paradox of feeling always one thing and its other—in and out, safe and exposed, contained and released—and the control required to convey them as nuanced contradictions.

Baldwin foreshadowed this syntactical paradoxical treatment of homosexuality in an essay published only two years before *Giovanni's Room* in 1954: "The Male Prison," a critique of a book by André Gide—although the original title of the essay, "Gide as Husband and Homosexual," suggests that this is a disquisition not solely on Gide's writing. In this extraordinary essay, Baldwin insists that it is not Gide's homosexuality that causes Baldwin unease, but his *Protestantism*. Yet the very paragraph in which he dismisses Gide's homosexuality as insignificant— really Gide's "own affair"—is filled with admonitory injunctions in the repetition of the reproachful "he ought":

And his homosexuality, I felt, was his own affair which he ought to have kept hidden from us, or, if he needed to be so explicit, he ought at least to have managed to be a little more scientific—whatever, in the domain of morals, that word may mean—less illogical, less romantic. He ought to have leaned less heavily on the examples of dead, great men, of vanished cultures, and he ought certainly to have known that the examples provided by natural history do not go far toward illuminating the physical, psychological, and moral complexities faced by men. If he were going to talk about homosexuality at all, he ought, in a word, to have sounded a little less *disturbed*.[80]

The essay ends with a wisdom that eludes David in *Giovanni's Room*: that masculinity itself is a prison. In the essay Baldwin suggests that the "door of hope" for Gide was the possibility, represented by his wife Madeleine, of "entering into communion with another sex"; the real danger for "the unlucky deviate" is "where the possibility of genuine human involvement has altogether ceased," universalizing, one might even say heterosexualizing, the problem of homosexuality.[81] *Giovanni's Room* also places much hope on the threshold—the *door*—as we have seen and shall see further.

What the novel shows is that the closet is not a simple binary of a safe but captive place, the leaving of which enclosure is liberation—but that the trap of the closet is the tyranny of the door: of ingress and egress. Of knowing where the room is and where one is in relation to it. Of needing to know that one can enter and exit at will, and often doing so for the sake of it—and not for what succor one will find inside or what freedom outside. In *Giovanni's Room* it is suggested early on that David is somehow aware of this:

It was after Joey. The incident with Joey had shaken me profoundly and its effect was to make me secretive and cruel. I could not discuss what had happened to me with anyone. I could not even admit it to myself; and, while I never thought about it, it remained, nevertheless, at the bottom of my mind, as still and as awful as a decomposing corpse. And it changed, it thickened, it soured the atmosphere of my mind.[82]

Here the protagonist who is also the narrator knows something and knows that he cannot admit it to himself. He knows that the encounter with Joey makes him "secretive" and he knows not only that he cannot talk about it, but that he cannot "admit it" even to himself. This is a kind of narrative splitting that allows a character to know what he is suppressing; although this is an epistemological contradiction, it suggests a paradigm of knowing and denying that is perhaps common not only to the dynamics of, especially, first-person literary narration, but also to the very dynamics of what we call denial and therefore sexual shame and humiliation.

David has a method, a mechanism, of a functioning door into and out of the closet. It is not pleasant, it does not make him happy, as control is hardly ever about happiness, but it allows him his homosexual relationships without being homosexual. It is perpetually humiliating but the reward is that he controls the threshold of humiliation. What matters is not that he keep himself from sex with men—though he does tell himself that this is what is at stake—but that in no way should it be said or recognized. He must not be *seen* to have homosexual desires.

And this is the important point about the closet in this book and about homosexuality and femininity: it is not shameful merely to be homosexual or effeminate, but to be seen to be. The closet has always been about what can be seen or hidden or denied. Here it is doing that same work but on the level of the ocular: at least, the ocular as the reigning metaphor. Writing about shame, Silvan Tomkins refers to this "interocular experience."[83] Shame is private; humiliation is public. Humiliation is the experience of the exposure of one's shame. Shame itself, however, can feel exposing, can feel visible. In fact, without the fantasy of exposure, shame has no currency. All of our responses to feeling shame, says Tomkins, involve a turning away of the head or lowering of the eyes that has the effect of reducing our exposure: the "shame response is an act which reduces facial communication"; shame produces a need "to cover" the body "from the stare of the other."[84]

Shame exists in the capacity to imagine that one is available to humiliation: that one's vulnerabilities can be exposed, seen. There are several examples in the novel, anticipating the carefree stroll in the streets with Giovanni, that suggest David's acute awareness of the exposure, the visibility, of his shame. When he has sex with Joey, he oedipally imagines the surveillance of Joey's mother: in bed with Joey, he "was ashamed. The very bed, in its sweet disorder, testified to vileness. I wondered what Joey's mother would say when she saw the sheets. Then I thought of my father, who had no one in the world but me, my mother having died when I was little."[85] He then thinks also of his own mother from the grave: "no matter what was happening in that room, my mother was watching it. She looked out of the photograph frame."[86] Desire is shameful; sex is humiliating. Yet somehow the humiliation does not have the sting that shame imagines it will—so shame is the sharper, deeper agony. At least in this novel, David is never ashamed of his actual sexual relations, only about how he imagines he is perceived.

When he first enters the bar where he will meet Giovanni, David concedes that the "bar was practically in my *quartier*"; and then that "I had many times had breakfast in the nearby working man's café"; and finally that "I had been in this bar, too, two or three times"; and then he recalls that, "once very drunk," he "had been accused of causing a minor sensation by flirting with a soldier."[87] Of course he barely remembers it—"my memory of that night was, happily, very dim," and he continues to insist that "no matter how drunk I may have been I could not possibly have done such a thing"—but nevertheless he has to admit that "my face was known and I had the feeling that people were taking bets about me."[88] In fact, he is sure he is being stared at: "it was as though they were the elders of some strange and austere holy order and were watching me in order to discover, by means of signs I made but which only they could read, whether or not I had a true vocation."[89] In this passage we can discern not only that the bar in which David meets Giovanni is probably a gay bar, for he admits only sheepishly that he has been there before, but also that what is unbearable to him in his dim memory of the night is that he is *known* as someone who flirts with men because he has been *seen* doing so.

Upon meeting Giovanni, David is able to declare that he is "glad … utterly, hopelessly, horribly glad," and although he drinks copiously "in the faint hope that … the ferocious excitement that had burst in me like a storm" might "spend itself," he declares again: "But I was glad." His qualm, however, is that his desire has been seen: "I was only sorry that Jacques had been a witness." He adds that this "made me ashamed."[90] This is the epistemology of the closet: that one might go to a lot of trouble to keep oneself hidden—keep one's "manhood" "immaculate"—but that one anyway, very drunk or not, might be *seen* to enact that hidden nature and therefore be *known* to have that nature, to be that thing. Although Sedgwick did not, as far as I can find, make a direct link between her writing on the closet and her later writing on paranoia, the continuity between these thought processes is that the closet is not only sustained by vigilance but that the name of that perpetual vigilance is paranoia.

The objective of paranoia is that there should be no bad surprises.[91] Humiliation is the price of failed paranoia—of not being paranoid *enough*—and therefore of being exposed. Shame underwrites a perpetual anxiety that one has something disgusting in oneself; humiliation comes when it is seen. "Thus," Tomkins tells us:

> in the paranoid and others who have been terrorized rather than simply shamed, the eyes may blink in fear at the direct gaze of the other or be rolled to the side away from the confrontation at the gaze of the other. Although there is a universal taboo on interocular intimacy this taboo is radically heightened in the paranoid condition so that there is an exaggerated awareness of both being looked at and the terrifying and humiliating consequences of such visibility.[92]

This is precisely what is mobilized in the scene where David "accidentally" cruises the sailor on the street. Upon the certainty that "he had seen some all-revealing panic in my eyes," and after the sailor "gave me a look contemptuously lewd and knowing," he narrates with unusually vague ascription: "And in another second, had our contact lasted, I was certain that there would erupt into speech, out of all that light and beauty, some brutal variation of *Look, baby. I know you.*"[93] It is not clear *who* would utter those words, for the suggestion is that they are recognizable to each other, that even though the contempt implies there is one who is looking and the other who is seen, the element here of cruising is that there is mutual recognition.

James Baldwin famously eschewed psychoanalysis; nevertheless it provides us with the insight that wrestling with a closet, as it were, is not a homosexual struggle but a far more common one, and *Giovanni's Room* is a lens through which this is especially evident. In Sedgwick's invocation of the thinking of mid-twentieth-century psychoanalyst Melanie Klein, the alternative to paranoia is reparation. In reparation, the position, or attitude, is not surveillant but depressive, that is, receptive.[94] Cruising seems to require both; perhaps Tomkins's use of the word "ambivalence" is useful here when he writes of the "ambivalence about looking and being looked at,"[95] for there is oscillation not only about who is looking and who is being seen, but about the fear and anticipation involved: the likelihood of bad surprises but also of good pleasures.

The closet is a trope of control—of inside/outside, knowledge/ignorance, revealing/keeping—and is in this way also a trope of shame and liberation.

However, while the closet and its breaches offer metaphors of shame and anxious control over the threshold of the closet, this dominion can also be understood as a kind of pleasure. There is said to be liberation in bursting out of the closet's enclosures, but this does not take into account the pleasures of staying in, or the mastery in deciding how far, how long, when, or whether. At the beginning of the novel, David proclaims, "for nothing is more unbearable, once one has it, than freedom."[96] Like an infant refusing food—the only control he or she might have in a household of adult rules and constraints—control over the threshold of the closet is its own puny satisfaction. Even though David is not happy, and does not get to claim his desires for men, what he does get is control. And like the infant who can only refuse food, the toddler gains agency by controlling what stays in and what goes out, under the jurisdiction of what Freud termed the anal stage of development.

In this regard, it turns out that everyone starts out with a closet and attempts to achieve mastery over it. Even before Klein, psychoanalysis gives us insight into the concomitance of this anxiety and pleasure. At 18 months to 3 years, the child, Freud tells us, in "producing … the contents of the bowels … can express his active compliance with his environment and, by withholding them, his disobedience."[97] So there is a prohibition not just over excretion but over exactly this control. "Educators are once more right," says Freud, "when they describe children who keep the process back as 'naughty.'"[98] Even before we are made to feel ashamed of sexual desires, "the first prohibition which a child comes across—the prohibition from getting pleasure from anal activity and its products—has a decisive effect on his whole development."[99] In fact, continues Freud, since "[s]mall children are essentially without shame,"[100] this early anal prohibition is fundamental to the very development of shame:

> This must be the first occasion on which the infant has a glimpse of an environment hostile to his instinctual impulses, on which he learns to separate his own entity from this alien one and on which he carries out the first 'repression' of his possibilities for pleasure.[101]

It is precisely these habits and exercises that become shameful as one gets older, as one becomes sexual in fact. And it is precisely this shame over the pleasure of mastery of withholding and releasing that governs the construction—the need for—the closet: "Further, the whole significance of the anal zone is reflected in the fact that few neurotics are to be found without their special scatological practices, ceremonies, and so on, *which they carefully keep secret*."[102] The pleasure of this control at the anal stage is caught up ultimately in the shame of exposure, even if that exposure is completely decided upon and under one's control; and the shame, of course, over the prospect of losing control, whether that ever even happens. And so the pleasure—and paranoia—of the closet is itself sexual.

Baldwin refused to call *Giovanni's Room* a homosexual novel. "While the novel is held up as a pioneering work of homosexual literature," Douglas Field tells us,

"Baldwin disavowed this interpretation, claiming it was about love."[103] We might say that just as the protagonist is disavowing homosexual desire throughout the novel, so is the author disavowing it as well. While Matt Brim refers to the "near-total failure of David's queer imagination"[104]—"gay, closeted David," Brim writes, "cannot *live* as a gay man"[105]—it seems rather that David's queer imagination is all too successful, all too vivid. At every point he knows exactly what he is disavowing. For in order to disavow something one must also recognize it on some level. He needs to want it and therefore to recognize it in order to refuse it.

The question of whether *Giovanni's Room* is a raceless novel re-emerges here at the site of shame. In a gesture of reverse engineering, we can understand C. Riley's Snorton's concept of the "glass closet," a "space [he] define[s] as marked by hypervisibility and confinement, spectacle, and speculation" as applying particularly, he argues, to Black sexuality.[106] In defining "the down low," a kind of racialized, closeted, AIDS-era homosexuality practiced particularly by African-American men who live heterosexual lives yet also engage in homosexual sex, Snorton claims that the media hype around this phenomenon not only renders Black sexuality a magnet for surveillance, but indeed "might actually characterize the condition for black sexual representation."[107]

Further, from similar premises, Darieck Scott suggests that Black sexuality is always already queer, given that Black bodies as sites historically of sexualization, sexualized violence, and surveillance are always already abject. Scott's use of abjection overlaps with the concept of shame as I am using it here: "for black people in general, but black men in particular, the abject is like the feminine, or is definitively feminine—that is, to be abject is to be feminized."[108]

Even through such readings that allow us to see *Giovanni's Room* as more racialized than is typically imagined, it nevertheless amplifies my point that sexual shame is projected onto those who are seen to be or who are willing to call themselves homosexual. It extends my argument by suggesting that the idea that there are bodies onto which queerness can be psychically displaced is a fantasy of being actually rid of it. Baldwin himself, in the last essay he published, in what we might see as a pose of ennui, dismisses sex itself and the breach of that closet door: "There is nothing more boring, anyway," he writes, "than sexual activity as an end in itself, and a great many people who came out of the closet should reconsider."[109]

Giovanni's Room exposes some fundamental anxieties over shame and exposure in the realm of sexuality. While the metaphor of the closet is particular to homosexual discourse, we are reminded by Sedgwick that the "epistemology of the closet has … been … inexhaustibly productive of modern Western culture and history at large."[110] In other words, as I have argued here, although the closet has become the ruling metaphor for the enclosure where homosexuals could hide their shameful desires, every sexual being is potentially at the mercy of and invested in the operation of a closet: if shame has to do with anxiety over exposure and "operates only after interest or enjoyment has been activated,"[111] then the closet is where anyone might hide. The closet functions not only in relation to deviant or obscure desires but to—desire. Paranoia ensures vigilance over the threshold of the closet and promises that there might always already be a "they" who must suffer shame so that there might be an imagined "we" who have less shame or—as David fantastically wishes—none.

Notes

1 Judith Butler, *Bodies That Matter: On the Discursive Limits of Sex* (London, Routledge, 1993), p. 226, italics in original.
2 Eve Kosofsky Sedgwick, *Touching Feeling: Affect, Pedagogy, Performativity* (Durham, NC, Duke University Press, 2003), p. 36; Silvan Tomkins, "Shame-Humiliation and Contempt-Disgust," in *Shame and Its Sisters: A Silvan Tomkins Reader*, ed. Eve Kosofsky Sedgwick and Adam Frank (Durham, NC, Duke University Press, 1995), p. 142.
3 James Baldwin, *Giovanni's Room* (1956) (New York, Penguin, 2001), p. 102.
4 *Ibid.*, p. 9.
5 *Ibid.*, p. 11.
6 *Ibid.*, p. 10.
7 *Ibid.*, p. 91.
8 *Ibid.*
9 *Ibid.*
10 *Ibid.*, p. 116.
11 *Ibid.*, p. 91.
12 *Ibid.*, p. 92.
13 *Ibid.*, italics in original.
14 *Ibid.*
15 *Ibid.*, p. 93.
16 *Ibid.*
17 *Ibid.*, p. 95.
18 *Ibid.*, pp. 96, 93.
19 *Ibid.*, p. 95.
20 *Ibid.*, p. 96.
21 *Ibid.*
22 *Ibid.*
23 See, for example, David M. Halperin, who writes "Effeminacy has often functioned as a marker of so-called sexual inversion in men, of transgenderism or sexual role reversal, and thus of homosexual desire"; "How to Do the History of Male Homosexuality," *GLQ: A Journal of Lesbian and Gay Studies*, 6:1 (2000), p. 92.
24 Baldwin, *Giovanni's Room*, p. 91, italics in original.
25 *Ibid.*, p. 30, italics in original.
26 *Ibid.*
27 *Ibid.*
28 *Ibid.*, pp. 13–14.
29 *Ibid.*, p. 14, italics in original.
30 *Ibid.*, p. 20.
31 *Ibid.*
32 *Ibid.*, p. 87, italics in original.
33 *Ibid.*, p. 88, italics in original.

34 *Ibid.*
35 *Ibid.*
36 *Ibid.*, p. 33, italics in original.
37 *Ibid.*, p. 100.
38 *Ibid.*, p. 88.
39 *Ibid.*, p. 89.
40 *Ibid.*
41 *Ibid.*
42 *Ibid.*, p. 12.
43 *Ibid.*, p. 13.
44 *Ibid.*, p. 14.
45 *Ibid.*, p. 12.
46 *Ibid.*, p. 14.
47 *Ibid.*, p. 15.
48 *Ibid.*, p. 25.
49 *Ibid.*, p. 80.
50 *Ibid.*, pp. 80–1.
51 *Ibid.*, p. 12.
52 *Ibid.*, p. 81.
53 *Ibid.*, p. 25.
54 *Ibid.*
55 *Ibid.*, p. 81.
56 *Ibid.*, p. 14.
57 *Ibid.*
58 *Ibid.*, p. 15.
59 *Ibid.*, p. 14, italics in original.
60 *Ibid.*, p. 15.
61 *Ibid.*
62 Colm Tóibín, "The Unsparing Confessions of 'Giovanni's Room,'" *The New Yorker*, 26 February 2016, www.newyorker.com/books/page-turner/the-unsparing-confessions-of-giovannis-room (accessed 15 June 2020).
63 Baldwin, *Giovanni's Room*, p. 112.
64 *Ibid.*, p. 9.
65 *Ibid.*, pp. 9–10.
66 Eve Kosofsky Sedgwick, *Epistemology of the Closet* (Berkeley, CA, University of California Press, 1990), p. 75.
67 Baldwin, *Giovanni's Room*, p. 11.
68 *Ibid.*
69 *Ibid.*
70 *Ibid.*, p. 25.
71 *Ibid.*, p. 64.
72 Marlon B. Ross, "Beyond the Closet as a Raceless Paradigm," in E. Patrick Johnson and Mae G. Henderson (eds.), *Black Queer Studies: A Critical Anthology* (Durham, NC: Duke University Press, 2005), p. 163.
73 Trudier Harris-Lopez, "Slanting the Truth: Homosexuality, Manhood, and Race in James Baldwin's *Giovanni's Room*," in Trudier Harris-Lopez (ed.), *South of Tradition: Essays on African American Literature* (Athens, GA, University of Georgia Press, 2002), p. 18; and see Ross, "Beyond the Closet."

74 Kathryn Bond Stockton, *Beautiful Bottom, Beautiful Shame: Where "Black" Meets "Queer"* (Durham, NC, Duke University Press, 2006), p. 172.

75 *Ibid.*, p. 168.

76 See, for example, Henry Louis Gates, Jr., "The Fire Last Time," in Harold Bloom (ed.), *James Baldwin: Bloom's Modern Critical Views* (New York, Chelsea House, 2007), who writes, "Perhaps not since Booker T. Washington had one man been taken to embody the voice of 'The Negro'" (p. 13).

77 E. Patrick Johnson and Mae G. Henderson, "Introduction: Queering Black Studies/ 'Quaring' Queer Studies," in Johnson and Henderson (eds.), *Black Queer Studies*, p. 11.

78 Baldwin, *Giovanni's Room*, pp. 110, 111.

79 *Ibid.*, p. 101.

80 James Baldwin, "The Male Prison" (1954), in *The Price of the Ticket: Collected Nonfiction 1948–1985* (New York: St. Martin's Press, 1985), p. 102, italics in original.

81 *Ibid.*, pp. 104, 105.

82 Baldwin, *Giovanni's Room*, pp. 20–1.

83 Tomkins, "Shame-Humiliation and Contempt-Disgust," p. 144.

84 *Ibid.*, p. 134.

85 Baldwin, *Giovanni's Room*, p. 14.

86 *Ibid.*, p. 18.

87 *Ibid.*, pp. 30, 31.

88 *Ibid.*, p. 31.

89 *Ibid.*

90 *Ibid.*, p. 44.

91 Eve Kosofsky Sedgwick, "Paranoid Reading and Reparative Reading, Or, You're So Paranoid, You Probably Think This Essay Is About You," in *Touching Feeling: Affect, Pedagogy, Performativity* (Durham, NC, Duke University Press, 2003), p. 130.

92 Tomkins, "Shame-Humiliation and Contempt-Disgust," p. 148.

93 Baldwin, *Giovanni's Room*, p. 88, italics in original

94 Sedgwick, "Paranoid Reading and Reparative Reading."

95 Tomkins, "Shame-Humiliation and Contempt-Disgust," p. 142.

96 Baldwin, *Giovanni's Room*, p. 11.

97 Sigmund Freud, "Infantile Sexuality," in *On Sexuality: Three Essays on the Theory of Sexuality and Other Works* (1905), Volume 7 of *The Penguin Freud Library*, ed. Angela Richards, trans. James Strachey (London, Penguin, 1977), pp. 103–4.

98 *Ibid.*, p. 103.

99 *Ibid.*, p. 104.

100 *Ibid.*, p. 110.

101 *Ibid.*, p. 104.

102 *Ibid.*, italics added.

103 Douglas Field, *All Those Strangers: The Art and Lives of James Baldwin* (Oxford, Oxford University Press, 2015), p. 2.

104 Matt Brim, *James Baldwin and the Queer Imagination* (Ann Arbor, MI, University of Michigan Press, 2014), p. 56.

105 *Ibid.*, pp. 63, 75, italics in original.

106 C. Riley Snorton, *Nobody's Supposed to Know: Black Sexuality On the Down Low* (Minneapolis, MN, University of Minnesota Press, 2014), p. 4.

107 *Ibid.*, p. 4.

108 Darieck Scott, *Extravagant Abjection: Blackness, Power, and Sexuality in the African American Literary Imagination* (New York, New York University Press, 2010), p. 29.

109 James Baldwin, "Here Be Dragons," in *The Price of the Ticket*, pp. 688–9.
110 Sedgwick, *Epistemology*, p. 68.
111 Tomkins, quoted in Eve Kosofsky Sedgwick with Adam Frank, "Shame in the Cybernetic Fold: Reading Sylvan Tomkins," in Sedgwick, *Touching Feeling*, p. 97.

Works Cited

Baldwin, James, *Giovanni's Room* (1956) (New York, Penguin, 2001).

————— "Here Be Dragons" (1985), in *The Price of the Ticket: Collected Nonfiction 1948–1985* (New York, St. Martin's Press, 1985), pp. 677–90.

————— "The Male Prison" (1954), in *The Price of the Ticket: Collected Nonfiction 1948–1985* (New York, St. Martin's Press, 1985), pp. 101–6.

Brim, Matt, *James Baldwin and the Queer Imagination* (Ann Arbor, MI, University of Michigan Press, 2014).

Butler, Judith, *Bodies That Matter: On the Discursive Limits of Sex* (London, Routledge, 1993).

Freud, Sigmund, "Infantile Sexuality," in *On Sexuality: Three Essays on the Theory of Sexuality and Other Works* (1905), Volume 7 of *The Penguin Freud Library*, ed. Angela Richards, trans. James Strachey (London, Penguin, 1977), pp. 39–72.

Gates, Jr., Henry Louis, "The Fire Last Time," in Harold Bloom (ed.), *James Baldwin: Bloom's Modern Critical Views* (New York, Chelsea House, 2007), pp. 11–22.

Halperin, David M., "How to Do the History of Male Homosexuality," *GLQ: A Journal of Lesbian and Gay Studies*, 6:1 (2000), pp. 87–123.

Harris-Lopez, Trudier, "Slanting the Truth: Homosexuality, Manhood, and Race in James Baldwin's *Giovanni's Room*," in Trudier Harris-Lopez (ed.), *South of Tradition: Essays on African American Literature* (Athens, GA, University of Georgia Press, 2002), pp. 18–30.

Johnson, E. Patrick, and Mae G. Henderson (eds.), *Black Queer Studies: A Critical Anthology* (Durham, NC, Duke University Press, 2005).

Ross, Marlon B., "Beyond the Closet as a Raceless Paradigm," in E. Patrick Johnson and Mae G. Henderson (eds.), *Black Queer Studies: A Critical Anthology* (Durham, NC, Duke University Press, 2005), pp. 161–89.

Scott, Darieck, *Extravagant Abjection: Blackness, Power, and Sexuality in the African American Literary Imagination* (New York, New York University Press, 2010).

Sedgwick, Eve Kosofsky, *Epistemology of the Closet* (Berkeley, CA, University of California Press, 1990).

————— "Paranoid Reading and Reparative Reading, Or, You're So Paranoid, You Probably Think This Essay Is About You," in *Touching Feeling: Affect, Pedagogy, Performativity* (Durham, NC, Duke University Press, 2003), pp. 123–52.

————— *Touching Feeling: Affect, Pedagogy, Performativity* (Durham, NC, Duke University Press, 2003).

Sedgwick, Eve Kosofsky, with Adam Frank, "Shame in the Cybernetic Fold: Reading Sylvan Tomkins," in *Touching Feeling: Affect, Pedagogy, Performativity* (Durham, NC, Duke University Press, 2003), pp. 93–122.

Snorton, C. Riley, *Nobody's Supposed to Know: Black Sexuality On the Down Low* (Minneapolis, MN, University of Minnesota Press, 2014).

Stockton, Katherine Bond, *Beautiful Bottom, Beautiful Shame: Where "Black" Meets "Queer"* (Durham, NC, Duke University Press, 2006).

Tóibín, Colm, "The Unsparing Confessions of 'Giovanni's Room,'" *The New Yorker*, 26 February 2016, www.newyorker.com/books/page-turner/the-unsparing-confessions-of-giovannis-room (accessed 15 June 2020).

Tomkins, Silvan, "Shame-Humiliation and Contempt-Disgust," in *Shame and Its Sisters: A Silvan Tomkins Reader*, ed. Eve Kosofsky Sedgwick and Adam Frank (Durham, NC, Duke University Press, 1995), pp. 133–78.

Contributor's Biography

Monica B. Pearl is Lecturer in Twentieth Century American Literature at the University of Manchester. She has written extensively on AIDS and AIDS representation, including her book *AIDS Literature and Gay Identity: The Literature of Loss* (Routledge, 2013) and essays on *Angels in America*, *Philadelphia*, *Zero Patience*, the photograph *Felix, June 5, 1994* by AA Bronson, and the AIDS Memorial Quilt. She has also published essays on Alison Bechdel's graphic memoir *Fun Home*, Audre Lorde's *Zami*, Janet Flanner's letters, Eve Sedgwick's essay "White Glasses" and another—"Queer Therapy"—on Sedgwick's account of her psychotherapy *A Dialogue on Love*, the writing of W. G. Sebald ("The Peripatetic Paragraph"), and two essays on opera: "The Opera Closet" and "Bliss: Opera's Untenable Pleasures."

GRADUATE STUDENT ESSAY AWARD WINNER

Baldwin's Kitchen: Food and Identity in His Life and Fiction

Emily Na   University of Michigan

Abstract

This article traces how the queer Black writer James Baldwin's transnational palate and experiences influenced the ways he wrote about Black domestic spaces in the late twentieth century. In the 1960s and 1970s, while Black feminist cooks and writers like Edna Lewis, Jessica B. Harris, and Vertamae Smart-Grosvenor developed new theories of soul food in relation to the Black American community and broader American cuisine, Baldwin incorporated these philosophies and transnational tastes into his lifestyle and works. He traveled and worked around Europe, settling in places like Paris, Istanbul, and Saint-Paul de Vence for years at a time. In Saint-Paul de Vence, where he spent his last years, he set up his own welcome table, at which he hosted internationally renowned guests and shared his love of cuisine. Inevitably, Baldwin's passion for cooking and hosting meals became a large, though scholarly neglected, component of his novels and essays. In his novels *Another Country*, which he finished in Istanbul and published in 1962, and *Just Above My Head*, which he finished in Saint-Paul de Vence and published in 1979, Baldwin's depictions of food and Black kitchens take a queer turn. Instead of lingering on traditional Black family structures, these texts specifically present new formulations of intimate home life and reimagine relationships between food, kitchens, race, and sex in the late twentieth century.

Keywords: food studies, cooking, soul food, welcome table, cuisine, Saint-Paul de Vence, James Baldwin

In one of Sedat Pakay's endearing photographs of James Baldwin in Turkey (Figure 1), Baldwin fries fish for Bertice Reading, an American-born international blues singer. He is wearing a white hat and a flared, printed ladies' apron. A Black man cooking for a Black woman, in Istanbul. While biographical information about Baldwin's love for cooking, hosting people in his homes in Istanbul and Saint-Paul de Vence, and his relationships with famous cooks and food writers reveals the profundity of his

James Baldwin Review, Volume 6, 2020, © The Authors. Published by Manchester University Press and The University of Manchester Library
http://dx.doi.org/10.7227/JBR.6.6

transnational taste, his novels regularly depict more traditional Black American food cultures. Scholarship on Baldwin's international lifestyle is largely silent about the relationship of his works to the concurrent food scene of the 1960s and 1970s. In the late twentieth century, Black feminist soul food cooks and writers began to make names for themselves, claiming the centrality of African heritage to soul food, and thereby, American food and identity.[1] Baldwin, whose lifestyle

Figure 1   Sedat Pakay, *James Baldwin, Writer, Istanbul, Turkey,* 1965. Baldwin cooks for Bertice Reading in his kitchen in Istanbul. He had many notable visitors, including Reading and her family, Marlon Brando, Beauford Delaney, and Alex Haley. Despite the fact that he and his friends in Turkey had hired help, they still loved to cook together.[2]

exemplified great passion for both soul food and international cuisine, had much in common with these women. I contend that he portrayed and transformed their culinary philosophies in his novels, allowing them to lead the way to new configurations of domesticity and intimacy.

In this article I argue that James Baldwin's international travels and homes, in Istanbul and especially in Saint-Paul de Vence, granted him a transnational palate and perspective that informed his writings about Black communities, sexualities, and constructions of home life. I focus on the works *Another Country* (1962) and *Just Above My Head* (1979) to show that by embodying a gender non-binary and feminist attitude toward food spaces in his life, Baldwin participated in a reshaping of Black American kitchen culture through the intersections of food, gender, and sexuality in his writings.

Much of late twentieth-century Black food theory revolves around the role of African-American women in defining and being defined by "soul food." In her book *High on the Hog* (2011), Jessica B. Harris defines soul food not only as traditional African-American food of the South, but as encompassing so much more:

> [it] depends on an ineffable quality. It is a combination of nostalgia for and pride in the food of those who came before [...] soul food looks back at the past and celebrates a genuine taste palate while offering more than a nod to the history of disenfranchisement of blacks in the United States.[3]

While a broad community of Black Americans partake in the sharing of soul food, the notion of soul food has particularly gendered aspects. Historically, Black women signified domestic servitude and inherent talent at cooking good meals. The transition from the Mammy figure to the Aunt Jemima figure in popular culture, flour advertisements, and pancake mixes in the first half of the twentieth century, for example, illustrates the burdens of both the white *and* Black American kitchen on the harmless, happy, African-American woman cook.[4] Black women cooks' association with domestic servitude, and specifically Southern and soul food expertise in the American imagination, allowed for Black feminist cooks and food writers like Jessica B. Harris, Vertamae Smart-Grosvenor, and Edna Lewis to pioneer more international, transatlantic implications of the term "soul food" and its geographies in the 1960s and 1970s.[5] I propose that James Baldwin himself, as a queer Black internationalist and food enthusiast, embodied the ideals of Black women food writers who worked to reportray soul food and expand its geographical influences.

Baldwin's own "welcome table" in Saint-Paul de Vence, where he spent the last seventeen years of his life, was one of many places at which he shared meals with people across differences. He had an outdoor and an indoor table, at which he famously hosted guests, and which his biographer David Leeming calls "a place of witness, where the exiles could come and lay down their souls."[6] He was close friends with his cook, Valerie Sordello, who served many of these meals. She became part of his family and the "heart of the house," staying with him to the very end, and he even took her on a trip to Paris.[7] Sordello and Baldwin would have worked together to accomplish the intimate domestic hosting aesthetic that was so pleasing to his guests. One of Baldwin's numerous guests at his welcome table was Jessica B. Harris. She makes the case that African and African-American culinary tradition has "marked the food of this country more than any other."[8]

In the context of the movements of the 1960s and 1970s, the reclamation of African-descended cultural roots that had withstood slavery and oppression was especially popular. However, Harris's insistence on the African origins of stereotypically Black American foods like okra, watermelon, and black-eyed peas might also sound racially essentializing.[9] Harris explains the blending of culinary traditions, particularly on the West African coast, between West African cultures and cuisines, and those of European adventurers and colonizers, to create a range of Afro-diasporic cuisine.[10] Tracing the journey that shunned the "slave foods"—referring to the diets of lower-class African-American people—Harris argues that after civil rights gains, "Black food in its increasing diversity was no longer segregated on the Blacks-only side of the menu, but squarely placed on the American table."[11] Harris's marketing of African/African-American food culture as a mobile, transnationally valued cuisine sheds new light on the appreciation of African food roots.

A meal in *Just Above My Head* reflects this shift toward the African roots of soul food cooking. Near the end of the nonlinear story but at the beginning of the book, Hall describes visiting his childhood friend Julia's home with his own children:

> The table is a darkly varnished, gleaming board […] There is a salad of raw spinach, lettuce, tomatoes, and radishes in one bowl, a fiery pale potato salad in the other bowl. The mahogany ribs are on the mahogany platter. There is a small bowl of African peppers, smoldering green and red, a wicker basket full of hot buttered rolls, and Coca-Cola, red wine, and beer. The table is in the center of the room […] There is a wooden African deity standing in a corner near the door.[12]

By describing this meal set-up, beginning with the table and ending with the table, even including the decorations around the table, such as "African deities," Hall and Julia portray—perhaps unconsciously on Baldwin's part—Baldwin's own meticulousness in setting up and presenting an inviting meal. Hall draws our attention to the perfect coordination of food with the interior space, calling both the ribs and the platter "mahogany," both the statues and the peppers "African." While Julia could be cooking with any kind of hot peppers, she seems to have intentionally included "African peppers," suggesting her personal return-to-Africa journey between her teenage years and contemporary life.[13] The distinctly "African" elements of the meal are placed alongside traditionally Southern dishes like potato salad and ribs, as if to represent the concurrent trends in the African genealogy of foods that women like Jessica Harris popularized and championed.

Baldwin conveyed this careful hosting aesthetic in his own cosmopolitan lifestyle while working on *Just Above My Head*. In a 2017 article for *Saveur* magazine, Harris describes visiting Baldwin in Saint-Paul de Vence in 1973 and being struck simultaneously by his charm—"the absolute seriousness backed by an elfin twinkle, and the enormous humanity of his smile every time I saw him"—as well as the perfection of the meal that his cook Valerie Sordello served at the outdoor welcome table: "an oh-so-splendid *soupe au pistou* that greeted us at the table. Dense with minced vegetables and heady with the pungent garlic that is the hallmark of the region's cooking, it was the perfect introduction to Provence."[14] Baldwin's long-established passion for food and entertaining allowed him to host such an ideal dining experience for a renowned food writer, and Sordello would surely have provided her culinary knowledge and labor to perfect the successful hosting endeavor.

Though he hosted and appreciated elegant French meals, Baldwin's conceptualization of food and identity complicated and challenged the binary of bourgeois European cuisine against "lower-class" soul food. He appreciated and enjoyed many different types of food, but by no means aspired to a colorblind fusion of all the foods he loved. He associated food with specific people, cultures, and experiences. In his 1972 nonfiction work *No Name in the Street*, Baldwin writes about homesickness and food-based identity:

> In the years in Paris, I had never been homesick for anything American—neither waffles, ice cream, hot dogs, baseball, majorettes, movies, nor the Empire State Building, nor Coney Island, nor the Statue of Liberty, nor the *Daily News*, nor Times Square […] I missed Harlem Sunday mornings and fried chicken and biscuits, I missed the music, I missed the style—that style possessed by no other people in the world. I missed the way the dark face closes, the way dark eyes watch, and the way, when a dark face opens, a light seems to go on everywhere.[15]

Here, Baldwin's lists comparing "America" and "Harlem" begin with food. He misses one, but not the other. In describing his homesickness, he compares waffles and ice cream to fried chicken and biscuits. He has no longing for the typical "American food" that other Americans abroad might miss. Instead, he misses food that he associates with "home," overlapping the location, Harlem, with the time, Sunday mornings, with the sounds and styles. He uses "dark face" and "dark eyes" to express his inherent connection to a unique community, a people like "no other people in the world." Subverting the notion of the nation and even geographical space, Baldwin defines his home as being with Black people, wherever they are, and the things he remembers sharing with them, like Sunday mornings, and chicken and biscuits. The conglomeration of his senses define home as transcending "America," or even "Harlem." Home, rather than being a physical structure or geographical location, is instead a feeling of kinship, expressed in solidarity with those he shares roots with, even after his many years spent abroad in France.

Regarding sense-based racial formation, Rachel Slocum explains embodied memory in her article "Race in the Study of Food": "Bodies are shaped in racial terms through their labor, what they eat and where they live […] Bodies produce knowledge by walking through a market, getting groceries, watching the ground for mushrooms and smelling the earth in an edible schoolyard."[16] She explains that "embodied memory" is a way for people to produce knowledge and form identities, specifically racial ones. Instead of "seeing race" visually in someone's body, race in this sense is something that is being created by one's interactions with the world through the senses, constantly forming and deeply malleable. Perhaps this type of racial identity through embodied memory is not unlike Baldwin's Sunday mornings. It is not the formation of race in a static, categorical way, but the formation of identity based on a strong sense of shared experiences, knowledge, tastes, and smells.

Cooking and eating, involving all five senses, are identity-making practices. Cookbook author Vertamae Smart-Grosvenor's conceptualization of "vibration cooking" is also in many ways a manifestation of the embodied memory that Slocum writes about. For Smart-Grosvenor, cooking—like race making—is not a calculated action. It's something one does by instinct, by feeling the "vibrations." She explains, "You can tell a lot about people and where they're at by their food habits. People who eat food with pleasure and get pleasure from the different stirring of the senses that a well-prepared food experience can bring are my kind of people."[17] According to Smart-Grosvenor, eating, cooking, and social identity are inextricably intertwined. In fact, they seem to create each other through experience, community, and shared meals.

Though she was born in Fairfax, South Carolina, Smart-Grosvenor positioned and marketed herself as an expert of Geechee culture, an island off the coast of Georgia and South Carolina inhabited by the Gullah people, who have a lineage of African descent that developed in "isolation" from the rest of the country.[18] Smart-Grosvenor's career was based on her proposal of a transatlantic, traveling notion of soul food, with roots in Africa as "home," yet an international presence and significance in cosmopolitan culture.[19] In her own work on vibration cooking, she closes the gap between the preparation of "fancy food" in France, and "simple food," by elucidating how they are actually one and the same thing.[20] Having spent time in Paris as a young woman, she was able to make many friends ("bohemians") from all over the world by sharing meals, and while living with a Swedish roommate, they cooked together and "gave the best dinner parties in the hotel."[21] These types of international culinary experiences allowed her to reconceptualize and remarket Black soul food.[22] Doris Witt explains, "Carefully distancing her understanding of soul food from the commodified interest in the 'slave' diet, she relocates African American dietary practices in the context of the culinary history of peoples of color around the world."[23]

Though Smart-Grosvenor's work advanced the dialogue around Black food roots at the time, her philosophy was also heteronormatively gendered, placing women at the forefront of the soul food movement, in a servile position. She is known for having written things like "Cooking for a man is a very feminine thing, and I can't understand how a woman can feed her man TV dinners."[24] Perpetuating the concept of the kitchen as the woman's sphere, Smart-Grosvenor sticks to a traditional understanding of food work as women's labor for men. While her work contributed to new formulations of soul food and cooking culture in vibrant and constructive ways, her essentializing gender politics and self-marketing as a woman of the Geechee community problematized Smart-Grosvenor's food ideologies. However, this specific rebranding of the feminine soul food cook also had empowering elements, as she put forward her expertise not only as the woman with an apron in the kitchen—an Aunt Jemima or Mammy figure, for example— but also as a mobile world-traveler who projected what was seen as regional soul food onto an international map of culinary formations.

Like Jessica B. Harris, Smart-Grosvenor was also friends with James Baldwin and attended dinners at his welcome table, even catering a party for him.[25] Of attending his funeral, she said,

> His funeral was the best home-going service, the most spectacular farewell I have ever witnessed or heard about […] Between the incense and the drums of Baabatunde Olatunji I thought I would faint and I almost did when at the end Jimmy sang "Precious Lord, take my hand." The funeral was so awesome. I told my friend, "Listen up. If you don't think you can have a funeral like Jimmy's, keep your black ass alive."[26]

Baldwin's funeral service, like Smart-Grosvenor's cooking, was a magnificent blend of African traditions and contemporary American religious practices. Her reverence for Baldwin shows in her deep appreciation for his funeral service, celebrating their mutual Black identity and what it means to leave the world after a lifetime of hard work in bringing people together through artistic creation—literary *and* culinary.

The impression that Baldwin made on famous Black cooks attests to his sociable, international renown. In a 1980 article for *People* magazine, Paul Gray writes of Baldwin's celebrity at the restaurants he frequented in Saint-Paul de Vence: "the local restaurateurs pamper him shamelessly. One exception to this regimen came on his recent birthday, when friends dropped by his house to celebrate and managed to eat 21 fried chickens. Jokes Baldwin: 'Fried chicken, soul food, sweeping the cuisine of southern France!'"[27] This instance of having fried chicken for his birthday in Saint-Paul de Vence is a lovely demonstration of Baldwin's intimate connection with "Harlem Sunday mornings and fried chicken," even in the midst of his intellectual and cosmopolitan lifestyle. He had wedded his internationalism to his love for soul food and its reminiscences of Black American community and friends.

Though Baldwin was living a gastronomically international lifestyle by the time he was writing *Another Country* and *Just Above My Head*, given his working-class upbringing and the breadth of his experiences of discrimination abroad and in the United States, he had a complicated relationship with soul food and recognizably Black American culture. In an interview with Baldwin in 1961, Studs Terkel calls attention to a line from Baldwin's *Nobody Knows My Name*:

> Now, here's the part, Jim: "I had never listened to Bessie Smith in America (in the same way that, for years, I never touched watermelon), but in Europe she helped me to reconcile myself to being a 'nigger.'"

Baldwin replies that he had been living in Switzerland at the time:

> One of the reasons I couldn't finish [my first novel] was that I was ashamed of where I
> came from and where I had been. I was ashamed of the life in the Negro church,
> ashamed of my father, ashamed of the Blues, ashamed of Jazz, and, of course, ashamed
> of watermelon: all of these stereotypes that the country inflicts on Negroes."[28]

Watermelon was one of many Black American stereotypes, among other precon-
ceived notions of soul food, that Baldwin had been ashamed of in his earlier years
abroad. He had escaped the shame of being Black in America, only to be haunted
by it in Europe. However, this interview clip importantly reveals a shift in Baldwin's
relationship with stereotypically "Black" foods. Initially, living in Switzerland had
made him hyper-aware of his Black Americanness, and hence disowning foods
associated with African Americans helped him dissociate himself from stereotypical Black culture.[29] It was Bessie Smith, a popular blues singer, who helped him
"reconcile" himself to "being a 'nigger.'" This transformation happened in Europe,
while he was working on *Go Tell It on the Mountain* (1953), a semi-autobiographical novel, particularly local to his childhood. The huge distance between living in a
homogeneous white Swiss town and the experiences of young John Grimes, his
protagonist in the novel, is in part bridged by his acceptance of Bessie Smith, blues,
and watermelon. Like Jessica B. Harris, he reclaims watermelon—and Blackness—
as his heritage, not necessarily to popularize or market that heritage, but to ground
himself undisguised and unashamed in something honest and authentic.

The impact of Baldwin's international travels on his American tastes was profound. In *No Name in the Street*, Baldwin writes about being home from abroad and
running into an old friend and his family: "I was no longer the person my friend and
his family had known and loved—I was a stranger now, and keenly aware of it, and
trying hard to act, as it were, normal."[30] He visits their home and is struck by the
profound changes in his life since they were at "P.S. 139" together, while his friend
and his mother seem "as though they had been trapped, preserved, in that moment
in time." Poignantly, Baldwin recounts, "They asked me if I wanted steak or chicken;
for, in my travels, I might have learned not to like fried chicken anymore. I said,
much relieved to be able to tell the truth, that I preferred chicken."[31] Both Baldwin
and his friends associate food with cultural and racial identity, and the question of
whether he prefers "steak or chicken" would ultimately reveal whether or not Baldwin can still be considered an insider in their Harlem community.

Though Baldwin honestly answers that he still prefers chicken, his admission of
being "much relieved to be able to tell the truth" discloses that perhaps he might
have considered lying, choosing chicken regardless of his genuine preference as a
way of performing closeness and identification. Or it could refer to the fact that he
had at one point in his life "buried" the stereotypically Black things that he genuinely enjoyed, and would lie to himself so as to renounce them.[32] Baldwin's international travels and residence allowed him to intentionally gel his lifestyle with
his writings about Harlem in particular. His writings about Harlem wouldn't

necessarily have to change in content based on his transatlantic perspective, but living abroad strengthened Baldwin's own self-identification with Blackness and soul food culture as well as his depictions of them. The reduction of his shame about Blackness allowed him to write more honestly, and to portray Black families and meals without the same biased reservations. As a result, his writings about Black family meals usually show them positively. Appearances of soul food throughout Baldwin's novels often play a role in expressing nostalgia for Black family life, shared meals, and unconscious racial formation through food culture.

In the opening pages of *Another Country*, Rufus wanders the streets of New York, lonely, hungry, and afraid. His predicament is unclear, but his desperation and anxiety are unmistakable. He passes a bar and hears people laughing inside:

> It made him remember [...] seeing his mother and his father and teasing his sister, Ida, and eating: spare ribs or pork chops or chicken or greens or cornbread or yams or biscuits. For a moment he thought he would faint with hunger and he moved to a wall of the building and leaned there. His forehead was freezing with sweat. He thought: this is got to stop, Rufus. This shit is got to stop.[33]

Though the reader has yet to learn Rufus's backstory and his reasons for haunting the streets anonymous and alone, they feel the intensity of his aching hunger. Baldwin depicts the basic human need for food, and in this moment Rufus almost faints from a lack of nourishment. Even harsher still is his lack of community. Specifically, Rufus remembers meals he ate as an integral part of the life he shared with his family.

The painful homesickness of this scene—Rufus's lost family life in Harlem, and his desire for soul food to recover it—represents a craving for Black communal life in his most desperate moments. When a man on the street offers to buy him a drink, Rufus responds that he would rather have a meal, and they proceed to a bar, where he orders and scarfs down a corned beef sandwich, the understanding being that he will exchange sexual favors for it. Afterwards, "the heavy bread, the tepid meat, made him begin to feel nauseous; everything wavered before his eyes for a moment; he sipped his beer, trying to hold the sandwich down."[34] Though he has eaten to stay alive, the prospect of a meal from yet another stranger in exchange for sex nauseates Rufus and makes him feel as though he has reached an all-time low. I read his unwilling sex-for-food work as a way in which he himself becomes consumed by poverty. His disgust is so great that he almost blacks out—this time not from an empty stomach, but from the implications of a full but conflicted stomach.[35]

The soul food that Rufus specifically remembers and longs for represents his craving for a return to the home he grew up in. While his hunger seems to indicate his nostalgia for his family, it may have more to do with his racial identity and experiences. As Rachel Slocum posits, "Eating and cooking as acts at once intimate and public, empowering and complicit, are constitutive of racial identity and its politics."[36] The premise that racial identity—like familial belonging—forms in part through food culture is something that Baldwin exemplified often in his life, as I have described above, and in his works, by representing his characters' nostalgia for moments at home through the characters' desires and appetites. This hunger for a hearty family meal is in strong contrast to Rufus and Leona's racially obsessed sexual desires for each other. They relate to each other's bodies through the language of appetite and consumption. Rufus describes Leona as having a "thin, insatiable body," and asks Vivaldo, "Did you ever have the feeling [...] that a woman was eating you up?"[37] Their relationship embodies unhealthy voraciousness, and though sexual appetite and desire are often healthy expressions of love in Baldwin's works, in the case of Rufus and Leona their individual frustrations combine to result in a harmful outcome. Instead of satisfying each other healthily, Leona devours Rufus psychologically, while Rufus devours her physically through violence.

Though in the aforementioned scene Baldwin depicts a nostalgic and hungry take on family meals, he does portray full and hearty meals at other points in his work. In *Just Above My Head*, Baldwin shows the warmth of food-based fellowship that characters like Rufus are sick for through Hall's memory of a Sunday dinner. The Millers have been over at the Montanas' house, and they have just left, leaving the Montanas to share a meal as a family. Hall recounts,

> Mama said, "Well come on, children, I know you must be hungry." Mama had baked a ham, and biscuits, we had collard greens and yams and rice and gravy and sweet potato pie, and there was more than enough, since the invited guests had gone. Arthur ate like a pig, and a spoiled one at that, but he meant it when he said that he was sorry Jimmy had had to go.[38]

Here, the memory of being with his family as a teenager appears near the beginning of the book. This meal brings together a community that has yet to be tainted by the pain of separation, loss, and abuse that Hall's narrative will later encapsulate. Hall playfully refers to Arthur as a "pig," with a tone of brotherly tenderness, and Arthur's own regret that Jimmy has to go reflects the genuine innocent disappointment at the end of a kids' play-date. The exit of guests and the quotidian—yet plentiful and joyful—convening of family members to eat characterize this scene, not too much unlike Rufus's own Harlem memories. Perhaps Baldwin situates this retrospective scene at the beginning of the book in order to present the memory of domestic bliss around food even more powerfully, before the ensuing sufferings of this particular group of people.

Like many of the instances described above, in traditional American family life and culture women labor in the kitchen as mothers and cooks for their households.[39] Black women have historically borne much of the burden of culinary work, as they cooked not only for their own families and communities, but also in white domestic environments. In his representations of home life in his novels, Baldwin portrays this history. However, given his enjoyment of soul food, family meals, and hosting and bringing people together through eating, Baldwin's novels also depict a unique movement toward non-traditional kitchen cultures. His writings demand a great amount of work to break down the obstacles of socially constructed genders, sexualities, and races. In what follows I will analyze the shift from a more typical Black domesticity to queer Black domesticity in *Another Country* and *Just Above My Head*, using Baldwin's own home in Saint-Paul de Vence as a lens.

In *Another Country*, there are not many communal meal scenes. However, after the depiction of Rufus's intense hunger, the most important food-related scene may be Eric and Yves's uneaten chicken in France. On their last night together before Eric leaves for New York, they stay together at home, for the most part cherishing the life and home they made together. They "had been together for more than two years and, from the time of their meeting his home had been with Yves. More precisely and literally, it was Yves who had come to live with him, but each was, for the other, the dwelling place that each had despaired of finding."[40] The notion of a person being the "dwelling place" is significant. Each ruptured or distanced from his own family, Eric and Yves have become alternative homes for each other. Madame Belet, their cook, makes them a chicken for their last night. While Yves speaks to her in the kitchen, "Eric munched again on the raw, garlic-flavored vegetables, thinking, *This is our last night here, Our last night.*"[41] While he eats his food, his mind is preoccupied with the loss of their home together, and though the vegetables are "garlic-flavored," one can imagine that Eric doesn't actually taste the flavor at all. Yves and Eric are in no rush to eat: "'She says the chicken is ready, we should not let it get cold.' [Yves] laughed, and Eric laughed. 'I told her it does not matter with chicken, if it is cold or hot, I like it either way.' They both laughed again."[42] On the next page they continue to laugh about the chicken while having sex on "the great haven of their bed," which "had never before seemed so much like a haven, so much their own."[43] Not only is their bed a haven for them in the sense of intimacy and comfort, but also as a symbol of having found a home with a partner in a non-heteronormative relationship. They never eat the chicken, and the table that Madame Belet set with the wine bottle, glasses, plates, and bread remains overnight as a sign of their completion with each other physically, ignoring the food and other material components of a typical household.

Baldwin's authorship of alternative domestic environments was inspired by his experiences living in a slew of different homes around the world, and the process of creating one that would ultimately serve and reflect him best. His prolonged residence in Paris, Istanbul, and Saint-Paul de Vence during his writing career gave him particularly useful vantage points from which to portray and critique American family life. It was in Istanbul that he finished *Another Country*, and in Saint-Paul de Vence that he finished *Just Above My Head*. He moved to Istanbul in 1961, seeking a writing haven to finish *Another Country*.[44] In Turkey, Baldwin was a popular public figure, especially as there were not many other Black men on the streets. He still sought solace in creating a home through "a series of apartments and houses," where he could write and host friends.[45] Despite his transition from dwelling to dwelling in Istanbul, writing was his home, and he had sought out a place away from the United States to realize it.

As Magdalena Zaborowska asserts in her book *Me and My House: James Bald-win's Last Decade in France*, Baldwin's works engage "the necessity to survive away from one's home and difficult childhood, and the desire to create alternative kinds of domesticity and modes of dwelling for Black bodies that do not fit normative gender, sexual, familial, religious, or social roles and designs."[46] Especially from his home in Saint-Paul de Vence, his final and most self-reflective dwelling place where he wrote most of *Just Above My Head*, Baldwin was able to create these depictions more vividly. Zaborowska maintains that "Of all his works, *Just above My Head* deals with Black queerness, and sexuality in general, most openly, at the same time as it makes clear deep prejudice against same-sex desire in the community, country, and the wider world around Arthur and Jimmy."[47] Reading this novel against the background of Baldwin's last domestic space—which also happened to be interna-tional—lends the freedom and security of Baldwin's own haven to the book's cri-tique, which blatantly challenged traditional American norms of domesticity.

Not only was Baldwin's home a place where he could write, live his life, and express his sexuality freely, it was also a place where he would host many meals for many guests. Both Zaborowska and David Leeming trace Baldwin's literal wel-come tables to his final play *The Welcome Table*, which was never published.[48] The festivity and community around Baldwin's two tables—the one indoors and one outdoors—reveal the safety and beauty of unique, set-apart spaces that honor the desires and identities of nonconforming individuals and artists.

While nostalgia and memory characterize many of Hall's descriptions of meals in *Just Above My Head*, these meals are often shared with family and friends, and Black women are still usually the ones who work in the kitchen. As young Arthur and Jimmy have yet to become conscious of their sexualities, they consume these Harlem childhood meals without thinking. However, as they begin to grow up, Baldwin reveals a relationship between food and sexuality. As Arthur develops into a young teenager his appetite and sexuality develop simultaneously. When he is in Tennessee with his gospel group, "Arthur is always hungry, and his stomach is growling as he keeps smiling."[49] With this appetite he begins to flirt with Sister Dorothy Green, and they make their way to the feast that the "church sisters" have set up in the church basement. Dorothy tells him to sit down: "'I'll serve you. What do you want?' 'Everything,' says Arthur, and looks up at her, and grins."[50] While Dorothy serves Arthur in a gender role that Vertamae Smart-Grosvenor would have encouraged, Arthur goes along and performs masculinity to the extent that he knows it is expected of him in his group of teenage boys, trying to gain sexual experience with girls. Insightfully, Hall narrates, "[Arthur] does not know what genius goes into the boiling and baking, the frying and broiling, the scouring—how hard it is to make oneself clean every day, and how hard it is to find and pre-pare the food."[51] Hall lists the domestic duties of women who prepare food for men in the church, and notes Arthur's ignorance of the women's labor that allows him to be able to safely and contentedly enjoy this meal. Baldwin speaks to Doris Witt here, in a Black feminist reading, as women produce the soul food and men have only to eat and enjoy.

As they begin to eat, the mingling of sex and food becomes even more explicit:

> He places the chicken wing, elaborately graceful, into her napkin, and he likes her more and more and wants her less and less [...] He begins to eat. He watches her breasts, beneath the beige cloth. His prick stiffens a little, twitches, but in a vacuum: he has no real curiosity about those breasts.[52]

This scene involves simultaneous food and body consumption—of a woman's breasts and chicken—through an emerging sexual appetite. While Arthur consumes the food the women's labor has provided for him in this scene, he self-consciously tries to develop a sexual desire for women. His body physically responds to hers, but he is confused and vexed about how he truly feels toward her. He acts upon the norms he knows are standard for Black men with Black women, but he is becoming conscious of the fact that perhaps this is not what he truly wants. This experience is a stepping stone in Arthur's sexual and social development, and through it Baldwin reveals the conflict between inherent personal identity and constructed social expectations as they relate to gender, race, and sexuality. As Arthur develops a more authentic sense of his sexual identity, he finds himself in a devoted relationship with Jimmy.

In the final meal of *Just Above My Head*, which Zaborowska calls a "glimpse" of "a utopian domestic space occupied by two Black men in love," Jimmy and Arthur are in love and share a home.[53] They cook together, sleep together, make music together. Zaborowska explains that *Just Above My Head* was the product of much labor from Baldwin's home in Saint-Paul de Vence, and that Arthur and Jimmy's artistic haven "contains furnishings that could have come from a room in Baldwin's own house; the colors are familiar, too, resembling the palette of the author's French abode."[54] Poignantly, "The only light in the room is the light around the piano, and the very faint light, filtering through the bedsheet, from the kitchen."[55] Much of the joy in their relationship comes out of the kitchen, and in this scene, Arthur proposes they stay in for dinner—that he will scrounge together what they have:

> "We got eggs and pork chops, some leftover red beans and rice, and a chicken wing." He leans up. "Bread, a little stale, but I can heat it up, you know. Some beer, a little whiskey. I mean—we don't have to go *out*, not unless you just *want* to go out." He grins. "I can *get* it together, now." [Jimmy:] "You want me to help you?"[56]

The intimate, easy back-and-forth of their dialogue is a reflection of their life together—their codependence and reciprocal service. Though the food that Jimmy gathers to cook isn't sumptuous fare, it is all they need to be satisfied, since they are happy staying home together rather than going out.

Arthur thinks about his hyper-awareness of joy with Jimmy, and Hall's unique retrospective, present-tense narration anticipates Arthur's premeditated actions:

> Arthur, now, stands at the window, knowing perfectly well that, in a moment, he will go behind the halfhearted partition, grab Jimmy by those two dimples just above his

ass, growl, and bite, into the nape of his neck, sniffing the hair there, just like a cat [...] and grind Jimmy's behind against his own prick, playfully, while Jimmy protests—playfully—and lets the onions burn while he turns and takes Arthur in his arms: too late. The pork chops, too, may burn, unless Jimmy, as he often does, exhibits great presence of mind, and turns down the one flame, while both calming, and surrendering to the other.[57]

The interplay of sexual energy with the cooking process parallels the cooking flames and physical arousal. Arthur's awareness of Jimmy's cooking consciousness—not wanting to burn the onions or the pork chops—imitates his awareness of Jimmy's sexual consciousness—wanting to give in to Arthur's kitchen foreplay. While in this scene food starts burning as physical intimacy begins, in Eric and Yves's case in *Another Country*, food starts getting cold. In neither environment does the food itself actually matter as food per se—instead it is the homes that these meals grace that transform them into meals of love, and symbols of queer domesticity.

The narration shifts into Jimmy's hands, and the pork chops are now starting to burn through his eyes and nose: Arthur

starts fooling around with me. I don't mind that, in fact, I dig that, but my hands are all slippery with grease and onions, and I can't move for a minute. He turns me around and he kisses me, long enough for the chops to start burning. So I push him away, and I try to laugh, and I turn the pork chops over.[58]

Earlier, Hall describes Jimmy's "great presence of mind" to make sure the chops don't burn through Arthur's consciousness of it. Here, Jimmy acts on his own presence of mind without explaining it. Baldwin layers the narration of the same moment through multiple perspectives, and the characters' consciousnesses of each other intermingle to emphasize Arthur and Jimmy's happiness together. Whereas earlier in his life Arthur had to self-consciously try to manipulate his feelings toward Sister Dorothy, who also served him food, here there are only natural feelings and instinctive actions. The "grease and onions" on Jimmy's fingers attract Arthur to him in a more genuine way than the set-up meal with the sisters in the church basement.

While domesticity makes food culture, food culture also makes domesticity. Both of these novels' queer domesticities show the work and the sacrifices required for them to materialize. The transition in *Another Country* from Rufus's far-off memories of family meals to Eric and Yves's French domestic bliss is in some ways at the cost of Rufus's suffering. Eric had to be separated from Rufus to move abroad to begin a new life with Yves. However, though it is most certainly a progression in terms of healthy domestic spaces, it is also a brief interlude in the middle of the book. The characters hardly eat together for the rest of the novel. When Vivaldo and Ida live together, or even in Cass and Richard's home, kitchen scenes for the most part involve preparing drinks, not food. The end of the book leaves the reader hanging right before Eric and Yves's reunification, wondering whether they will return to the relational home they had been for each other in France.

In *Just Above My Head*, the narrative of the story is nonlinear; therefore, some of the memories at the beginning of the book, like the meal with African peppers in Julia's house, actually happen after the final scene in Arthur and Jimmy's kitchen. Arthur's death lies between the two. Hall is able to recreate these memories through the lens of Arthur's loss, and this distance renders the meals—all of them—even more sentimental. Regardless of the chronological order of events in *Just Above My Head*, in Baldwin's movement from traditional family meals to heating up leftovers in a queer domestic environment, the latter becomes a place of healing for these characters from their childhood wounds—Jimmy's loss of his mother, his father's abusiveness, and being sent to live with his aunt in New Orleans, and Arthur's trauma from being sexually abused as a young boy by a stranger on the streets. The home they create with each other brings their vulnerability and experiences of abuse into a safe, creative environment.

While most of this essay has been about Baldwin's relationship with food through international travel, memory, and domesticity, to conclude I will discuss one more important instance in which Baldwin uses food to draw our attention to bigger concepts, in *If Beale Street Could Talk* (1974), which Baldwin also finished in Saint-Paul de Vence. In a memorable and disturbing scene, Tish is shopping for tomatoes at a vegetable stand when someone touches her buttocks from behind. She turns around to face a "small, young, greasy Italian punk. 'I can sure dig a tomato who digs tomatoes,' he said, and he licked his lips, and smiled." Tish looks frantically for Fonny and tries to pay and leave. The boy repeats, "Hey, sweet tomato. *You* know I dig tomatoes."[59] Through his gaze and words, Tish becomes an ingestible object, available for his pleasure as a Black woman in public. The ensuing altercation between Tish, the boy, and Fonny ends with "the white boy [laying] bleeding and retching in the gutter," and a cop coming after Fonny. Fonny's actions were of masculine protection of Tish, but when the cop appears, Tish uses her body to protect Fonny from physical harm. Her tomatoes left on the scale become a witness to her story, which the cop initially doubts. Finally, as Tish and Fonny are free to go, the shopkeeper gives her the tomatoes to take home.[60]

Fonny, having unleashed his anger on the Italian assailant, has not been able to freely speak or move in front of the policeman, due to Tish's protectiveness. He feels emasculated by Tish's covering for him and "takes the bag of tomatoes and smashes them against the nearest wall" as the two of them walk home alone.[61] In a patronizing and masculinist act, he violently reprimands her for trying to protect him. This scene, which is a genesis of sorts in Fonny and Tish's collective clash with law enforcement, is not only important in its depiction of gender roles before the police, but also in the way that tomatoes, as material objects, have over the course of a few pages gone from instigating derogatory sexual remarks, to becoming evidence of the harassment, to silently testifying to the injustice that has passed—a symbol of Fonny's anger, red and splattered against the wall. Food is more than a metaphor for women and sexual consumption; food is a witness to injustice, and an object that absorbs anger and violence.

Baldwin's tomatoes in *If Beale Street Could Talk* operate on multiple layers of meaning making. But what do these ruined ingredients have to do with Baldwin's international experiences, Black feminist food writers, and queer domesticities? I propose that the tomatoes suggest a loss of appetite, the same loss of appetite that Baldwin experiences in Montgomery when he walks into a restaurant only to be barked at by white servers to leave and enter through the "colored" entrance. He sits and orders food only because he wants to see how Black people are served in such establishments, set apart from the rest of the restaurant, behind the counter, behind some mesh. The food arrives wrapped in paper so the white servers don't have to wash their hands while serving Black and white people one after the other.[62] Baldwin is disgusted, demoralized. He writes, "My stomach was as tight as a black rubber ball. I took my hamburger and walked outside and dropped it into the weeds. The dark silence of the streets now frightened me a little, and I walked back to my hotel."[63]

The hamburger in the weeds, the tomatoes on the wall. Both instances of destruction reveal the intensity of Baldwin's righteous anger toward the greater American project. While living abroad and eventually working himself up to an appealing gastronomical lifestyle, Baldwin's distaste for the corruption of the American system, which led him abroad in the first place, persists. In the documentary *The Price of the Ticket*, Baldwin is recorded saying that he originally went to Paris to "vomit up a great deal of bitterness." He also writes in his 1960 essay, "They Can't Turn Back," "It took many years of vomiting up all the filth I'd been taught about myself, and half-believed, before I was able to walk on the earth as though I had a right to be here."[64] He characterizes American beliefs about Blackness as unappetizing, as filth, tipping the critique of Black soul food as filth on its head. While the transnational distance allowed him to write heartfelt, nostalgic scenes about family, soul food, and community, it also allowed him to gain insight into the injustices of the U.S., and to channel that anger into the hearty literary meals that would feed American social consciousness, from his lifetime onward.

Notes

1 Examples of Black women cooks and food writers include Vertamae Smart-Grosvenor, *Vibration Cooking: Or, the Travel Notes of a Geechee Girl* (1970) (Athens, GA, University of Georgia Press, 2011); Jessica B. Harris, *High on the Hog* (New York, Bloomsbury, 2011) and *The Africa Cookbook: Tastes of a Continent* (New York, Simon and Schuster, 1998); Edna Lewis, *The Taste of Country Cooking* (1976) (New York, Alfred A. Knopf, 2006). For more on food theory and Black feminism, see Rafia Zafar, "The Signifying Dish: Autobiography and History in Two Black Women's Cookbooks," *Feminist Studies*, 25:2 (1999), pp. 449–69; Jennifer Jensen Wallach (ed.), *Dethroning the Deceitful Pork Chop: Rethinking African American Foodways from Slavery to Obama* (Fayetteville, AK, University of Arkansas Press, 2015); Psyche A. Williams-Forson, *Building Houses out of Chicken Legs: Black Women, Food, and Power* (Chapel Hill, NC, University of North Carolina Press, 2006); and Kimberly D. Nettles-Barcelón, Gillian Clark, Courtney Thorsson, Jessica Kenyatta Walker, and Psyche Williams-Forson, "Black Women's Food Work as Critical Space," *Gastronomica: The Journal for Food Studies*, 15:4 (2015), pp. 34–49.

2 Magdalena Zaborowska, *James Baldwin's Turkish Decade: Erotics of Exile* (Durham, NC, Duke University Press, 2009), pp. 10, 66.

3 Harris, *High on the Hog*, p. 208. Harris also includes her formulation of the concept of "soul" in the 1960s as stemming from the civil rights movement and the Black Power movement: "a growing pride in things Black and in the culture that had survived enslavement. It went hand in hand with a national feeling of solidarity among Blacks" (p. 207).

4 Alice A. Deck, "'Now Then—Who Said Biscuits?' The Black Woman Cook as Fetish in American Advertising, 1905–1953," in Sherri A. Inness (ed.), *Kitchen Culture in America: Popular Representations of Food, Gender, and Race* (Philadelphia, PA, University of Pennsylvania Press, 2001), p. 71.

5 While women dominated the soul food cooking and writing scene at the same time that Baldwin was writing his novels—especially his later works—the food discourse created a complicated space for men. Black men were notoriously complicit in keeping food and the aptitude for cooking as the work of Black women. In addition, homophobia and anti-miscegenation beliefs acted in conjunction to racialize and sexualize people like Baldwin who fit outside the norms, and these beliefs were also transcribed onto the "soul food" that was in the margins. In her section on "Soul Food and Black Masculinity," Doris Witt traces the connections between viewing soul food as "filth" because of its derivation from slavery, and the practices of movements like Black Power and the Nation of Islam in simultaneously preaching against soul food and marginalizing Black women. Doris Witt, *Black Hunger: Food and Politics in U.S. Identity* (Minneapolis, MN, University of Minnesota Press, 1999), p. 81.

6 David Leeming, *James Baldwin: A Biography* (New York, Alfred A. Knopf, 1994), p. 374.

7 Cecil Brown, "With James Baldwin at the Welcome Table: A Protégé of Baldwin Remembers the Writing of *If Beale Street Could Talk*," *The Common Reader: The James Baldwin Issue*, 23 September 2019, https://commonreader.wustl.edu/c/with-james-baldwin-at-the-welcome-table/ (accessed 6 June 2020), and Magdalena Zaborowska, *Me and My House: James Baldwin's Last Decade in France* (Durham, NC, Duke University Press, 2018), p. 133.

8 Harris, *High on the Hog*, p. 1.

9 *Ibid.*, p. 18. In her book, Harris is meticulous about the origins of specific foods. For example, she distinguishes between "true yams" (from Africa) and American "sweet potatoes." In some ways, the insistence on the authenticity of a "true" African nature fails to complicate the evolution and retention of culture with migration and time.

10 *Ibid.*, p. 26.

11 *Ibid.*, p. 216.

12 James Baldwin, *Just Above My Head* (1979) (New York, Dell, 2000), p. 29.

13 By "return to Africa" I refer to the increased interest in African genealogy for Black Americans in the late twentieth century. Works like Alex Haley's book (1974) and television series *Roots* (1977) inspired many African Americans to seek to "reclaim" and reconnect with their heritage by traveling to Africa. Baldwin published *Just Above My Head* in 1979, contemporaneously with the cultural wave of *Roots* and the ensuing Black heritage tourism, or "roots tourism."

14 Jessica B. Harris, "Dining with James Baldwin," *SAVEUR*, 15 May 2017, www.saveur.com/dining-with-james-baldwin (accessed 6 June 2020). In her memoir, *My Soul Looks Back* (New York, Scribner, 2017), Harris spends much of her first chapter describing her experience of staying at Baldwin's home in Saint-Paul de Vence.

15 James Baldwin, *No Name in the Street* (1972), in *The Price of the Ticket: Collected Nonfiction 1948–1985* (New York, St. Martin's/Marek, 1985), p. 486.

16 Rachel Slocum, "Race in the Study of Food," *Progress in Human Geography*, 35:3 (2011), p. 318.

17 Smart-Grosvenor, *Vibration Cooking*, p. xxxix.

18 Doris Witt, "Vertamae Smart Grosvenor's Geechee Diaspora," in Inness (ed.), *Kitchen Culture in America*, p. 229.

19 *Ibid.*, p. 243.

20 Smart-Grosvenor, *Vibration Cooking*, p. xxxviii. Smart-Grosvenor recounts a story of expectantly being served a delicacy at a restaurant in France, and realizing that it was just chitterlings in the form of sausage called andouillettes (p. xxiii). She also writes about the very similar ways that French and Americans prepare shared foods like sweet potatoes (p. xxxviii).

21 *Ibid.*, p. 55.

22 Another Black feminist writer who popularized the harmonious fusion of soul food and French cuisine was Edna Lewis. Known as the "grand dame" of Southern cooking, Lewis's international travels allowed her to bring French techniques to Southern food, contributing soul food to the movement of white cosmopolitan cooking. She is known for her lyrical essay "What is Southern?," and her close relationship with the much younger white chef Scott Peacock, her protégé, cookbook co-author, and good friend, epitomizes the fluid boundaries Lewis embodied in Southern identity. Lewis's life as a chef and food writer was characterized by bringing people together across differences to share food and community, creating alliances, understanding, and new forms of intimacy via Southern food. Sara B. Franklin, "Introduction," in Sara B. Franklin (ed.), *Edna Lewis: At the Table with an American Original* (Chapel Hill, NC, University of North Carolina Press, 2018), pp. 1–14.

23 Witt, "Vertamae Smart Grosvenor," p. 233

24 Smart-Grosvenor, *Vibration Cooking*, p. xxxix.

25 Zaborowska, *Me and My House*, pp. 57, 197.

26 Smart-Grosvenor, *Vibration Cooking*, p. 204.

27 Paul Gray, "Author James Baldwin Defines Life: 'You Learn to Make Love with Whatever Frightens You,'" *PEOPLE.com*, 7 January 1980, people.com/archive/author-james-baldwin-defines-life-you-learn-to-make-love-with-whatever-frightens-you-vol-13-no-1/ (accessed 6 June 2020).

28 James Baldwin, *James Baldwin: The Last Interview and Other Conversations* (New York, Melville House, 2014), p. 4.

29 James Baldwin, "Stranger in the Village" (1953), in *The Price of the Ticket*, pp. 79–90.

30 Baldwin, *No Name in the Street*, p. 456.

31 *Ibid.*, p. 457.

32 Baldwin, *James Baldwin: The Last Interview*, p. 4.

33 James Baldwin, *Another Country* (1962), in *Early Novels and Stories*, ed. Toni Morrison (New York, Library of America, 1998), p. 369.

34 Baldwin, *Another Country*, p. 402.

35 The relationship between food and sex work, more specifically gay or queer sex work, is something that Baldwin points out in other works as well. In *Giovanni's Room*, David and Giovanni go to a restaurant with Jacques and Guillaume, where older, richer men flirt with younger men, indicating that they will buy them dinner if the younger men make themselves available sexually (p. 62). Giovanni's employment at Guillaume's bar is a result of Guillaume knowing that he will bring in money as a young man attractive to older richer men, and he entices him with a work visa and payment. Giovanni is more than a barman at the restaurant; he is a sexual symbol, a symbol of the fleeting exchange

of desires, alcohol, food, and money in this elusive, non-heteronormative space. James Baldwin, *Giovanni's Room* (1956) (New York, Vintage, 2013).

36 Slocum, "Race in the Study of Food," p. 305.
37 Baldwin, *Another Country*, p. 410.
38 Baldwin, *Just Above My Head*, p. 77.
39 Sherry A. Inness, "Introduction," in Inness (ed.), *Kitchen Culture in America*, p. 3.
40 Baldwin, *Another Country*, p. 530.
41 *Ibid.*
42 *Ibid.*, p. 566.
43 *Ibid.*, p. 567.
44 Zaborowska, *James Baldwin's Turkish Decade*, p. 42.
45 *Ibid.*, p. 44.
46 Zaborowska, *Me and My House*, p. 56.
47 *Ibid.*, p. 97.
48 Baldwin worked on his play *The Welcome Table* from his home in Saint-Paul de Vence. Some of the people around him were inspirations for characters in his play, which was set in a house not unlike his own, and rehearsed in his actual house (Leeming, *James Baldwin: A Biography*, p. 374). Magdalena Zaborowska writes, "it embraces African Americans as part of a larger, transnational community of émigrés, and transient artists" (*Me and My House*, p. 182). Fittingly enough, the "culminating event" is an elderly woman's birthday party. The themes of *The Welcome Table* reflect Baldwin's transnational hospitality, community, and social life.
49 Baldwin, *Just Above My Head*, p. 177.
50 *Ibid.*, p. 178.
51 *Ibid.*, p. 179.
52 *Ibid.*, p. 181.
53 Zaborowska, *Me and My House*, p. 95.
54 *Ibid.*, p. 96.
55 Baldwin, *Just Above My Head*, p. 570.
56 *Ibid.*, p. 571.
57 *Ibid.*, p. 574.
58 *Ibid.*
59 Baldwin, *If Beale Street Could Talk* (1974) (New York, Vintage, 2006), p. 136.
60 *Ibid.*, p. 139.
61 *Ibid.*, p. 140.
62 Baldwin, *No Name in the Street*, p. 488.
63 *Ibid.*
64 James Baldwin, "They Can't Turn Back," (1960) in *The Price of the Ticket*, p. 227.

Works Cited

Baldwin, James, *Another Country* (1962), in *Early Novels and Stories*, ed. Toni Morrison (New York, The Library of America, 1998), pp. 361–756.
_____ *Giovanni's Room* (1956) (New York, Vintage, 2013).
_____ *If Beale Street Could Talk* (1974) (New York, Vintage International, 2006).
_____ *James Baldwin: The Last Interview and Other Conversations* (New York, Melville House, 2014).
_____ *Just Above My Head* (1979) (New York, Dell, 2000).

_____ *No Name in the Street* (1972), in *The Price of the Ticket: Collected Nonfiction 1948–1985* (New York, St. Martin's/Marek, 1985), pp. 449–552.

_____ "Stranger in the Village" (1953), in *The Price of the Ticket: Collected Nonfiction 1948–1985* (New York, St. Martin's/Marek, 1985), pp. 79–90.

_____ "They Can't Turn Back" (1960), in *The Price of the Ticket: Collected Nonfiction 1948–1985* (New York, St. Martin's/Marek, 1985), pp. 215–28.

Brown, Cecil, "With James Baldwin at the Welcome Table: A Protégé of Baldwin Remembers the Writing of *If Beale Street Could Talk*," *The Common Reader: The James Baldwin Issue*, 23 September 2019, https://commonreader.wustl.edu/c/with-james-baldwin-at-the-welcome-table/ (accessed 6 June 2020).

Deck, Alice A., "'Now Then—Who Said Biscuits?' The Black Woman Cook as Fetish in American Advertising, 1905–1953," in Sherrie A. Inness (ed.), *Kitchen Culture in America: Popular Representations of Food, Gender, and Race* (Philadelphia, PA, University of Pennsylvania Press, 2001), pp. 69–94.

Franklin, Sara B., "Introduction," in Sara B. Franklin (ed.), *Edna Lewis: At the Table with an American Original* (Chapel Hill, NC, University of North Carolina Press, 2018), pp. 1–14.

Gray, Paul, "Author James Baldwin Defines Life: 'You Learn to Make Love with Whatever Frightens You,'" *PEOPLE.com*, 7 January 1980, people.com/archive/author-james-baldwin-defines-life-you-learn-to-make-love-with-whatever-frightens-you-vol-13-no-1/ (accessed 6 June 2020).

Haley, Alex, *Roots: The Saga of an American Family* (1974) (Boston: Da Capo, 2014).

Harris, Jessica B., *The Africa Cookbook: Tastes of a Continent* (New York, Simon and Schuster, 1998).

_____ "Dining with James Baldwin," *SAVEUR*, 15 May 2017, www.saveur.com/dining-with-james-baldwin (accessed 6 June 2020).

_____ *High on the Hog* (New York, Bloomsbury, 2011).

_____ *My Soul Looks Back: A Memoir* (New York, Scribner, 2017)

Inness, Sherrie A., "Introduction," in Sherrie A. Inness (ed.), *Kitchen Culture in America: Popular Representations of Food, Gender, and Race* (Philadelphia, PA, University of Pennsylvania Press, 2001), pp. 1–12.

_____ (ed.), *Kitchen Culture in America: Popular Representations of Food, Gender, and Race* (Philadelphia, PA, University of Pennsylvania Press, 2001).

Jensen Wallach, Jennifer (ed.), *Dethroning the Deceitful Pork Chop: Rethinking African American Foodways from Slavery to Obama* (Fayetteville, AK, University of Arkansas Press, 2015).

Leeming, David, *James Baldwin: A Biography* (New York, Alfred A. Knopf, 1994).

Lewis, Edna, *The Taste of Country Cooking* (1976) (New York, Alfred A. Knopf, 2006).

Nettles-Barcelón, Kimberly D., Gillian Clark, Courtney Thorsson, Jessica Kenyatta Walker, and Psyche Williams-Forson, "Black Women's Food Work as Critical Space," *Gastronomica: The Journal for Food Studies*, 15:4 (2015), pp. 34–49.

Slocum, Rachel, "Race in the Study of Food," *Progress in Human Geography*, 35:3 (2011), pp. 303–27.

Smart-Grosvenor, Vertamae, *Vibration Cooking: Or, the Travel Notes of a Geechee Girl* (1970) (Athens, GA, University of Georgia Press, 2011).

Thorsen, Karen (dir.), *The Price of the Ticket* (Maysles Films & PBS/American Masters, 1990).

Williams-Forson, Psyche A., *Building Houses out of Chicken Legs: Black Women, Food, and Power* (Chapel Hill, NC, University of North Carolina Press, 2006).

Witt, Doris, *Black Hunger: Food and Politics in U.S. Identity* (Oxford, Oxford University Press, 1999).

_____ "'My Kitchen Was the World': Vertamae Smart Grosvenor's Geechee Diaspora," in Sherrie A. Inness (ed.), *Kitchen Culture in America: Popular Representations of Food, Gender, and Race* (Philadelphia, PA, University of Pennsylvania Press, 2001), pp. 227–50.

Zaborowska, Magdalena, *James Baldwin's Turkish Decade: Erotics of Exile* (Durham, NC, Duke University Press, 2009).

_____ *Me and My House: James Baldwin's Last Decade in France* (Durham, NC, Duke University Press, 2018).

Zafar, Rafia, "The Signifying Dish: Autobiography and History in Two Black Women's Cookbooks," *Feminist Studies*, 25:2 (1999), pp. 449–69.

Contributor's Biography

Emily Na is a PhD student in American Culture at the University of Michigan. Her research focuses on African-American literature and the contemporary memory of slavery in the U.S. through literature, visual culture, and museums.

GRADUATE STUDENT ESSAY

The Warrior and the Poet: On James Baldwin and the Many Roles in Revolution

Nicholas Binford   Washington State University

Abstract

Artists, scholars, and popular media often describe James Baldwin as revolution-ary, either for his written work or for his role in the civil rights movement. But what does it mean to be revolutionary? This article contends that thoughtlessly calling James Baldwin revolutionary obscures and erases the non-revolutionary strategies and approaches he employed in his contributions to the civil rights movement and to race relations as a whole. Frequent use of revolutionary as a synonym for "great" or "important" creates an association suggesting that all good things must be revolutionary, and that anything not revolutionary is insufficient, effectively erasing an entire spectrum of social and political engagement from view. Baldwin's increasing relevance to our contemporary moment suggests that his non-revolutionary tactics are just as important as the revolutionary approaches employed by civil rights leaders such as Malcolm X or Martin Luther King, Jr.

Keywords: revolution, Malcolm X, Martin Luther King, Jr., civil rights movement, James Baldwin, rhetoric

> The poet and the people get on generally very badly, and yet they need each other. The poet knows it sooner than the people do. The people usually know it after the poet is dead; but that's all right.
>
> James Baldwin[1]

At James Baldwin's funeral, Amiri Baraka declared: "Jimmy wrote, he produced, he spoke, he sang. No matter the odds, he remained man, and spirit, and voice, ever expanding, and evermore conscious. Let us hold him in our hearts and minds. Let us make him a part of our invincible black souls … The intelligence of our transcendence."[2] Baldwin's legacy is significant, but we are only now beginning to

James Baldwin Review, Volume 6, 2020, © The Authors. Published by Manchester University Press and The University of Manchester Library
http://dx.doi.org/10.7227/JBR.6.7

understand just how vast it really is. Ongoing political events continue to reveal the prophetic nature of Baldwin's words, and scholars, artists, and activists around the world have taken notice. A Baldwin renaissance is taking place and has been for the last ten or fifteen years. Numerous new scholarly books are finding publication, revivals and derivations of his plays are being performed, and his writing is more visible than ever before, scrawled across protest signs and shared across the internet in tweets and images. "Each triumph of broadening access and exposure to his brilliant writing is a moment for celebration," write Justin A. Joyce, Dwight A. McBride, and Douglas Field in the introduction of the inaugural issue of *James Baldwin Review*, "yet each time the social and political landscape of a moment calls out for Baldwin's critical insight we are reminded of the ongoing necessity for change."[3] It is worth asking: why Baldwin, and why now? His role in the civil rights movement notwithstanding, what about Baldwin reaches out across the span of decades to speak so clearly, so prophetically, to our current moment? What separates Baldwin from his contemporaries?

Malcolm X once said to Baldwin, "I am the warrior of this revolution, and you are the poet."[4] Baldwin's position during the civil rights movement is quite different from that of its other major figures, including Malcolm X, Martin Luther King, Jr., or Black Panther founders Bobby Seale and Huey P. Newton. Amiri Baraka proclaimed that Baldwin was "God's black revolutionary mouth, if there is a God. And revolution, his righteous natural expression."[5] But is this true; is James Baldwin a revolutionary? Despite his interest in civil rights, he never aligned himself with any of its revolutionary movements. Baraka is not the only person to describe Baldwin as revolutionary; popular descriptions of Baldwin as a "revolutionary humanist" or a "self-created revolutionary" are common.[6] Academics, too, often refer to him in this way: biographer Bill Mullen describes him as "a revolutionary for our times" in his preface to *James Baldwin: Living in Fire* (2019), Professor Davis W. Houck argues for Baldwin's "revolution from within," and critic Stuart Hall called him a "middle-aged black revolutionary."[7] I challenge this characterization of Baldwin as a revolutionary, as neither his message nor his methods have much in common with revolutionary contemporaries like Martin Luther King, Jr. or Malcolm X. I also contend that it is in fact the non-revolutionary nature of his message that is responsible for Baldwin's ongoing relevance.

In the context of James Baldwin and the civil rights movement, "revolutionary" and "revolution" are highly charged and hotly contested terms deployed strategically by the movement's most prominent voices. Their frequent or else sparing use of these terms signified how far they were willing to go in their opposition to the status quo. Playing out in the background of the civil rights movement were the numerous African revolutions and the Vietnam War. Algeria, Egypt, Rwanda, Sudan, and other nations were experiencing violent political upheavals and dramatic changes in governance. *Coups d'état*, insurgency, and even outright war were the order of the day, and imperialist nations such as France and the United States were acting to quell these uprisings. So it should be unsurprising, perhaps even inevitable, that many drew parallels between events across the Atlantic and the

burgeoning civil rights movement in the U.S. While many activists took inspiration from these countries, those in power grew more wary. This global political
climate made revolution a loaded word, characterized by violence and political
upheaval, and the manner in which it was deployed played a major role in shaping
the discourse of the various movements.

Malcolm X claimed "revolution" and all its implications outright. In his historic
"Message to Grassroots," he declares that revolution is "the land-less against the
landlord," and argues that it can only be achieved through "bloody battle."[8] He
claimed kinship with the African revolutions and all revolutions by non-whites
against their white oppressors, calling it a worldwide Black revolution, of which he
considered himself and his followers a part. In his speech he distinguishes the
"black revolution" from the "negro revolution," his scornful name for King's movement, which he mocked for its insistence on loving their oppressors. He even
argues that King and his followers should not call themselves a revolution at all:

> First, what is a revolution? Sometimes I'm inclined to believe that many of our people
> are using this word "revolution" loosely, without taking careful consideration [of]
> what this word actually means, and what its historic characteristics are. When you
> study the historic nature of revolutions, the motive of a revolution, the objective of a
> revolution, and the result of a revolution, and the methods used in a revolution, you
> may change words. You may devise another program. You may change your goal and
> you may change your mind.[9]

"A revolution is bloody," Malcolm X declared, "revolution is hostile. Revolution
knows no compromise. Revolution overturns and destroys everything that gets in
its way."[10] This version of revolution would later be revised by the Black Panthers
Party for Self-Defense into a more explicitly political position in their "Ten Point
Program," in which they demanded land as reparation for centuries of mistreatment and claimed the right to resist violence by any means necessary.[11]

Dr. Martin Luther King, Jr. was far more circumspect than Malcolm X in his use
of the term "revolution," but he appears to have defined it in a similar way. He too
invokes the political revolutions of Africa and warns of "a time when the cup of
endurance runs over and men are no longer willing to be plunged into an abyss of
injustice" as a means of foreshadowing the violent consequences of continued
oppression.[12] But unlike Malcolm X, King couches the idea of revolution in the
precise, strategic language of his movement. In "Letter From a Birmingham Jail"
he briefly identifies his movement as a "social revolution," then writes: "In any
nonviolent campaign [note how "revolution" has now become "campaign"] there
are four basics steps: collection of the facts to determine whether injustices are
alive, negotiation, self-purification, and direct action."[13] Direct action is King's
revolutionary approach, his substitute for Malcolm X's violence as the means of
"overthrowing." King would continue to be just as strategic in future orations. In a
1967 speech on the Vietnam War he advocated for a "revolution of values," and in
a sermon one year later, he declared that "a great revolution is taking place in the

world today."[14] He elaborates in a 1968 speech: "We must come to see that the roots of racism are very deep in our country, and there must be something positive and massive in order to get rid of all the effects of racism and the tragedies of racial injustice."[15] King avoids using the word revolution outright. It is always carefully qualified as explicitly nonviolent, a "social revolution," or abstract, a "revolution of values," or else he substitutes it with any number of synonyms or equivalent phrases. What this reveals is King's recognition that the term revolution, at this time, connoted violence, and he could not afford to have his movement associated with that. Thus, King complicated the meaning of revolution in order to harness its rhetorical force while disarming its threat of violence.

This leaves two dominant versions of revolution: Malcolm X's land and bloodshed and King's "something positive and massive." Despite disagreeing on the actual method of resistance, the two have some common characteristics. Both identify an enemy or oppressor, delineate a method of combating them, and define conditions for victory which require paradigmatic sociopolitical shifts. In other words, revolution in the civil rights movement is a method of engaging with structures of power, such as white hegemony, that seeks to overturn social or institutional systems, such as racism and segregation. Meanwhile, a revolutionary is someone who practices or advocates for this method of engagement.

We have seen how careful civil rights leaders were in their use of the terms, but nowadays we are much less scrupulous. In the United States, at least, our history has instilled the words "revolution" and "revolutionary" with significant connotative baggage—including concepts of goodness, justice, underdog, or martyrdom—often leading us to conflate two vocabularies: words describing sudden, major impacts on society—revolutionary, radical, subversion, rebellion—and words describing forces of positive change—intellectual, free thinker, advocate, poet. What I am suggesting is that "revolution" and "revolutionary" have become words to describe all forces for positive change. If a change is good, it must be revolutionary. The exigency here is that by calling all good change revolutionary, we begin to forget that there are other ways to effect positive change. Anything short of revolution becomes insufficient. Yet, as Baldwin shows us, this is not always the case.

The life and work of James Baldwin defies the implicit and often unrecognized belief in the imperative of revolution and shows us alternative methods to fight for change, but only if we recognize his approach accurately. Baldwin certainly recognized his own approach; he was always careful in his speeches and his writing not to overly associate himself with revolution. In fact, he rarely used the word, though if he did, he would always qualify it in a way that expressed his misgivings. When Malcolm X called revolution land and bloodshed, Baldwin was quick to caution everyone in his own 1963 speech, "We Can Change the Country," that

we are not—we who are on the barricades in this unprecedented revolution—in the position of someone in the Congo or someone in Cuba. That is, we cannot take over the land. The terms of this revolution are precisely these: that we will learn to live together here or all of us will abruptly stop living.[16]

In an interview two years later for *Who Speaks for the Negro?* (1965), he insists that the situation constitutes a "complicated revolution," because "here it's your brothers and your sisters, whether or not they know it, they are your brothers and your sisters … It complicates it so much that I can't possibly myself quite see my way through this."[17] And two years later still, in a letter for *Freedomways*, he commented

> no people have ever been in a revolutionary situation so bizarre. It is a revolution which has all the aspects of a civil war; but at the same time, it is happening all over the globe, and America is fighting it all over the globe—using, by no means incidentally, vast numbers of its surplus and despised population.[18]

Baldwin avoided referring to the civil rights movement as an outright revolution, but always one "unprecedented," "complicated," and "bizarre," in which the "surplus and despised populations" would suffer the most in their attempts to reproduce current or historical revolutions whose circumstances were not compatible with their own. In one interview, he even offered up an explicit alternative to revolution: "We represent around 10% of the American population. Without talking about starting a revolution, it is certainly enough to destroy society … It is easy for us, for example, to make the cities uninhabitable. It is the Blacks who form the bulk of the urban services."[19] In an age when revolution was on the tip of every tongue, Baldwin's repeated decision to avoid or disarm the term is conspicuous and significant.

While he always acknowledged and sympathized with the injustices that inspired a revolutionary attitude, Baldwin greatly feared the consequences of such a course of action, both for the physical violence it would inevitably provoke and for the spiritual damage it would inflict on society as the rift between Black and white grew ever larger. In *The Devil Finds Work* (1976), Baldwin describes an early education in film given to him by his teacher, Orilla (Bill) Miller, a radical female leftist. She took him to see a film production of *A Tale of Two Cities*, and Baldwin's response to the film is worth quoting at length:

> I understood, as Bill had intended me to, something of revolution—understood, that is, something of the universal and inevitable human ferment which explodes into what is called a revolution. *Revolution*: the word had a solemn, dreadful ring: what was going on in Spain was a *revolution*. It was said that Roosevelt had saved America: from a revolution. Revolution was the only hope of the American working class—the *proletariat*; and world-wide revolution was the only hope of the world. I could understand (or, rather, accept) all this, as it were, negatively. I could not see where I fit in this formulation, and I did not see where blacks fit.[20]

Here Baldwin recognizes the complex history behind the word revolution, the ways in which it is invoked by different groups at different times for different purposes. It is always formed by the explosion of "universal and inevitable human ferment" but that explosion is harnessed, shackled even, when it is named a revolution. Baldwin continues,

In the film, I was not overwhelmed by the guillotine. The guillotine had been very present for me in the novel because I already wanted, and for very good reasons, to lop off heads. But: once begun, how to distinguish one head from another, and how, where, and for what reason, would the process stop? Beneath the resonance of the word, *revolution*, thundered the word, *revenge*. But: *vengeance is mine, saith the Lord*: a hard saying, the identity of *the Lord* becoming, with the passage of time, either a private agony or an abstract question. And, to put it as simply as it can be put, unless one can conceive of (and endure) an abstract life, there can be no abstract questions. A question is a threat, the door which slams shut, or swings open: on another threat.[21]

Revolution is revenge, and revenge belongs to the Lord. How, Baldwin wonders, could anyone as fallible as a human being be entrusted with such authority? Perhaps these doubts are responsible for some of Baldwin's harshest characterizations of revolutionaries. Later in *The Devil Finds Work*, he describes the revolutionaries as "superior and dedicated gangster[s]," and in *No Name in the Street* (1972), as "suicidal," equating them with "fanatics."[22] The revolutionaries Baldwin is envisaging are those who have abandoned the fight for a just society in favor of a new social order in which *they* are in power, a shift which only perpetuates the cycle of violence between whites and Blacks. And in *The Fire Next Time* (1963), he writes,

We should certainly know by now that it is one thing to overthrow a dictator or repel an invader and quite another thing really to achieve a revolution. Time and time and time again, the people discover that they have merely betrayed themselves into the hands of yet another Pharaoh.[23]

And still later, in "An Open Letter to My Sister Angela Y. Davis," he expresses uneasiness and resignation toward the seemingly inevitable revolution to come, writing that "The enormous revolution in black consciousness which has occurred in your generation, my dear sister, means the beginning or the end of America."[24] Where Malcolm X and King saw "revolution" as a desirable and effective solution, Baldwin viewed it as dangerous and destructive. Of course, he would never condemn those seduced by its call, for revolution is the inevitable outcome of intolerable oppression, but he would advocate desperately for another path.

While the relationship between King and Malcolm X has long been the subject of extensive analysis, our understanding of Baldwin's position in relation to the two of them is still developing and disrupts the comfortable narrative that there are only two approaches to confronting and counteracting racism. Fredrick Harris characterized Baldwin as "standing in between the titans of non-violent resistance and any-means-necessary self-defense" and contends that Baldwin "saw limitations to King's edict of love for the oppressor and Malcolm X's condemnation of 'White Devils.'"[25] Baldwin refused to accept the simple revolutionary narrative that there are "two sides" to the problem of race, and even that race is a problem that can be "solved." His call in *The Fire Next Time* for the "relatively conscious whites" and the "relatively conscious blacks" to come together "like lovers" points instead toward an identity-affirming world of universal brotherhood as a solution to perpetual racial conflict.[26] "We are capable of bearing a great burden," Baldwin writes, "once we discover that the burden is reality and arrive where reality is."[27] I propose that "reality" here is his belief that race is a pervasive, complex social construction that cannot be "solved" in the sense that King and Malcolm X believe it can. Race is not a battle for one side to win; instead, it is a burden we all must bear. Baldwin takes a fundamentally different approach to the issue of race compared to King and Malcolm X, one that has no "us" and "them," and one that acknowledges the immensity of a problem which will take far more than desegregation, and far more than Black nationalism, to solve.

Baldwin's skepticism of political and social revolution was not about its feasibility or impact, it was about whether revolution would actually solve a problem or just generate more conflict. He fully acknowledged the energy and emotion both King and Malcolm X had harnessed, writing:

> we are living in an age of revolution, whether we will or no, and ... America is the only Western nation with both the power and, as I hope to suggest, the experience that may help to make these revolutions real and minimize the human damage. Any attempt we make to oppose these outbursts of energy is tantamount to signing our death warrant.[28]

Baldwin's concern about human damage was warranted; Malcolm X and Martin Luther King, Jr. were both assassinated within five years of *The Fire Next Time*'s publication. In "Message to Grassroots," Malcolm X had asked, "How do you think [the white man] will react when you learn what a real revolution is?"[29] Baldwin, a student of literature, knew well that revolution always comes at a cost; the candle that burns twice as bright burns half as long.

It was this human damage that Baldwin hoped to mitigate through his essays and speeches, and, as we will see, in his fiction. The "burning out" of a bright individual is a consistent theme in Baldwin's novels and serves as both an argument for and illustration of the necessity of non-revolutionary ideology. Baldwin's novels feature a number of characters who very closely resemble the revolutionaries in their uncompromising attitudes toward society, but these characters typically meet tragic and unhappy ends precipitated by their inability to recognize the shared humanity in all people. It would be more accurate to describe these characters as pre-revolutionary, as they have the prerequisite attitude of "us versus them" and significant justified anger at the current state of society, but have not attached themselves to any particular movement. Through the fates of these characters, Baldwin illustrates his belief that revolutionary ideologies will only generate more conflict.

Of all Baldwin's characters, the one most representative of this pre-revolutionary archetype is Rufus Scott in *Another Country* (1962). Rufus is a jazz musician living in New York who begins an affair with a white woman named Leona, and though it begins as a casual relationship, it becomes gradually more serious as they begin living together. Over time, Rufus becomes increasingly violent with Leona, eventually hurting her so badly that her family takes her away and places her in an asylum. Overcome with guilt, Rufus disappears into the streets of New York for several weeks before leaping off a bridge to his death. Rufus's downfall was brought about by his hatred of white people and his inability or refusal to recognize the humanity in his "enemies": "How I hate them–all those white sons of bitches out there. They're trying to kill me, you think I don't know? They got the world on a string, man, the miserable white cock suckers, and they tying that string around my neck, they killing *me*."[30] To use Baldwin's words, Rufus has "accept[ed] the same criteria" and "share[s] the same beliefs" as his oppressors. He is convinced that white is out to kill Black, and in accepting this he perpetuates the violence by lashing out at Leona. This is the trap Baldwin fears, the trap of creating an "other" who is fundamentally different, and in doing so reinforcing the racial paradigm from which the conflict originates. "Black and white can only thrust and count-er-thrust, [and] long for each other's slow, exquisite death," warns Baldwin, "so that they go down into the pit together."[31] To accept such a myth is tantamount to a slow suicide, because it ensnares the victim and drags them down. Leona speaks to this as Vivaldo rescues her from Rufus's apartment: "But, Rufus, he's all the time looking for it, he sees it where it ain't he don't see nothing else no more."[32] Rufus's acceptance of this intractable Black/white binary leads him to act in ways for which he is unable to forgive himself, ultimately leading to his demise.

While this reading of Rufus's character may seem harsh, it is important to note that Baldwin does not place blame on his shoulders. The judgement and alienation Rufus and others face for their various social transgressions is overwhelming, and Baldwin takes care to thoroughly illustrate this for his readers. Additionally, every character who knew Rufus insisted that he was a kind and good man, even Leona, despite his misdeeds. People like Rufus are not wrong to feel the way they feel, according to Baldwin, but they must recognize the impotency of unconstructive rage. "I think that we all commit our crimes," says Cass to Rufus shortly before his suicide:

> The thing is not to lie about them—to try to understand what you have done, why you have done it … That way, you can begin to forgive yourself. That's very important. If you don't forgive yourself you'll never be able to forgive anybody else and you'll go on committing the same crimes forever.[33]

Anger is a natural reaction to an unjust society, but anger alone only feeds back into the system, as it did for Rufus.

Go Tell It on the Mountain (1953) also features a character much like Rufus in the form of Elizabeth's first love, Richard. Richard and Elizabeth meet in Maryland before moving to New York, ostensibly to get married. There they live happily for a time before Richard is arrested on suspicion of committing a robbery, though his only crime was to be present when the police were arresting other Black suspects. Richard refuses to sign a confession for a crime he did not commit and is beaten for it, but he is eventually released when his involvement cannot be proven. The next night he commits suicide. Richard expresses many of the same sentiments that Rufus does, as exemplified by his monologue at the museum:

> I just decided me [*sic*] one day that I was going to get to know everything them white bastards knew, and I was going to get to know it better than them, so could no white son-of-a-bitch *nowhere* never talk *me* down, and never make me feel like I was dirt, when I could read him the alphabet, back, front, and sideways. Shit—he weren't going to beat my ass, then. And if he tried to kill me, I'd take him with me, I swear to my mother I would.[34]

Here can be seen the same preoccupation with the "two sides" of white and Black, and the same assumption that there can only ever be violence between the two groups. Like Rufus, Richard has accepted the myth, but where Rufus was driven to actions for which he could not forgive himself, Richard succumbs to a despair based on his belief in the impenetrable inhumanity of his fellow men. And like Rufus, Richard is not entirely to blame for this belief, as he was shown little enough humanity by the shopkeeper and white officers who arrested him.

The purpose in comparing these characters is to establish the existence of a pattern in Baldwin's fiction that reveals meaningful social commentary consistent with his political beliefs. The fate of characters like Rufus and Richard illustrates Baldwin's firm belief in the futility of trying to live in the world while cultivating a hatred of our fellows, Black or white. Both of these tragic characters commit suicide literally as a result of this perspective, since fiction is an arena appropriate for such theatrics, but Baldwin makes clear in his other writings that the suicide is figurative, a mutilation of the soul that makes one into the very thing one had hoped to destroy. And one can also see in Richard's story Baldwin's fear of the white oppressors crushing those who dare to oppose too strongly their absolute authority, a fear which came to pass an appalling number of times, most notably in the assassinations of Malcolm X and Martin Luther King, Jr. These are the consequences of revolution that Baldwin foresaw, and thus he modeled his own activism in such a way that it would *not* be construed as revolutionary, his extensive F.B.I. file notwithstanding. He did not do so out of fear, he simply believed that the world did not need yet another revolution.

But strongly opposed as Baldwin was to revolution, he could hardly deny that revolution was, in truth, the course upon which the United States seemed to have set itself. As the years passed it became more and more clear that white Americans would never meet their Black brothers and sisters at the table, and his writing and politics began to reflect his frustrations. It has generally been accepted that Baldwin's despair over the racial situation in the United States contributed to a low point in his later career, a time when he abandoned, never to return to, his message of universalism and brotherhood as his writing became angry and bitter, and, thus, less complex and insightful. In his article "God's Black Revolutionary Mouth: James Baldwin's Black Radicalism," Bill Lyne joins other critics who have lately challenged this narrative of Baldwin's development, arguing instead that his later work is as skillful and powerful as ever, but that the white-dominated critical majority no longer liked his message. "The problem is not that Baldwin relinquished art for politics," writes Lyne, "but that his politics moved from a stance that made him the darling of the white liberal establishment to one that pushed him beyond the boundaries of canonization."[35] Lyne contends that dismissing Baldwin's turn to Black radicalism as bad art is a technique employed by white-dominated culture to preserve the image of Baldwin as exclusively a liberal integrationist rather than acknowledging his complex political journey. Lyne's argument is a good one and is worth addressing, as my own argument draws heavily on Baldwin's earlier career. While Baldwin may have turned his attentions toward Black radicalism later in life, I argue that he was never permitted to act on those ideals thanks in no small part to the way his homosexuality was received at the time, and, without acting on them, he cannot truly be said to have donned the mantle of a "revolutionary."

Thus far I have largely represented Baldwin's non-revolutionary civil rights approach as a conscious strategy for navigating a perilous political environment, but it is also the case that he had little choice in the matter. Baldwin's sexuality is almost entirely absent from all of the pieces discussed so far—other than *Another Country*—but it is an important part of his identity and played a critical role in his relationship with revolutionaries and the radical left. In his article, "Looking for Jimmy Baldwin: Sex, Privacy, and Black Nationalist Fervor," Douglas Field suggests that Baldwin's sexuality was the most important factor in determining his political trajectory. Much of Field's essay is dedicated to exploring Baldwin's troubled history with homosexuality, including his refusal to accept the terms gay or homosexual, his insistence that his work was not about homosexuality, and his repeated statement that race is more important than sexuality. But despite these efforts to downplay his orientation, numerous contemporaries and critics have noted that Baldwin's potential as a civil rights leader was subverted by his orientation. James Campbell wrote that Baldwin's "value to the [civil rights] movement was mainly symbolic,"[36] and Ishmael Reed and Amiri Baraka criticized his writing "for not being sufficiently politically engaged," likely because Baldwin felt that his sexuality forced him to temper his position.[37] But Baldwin *did* try to participate in King's "social revolution," only to be stonewalled by King himself, who "felt that Baldwin was uninformed regarding his movement," even going so far as to exclude Baldwin from speaking at the March on Washington event in 1963.[38] And though Baldwin and Malcolm X's relationship was one of mutual respect and good will, the Black nationalist opinion on Baldwin and his homosexuality was less than welcoming. When Eldridge Cleaver attacked Baldwin for being effeminate and weak, Field argues that Baldwin's message took a sharp turn toward the radical rhetoric of the Black Panthers, an argument echoed by Lyne and other critics. This might also have been due in part to the assassinations of Malcolm X and Martin Luther King, Jr., which broke Baldwin's faith in his message of love. Despite Baldwin's support of Black nationalism, he was still unable to achieve status within the movement. It is especially ironic that Jean Genet, celebrated French homosexual writer and strong supporter of the Black Panthers, was invited to speak at their events, while Baldwin was sidelined. Field writes, "On the one hand, Baldwin was frequently criticized for being politically too vague, but … unlike Genet, Baldwin's sexuality was a direct hindrance to his contribution to Black politics," which led Baldwin to be "seen less as a revolutionary, and more … as a source of poetic inspiration."[39] As much as Baldwin came to embrace Black nationalism and, however apprehensively, the inevitability of revolution, he was prevented from fully engaging in it, and thus from ever truly becoming a revolutionary.

Baldwin's continued importance to our political moment has not gone unnoticed by contemporary scholars. An important aspect of the "Baldwin renaissance" Joyce, McBride, and Field identified is the deep examination and comparison of Baldwin to other civil rights leaders. Historically, most attention has been paid to revolutionaries such as Malcolm X, Martin Luther King, Jr., and activist groups like the Nation of Islam and Black Panthers, because these groups presented clear, concrete objectives and methods which made it easy to evaluate their successes and failures. But James Baldwin was always an outlier, his philosophy abstract and, perhaps, even more demanding and intimidating than the other approaches available at the time. He did not offer a simple solution, an enemy to combat, or a single explicit obstacle to overcome, yet his relevance only continues to grow. An examination of recent scholarly publications will reveal that, consciously or otherwise, many scholars mark Baldwin's philosophy as fundamentally different than those belonging to the revolutionaries, and it is this difference which makes Baldwin so important.

In the essay, "Cleaver/Baldwin Revisited: Naturalism and the Gendering of Black Revolution," Nathaniel Mills closely examines the relationship between Eldridge Cleaver and James Baldwin. In the 1960s, Baldwin was on relatively good terms with King and Malcolm X, with whom he did not entirely agree, but by the 1970s Black nationalism was in full force, and outright condemned Baldwin as weak and effeminate. Despite this, Baldwin had become much more sympathetic to the Black nationalist movement after the assassinations of King and Malcolm X. Mills argues that Baldwin's novel, *If Beale Street Could Talk* (1974), "shows Baldwin revising black nationalism's separatist, heteropatriarchal, and masculinist tendencies while appropriating its revolutionary militancy."[40] Mills contends that Baldwin served as a "midwife" to help deliver Black nationalism's message by recasting their politics in a less divisive light.

While Mills's argument helpfully illustrates the distinction I was drawing earlier—Baldwin adapting revolutionary rhetoric to be less divisive certainly fits his non-revolutionary identity—I find the method by which Mills makes his argument to be even more relevant. He is very deliberate in his use of the term "revolutionary"; it is only reserved as a descriptive term for Cleaver. Baldwin is *always* referred to as the "artist." Mills's ultimate point is that *both* parties are needed, that "Revolution requires the artisanal and political labor of revaluing realities and relationships while organizing communities."[41] This point echoes Malcolm X's assertion that he was the warrior of the revolution and Baldwin was the poet. But the relationship between the warrior/revolutionary and the poet/artist is not always as good natured and respectful as it was for Malcolm X and Baldwin.

Cleaver's *Soul on Ice* was an outright attack on Baldwin, on his sexuality as a "political backstabbing" and "white aberrancy," but also on "what [Cleaver] sees as Baldwin's emasculated, non-violent politics of 'Martin Luther King-type' supplication to white rule."[42] Baldwin's approach was not revolutionary enough for Cleaver, and so it was insufficient. Yet it is Baldwin, not Cleaver, who is seeing a significant resurgence in our modern racial discourse.

The distinction that Mills made in his article can be found in the work of other Baldwin scholars. In "James Baldwin, 1963, and the House that Race Built," Fredrick Harris sets out to distinguish Baldwin's rhetoric from that of his contemporaries by covering the political events of 1963 and comparing King, Malcolm X, and Baldwin. Harris's real focus, however, is on the present, and the numerous incidents of racial conflict that have erupted in recent years. Harris details instances of racism and racial profiling from the last couple of decades, including the shooting of Trayvon Martin, to demonstrate that King's and Malcolm X's approaches have not been enough to change things. Harris then cites Deborah Hughes, a Black woman who threw herself over the body of a white man being attacked by residents of a predominantly Black neighborhood after accidentally striking a boy with his car. When asked why she came to help when no one else would, Hughes, Harris argues, "responded in words that transcended—as Baldwin commanded—'the realities of color, of nation, and of altars' by answering plaintively, gracefully, without irony and in words Baldwin might have whispered into her ear, 'He was a man, he wasn't white.'"[43] Harris goes beyond simply arguing that Baldwin's philosophy is different than his contemporaries; he contends that it is in fact more important than theirs for our particular cultural moment. Baldwin's instruction to rise above social boundaries and recognize that we are all people, that we all live in the same house, provides us a path toward healing the racial divide where previous attempts to overthrow it failed. Harris concludes that "Baldwin speaks more to America's current state of racial quagmire than the insights of either King or Malcolm X."[44]

James Miller adopts a similar approach in "Integration, Transformation and the Redemption of America: *The Fire Next Time* and 'A Letter from Birmingham Jail,'" to argue for the significance of Baldwin's contributions to civil rights discourse. Miller compares both pieces for their themes on family, love, and the Church, and notes that Baldwin was more interested in exploring personal issues, and that Baldwin was consistently more abstract and less pragmatic than King. Miller writes, "King's emphasis on the public sphere forms a practical appeal for ending the social reality of segregation. Baldwin, in contrast, presents the social sphere as the material contradiction of much more involved and complicated ideologies."[45] Where King pushes a series of pragmatic political goals, Baldwin advocates for a "recognition of a common American heritage," that will "allow white and black to affirm each other on a personal level," and lead to broader and more permanent social change.[46] Miller's distinction between the pragmatic and ideological approaches points toward the differing objectives of the two men. King had clearly identified an adversary, a system of power, and had drawn battle plans with which to fight back, even if the fighting was not martial. Baldwin, on the other hand, was preaching abstractions, new perspectives on America and the people in it. It is much more difficult to identify the "utility" of Baldwin's ideas than it is King's, because King's are grounded in pragmatic goals and specific strategies against a specific legal regime, segregation.

Yet Miller concludes that Baldwin "proposes a more far-reaching vision of integration than the pragmatic politics of King's actual Civil Rights campaign."[47] He argues that King's determination to make a difference in the day-to-day lives of African Americans ultimately limited the impact of those pragmatic goals, while Baldwin "enlarged the circumference of what was considered 'political'" by "demonstrating the ways in which psychological problems of race and racism blur the margins of conventional political discourse."[48] Like Mills in his comparison of Baldwin and Cleaver, Miller emphasizes the importance of Baldwin's contributions to the civil rights movement, even if their impact was not as immediately clear as King's. Baldwin did not view race as a problem that could be solved simply by changing some laws; instead, he focused his energies on developing the racial discourse, on supplying us with the tools we need to one day make the personal changes that we all must make in order to live together in a country built upon the "mythology of race."

Baldwin does not give his reader a simple task, or inform them of an adversary, or a concrete obstacle to overcome. Instead, as Harris put it, he transcends the boundaries of these systems to teach us how to live our lives and how to heal society. For this reason, time has proven Baldwin to be an essential voice of the civil rights era. Alone, his non-revolutionary approach may not be enough. But the same might very well be said of the activism of King, Malcolm X, and other revolutionaries. A common theme among scholars comparing Baldwin with other civil rights leaders is that regardless of their ideological differences, all of their voices are needed to represent the entire scope of racial injustice and conflict. And so it must be recognized that the revolutionary needs the artist, and that the artist is not worth less because he is not a revolutionary. Baldwin once said, "The poet or the revolutionary is there to articulate the necessity, but until the people themselves apprehend it, nothing can happen … Perhaps it can't be done without the poet, but it certainly can't be done without the people."[49] The path forward may not be simply a choice of which activist to follow. It may instead be a recognition that Baldwinian artists and revolutionaries must go hand in hand. Together they form the body and soul of a powerful social movement, fighting for concrete change while guided by a transcendent conscience.

Notes

1 "The Black Scholar Interviews: James Baldwin," *The Black Scholar,* 5:4 (1973), p. 40.
2 Karen Thorsen and William Miles (dir.), *James Baldwin: The Price of the Ticket* (California Newsreel, 1990).
3 Justin Joyce, Dwight A. McBride, and Douglas Field, "Baltimore Is Still Burning: The Rising Relevance of James Baldwin," *James Baldwin Review*, 1 (2015), p. 3.
4 James Campbell, *Talking at the Gates: A Life of James Baldwin* (New York, Viking, 1991), p. 206.

5 Karen Thorsen (dir.), *James Baldwin: The Price of the Ticket* (1990).

6 Adam Barnett, "James Baldwin, Revolutionary Humanist," *Little Atoms*, 4 May 2017, http://littleatoms.com/culture-film-music/james-baldwin-revolutionary-humanist (accessed 31 January 2020); Emil Wilkebin, "James Baldwin: Revolutionary Reflections," *AFROPUNK*, 2 August 2018, https://afropunk.com/2018/08/james-baldwin-revolutionary-reflections/ (accessed 2 January 2020).

7 Bill V. Mullen, *James Baldwin: Living in Fire* (London, Pluto Press, 2019); Davis W. Houck, "'Who's the Nigger Now?': Rhetoric and Identity in James Baldwin's Revolution from Within," *James Baldwin Review*, 3 (2017), pp. 110–30; Stuart Hall, "'You a Fat Cow Now,' Review of *Tell Me How Long the Train's Been Gone*, by James Baldwin," *New Statesman*, 28 June 1968, p. 871.

8 "Malcolm X: Message to Grassroots," Teaching American History, http://teachingamericanhistory.org/library/document/message-to-grassroots/ (accessed 31 January 2019).

9 *Ibid.*

10 *Ibid.*

11 Joshua Bloom and Waldo E. Martin, *Black Against Empire* (Berkeley, CA, University of California Press, 2013).

12 Martin Luther King Jr., "Letter From a Birmingham Jail," p. 7, The Martin Luther King, Jr. Research and Education Institute, https://kinginstitute.stanford.edu/king-papers/documents/letter-birmingham-jail (accessed 1 March 2020).

13 *Ibid.*, p. 4.

14 Martin Luther King, Jr., "Beyond Vietnam," The Martin Luther King, Jr. Research and Education Institute, http://kinginstitute.stanford.edu/king-papers/documents/beyond-vietnam (accessed 22 January 2019).

15 Martin Luther King, Jr., "Remaining Awake Through a Great Revolution," The Martin Luther King, Jr. Research and Education Institute, https://kinginstitute.stanford.edu/king-papers/publications/knock-midnight-inspiration-great-sermons-reverend-martin-luther-king-jr-10 (accessed 15 June 2020).

16 James Baldwin, "We Can Change the Country" (1963), in *The Cross of Redemption: Uncollected Writings*, ed. Randall Kenan (New York, Pantheon Books, 2010), p. 48.

17 Robert Penn Warren, *Who Speaks for the Negro?* (New York, Random House, 1965), p. 280.

18 James Baldwin, "Anti-Semitism and Black Power" (1967), in Kenan (ed.), *The Cross of Redemption*, p. 204.

19 David Leeming, *James Baldwin: A Biography* (New York, Alfred Knopf, 1994), p. 308.

20 James Baldwin, *The Devil Finds Work* (1976), in *Collected Essays*, ed. Toni Morrison (New York, Library of America, 1998), p. 488.

21 *Ibid.*, pp. 488–9.

22 *Ibid.*, p. 498; James Baldwin, *No Name in the Street* (1972), in Morrison (ed.), *Collected Essays*, p. 409.

23 James Baldwin, *The Fire Next Time* (New York, Vintage International, 1993), p. 90.

24 James Baldwin, "An Open Letter to My Sister Angela Y. Davis" (1970), in Kenan (ed.), *The Cross of Redemption*, p. 211.

25 Fredrick Harris, "James Baldwin, 1963, and the House That Race Built," *Transition*, 115 (2014), p. 54.

26 Baldwin, *Fire Next Time*, p. 105.

27 *Ibid.*, p. 91.

28 *Ibid.*

29 "Malcolm X: Message to Grassroots."
30 James Baldwin, *Another Country* (New York, Dial Press, 1962), p. 67.
31 *Ibid.*, pp. 584–5.
32 *Ibid.*, p. 58.
33 *Ibid.*, p. 79.
34 James Baldwin, *Go Tell It on the Mountain* (New York, Dell, 1969), p. 167.
35 Bill Lyne, "God's Black Revolutionary Mouth: James Baldwin's Black Radicalism," *Science & Society*, 74:1 (2010), p. 14.
36 Campbell, *Talking at the Gates*, p. 175, quoted in Douglas Field, "Looking for Jimmy Baldwin: Sex, Privacy, and Black Nationalist Fervor," *Callaloo*, 27:2 (2004), p. 460.
37 Quoted in Field, "Looking for Jimmy Baldwin," p. 460.
38 *Ibid.*
39 *Ibid.*, p. 472.
40 Nathaniel Mills, "Cleaver/Baldwin Revisited: Naturalism and the Gendering of Black Revolution," *Studies in American Naturalism*, 7:1 (2012), p. 52.
41 *Ibid.*, p. 73.
42 *Ibid.*, p. 55.
43 Harris, "James Baldwin, 1963, and The House That Race Built," p. 60.
44 *Ibid.*, p. 66.
45 James Miller, "Integration, Transformation and the Redemption of America: *The Fire Next Time* and 'A Letter from Birmingham Jail,'" *European Journal of American Culture*, 28:3 (2009), p. 253.
46 *Ibid.*, p. 258.
47 *Ibid.*, p. 247.
48 *Ibid.*, p. 246.
49 "The Black Scholar Interviews," p. 40.

Works Cited

Baldwin, James, *Another Country* (New York, Dial Press, 1962).
_____ "Anti-Semitism and Black Power" (1967), in *The Cross of Redemption: Uncollected Writings*, ed. Randall Kenan (New York, Pantheon Books, 2010), pp. 203–5.
_____ "The Devil Finds Work" (1975), in *Collected Essays*, ed. Toni Morrison (New York, Library of America, 1998), pp. 479–572.
_____ *The Fire Next Time* (New York, Vintage International, 1993).
_____ *Go Tell It on the Mountain* (New York, Dell, 1969).
_____ *No Name in the Street* (1972), in *Collected Essays*, ed. Toni Morrison (New York, Library of America, 1998), pp. 353–475.
_____ "An Open Letter to My Sister Angela Y. Davis" (1970), in *The Cross of Redemption: Uncollected Writings*, ed. Randall Kenan (New York, Pantheon Books, 2010), pp. 206–11.
_____ "We Can Change the Country" (1963), in *The Cross of Redemption: Uncollected Writings*, ed. Randall Kenan (New York, Pantheon Books, 2010), pp. 48–52.
Barnett, Adam, "James Baldwin, Revolutionary Humanist," *Little Atoms*, 4 May 2017, http://littleatoms.com/culture-film-music/james-baldwin-revolutionary-humanist (accessed 31 January 2020).
"The Black Scholar Interviews: James Baldwin," *The Black Scholar*, 5:4 (1973), pp. 33–42.
Bloom, Joshua, and Waldo E. Martin, *Black Against Empire* (Berkeley, CA, University of California Press, 2013).

Campbell, James, *Talking at the Gates; A Life of James Baldwin* (New York, Viking, 1991).

Field, Douglas, "Looking for Jimmy Baldwin: Sex, Privacy, and Black Nationalist Fervor," *Callaloo*, 27:2 (2004), pp. 457–80, doi:10.1353/cal.2004.0063.

Gates, Jr., Henry Louis, "The Black Man's Burden," in Michael Warner (ed.), *Fear of a Queer Planet: Queer Politics and Social Theory* (Minneapolis, MN, University of Minneapolis Press, 1993), pp. 230–8.

Hall, Stuart, "'You a Fat Cow Now,' Review of *Tell Me How Long the Train's Been Gone*, by James Baldwin," *New Statesman*, 28 June 1968, p. 871.

Harris, Fredrick, "James Baldwin, 1963, and the House That Race Built," *Transition*, 115 (2014), pp. 52–67, doi:10.2979/transition.115.52.

Houck, Davis W., "'Who's the Nigger Now?': Rhetoric and Identity in James Baldwin's Revolution from Within," *James Baldwin Review*, 3 (2017), pp. 110–30, doi:10.7227/jbr.3.7.

Joyce, Justin A., Dwight A. McBride, and Douglas Field, "Baltimore Is Still Burning: the Rising Relevance of James Baldwin," *James Baldwin Review*, 1 (2015), pp. 1–9, doi:10.7227/jbr.1.1.

King, Martin Luther, Jr., "Beyond Vietnam," The Martin Luther King, Jr. Research and Education Institute, http://kinginstitute.stanford.edu/king-papers/documents/beyond-vietnam (accessed 22 January 2019).

———— "Letter From a Birmingham Jail," The Martin Luther King, Jr. Research and Education Institute, https://kinginstitute.stanford.edu/king-papers/documents/letter-birmingham-jail (accessed 1 March 2020).

———— "Remaining Awake Through a Great Revolution," The Martin Luther King, Jr. Research and Education Institute, https://kinginstitute.stanford.edu/king-papers/publications/knock-midnight-inspiration-great-sermons-reverend-martin-luther-king-jr-10 (accessed 2 January 2020).

Leeming, David, *James Baldwin: A Biography* (New York, Alfred Knopf, 1994).

Lyne, Bill, "God's Black Revolutionary Mouth: James Baldwin's Black Radicalism," *Science & Society*, 74:1 (2010), pp. 12–26.

"Malcolm X: Message to Grassroots," Teaching American History, http://teachingamericanhistory.org/library/document/message-to-grassroots/ (accessed 31 January 2019).

Miller, James, "Integration, Transformation and the Redemption of America: *The Fire Next Time* and 'A Letter from Birmingham Jail,'" *European Journal of American Culture*, 28:3 (2009), pp. 245–62, doi:10.1386/ejac.28.3.245_1.

Mills, Nathaniel, "Cleaver/Baldwin Revisited: Naturalism and the Gendering of Black Revolution," *Studies in American Naturalism*, 7:1 (2012), pp. 50–79, doi:10.1353/san.2012.0002.

Mullen, Bill V., *James Baldwin: Living in Fire* (London, Pluto Press, 2019).

Thorsen, Karen, and William Miles (dir.), *James Baldwin: The Price of the Ticket* (California Newsreel, 1990).

Warren, Robert Penn, *Who Speaks for the Negro?* (New York, Random House, 1965).

Wilbekin, Emil, "James Baldwin: Revolutionary Reflections," *AFROPUNK*, 2 August 2018, https://afropunk.com/2018/08/james-baldwin-revolutionary-reflections/ (accessed 2 January 2020).

Contributor's Biography

Nicholas Binford is a graduate student at Washington State University completing his master's thesis on representations of deviance in literature.

GRADUATE STUDENT ESSAY

Baptism by History: Reading James Baldwin's Existential Hindsight in *Go Tell It on the Mountain*

Miller Wilbourn   University of Texas at Austin

Abstract

This essay reads James Baldwin's first novel, *Go Tell It on the Mountain*, through the lenses of European existentialism and Black existential thought to arrive at a new understanding of the novel itself as well as essential stages of its development. Archival sources and close reading reveal Baldwin's historically and existentially informed artistic vision, summed up in the terms *hindsight* and *insight*. His thoughtful, uncomfortable engagement with the past leads to a recuperated relationship to the community and constitutes existential hindsight, which informs his inward understanding of himself—his insight. This investigation draws on various works from Baldwin's fiction, essays, interviews, and correspondence to arrive at a better understanding of the writer's intellectual and artistic development, focusing especially on the professed objectives behind, and major revisions of, the novel. I conclude the essay through a close reading of the conversion scene that constitutes Part Three of *Go Tell It on the Mountain*.

Keywords: James Baldwin, Jean-Paul Sartre, existentialism, Black existentialism, *Go Tell It on the Mountain*, Christianity

On 11 November 1948, James Baldwin left for Paris with only forty dollars to his name. He waited until the day of departure to inform his mother and sisters of his flight from Harlem, and then boarded the plane despite their tears and protests with a one-way ticket.[1] The young writer left not because of what he hoped to find in Paris, but because of what he had to escape in America. In his own words, "I left America because I doubted my ability to survive the fury of the color problem there."[2] In a later interview, Baldwin put it more bluntly: "I didn't know what was going to happen to me in France but I knew what was going to happen to me in

James Baldwin Review, Volume 6, 2020, © The Authors. Published by Manchester University Press and The University of Manchester Library
http://dx.doi.org/10.7227/JBR.6.8

New York. If I had stayed there, I would have gone under, like my friend on the George Washington Bridge."[3]

As Baldwin's plane landed in Paris, four men were drinking coffee at Les Deux Magots, a famous Parisian café known as the favorite meeting spot of many of the city's intellectual elite. Among the four were Richard Wright, renowned American author of *Native Son* (1939) and Baldwin's literary mentor, and existentialist philosopher Jean-Paul Sartre, who is less commonly associated with Baldwin.[4] Wright left to meet Baldwin upon his arrival, but the other men kept talking.[5] It is easy to imagine the heat of the conversations in similar cafés between the intellectual giants of Paris in those years—minds like Sartre and Simone de Beauvoir exchanging ideas with writers like Baldwin or Wright, debating politics, discussing philosophy, dissecting literature, and sharing stories. Perhaps the meetings occasionally involved more than a few drinks. Perhaps voices were raised, or feelings were hurt, epiphanies reached, and friendships were forged and broken. We can be sure that writers, philosophers, and activists grappled with many of the same questions, and came to disparate conclusions.

This essay brings together two questioners in particular, reading the works of Baldwin and Sartre side-by-side in order to shed light on similarities in the two thinkers' questions as well as significant differences in the answers they seem to have found. More specifically, it draws a comparison between the existential dimensions of Baldwin's thought and the model of existential humanism of which Sartre is the primary architect. This comparison is especially relevant when coupled with questions concerning the literary challenges that Baldwin appears to have faced during the decade-long struggle to write his seminal novel, *Go Tell It on the Mountain* (1953), and the climactic nervous breakdown and recovery, as told by Baldwin, that led to its ultimate completion.

Baldwin's participation in Paris's salon culture is undeniable, but there is less information available as to the specific questions he asked and answered in those days. Baldwin and Wright's relationship is well documented and the subject of much critical discussion. Wright took Baldwin under his wing when the fledgling author was still living in Harlem, and even landed him his first writing fellowship for a project that would eventually become *Go Tell It*.[6] He also facilitated Baldwin's debut in Parisian social and literary circles and helped him find lodging in the city.[7] The more turbulent years of the two writers' friendship began with the publication of Baldwin's essay, "Everybody's Protest Novel," in 1949, which critiqued Wright's novel, *Native Son*, as a simplistic work of protest fiction, and the resulting fallout between Baldwin and Wright has been discussed at length.[8]

Considerably less work, however, explores the relationship between Baldwin and Sartre, two men of widely different backgrounds and literary dispositions, who nevertheless ran in some of the same circles in the Paris of the 1940s and 1950s. The record of communication between the novelist and the philosopher is slim—apparently the two did not meet on the day of Baldwin's arrival in Paris— but sources attest to the acquaintance of the two, and Baldwin mentions Sartre briefly and disparagingly in his writing.[9] He told Julius Lester in a 1984 interview that he thought Richard Wright "was much, much better than a lot of the company he kept," particularly "the French existentialists … Simone de Beauvoir [and] Jean-Paul Sartre."[10] In his essay, "Alas, Poor Richard," in which he addresses his relationship with Wright, Baldwin admits that he "distrusted [Wright's] association" with Sartre and de Beauvoir.[11] He explains his distaste in the same essay: "It has always seemed to me that ideas were somewhat more real to [the French existentialists] than people."[12] This criticism is consistent with Baldwin's assertion throughout his oeuvre that the complexity and uniqueness of the individual is more important for a writer than any ideology or system of beliefs.[13]

It is useful to remember Baldwin's own admission of his tendency to "argue with people who do not disagree with [him] too profoundly" from the autobiographical notes that introduce his 1955 essay collection, *Notes of a Native Son*.[14] Certainly Baldwin levels harsh critiques at other writers and public intellectuals throughout his writing, but, as Leeming documents, he also considered many of those with whom he voiced the most significant differences his closest friends.[15] In his essay "Alas, Poor Richard," Baldwin confesses that he did not think that he had "attacked" Wright in "Everybody's Protest Novel," and that he did not consider that he had "even criticized [Wright's novel]."[16] The writer goes on to confess that Wright's work was "a road-block … the sphinx, really, whose riddles I had to answer before I could become myself," and that he "used [Wright's] work as a springboard into [his] own."[17] In the same spirit, reading Baldwin's work alongside Black existential thought's criticism of, and innovation upon, European existentialism offers insights that are productive, often through contrast.

It is also important to recognize that by 1948, existentialism in general, and its more specific articulation as existential humanism by Sartre, were being discussed by intellectuals throughout Paris and internationally—and Baldwin was an active participant in the literary, artistic, and philosophical culture in Paris, as documented by George Cotkin and Douglas Field.[18] Field thoughtfully surveys Baldwin's journey to, and life in, Paris, traces Baldwin's developing thoughts on American identity, and explores the ways that his sojourn abroad contributed to these thoughts. Field also discusses Baldwin's motivations for leaving the "racial and social nightmare" in America and his decision to invest in his growth as an artist at a distance from such turmoil.[19] Field's contribution is particularly useful in its study of Baldwin's essays on Paris, beginning with "Everybody's Protest Novel," which attests to his feeling of isolation abroad.[20] Especially relevant is Field's work in explaining the various dimensions of Baldwin's sense of isolation in Paris: personal, as evidenced in his "strained" relationship with Wright and lack of close friendships in the early Paris years; racial, as Baldwin articulated the self-imposed alienation between Black Americans who avoid one another to avoid painful thoughts of home; and intellectual, as Baldwin deliberately distanced himself from "established intellectual and artistic communities" in the city.[21]

In his more recent work, *All Those Strangers: The Art and Lives of James Baldwin*, Field attempts to make sense of the often contradictory and confusing web of Baldwin's life by reading him through different and evolving "lives" or identities, rather than trying to reconcile the seemingly disparate personas of Baldwin into one. The work includes chapters on Baldwin's Marxist background in New York, the record of his life through the F.B.I. file that was active from 1960 to 1974, the central religious themes of his corpus, and Baldwin's transnational life and writing. Notable particularly to this essay is Field's observation from the work's final chapter that contemporary "discussions in existentialism" in the 1940s and 1950s likely spoke to the way that "rigid identity categories were not only stifling but dangerous for Baldwin."[22] Field identifies Baldwin's works at the end of the 1940s and beginning of the 1950s as discussing "the ways that mainstream culture created and perpetuated myths about what it meant to be American," especially surrounding race, gender, and sexuality.[23]

Field does not go so far as to claim that Baldwin engaged intentionally or consciously with the philosophy of existentialism, and neither does this essay; however, it is probably not a coincidence that Baldwin, writing in the same historical moment that existentialism formally emerged on the intellectual scene, explores many questions and concepts through his work that seem to be existentially concerned. Lewis Gordon's work on Black existential philosophy is helpful in this distinction. He writes that Black thinkers at various points in history "have a reason to raise existential questions" concerning existence, identity, and humanity "by virtue of the historical fact of racial oppression."[24] These questions may not fall under the philosophical umbrella of European existentialism, but they are certainly *existential*. This essay will make the same distinction in comparing texts by Sartre or other philosophers that clearly participate in existentialism as a philosophy with aspects of Baldwin's writing that do not explicitly treat existential philosophy per se, but are existential in nature.

Bruce Lapenson's article, "Race and Existential Commitment in James Baldwin," argues generally for an affinity to existentialism in Baldwin's thought, with attention paid to philosophers such as Sartre, Martin Heidegger, and Albert Camus. Lapenson addresses anticipated objections to establishing Baldwin's existential commitment: existentialism's reputation for nihilist, lackadaisical moral attitudes seems incompatible with Baldwin's strong moral voice.[25] He addresses this and similar objections, arguing that they are based on a misunderstanding of existentialist doctrine, before proceeding to call attention to Baldwin's emphasis on community, his religious decentering, sense of forlornness, and call for eliminating self-delusion in personal and national contexts, all of which he identifies as examples of Baldwin's existentialism.[26] Lapenson also broaches some of the temporal relations that this essay will explore in greater depth in Baldwin's existentialism: the belief that the present and future are anchored in the past, and that we as a society have the responsibility and capability to create the future.[27] Lapenson's article is a useful introduction to certain aspects of Baldwin's existential thought, but does not examine any single work in depth, and fails to consider the relevant innovations of Black existentialism as useful models for understanding the author's work.

Radiclani Clytus's essay, "Paying Dues and Playing the Blues: Baldwin's Existential Jazz," conducts a particularly thoughtful analysis that unites Baldwin's existentialism with his discussion of music in a few essays, interviews, and the short story "Sonny's Blues." Through various examples, Clytus explores jazz as a vehicle used by Baldwin for reflecting on certain tenets of existentialism. The essay also puts Baldwin in dialogue with other contemporary writers like Ralph Ellison, as Clytus argues that both of the authors' work illustrates the fact that "black existence is struggle."[28] Sartre's 1946 essay, "Existentialism is a Humanism," features prominently in Clytus's examination of Baldwin's engagement with existentialism, and he illustrates the presence of Sartre's concepts of self-creation and rejection of determinism in Baldwin's oeuvre.[29] Clytus's most insightful contribution to the study of Baldwin's existentialism is his analysis of "Sonny's Blues." He identifies Baldwin's illustration of existential isolation in the story through the two brothers' strained relationship, as well as the challenge of existential awareness and the resulting anguish for the artist, as seen in Sonny's distressed state. Ultimately, Clytus demonstrates the ability of jazz to accomplish a kind of existential reconciliation between the brothers in the story's final scene at the jazz club.[30] Clytus's use of Baldwin's existential thought as a lens to better understand the author's reflections on jazz is productive, and supplements Lapenson's introductory exploration. It also serves as a useful foundation for this essay, as I explore the work of Baldwin in comparison to Sartre's existential humanism to clarify certain questions and obscurities in *Go Tell It on the Mountain* in similar fashion.

The work of Field, Lapenson, and Clytus constitutes a solid foundation for the application of an existential lens to Baldwin's work. The place for an intervention exists, however: whereas Field seeks to paint a more general picture of Baldwin's sojourn and suggests a possible overlap between the concerns of Baldwin and existentialist thought, this project seeks to investigate more deeply the contrast between Baldwin's uniquely Black existential concerns and those of the dominant forms of European existentialism. Lapenson's article offers a general and traditional existentialist reading of Baldwin's corpus, but does not take the focused approach this project will employ. Finally, Clytus's essay is an excellent example of the way that an existential lens can enhance our reading of Baldwin; my essay strives to both emulate its close reading and to identify fruitful connections between the works of Baldwin and Sartre by examining the development of *Go Tell It*.

A basic understanding of Sartre's essay "Existentialism is a Humanism" is necessary for our forthcoming comparison.[31] Sartre opens the essay by stating his purpose: "to offer a defense of existentialism against several reproaches that have been laid against it."[32] These are as follows: that the existentialist outlook encourages quietism and despair; that it is unnecessarily morbid and ignores "the brighter side of human nature"; and that it denies "the reality and seriousness of human affairs."[33] Sartre responds with the claim that existentialism is in fact a humanism because it places humans in control of their own fate and enables their self-realization through a process of "seeking, beyond [themselves], an aim" which they choose.[34] He clarifies that existentialism is not compatible with the brand of humanism that holds that the human is "the end-in-itself" or "the supreme value."[35] Sartre's existentialism is humanist in that it puts humans at the center, but it does not seek to deify them.

The bulk of the essay explores the humanist implications of the existentialism Sartre articulates. He begins with the primary doctrine of existentialism: "*existence comes before essence*."[36] For Sartre, humans are first born and define themselves afterwards; no one has predetermined a meaning or purpose for their lives. This is in contrast to the doctrine of human nature—which, to simplify here, holds that humans have a foundational, predestined character in common with one another—and divine sovereignty—which holds that God creates humans with a certain nature and trajectory. Since nothing is predetermined, Sartre writes, the human reality is one of choice. Humans must choose what to do and how to conceive of themselves. Sartre writes, "Man is nothing else but that which he makes of himself," and adds that humans must create themselves by choosing.[37] In other words, "man is condemned to be free."[38]

The realization of this freedom is central to Sartre's essay. He argues that people must come to terms with their existential condition—the lack of any predetermined meaning for their lives and the necessity of choice and self-creation—in order to fully understand themselves. And, Sartre argues, through self-discovery one "also discovers all the others," and "the intimate discovery of myself is at the same time the revelation of the other."[39] The process of self-discovery is also a process of understanding other people.

The necessity of choice for Sartre means that freedom is an unavoidable reality. He writes of the "complete and profound responsibility" that comes with such liberty.[40] Because humans must choose, they are also responsible for what their choices entail. In choosing something, they cannot avoid assigning value and meaning to it. And since nothing is predetermined, no concrete morality can serve as a guide for such choices: "No rule of general morality can show you what you ought to do."[41] The implication of this is that since there is no God "to invent values," the burden falls on our shoulders.[42] Accordingly, humans must invent their own morality in the same way that art is accomplished through "creation and invention."[43]

Sartre also emphasizes freedom as relational; he argues that one's freedom "depends entirely upon the freedom of others," so that one is "obliged to will the liberty of others at the same time as [one's] own."[44] The unavoidable reality of freedom—the fact that humans cannot avoid choice—means that humans cannot use any external factor to explain their actions. To do so would be "a dissimulation of man's complete liberty of commitment," Sartre writes, emphasizing humans' responsibility for their choices.[45] He argues that to use any excuse "by inventing some deterministic doctrine" is self-deception.[46] This is because the only determining factor is one's own will. The culmination of all of these doctrines of Sartre's existential humanism is as follows: the future is what we make it—that is to say, we can and must make it—and we cannot hide behind hope in God. We are our own only hope.[47] Of the various doctrines I have reviewed from Sartre's essay, the concepts that will be most important for our purposes are the necessity of self-discovery facilitated by others, revelation of the other as the consequence of self-discovery, and the ability of humans to create the future.

Now we can proceed to explore the ways that an understanding of Baldwin's existential hindsight, which bears key affinities to and differences from Sartre's philosophical worldview, serves as a lens for reading *Go Tell It on the Mountain*. First I will explore the course of *Go Tell It*'s evolution in order to better understand Baldwin's aims for the novel before proceeding to a close reading of the prolonged dramatic scene that comprises its third part. Building on Field's evaluation of Baldwin's completion of the semi-autobiographical novel as both "something akin to the experience of religious conversion," and "an attempt to come to terms with and exorcise his Sanctified past," I argue that this scene in particular signifies a kind of existential conversion beneath the surface of the religious imagery that pervades it.[48] In this scene the protagonist undergoes a personal but community-oriented episode that involves confronting the past and his place in a racist world. The novel proceeds through rising action and tension to a climactic moment of self-realization, resulting ultimately in a state of existential and intellectual freedom, and a more authentic relationship to the community.

It took ten years for Baldwin to write this novel. He cited the harrowing impact of racism on his life in New York as one impediment to his writing, but his departure for Paris did not result in an immediate "breakthrough"—Baldwin did not finish the manuscript until February of 1952, over three years after his arrival in Europe.[49] In his essay, "The Discovery of What It Means To Be an American," Baldwin writes about a nervous breakdown he experienced in 1951 and his subsequent recovery in the small Swiss village of Loèche-les-Bains, where he finished the manuscript for *Go Tell It*. He writes that in Paris he shed his "social paranoia" and "began to see" that "he [was] accessible to everyone and open to everything."[50] Specifically in reference to his breakdown, Baldwin describes his realization that for both Black and white people, "no matter where our fathers had been born, or what they had endured, the fact of Europe" was "a part of our identity and part of our inheritance."[51] These two recognitions—first of the fact of community and connectedness and second of the unavoidability of historical legacy—can be read to signify Baldwin's "breakthrough" in the village.

Many aspects of Baldwin's plan for *Go Tell It* changed over the years of its development, but the author's notes show that John Grimes's familial and racial background were central from the start. In an "Outline for a Novel" contained in Baldwin's recently acquired papers at the Schomburg Center for Research in Black Culture, he writes that John's history includes "generations and centuries of unfulfilled hatred," and elaborates that this hatred is "so deep as to be almost wholly inarticulate and even unsuspected."[52] Baldwin refers to the unresolved emotion present in the psyche of Black people that inevitably results from four hundred years of their ancestors' enslavement. He explains that it runs so deep that it is nearly impossible to recognize. "[B]ecause it has lived under-ground so long," this hatred has a special "subtle and distorting power" that pervades John's experience of reality, making the world "ambiguous and full of terror."[53] Since this force is so subtle and destructive at the same time, it constitutes a significant part of the barrier between John and his self-realization—he must face his history to overcome it.

In his outline, Baldwin continues to explain that no one is able to "break through the web of centuries of anger and guilt and terror and desire to be united with his own experience."[54] This, he writes, "might be called the American dilemma."[55] In his 1962 essay, "The Creative Process," Baldwin articulates the problem more personally: "whoever cannot tell himself the truth about his past is trapped in it, is immobilized in the prison of his undiscovered self."[56] Although he and others of his generation did not directly experience centuries of slavery, its impact on the world they inhabit is undeniable. The legacy of American slavery, as well as the continued injustice visited on Black people, has an alienating effect, Baldwin argues. If one cannot come to terms with the history of American racism, then one cannot hope to confront one's own experience. Similarly, in his 1950 essay, "Encounter on the Seine," Baldwin states that "[t]his depthless alienation from oneself and one's people is, in sum, the American experience."[57] He adds that this experience leads to a "battle for [one's] own identity" and a fight to "articulate to [oneself] or to others the uniqueness of [one's] experience."[58] This struggle of alienation from history is central to the novel from its earliest conception, and we will see that Baldwin's success in directly facing the past constitutes his existential hindsight.

Thus far Baldwin's notes have mostly addressed themes that are apparent in the novel that was ultimately published. However, a closer look at the major differences that appear between Baldwin's earlier plans as articulated in his "Outline for a Novel" from 1950 and the published work offers insight into the objectives the author prioritized. By assuming that Baldwin's thematic objectives remained relatively consistent, it is possible to surmise that he changed his plans for the novel's plot in order to better accomplish his vision for the work. A comparison of the early and final versions yields a better understanding of this vision.

Baldwin's notes in 1950 show that the earlier plan for the novel narrated the involvement of Roy, the protagonist's stepbrother, with a gang, including a robbery for which he is caught and sentenced to reform school.[59] This version also described his romantic involvement with a girl from the neighborhood in which John's family lives, and ultimately his fathering of a child with her.[60] Simultaneous with Roy's struggles with law and family, John would be losing his faith. Baldwin explains, "For his belief, primitive and powerful, is not strong enough to withstand his own increasing sophistication, the force of the outside world, the force of his own needs."[61] It appears that Roy serves as a foil to clarify John's position: as John watches his brother fall prey to the dangers of growing up in Harlem, he begins to abandon his faith in order to face and overcome these dangers. This is in contrast to the published version of the novel, where Gabriel and family history serve to illustrate the danger of John's position in the world.

After Roy's return from reform school, the notes describe a conversation between the two brothers in which John realizes and says aloud that he "no longer believes."[62] This "lost salvation" becomes his "first release" according to the notes, and "it explodes something in his spirit, in his mind."[63] John's departure from faith acts as an existential springboard that catapults him into a brighter, freer future. John finds that "he has never been so close" with Roy.[64] The notes elaborate:

[H]e recognizes dimly, with horror and with exultation, the *depths of his alienation* and, at the same time, the passion and the *power and the hope of his involvement*. John goes back to his books, daring consciously now to dream of the day he will be free of his father and his fathers' God.[65]

John's comprehension of his alienation leads to his realization of power and hope, and allows him to see the possibility of future freedom, just as Sartre describes in his essay; coming to terms with our position in the universe is difficult, but it also empowers us by placing our fate in our own hands.[66] Despite the existential significance of the protagonist's self-realization, this version is much less dramatic than the one that is ultimately narrated in the published novel's final section, "The Threshing Floor."

As has been established, the completed novel takes a course markedly different from the outline contained in Baldwin's papers, but I maintain that the transformation John experiences in *Go Tell It on the Mountain* holds essentially the same significance as the one described above. In the final version, Baldwin decides to couch the conversion experience in the diction and imagery of an enthusiastic Pentecostal tradition, rather than take the earlier, more explicit approach of breaking John free from the Church.[67] This approach runs counter to the autobiographical knowledge we have of Baldwin's experience of ultimately leaving the Church rather than experiencing conversion or revival at this stage of life.[68] The original plan would seem to show a stronger resemblance to Sartre's model for self-realization, while the published novel demonstrates Baldwin's own existential vision in emphasizing the importance of confronting the past in the process of self-realization.

Many of the same elements in this early version of the story are found in the eventual novel: John's confrontation with his alienation, a rejection of the determinist forces of Harlem and Gabriel's religion, mediation of self-discovery by others, and the sense of empowerment that follows from existential realization. A comparison shows that Baldwin revised his original plan by giving considerably more time and attention to John Grimes's encounter with his family history. From his early notes it is apparent that Baldwin planned all along on using the novel to address "the American inability to comprehend or be related to the past," but only later determined how to best do so.[69]

Baldwin's notes from 1950 make it clear that John is the story's protagonist, and that the author plans to spend the bulk of the novel telling his story.[70] Other characters will occupy some portion of the spotlight, but only insofar as they develop and contextualize John's story. Gabriel and Elizabeth both play important parts, and it seems that Baldwin knew from the start that Gabriel's past would be largely responsible for John's torment and an obstacle to his coming to terms with the past. But in the novel eventually published, Gabriel's own story, beginning years earlier, comes to occupy almost as much space as John's, and serves to explain the convoluted, bitter relationship between stepfather and son. It follows that at some point, or over some period, Baldwin drastically revised his plan for the novel.

A letter from the James Baldwin Papers at the Schomburg Center for Research in Black Culture in Harlem, signed R. N. Linscott (whom the archive designates an "unknown author"), advises an also unknown third party on how Baldwin might revise an early draft of the novel.[71] Linscott's letter implies that he does not know Baldwin personally but has acquired and read the draft through the unknown third party. He writes that it is "an honest book" but says that he sees no reason to believe the claim that Baldwin "is an authentic genius and the most promising of all negro writers."[72] Linscott continues, "Its [sic] my own feeling … that he will never make Johnny's story into a good novel as this is the part thats [sic] all autobiography and self pity."[73] Stopping here, a reader might write off Linscott's harsh words, considering the monumental success the novel enjoyed when published. We may be tempted to object that Baldwin's autobiographical input is exactly what makes the book so personal and powerful—but this would be getting ahead of ourselves.

Further reading reveals the debt Baldwin may in fact owe to Linscott, despite the critic's harsh tone:

> What I wish he would do is reconstitute it entirely, make it the life story of Gabriel Grimes … have his life one long desperate battle between sin and repentence … Theres [sic] a real novel in Gabriel, the story of a vital, facinating [sic], complex character; … This novel would excite me; the story of Johnny would, I'm afraid, only bore me.[74]

All the archive offers is the letter, undated, by an author whose name is unfamiliar. Simply by comparing the notes from 1950 (also present in the archive) with the final version of *Go Tell It*, I must surmise that the letter came to Baldwin prior to his major revision of the novel, and I wager that the letter inspired his changes to a considerable degree. Baldwin certainly did not turn his novel exclusively into the story of Gabriel, but the final work covers much more that is seemingly extraneous to the story of John than the outline from 1950 would suggest.

Of the novel's 226 pages in the 2013 Vintage edition, at least 100 are devoted to the stories of Gabriel and, more peripherally, of Elizabeth and John's biological father, Richard.[75] The novel's exploration of these characters' pasts is essential to its presentation of John's transformation, as well as its symbolic statements about the nation: in a letter to his publisher from the end of 1952 discussing edits to the final manuscript, Baldwin stresses that the novel's narration of Gabriel's story is central because it seeks "to suggest, symbolically, the history of the Negro people in America."[76] Perhaps the first version might have been a bit boring, without the background and foils necessary to bring John's story to life. Only a thoughtful, complex meditation on the religious and racist forces that so restricted and tormented Gabriel can illuminate the struggles that John inherits from his stepfather. And only then does the throwing off of such chains gain a powerful, dramatic effect—when the reader sees how many miles and years backward they stretch. With this revision, the consequences of Baldwin's existential hindsight become clear—that the look inward must necessarily involve a long and painful look backward, even generations beyond one's birth. Otherwise *Go Tell It* might have turned out to be "all autobiography and self pity" after all.

Baldwin's breakthrough with *Go Tell It* can be usefully read alongside an account of Black existentialism and its critique of European existentialism. Linwood G.

Vereen et al. note in their article, "Black Existentialism: Extending the Discourse on Meaning and Existence," that while European and Black existentialism are concerned with many of the same questions—concerning human identity, agency, and meaning—Black existentialism sees the European model as insufficient for those who are subject to the ubiquitous anti-Black violence of a racist world. The authors argue that "[European existentialist] premises fail to consider the influence and dynamic of social constructions, such as marginalization and racialization, on the individual's developmental understanding of self and others."[77] These social constructions ensure that Black people inhabit a world which, from birth, seeks constantly to impose on them an oppressive, subhuman essence. In such a world, it is impossible to follow Sartre's advice and simply assert an essence; one is reminded of Baldwin's critique that the European existentialists fail to grasp human realities.[78] Afro-pessimist thinkers such as Calvin Warren argue that humanism as a philosophy excludes Black people altogether—or rather, it depends upon Blackness as an essential opposite to the positive characteristics of the human. In Warren's words, humanism "allows the Human to differentiate himself from and define himself against an ultimate other," which is the Black nonhuman.[79]

While some Afro-pessimists are skeptical of any potential for liberation within humanism because it constitutes a state of nonhumanity for Black people, other Black existential thinkers theorize a path forward that resists the erasure of Black humanity. The reality of Blackness and the violent anti-Black structures upon which society is built must be addressed directly through what Vereen et al. call "truth-telling," so that affirmative, humanizing conceptions of Blackness and, thus, people who are Black may be restored.[80] In the space created by this process of truth telling—called *homeplace* by bell hooks in the context of the oppression of Black women in particular—the enterprise of claiming a fully human identity independent of anti-Black definitions can take place.[81] In sum, Black existentialism answers Sartre's claim that "existence precedes essence" with an assertion of the value of the individual's relationship to the collective, best summed up in the African Ubuntu maxim, "I am because we are."[82] Scholar Ed Pavlić identifies a similar concept in his study of Baldwin, which he calls "mutual consequence," and defines as "a people's affirmative sense of itself, grounded in their transformed sense of each other."[83] Black existentialism's emphasis on the value of the collective as well as the individual makes space for the search for identity, while it also "honors the humanity in others revealing the interconnectedness of all that is, was, and will be," according to Vereen et al.[84]

Having studied Baldwin's aims for his novel as articulated in his notes and keeping in mind our discussion of Black existential thought's innovation upon European existentialism, the stage is set to engage in a close reading of Part Three from *Go Tell It*, entitled "The Threshing Floor." Immediately following the novel's prolonged narration of the life stories of Gabriel and Elizabeth, the narrator turns to a particularly charismatic evening church service where John finds himself collapsed on the floor of the Temple of the Fire Baptized in a fit of religious fervor, surrounded by the congregants who are likewise overcome with zeal.[85] Baldwin uses obscurely symbolic language throughout "The Threshing Floor," but the existential lens offers a clarifying reading of the stages of John's conversion as well as the salient symbols involved. First, John finds himself under the power of Gabriel's determinist religion, then challenges and overcomes it. Next he encounters the symbol of the "cloud of witnesses," which represents the community and history through which he must come to self-knowledge. John's realization of his relationship to the community through this "cloud of witnesses" corresponds with a realization of identity, and leads into the culmination of his existential conversion.

As the scene begins, it quickly becomes apparent that John's conversion is not a typical altar call. Nor is it as simple as an adoption or rejection of the Christian God; Baldwin has departed from the plan set out in his earlier notes. John finds himself in anguish, suspended between two competing powers—the imposing force of Gabriel's bitter, guilt-inspiring God, and his own desire for Elisha, and for salvation. Instead of portraying a flat, simplistic struggle simply to be liberated on the grounds of faith and doubt by rejecting Christianity, John's struggles against determinist spiritual, paternal, and sexual powers are intertwined.

Elevated, biblical language lends dramatic power to the scene. This framework is ironic, considering that Baldwin is not ultimately describing a Christian conversion. He said explicitly on many occasions that he had left the Church and abandoned Christianity, and his notes for the novel confirm that John's struggle culminates with religious disillusionment of some kind at least.[86] In John's struggle, the version of Christianity that Gabriel imposes is usefully read as analogous to the kinds of violent anti-Black structures identified as the primary obstacles to self-realization by Black existentialism. Elisha, as the object of John's sexual desire, and as John's helper in the conversion experience, represents a competing force for existential freedom.

John struggles to be free from the determinist theology of Gabriel's God, which attempts to convince John of his own doom. The narrator describes John's anguish:

> And he knew ... that his father had thrust him out. His father's will was stronger than John's own. His power was greater because he belonged to God. Now, John felt no hatred, nothing, only a bitter, unbelieving despair: all the prophecies were true, salvation was finished, damnation was real.[87]

Superficially, John's struggle is a religious one. Through a European existential lens, it mirrors the Sartrean assertion that existence precedes essence. Gabriel would have it backward, and impose a predetermined essence on his stepson before existence. Gabriel identifies himself with an angry, judgmental God and convinces John of his guilt, which can only be met with damnation. Elisha is the hopeful intercessor who wishes John to arrive at salvation and take his place in the religious community. John's inner dialogue reveals that the religious struggle serves to dramatize personal and racial questions of identity; when John asks himself, in a moment of despair, "if he believed that he was cursed," an inner voice asserts, "All niggers had been cursed."[88] Through the Black existential lens, the anti-Black violence upon which society depends embodies this curse; in Baldwin's lived reality, it existed as the American racial nightmare that the author fled, and sought to overcome through his writing. John's struggle in this scene is to overcome the curse—the alleged damnation of himself and his community—and to be "saved" by finding his own identity, independent of racist or religious definitions imposed by society and Gabriel.

In order to do so, John must confront his family's history and come to terms with his place in the community. In the vision that dominates the "threshing floor" scene, John finds himself in a graveyard, where he discovers "his mother and his father" along with "a cloud of witnesses" behind them.[89] John's parents represent his link to the past, and the "cloud of witnesses" includes the many ancestors before them. His Aunt Florence and Gabriel's first, deceased wife, Deborah, are present too, while Roy lies stabbed and dead on the ground. John sees the cloud of witnesses, including his immediate family members, alternatively as "the despised and rejected, the wretched and the spat upon," and as "a multitude of people, all in long, white robes" recognized as "the saints."[90] John is sure that despite efforts to flee, "he was in their company," but an inner voice asks, "*Who are these? Who are they?*" and it is upon this question that John's salvation depends.[91] After a few more moments of protracted spiritual struggle, John briefly sees God and wakes in the morning to find that he is saved. Awakening, he sees the saints neither as a wholly wretched, nor a wholly blessed people; their "joyful feet" are nevertheless "bloodstained forever, and washed in many rivers."[92] At the moment of John's self-realization, he knows both that "the terrors of the night … were not finished" and that he belongs as "one of [the saints'] company now."[93]

The scene illustrates the unity of past and present that constitutes Baldwin's mutually dependent existential hindsight and insight. Roy, dead on the ground, signifies the present state of despair in which John and his family live, as people who are Black and thus "cursed" by the world. Likewise, Gabriel and Aunt Florence represent the generation that connects John to the past which he confronts throughout his mystical episode, and Deborah, no longer alive but remembered, recalls the past that is remote from John but which Gabriel has never reconciled with and which therefore haunts the Grimes family. Through the Black existential lens, John's confrontation with history and community is a form of "truth telling," which directly identifies the oppressive racist forces of the society that John and his ancestors have lived in. Truth telling yields grim truths, and Roy is only the latest casualty at the hands of an anti-Black world. However, truth telling also engenders a more authentic relationship between John and his community, creating a "homeplace" for his ultimate assertion of identity. Further, the necessity of these characters' presence in the climactic conversion experience of John Grimes illustrates the importance of the revision suggested by Linscott, as the story of Gabriel sets the stage for the conversion of John.

I have referred to the scene as one of existential conversion because of the way it portrays John's throwing off of his father's religion and simultaneous assumption of his own agency and self-knowledge. However, the metaphor of existential baptism is perhaps more apt: John has bathed in the waters of his family's history and has felt keenly the suffering and death of his ancestors. He has arisen from the waters with an honest, empowering relationship to the community and the space to make a way forward, and goes forth from the threshing floor with a new life and a new vision. John's story is the story of Baldwin's *hindsight*, where an honest, painful encounter with the past is necessary for an empowered, *insightful* step forward.

Sartre's vision of existential humanism is a philosophical worldview—an intellectual lens through which one can perceive reality. Baldwin denies having adopted any "ideology," but is deeply concerned with the way that he as an artist sees the world: in other words, the integrity of his vision. The two share certain questions and concerns about themselves and the place of the human in the world, but they come from vastly different backgrounds. Thus it is fruitful to determine how Sartre's existential humanism compares with Baldwin's artistic vision, and the ways that Baldwin's vision in turn differs from and widens its scope in comparison to the Sartrean worldview. The result of Baldwin's existential innovation is a bipartite vision in which the author's historically focused *hindsight* informs his self-realizing *insight*. *Go Tell It* both dramatizes and owes its existence to a kind of existential breakthrough, and this understanding casts light on the development of the novel, the assertion of Baldwin's identity as a writer, and yields a fresh reading of the novel's enigmatic third part, "The Threshing Floor."

The existential lens that I have used throughout this essay in order to clarify the development of *Go Tell It* as well as to yield a fresh reading of its final chapter is comparative. Baldwin's breakdown and breakthrough, likely facilitated by Linscott's letter, mirrors the innovation of Black existentialism on European existentialism. The resulting revision of the novel illustrates the importance of truth telling concerning racist realities in order to create community-empowered spaces for exploration of the self, and it is best understood in this light. Finally, my investigation sets the stage for further application of an existential lens to Baldwin's subsequent writing as it increasingly reflects on the mutual consequence of the beliefs and actions of Black and white people as reciprocal elements in what Baldwin calls the American dilemma.

Notes

1 David Leeming, *James Baldwin: A Biography* (New York, Arcade, 2015), p. 55.
2 James Baldwin, "The Discovery of What It Means To Be an American," in *Collected Essays*, ed. Toni Morrison (New York, Library of America, 1998), p. 137.
3 James Baldwin, "The Art of Fiction," *Paris Review*, 91 (1984), p. 1. Baldwin's close friend, Eugene Worth, committed suicide in 1946. Leeming, *James Baldwin*, p. 46.
4 Leeming, *James Baldwin*, p. 57.
5 *Ibid.*
6 *Ibid.*, pp. 49–50.
7 *Ibid.*, pp. 57–8.
8 See, for example, Leeming, *James Baldwin*, pp. 64–7, and James Baldwin, "Alas Poor Richard," in Morrison (ed.), *Collected Essays*, pp. 256–8.

9 Leeming, *James Baldwin*, p. 68; Baldwin, "Alas Poor Richard," p. 249.

10 Julius Lester, "James Baldwin—Reflections of a Maverick," *New York Times*, 27 May 1984, p. 1.

11 Baldwin, "Alas, Poor Richard," p. 249.

12 *Ibid.*

13 See, for example, James Baldwin, "Autobiographical Notes," in Morrison (ed.), *Collected Essays*, pp. 6–9; James Baldwin, "Everybody's Protest Novel," in Morrison (ed.), *Collected Essays*, pp. 12–18.

14 Baldwin, "Autobiographical Notes," p. 9.

15 Baldwin wrestled with his objections to the ideologies of both Dr. Martin Luther King, Jr. and Malcolm X, but still allied himself with each at crucial points in their respective activist careers; Leeming, *James Baldwin*, pp. 219, 289, 294.

16 Baldwin, "Alas, Poor Richard," p. 256.

17 *Ibid.*

18 George Cotkin, "French Existentialism and American Popular Culture," *The Historian*, 61:2 (1999), pp. 330–33; Douglas Field, *James Baldwin* (Tavistock, Northcote House, 2011), p. 13.

19 Field, *James Baldwin*, p. 13.

20 *Ibid.*, pp. 15–21.

21 *Ibid.*, pp. 17–19.

22 Douglas Field, *All Those Strangers: The Art and Lives of James Baldwin* (Oxford, Oxford University Press, 2015), p. 119.

23 *Ibid.*

24 Lewis Gordon, "Introduction: Black Existential Philosophy," in Lewis Gordon (ed.), *Existence in Black: An Anthology of Black Existential Philosophy* (New York, Routledge, 1997), p. 3.

25 Bruce Lapenson, "Race and Existential Commitment in James Baldwin," *Philosophy and Literature*, 37:1 (2013), p. 199.

26 *Ibid.*, pp. 200–7.

27 *Ibid.*, pp. 203–8.

28 Radiclani Clytus, "Paying Dues and Playing the Blues: Baldwin's Existential Jazz," in Michele Elam (ed.), *The Cambridge Companion to James Baldwin* (Cambridge, Cambridge University Press, 2015), p. 72.

29 *Ibid.*, pp. 74–5.

30 *Ibid.*, pp. 77–81.

31 One should also note that this is not to say that Baldwin ever wrote with the intention of referencing the essay, nor does it mean that Baldwin's thought does not interact with any of Sartre's other works. The conversation ahead concentrates on this essay because Baldwin's writing seems to most closely relate to the account of existential humanism set out therein, and because of its concise summation of Sartre's philosophy.

32 Jean-Paul Sartre, "Existentialism is a Humanism" (1946), in Walter Kauffman (ed.), *Existentialism: From Dostoevsky to Sartre* (New York, Plume, 2004), p. 345.

33 *Ibid.*, pp. 345–6.

34 *Ibid.*, p. 369.

35 *Ibid.*

36 *Ibid.*, p. 348.

37 *Ibid.*, p. 349.

38 *Ibid.*, p. 353.

39 *Ibid.*, p. 361.

40 *Ibid.*, p. 351.

41 *Ibid.*, p. 356.

42 *Ibid.*, p. 367.

43 *Ibid.*, p. 364.

44 *Ibid.*, p. 366.

45 *Ibid.*, p. 365.

46 *Ibid.*

47 *Ibid.*, p. 369.

48 Field, *All Those Strangers*, p. 100.

49 Baldwin, "The Discovery," p. 137; Leeming, *James Baldwin*, p. 79.

50 Baldwin, "The Discovery," p. 140.

51 *Ibid.*, p. 138.

52 James Baldwin, "Outline for a Novel," Box 12, Folder 2, James Baldwin Papers 1936–1992, New York Public Library, Schomburg Center for Research in Black Culture, pp. 1–2.

53 *Ibid.*

54 *Ibid.*, p. 2.

55 *Ibid.*

56 James Baldwin, "The Creative Process," in Morrison (ed.), *Collected Essays*, p. 672.

57 James Baldwin, "Encounter on the Seine: Black Meets Brown," in Morrison (ed.), *Collected Essays*, p. 89.

58 *Ibid.*, p. 88.

59 Baldwin, "Outline for a Novel," pp. 12–15.

60 *Ibid.*

61 *Ibid.*, p. 14.

62 *Ibid.*, p. 15.

63 *Ibid.*

64 *Ibid.*

65 *Ibid.*, emphasis added.

66 Sartre, "Existentialism is a Humanism," pp. 353, 360.

67 See Field's chapter, "James Baldwin's Religion: Sex, Love, and the Blues," from his recent book, *All Those Strangers*, for a discussion of the significance of Baldwin's Pentecostal background.

68 Leeming, *James Baldwin*, p. 213; This is not to discount the ongoing and complicated importance of Christianity in Baldwin's life and writing—a topic that is well treated in Field's recent book, *All Those Strangers*.

69 Baldwin, "Outline for a Novel," p. 2.

70 *Ibid.*, pp. 1–3.

71 R. N. Linscott, "Criticism about the Book," Box 12, Folder 2, James Baldwin Papers 1936–1992, New York Public Library, Schomburg Center for Research in Black Culture, p. 1.

72 *Ibid.*

73 *Ibid.*

74 *Ibid.*

75 James Baldwin, *Go Tell It on the Mountain* (1953) (New York, Vintage International, 2013).

76 James Baldwin, "Letter to Phil," 121.2, Alfred A. Knopf, Inc. Records, University of Texas at Austin, Harry Ransom Center, p. 2.

77 Linwood Vereen, Lisa A. Wines, Tamiko Lemberger-Truelove, Michael D. Hannon, Natasha Howard, and Isaac Burt, "Black Existentialism: Extending the Discourse on Meaning and Existence," *The Journal of Humanistic Counseling*, 56 (2017), p. 74.

78 Baldwin, "Alas, Poor Richard," p. 249.

79 Calvin Warren, "Onticide," *GLQ: A Journal of Lesbian and Gay Studies*, 23:3 (2017), p. 397.

80 Vereen et al., "Black Existentialism," p. 79.

81 bell hooks, "Homeplace: A Site of Resistance," in *Yearning: Race, Gender, and Cultural Politics* (New York, Routledge, 2015), p. 43.

82 Vereen et al., "Black Existentialism," p. 74.

83 Ed Pavlić, "On James Baldwin's Dispatches from the Heart of the Civil Rights Movement," *LitHub*, 10 December 2018, https://lithub.com/on-james-baldwins-dispatches-from-the-heart-of-the-civil-rights-movement/ (accessed 15 March 2019).

84 Vereen et al., "Black Existentialism," p. 74.

85 Throughout the close reading of this scene, it is important to remember that John experiences everything in a state of spiritual hallucination, while he remains prostrate on the floor of the church.

86 Leeming, *James Baldwin*, p. 213; Baldwin, throughout his oeuvre, is concerned with the tension between hypocritical religion and the ideal of love that Christianity is supposed to embody. It is important to read Baldwin's disavowals of Christianity and the Church with the knowledge that despite his negative feelings, Christianity remains a constant theme throughout Baldwin's writings. See Field's chapter, "James Baldwin's Religion: Sex, Love, and the Blues," from his recent book, *All Those Strangers*.

87 Baldwin, *Go Tell It*, p. 198.

88 *Ibid.*, p. 200.

89 *Ibid.*, p. 202.

90 *Ibid.*, pp. 204–7.

91 *Ibid.*, p. 204.

92 *Ibid.*, p. 207.

93 *Ibid.*, p. 209.

Works Cited

Baldwin, James, "Alas, Poor Richard" (1961), in *Collected Essays*, ed. Toni Morrison (New York, Library of America, 1998), pp. 247–68.

———— *The Amen Corner* (1954) (New York, Vintage International, 1968).

———— "The Art of Fiction No. 78," interview with James Elgrably, *Paris Review*, 91 (1984), www.theparisreview.org/interviews/2994/the-art-of-fiction-no-78-james-baldwin (accessed January 2018).

———— "Autobiographical Notes" (1955), in *Collected Essays*, ed. Toni Morrison (New York, Library of America, 1998), pp. 5–10.

———— "The Creative Process" (1962), in *Collected Essays*, ed. Toni Morrison (New York, Library of America, 1998), pp. 669–72.

———— "The Discovery of What It Means To Be an American" (1959), in *Collected Essays*, ed. Toni Morrison (New York, Library of America, 1998), pp. 137–42.

———— "Encounter on the Seine: Black Meets Brown" (1950), in *Collected Essays*, ed. Toni Morrison (New York, Library of America, 1998), pp. 85–90.

_____ "Everybody's Protest Novel" (1949), in *Collected Essays*, ed. Toni Morrison (New York, Library of America, 1998), pp. 11–18.

_____ *The Fire Next Time* (1963) (New York, Vintage International, 1993).

_____ *Go Tell It on the Mountain* (1953) (New York, Vintage International, 2013).

_____ *If Beale Street Could Talk* (1974) (New York, Vintage International, 2006).

_____ "Letter to Phil," Box 121, Folder 2, Alfred A. Knopf, Inc. Records, Harry Ransom Center, University of Texas at Austin, 25 October 2019.

_____ *Notes of a Native Son* (1955) (Boston, Beacon Press, 2012).

_____ "Outline for a Novel," Box 12, Folder 2, James Baldwin Papers, Schomburg Center for Research in Black Culture, New York Public Library, 16 November 2017.

Clytus, Radiclani, "Paying Dues and Playing the Blues: Baldwin's Existential Jazz," in Michele Elam (ed.), *The Cambridge Companion to James Baldwin* (New York, Cambridge University Press, 2015), pp. 70–84.

Cotkin, George, "French Existentialism and American Popular Culture," *The Historian*, 61:2 (1999), pp. 327–40.

Field, Douglas, *All Those Strangers: The Art and Lives of James Baldwin* (Oxford, Oxford University Press, 2015).

_____ *James Baldwin* (Tavistock, Northcote House, 2011), pp. 12–27.

Gordon, Lewis, "Introduction: Black Existential Philosophy," in Lewis Gordon (ed.), *Existence in Black: An Anthology of Black Existential Philosophy* (New York, Routledge, 1997), pp. 1–9.

hooks, bell, "Homeplace: A Site of Resistance," in *Yearning: Race, Gender, and Cultural Politics* (New York, Routledge, 2015), pp. 41–9.

Lapenson, Bruce P., "Race and Existential Commitment in James Baldwin," *Philosophy and Literature*, 37:1 (2013), pp. 199–209.

Leeming, David, *James Baldwin: A Biography* (1994) (New York, Arcade, 2015).

Lester, Julius, "James Baldwin—Reflections of a Maverick," *New York Times*, 27 May 1984, p. 1.

Linscott, R. N., "Criticism about the Book," Box 12, Folder 12, James Baldwin Papers, Schomburg Center for Research in Black Culture, New York Public Library, 16 November 2017.

McAra, Catriona, "Introduction: Excavating an Abyss," in *A Surrealist Stratigraphy of Dorothea Tanning's Chasm* (New York, Routledge, 2017), pp. 1–16.

Pavlić, Ed, "On James Baldwin's Dispatches from the Heart of the Civil Rights Movement," *LitHub*, 10 December 2018, https://lithub.com/on-james-baldwins-dispatches-from-the-heart-of-the-civil-rights-movement (accessed 15 March 2019).

Sartre, Jean-Paul, "Existentialism is a Humanism" (1946), in Walter Kauffman (ed.), *Existentialism: From Dostoevsky to Sartre* (New York, Plume, 2004), pp. 345–68.

Vereen, Linwood, Lisa A. Wines, Tamiko Lemberger-Truelove, Michael D. Hannon, Natasha Howard, and Isaac Burt, "Black Existentialism: Extending the Discourse on Meaning and Existence," *The Journal of Humanistic Counseling*, 56 (2017), pp. 72–84.

Warren, Calvin, "Onticide," *GLQ: A Journal of Lesbian and Gay Studies*, 23:3 (2017), pp. 391–418.

Contributor's Biography

Miller Wilbourn is a first-year Ph.D. student in English at the University of Texas at Austin studying twentieth-century American and African American literature with a focus on post-secular expressions of faith in fiction.

Manchester University Press

DISPATCH

The Disorder of Life: James Baldwin on My Shoulder

Karen Thorsen

Abstract

Filmmaker Karen Thorsen gave us *James Baldwin: The Price of the Ticket*, the award-winning documentary that is now considered a classic. First broadcast on PBS/American Masters in August, 1989—just days after what would have been Baldwin's 65th birthday—the film premiered at the Sundance Film Festival in 1990. It was not the film Thorsen intended to make. Beginning in 1986, she and Baldwin had been collaborating on a very different film project: a "nonfiction feature" about the history, research, and writing of Baldwin's next book, *Remember This House*. It was also going to be a film about progress: how far we had come, how far we still had to go, before we learned to trust our common humanity. The following memoir explores how and why their collaboration began. This recollection will be serialized in two parts, with the second installment appearing in *James Baldwin Review*'s seventh issue, due out in the fall of 2021.

Keywords: *The Price of the Ticket*, Albert Maysles, James Baldwin, film, screenwriting

After two months of phone calls and occasional faxes, I sat down facing the entrance to wait for James Baldwin. It was April 1986, and this was The Ginger Man: the fabled watering hole across from Lincoln Center named after J. P. Donleavy's 1955 novel of the same name—a "dirty" book by an expatriate author that was banned in Ireland, published in Paris, censored in the U.S., and is now considered a classic. Appropriately, Baldwin called the place his "New York office."

Also appropriately, Baldwin was late. I had been forewarned by some who already knew him to expect this; indeed, I nursed iced water for close to forty minutes before he appeared in the doorway, searching the room for his not-yet-met collaborator-to-be. My first thought was an astonished, "He's tiny!," quickly followed by a rush of delight: reactions inspired by his unexpectedly diminutive

James Baldwin Review, Volume 6, 2020, © The Authors. Published by Manchester University Press and The University of Manchester Library
http://dx.doi.org/10.7227/JBR.6.9

stature and the unforgettable grin that lit up the room as soon as he spotted me. He felt epic.

In my mind, he had always been larger than life. I first read him in college: I had signed up for an African-American Studies elective; *Notes of a Native Son* (1955) was the first book assigned. It was a head-on collision. I was young, white, and female, just returned to Vassar from a junior year in Paris and a summer of back-packing, still processing the countless reminders of my status as an "Ugly American." He was young, Black, and male, still living in Paris and still processing the count-less reminders of his status as an unwanted "Native Son." He was, of course, far more wounded than I, but back then I was struck more by our similarities than our differences. We had both grown up poor, witnessed injustice, and felt shame for our nation; we had both escaped to France, trying to gain perspective on our own deeply conflicted identities. He felt like a fellow traveler. And—for me, most impressive of all—he was a writer, a good writer, the one thing I'd always said I wanted to be ever since I learned to read.

The impact stayed with me.

Like him, I found work as a New York-based writer-for-hire—first in book pub-lishing, then magazine journalism—and finally returned to Paris where I once again severed connections and tried to start over, this time as a screenwriter and aspiring filmmaker. I hitchhiked to the Cannes Film Festival and fell in with a crowd of French *cinéphiles* who took me to dinner up in Saint-Paul de Vence, a medieval walled village perched in the hills above Nice. On the way into town, they pointed out the farm-house where James Baldwin had been living since 1971, a seventeenth-century refuge from pain after the assassination of his friends in the 1960s. When I shared my admi-ration for the man and his work, they told me that Baldwin often hung out at La Colombe d'Or, the restaurant where we were about to eat … but we didn't see him.

That near miss in the Alpes-Maritimes led me to reread *Notes of a Native Son*—where I found new layers of content that matched my own evolution. There it was, staring at me, in Baldwin's "Autobiographical Notes": he wanted "to re-create out of the disorder of life that order which is art" and "to own a sixteen-millimeter camera and make experimental movies."[1]

It was what his biographer, David Leeming, later called "a lifelong fascination with the cinema."[2]

* * * * * *

The fascination began with Baldwin's extraordinary, nearly five-year friendship with Orilla ('Bill') Miller, a teaching intern at P.S. 24 on East 128th Street in Harlem. Despite his stepfather's palpable disapproval, this college-age white woman became the young Baldwin's mentor. Starting when he was in sixth grade, she made him her "assistant." She directed his first play; she took him to see plays and films, both uptown and downtown; she schooled him on politics and society, both local and global.

He wrote about the films they saw together in both *Notes of a Native Son* and *The Devil Finds Work* (1976). Plenty of people went to "the movies," he recalled, but for him the experience was life-changing: those Saturday afternoons in the dark were "my first entrance into the cinema of my mind."[3] Like the books from the library on 135th Street that he read so obsessively, "they had something to tell me."[4]

When Baldwin was 12, he and Bill went to see the 1935 version of Dickens's eighteenth-century historical fiction, *A Tale of Two Cities*. It struck him like thunder: the death of the peasant boy, the guillotines that chopped heads turned the book that he had already read and reread into absolutely believable life. Cinema of the mind, indeed. "My first director," as Baldwin called the film's actor-turned-MGM director, Jack Conway, "was instructing me in the discipline and power of make-believe."[5]

He and Bill also saw the 1932 drama *20,000 Years in Sing Sing*, starring the not-yet-famous Spencer Tracy and newcomer Bette Davis. Now, even more than the heartbreak behind bars, it was Davis who stunned him: he had been repeatedly told by his stepfather that his bulging "frog-eyes" were ugly—those "big world-absorbing eyes" so eloquently eulogized by Amiri Baraka at Baldwin's funeral a half-century later—and yet here was an actual movie star, a *white* movie star, with eyes that looked just like his ... *and* his mother's![6]

The sight filled the young misfit with hope. "Perhaps I could find a way to use my strangeness," he wrote about his reaction to Bette Davis. "My infirmity, or infirmities, might be forged into weapons."[7]

From age 10 to 14, films helped shape Baldwin's future. Then came a detour: driven by a mix of stepfather pressure, sexual panic, and a strong dose of self-loathing, he "found the Lord," became a boy preacher and no longer indulged in such "ungodly activities." He and his beloved Bill Miller lost touch, but later reconnected and remained friends for life. She had given him a gift beyond measure, the "language of the camera"—what he ultimately came to call "the language of our dreams."[8]

******

Slowly but surely, Baldwin became one of my touchstones, both for artistic guidance and for how to live *life*. Over the next several years—between my own forays into the world of film—I went on a Baldwin binge. *Nobody Knows My Name* (1964), *The Fire Next Time* (1963), *No Name in the Street* (1972), *The Devil Finds Work*. All nonfiction, all focused on what Baldwin called his "central premise, which is that all men are brothers," all probing the "horror of the black condition," all urging us to "trust our common humanity."[9] All "obeying the dictum laid down by the great Ray Charles ... tell the truth."[10]

At times, to be honest, I struggled. The sentences were so long, the ideas so dense, so elliptical—and with so many commas!—I sometimes had to start a paragraph over just to digest its conclusion. Sometimes he referred to events not yet familiar to me; sometimes he critiqued films that I hadn't heard of. Sometimes I winced: twinges of shame. White guilt. Outright pain. Even so, I kept reading.

> These innocents who believed that your imprisonment made them safe ... are your brothers—your lost, younger brothers. And if the word *integration* means anything, this is what it means: that we, with love, shall force our brothers to see themselves as they are, to cease fleeing reality and begin to change it.[11]

Such fervent lucidity! Every line I read rang true. It was painful truth, yes: between injustice now and future ideals, between what is and what *could* be, it was hard to avoid mental whiplash, even harder to see a clear path toward change—but he won me over.

It was Baldwin's ability to embrace contradictions that got me, his capacity to dissect the dualities that fill our lives, to analyze both the factors that caused them and the fruit they bore. For me, it was mind-expanding; for him, it was survival. In his life he was forced to confront these dichotomies on a near-daily basis: pain laced with love, horror infused with hope, "questions louder than drums" explored with impeccable objectivity.[12] Plus his commitment to artistry and the risks that came with it: existential screams of consciousness in those long paragraphs built like jazz that were so incredibly, painfully costly.

Baldwin understood "the price of art."[13]

"Anyone who has ever struggled with poverty knows how extremely expensive it is to be poor," he wrote in his searing essay "Fifth Avenue, Uptown," in *Nobody Knows My Name*.[14] This almost laughable irony was and still is a given, particularly for those he described as "captive populations," people victimized simply by the color of their skin. It is also, he took care to point out, a given for artists—especially for Black artists.[15]

He made this point clear for me in his essay about the writer Norman Mailer, "The Black Boy Looks at the White Boy": like Mailer, as I was beginning to understand, I had the luxury of white privilege, centuries rich with stories of "struggling artists" who had conquered the odds—but for many, including Baldwin, this was uncharted territory. "To become a Negro Man, let alone a Negro artist, one had to make oneself up as one went along ... The world had prepared no place for you, and if the world has its way, no place would ever exist."[16]

As with so much of his writing, Baldwin spoke from his own experience as a Black American, and wound up with the universal. Was he speaking to me? Obliquely, yes. Was it one more sign of white hubris that I presumed such an honor? Probably. But even as I became more aware of the nearly unbridgeable chasm that separated our lives, he bridged it. His message was simple: all people struggle, all people suffer, all are connected.

> You think your pain and your heartbreak are unprecedented in the history of the world, but then you read. It was Dostoyevsky and Dickens who taught me that the things that tormented me most were the very things that connected me with all the people who were alive, who had ever been alive.[17]

James Baldwin did far more than "expand my mind." He validated my confusions, he gave voice to my fears, he supported my quest as a developing filmmaker.

He focused on "the condition of the artist," the state you find yourself in once you have chosen to be one. In his essay on Mailer, he stated bluntly, "A writer who is worried about his career is also fighting for his life."[18] In "The Northern Protestant"—his essay about Ingmar Bergman, "one of the very few genuine artists now working in film"—both he and Bergman agreed that artists are "always on the very edge of disaster."[19] In *The Devil Finds Work*—as part of his critique of *Lady Sings the Blues*, the Hollywood version of Billie Holiday's life—he underscored the hard fact that "the film suggests nothing of the terrifying economics of a singer's life."[20]

But this terror wasn't just about financial survival. This was about artistic achievement, the struggle for meaning. Purpose. He wrote about "the glory and torment of every writer": the hope that their experience "might be turned to good account"—and the fear that grips their "wilderness of the soul" when great content doesn't follow.[21] He described how artists are "always on the very edge of great things," always "trembling on the edge of great revelations." How their real *raison d'être* is "to disturb the peace."[22]

He made disturbing sound good. And as for that "wilderness of the soul," I had barely begun to explore it—but despite all the pitfalls, I wanted in.

******

Baldwin also described how easy it is for artists to fall short. Particularly when dealing with "the arid plains of Hollywood," the "machinery" that required the sale of the soul.[23]

When he dismissed *Lady Sings the Blues* as "empty as a banana peel, and as treacherous," that was just one example.[24] He accused it and so many other Tinseltown "products" of existing only to make money, to stifle emotional truth. He blasted "the brutally crass and commercial."[25] He bristled at scenes that he deemed "pure bullshit."[26] He pitied the screenwriters, paid to turn serious content into "hints of reality, smuggled like contraband into a maudlin tale."[27]

He had been down that road himself, more than once.

Despite his disgust with Hollywood's "absolutely appalling distance from reality," he never stopped trying to add his own storytelling skills—and a reflection of the life *he* knew—to the film industry's undeniable whitewash (#ScreensSoWhite!).[28] "Black people need witnesses," he stated repeatedly, "in this hostile world which thinks everything is white."[29]

Over the course of his lifetime, he made deal after deal. But it wasn't until 1985, when Baldwin was 60, less than three years before his death at age 63, that he got to see his words come to life on screen: the PBS/American Playhouse production of *Go Tell It on the Mountain*, adapted from his first work of fiction published more than thirty years earlier. Directed by the now well-known Stan Lathan, the result touched him deeply. "I'm very, very happy about it. It did not betray the book ... I still see myself there."[30] Baldwin didn't write the PBS script for *Go Tell It*—it was adapted by Gus Edwards and Leslie Lee—but he *did* write a number of screenplays that were never produced.

His first attempt was a teleplay adapted from his 1955 autobiographical essay, "Equal In Paris" (first published in *Commentary*, then in *Notes of a Native Son*), about his time in a French jail due to a friend's stolen bedsheet. Written in 1957 in collaboration with Sol Stein—the "high school buddy, editor, novelist, playwright" who had edited *Notes* for Beacon Press—the script turned Baldwin's protagonist into a heterosexual male with a love interest in hopes that it might appeal to

U.S. Steel Hour, the Emmy Award-winning series which had already broadcast one of Stein's plays.[31] It didn't. A drama about a Black man in Paris was beyond the pale.

Trouble was, all of Baldwin's content was 'risky.' Beginning in 1957, he wrote multiple drafts of a script from his 1956 novel, *Giovanni's Room*—with Marlon Brando initially slated to play the role of David, the ambivalent lover, then (as Brando aged) Guillaume, owner of the gay bar where much of the drama unfolds.[32] In the 1960s Baldwin sold the rights to his interracially steamy 1962 novel, *Another Country*, stipulating himself as the screenwriter—but funding never materialized and no script was written. In the 1970s he filled the first few pages of a leather-bound notebook with plans for a film version of *If Beale Street Could Talk*, his 1974 novel about a pregnant 19-year-old whose fiancé has been unjustly arrested and jailed—reflecting on which scenes to cut, how to turn certain monologues into scenes, when to use Tish's voice as voiceover. He even listed potential directors: François Truffaut, Louis Malle, Gordon Parks, Lloyd Richards... And the cast, he noted, should include Ruby Dee. But again, no film was made—that is, not until 2018 when director Barry Jenkins turned *Beale Street* into an Academy Award nominee.

The closest Baldwin came to the "business" of filmmaking was in 1968, when Columbia Pictures tapped him to adapt Marvin Worth's production of Alex Haley's "as-told-to" bestseller, *The Autobiography of Malcolm X*. Friends and family advised him not to take the gig, but he couldn't resist. Malcolm had been his close friend; he felt like "the custodian of a legend."[33] He had already outlined the draft of a play based on Haley's book—with Elia Kazan as director—so a screenplay would be a natural continuation. "An act of love."[34]

In his words, he was "both fascinated and challenged" by Hollywood.[35] Part of him hoped he could "change this town"; part of him had "grave doubts and fears" despite "the distances covered since *Birth of a Nation*."[36] His fears were justified. Month after month—despite the near-constant pain caused by current events, from the targeting of Black Panthers to the assassination of Martin Luther King, Jr.—Baldwin battled the studio, insisting on writing the Malcolm script his way "or not at all."[37] His employers responded by hiring a "technical" co-writer to review his scenes. The result was beyond painful. "My scenes were returned to me, 'translated' ... all meaning was being siphoned out of them."[38]

Tensions escalated. Baldwin wanted to cast the little-known Billy Dee Williams as Malcolm; the studio wanted a star. Baldwin was determined not to betray Malcolm's narrative; his producers were disenchanted with the writer they had hired. Biographer David Leeming explains their logic bluntly: Baldwin's 200-page treatment "read more like a novel than a screenplay. Furthermore, his presence was disruptive, his working habits deplorable, and his life-style expensive."[39]

Despair set in.

Weighed down by assassinations, friends imprisoned, love gone wrong, Baldwin tried to solve his problems with sleeping pills. The overdose nearly killed him, but friends rushed him to the hospital just in time; not long after, he left Hollywood, taking his screenplay with him. "I simply walked out," he wrote later. "I did not wish to be party to a second assassination."[40]

The fallout didn't end there. Warner Bros. bought Columbia's rights to Haley's book; producer Marvin Worth and Baldwin's co-writer, the once-blacklisted Arnold Perl, jumped with it. In 1972, under the Warner logo, Worth released *Malcolm X*, an Oscar-nominated documentary directed by Perl and narrated by James Earl Jones. The same year, Baldwin published his own version of Malcolm's life: *One Day, When I Was Lost*, based on his original screenplay, pre-Perl. Over the next two decades, award-winning luminaries from David Mamet to Sidney Lumet tried to adapt Baldwin's script. Lumet's version was to feature Richard Pryor as Malcolm and Eddie Murphy as Alex Haley—an intriguing prospect—but again, no go. It took the director Spike Lee, with Marvin Worth as producer, to make it happen.

By the time Spike Lee's *Malcolm X* was released, it was 1992—and Baldwin had been dead five long years. Lee wanted to credit Baldwin as one of the writers, along with himself and the late Arnold Perl; Baldwin's family said no, because Lee hadn't filmed Baldwin's script exactly as written. As for Lee's film, it went on to win multiple awards, and even now, almost thirty years later, both the 1992 feature *and* the 1972 documentary are available on Amazon Prime.

******

Despite his hopes, Baldwin failed to change Hollywood in his lifetime—"it was a gamble I knew I might lose, and which I lost"—but he helped shape its future.[41] And, inadvertently, mine.

Four years after publishing his screenplay on Malcolm, he wrote *The Devil Finds Work*. Both a cautionary tale and a personal memoir, it was also an ode to filmmaking. His passion leapt off every page. His affection for what *could* be—for the "language of our dreams," for the creative possibilities inherent in film, for the intensely private joys that he had discovered way back in boyhood—was still with him. And I knew just what that meant.

With his words as fuel, I put myself through my own version of film school.

I joined a French team on a feature film shoot in Asia. I launched a Super 8 Film Festival that played in New York, Houston, and Paris. I co-wrote a screenplay that got optioned (twice) by Hollywood—but then the producer died and the option died with him. I won a Financial World Silver Medal by writing an annual report for Warner Communications, then fell in love (almost) with the studio's maverick-but-brilliant head of production, the late great John Calley. I flirted with advertising: I wrote, directed, and/or produced a year's worth of commercials—including one "starring" Bill Cosby (yes, he was difficult) for Jello Pudding Pops.

And in the midst of all that, I met the legendary filmmaker Albert Maysles: the man who, ten years later, would make my collaboration with James Baldwin "possible"—and who would, after Baldwin died unexpectedly in 1987, become the executive producer of my first feature-length documentary, *James Baldwin: The Price of the Ticket*. I certainly knew who he was. I admired the nonfiction films that he made with his brother, David. I had stood in line to see their Rolling Stones tour de force, *Gimme Shelter* (1970); I had been deeply moved by *Grey Gardens* (1975), their mother–daughter portrait of two "upper crust" recluses in a decaying

East Hampton mansion. I was soon to be amazed by *Running Fence* (1977), their exploration of Christo's breathtaking art installation that crowned sheep pastures and hillsides all the way down to the Pacific. But...

Fate was knocking, and I wasn't listening. My mind was firmly focused on fiction.

Thanks to my various film gigs, I learned a lot. My writing skills helped, my naïveté was a plus, and my disenchantment with the commerce required by art was deep. On a far lesser scale than any of Baldwin's battles, this was my own love–hate dance with Hollywood. And yet even so, I still believed—as artists must—that I might prevail. Not just to make a mark, but to make a *difference*.

Trouble was, and is, I'm female: white, yes, but female. I like to joke that if only I had big hair I would be head of a studio, but the real truth is—even though my parents took care to assure me that women could achieve whatever they set their mind to—I found it hard to advance.

My achievements peaked when I scored a call-back from Jane Fonda's assistant, asking for a meeting because her boss liked the film treatment I had sent them. My first screenplay, *Territory*—the one whose producer died—was a dramatized version of Clarence Darrow's last case, a 1931 rape-and-murder whodunit that pitted East Coast socialites against Hawaiian natives. (Guess who won that fight?) My second script, *Common Sense*, offered a different experiment in historical fiction: a fantasized six-month slice-of-life that fit neatly into the events of its time. My subject was Thomas Paine, the bankrupt British-born corsetmaker who, after shipping out to the Colonies, wrote the essay that launched the American Revolution. Set in New York's rural outskirts, it was about wartime love and the ethics of infidelity—with a female spy as the leading role.

Perfect for Fonda, right? I never even made it up to her office. Our meeting took place in her NYC lobby, while she was en route from one pitch to the next. When she lowered her sunglasses, I knew it was over.

Was it time to give up? My freelance life was hard to maintain, I had to scramble for money and withstand rejection. I found myself losing steam—and, once again, turned to Baldwin. Maybe his struggles, his persistence, his refusal to abandon his vision, could help. I flipped through his pages, skimming the phrases I had starred in red ink:

"The typewriter would be there, staring at me..."[42]

That helped. So did:

"About a year and several overflowing wastebaskets later..."[43]

Just knowing that someone with his talent hit roadblocks was enough to sustain me.

Marking up books is a habit of mine. When I read something I like, I start folding down corners of pages—and, if folded corners start to accumulate, I go back with a pen and start underlining, writing in margins. I even switch colors when I reread an old favorite: it gives me a timeline of my own evolution.

It also means that I don't often share books. My copy of *The Devil Finds Work* is especially dog-eared: on page after page, I've marked whatever struck me during my latest reading—including one passage that hit me during my frustrations with Hollywood. That particular segment was part of Baldwin's critique of the Academy Award-winning drama *In the Heat of the Night* (1967). It's his description of a feeling he had while watching Sidney Poitier and Rod Steiger trying to find common ground, the feeling of "something choked and moving, something sensed through a thick glass, dimly," "something strangling, alive, struggling to get out."[44]

That passage spoke to me somewhere deep in my psyche.

I felt like Steiger and Poitier: full of promise, maybe, but stuck. Again, I had found a description of roadblocks—but this one went deeper. It focused on our search for identity, our need to understand who we are. How we need to accept each other before we can accept ourselves. How our fulfillment depends on this—but we have yet to face the truths that will help us achieve it. I wanted to achieve that *and* artistic fulfillment.

Maybe there was a way to do both.

* * * * * *

I decided to try documentaries. I knew that docs paid less than fiction, but I wasn't earning enough as it was… And the few female filmmakers I knew in the doc world told me they felt respected.

My first gig-for-hire was a film about money (irony noted!), with the Oscar-winning painter-turned-filmmaker Francis Thompson as producer and me as his screenwriter. Francis and his partner Sasha Hammid had won their Oscar for the 70mm multi-screen wonder *To Be Alive!*, co-directed for the Johnson's Wax Pavilion at New York's 1964 World's Fair: an understandable win. But their lyrical 1957 short film, *N.Y., N.Y.*—a entire city reflected through special lenses, prisms and mirrors, even on the back of a spoon—was my inspiration. Our subject was "The Fed"; I wrote a script that followed a single dollar bill through the system. The end result, alas, was a bit more literal than we had imagined. Hardly surprising: our client was the federal government, and our vision of finance was more poetic than theirs. Even so, the film did win a Cine Golden Eagle … and my future husband was part of the film crew.

Then came another life-changer. I went to see Albert Maysles, the documentary filmmaker who had come up to me at the end of one of my Super 8 Film Festival screenings to thank me for the films I had chosen and to give me his business card. "Come by our office sometime." A few years had passed since that first encounter, but Albert remembered—and within a few weeks, after an interview with his younger brother, David, I had a job offer.

The Maysles Brothers were already famous. In collaboration with their co-directors/ editors, they produced groundbreaking documentaries which swiftly became cult films, then classics. These were docs, yes, but instead of intoning some fact-heavy lesson, they felt more like fiction. Each film explored human nature—and each film revealed life "as it happened," without scripts, sets, or imposed direction. And they all, as Al Maysles put it, had "the power of truth and the romance of discovery."[45]

The pair called their approach Direct Cinema. In the tradition of Russia's *kino-pravda* ("cinema truth"), Britain's free cinema and France's *cinéma vérité*, Al handheld his camera and David strapped on his synch-sound gear in order to capture real life as it unfolded before them. Their goal was to remain unobtrusive, to record people's lives, and to rely on the power of editing once filming was done. Narration—the traditional documentary tool of the time, where some anonymous voice told viewers what to think—was *not* an option.

When I began to learn more, I was embarrassed by how little I knew. I had been so focused on the world of fiction that documentaries felt like a distant cousin—and yet here was a form of filmmaking that checked all my boxes. Relatively affordable. Ethically rigorous. Anti-establishment. The opposite of the studio system. It was like Super 8 filmmaking on a grander scale, a way to explore human emotions and craft a strong narrative with minimal artifice. Power to the People.

The irony for me was that Maysles Films had no need of a screenwriter—but I jumped at the chance to be part of their entourage. To earn my keep, I served as "film rep" and grant writer, soaking up the philosophy that defined my new job. It was a great place for learning. The office was a penthouse, full of windows, with a huge open floor plan: at one end, Albert and David sat facing the room; desks for the rest of us lined the remaining walls. Everyone heard almost everything. We even ate lunch together, sharing stories, trading laughs, often squeezed round a large single table. Sure, there was friction, petty jealousies, even nasty gossip and family infighting—but overall, and certainly more than anywhere else, this was filmmaking done right. Art hung on all available surfaces; music often played in the background; a large roof terrace was perfect for parties. Plus, down the hall, smaller rooms pulsed with the thrill of production: editing suites, equipment alcoves, racks crammed full of canisters with intriguing film titles—and a screening room where we could hold private meetings.

I felt as if I'd finally come home. Everyone there was some shade of eccentric; the brothers were benevolent bosses. David was the extrovert: he loved hanging with artists; he valued flamboyance; he had a big heart. Albert was quieter, still water runs deep. His mind was keen, his soul was wise; he soon became my close friend and mentor.

In my mind, Al resembled Baldwin's description of the great Ingmar Bergman, only warmer. He too was "possessed by a vision"; he too "was not to be sidetracked."[46] He too didn't want "to be guilty of the world's indifference"—and, perhaps most important, "what he saw when he looked at the world did not seem very different from what *I* saw."[47]

Now I had *two* mentors: Albert Maysles in his corner, just a few yards away—and James Baldwin, still on my shoulder, the sustaining presence whom I'd never met. I couldn't help comparing the two.

Albert Maysles:	"Knowledge of the real world is exactly what we need to better understand and therefore love one another. It's my way of making the world a better place."[48]
James Baldwin:	"The unexamined life is not worth living." "If you can examine and face your life, you can discover the terms in which you're connected to other lives." "Neither of us, truly, can live without the other."[49]

They both believed in human potential—and they both believed in truth-telling as a way to unlock it.

******

What's the best way to communicate truth?

In our "World-According-to-Maysles," it was simple: find a compelling character, someone you like to listen to, someone believable. Someone with light in their eyes and warmth in their voice, someone with passion about their particular take on the universe. Someone *interesting.* In other words, a good storyteller. And then follow that person or persons until something happens—which, as Al Maysles would assure you, *will* happen.

It also helped, as the brothers knew well, to focus on a celebrity, someone with name recognition. They didn't *just* do that—their extraordinary 1969 film, *Salesman*, a surprisingly moving feature-length portrait of four door-to-door Bible salesmen, is ample proof of their fascination with human nature of all stripes—but since celebrities often become famous *because* of their talent and inherent charisma, it made sense to film them.

It was Albert who started it all. He began as a college professor, teaching psychology—but after falling in love with cinematography during three trips to Russia, he switched to filmmaking. He joined forces with *vérité* pioneers Robert Drew, Richard Leacock, and D. A. Pennebaker; their first production was *Primary*, a behind-the-scenes glimpse of John F. Kennedy and Hubert Humphrey, two presidential candidates competing for the Democratic nomination. Released in 1960, after Kennedy defeated Nixon, the film transformed the world of nonfiction journalism—and inspired Albert and David to make their own films. From 1963 on, many of their subjects were artists, from Marlon Brando and Truman Capote to the Beatles and the Rolling Stones—all filmed with minimal intervention. Personal truth was the goal.

The two brothers became an institution. In order to fund their art, they began making "real people" commercials and corporate films—and by the time I joined the team, client meetings were as frequent as celebrity sightings. The best times for me were my own "close encounters" with the writers and filmmakers who dropped by our office, and the hours I spent in our edit rooms.

I got to sit beside some of the greats: Charlotte Zwerin, Kathy Dougherty, Ellen Hovde, Muffie Meyers, Susan Froemke, Deborah Dickson… Looking over their shoulders while they drove the Steenbecks, adjusting image and sound one frame at a time, I learned the patience that goes with long hours of screening, the challenge of choosing what scene should go where. I learned the anguish of an inaudible word and the joy of figuring out how to save it, the thrill found in moments that light up the screen. To this day, even though digital editing no longer involves the physical cutting of film, I can still hear the sound of a guillotine splicer—and I'm *still* awed by the difference two frames can make.

I took pride in the fact that I was a Maysles filmmaker. Beyond my grant-writing, beyond sharing opinions on rough cuts, I'd even managed to make a film for one of our corporate clients: a dubious honor, but still…

I wondered how to put it all to good use.

Outside of the office, I was still developing my own projects: a book version of my first screenplay, *Territory*; a new script about a Love Canal teacher/activist and chemical waste; a rewrite of my Thomas Paine drama. But, much like Baldwin's film ventures, my efforts led to signed contracts without end result, and I kept working at Maysles.

Then fate intervened. Someone sent a letter to our penthouse office—I have no idea who, I no longer have the letter—suggesting a number of famous people as ideal subjects for a Direct Cinema portrait … and James Baldwin was on the list.

My heart literally skipped a beat. *That* was what I wanted to do. I had no idea where in the world Baldwin was, but I figured he was still writing: his book on the Atlanta child murders, *The Evidence of Things Not Seen* (1985), had just been published, along with a huge tome of collected essays, *The Price of the Ticket* (1985). They were on my to-buy list. Without further research—remember, these were pre-Google days, you couldn't find information with the tap of a finger—I broached the idea to Albert and David. After a brief back-and-forth, they agreed that if I could raise the money for a film on "James Baldwin Today," they would helm it with me as producer.

I went home that night, elated. Both to share my news with Doug, that wonderfully smart, funny guy from "The Fed" crew whom I was now living with—and to dust off the Baldwin books still lining my bookcase, to flip through the pages and my notes in the margins, just to refresh my memory. To make sure that his words still held their original magic.

They did.

Finally, I'd found a path that matched my convictions—but first, I had to find Baldwin.

* * * * * *

Note to the Reader: Part Two will explore my collaboration with Baldwin. For 22 months, from early 1986 to his death on 1 December 1987, we worked on a *cinéma vérité* version of his next book, "Remember This House." For 25 months, from 1 December 1987 to January 1990, we worked on his posthumous biographical portrait, *James Baldwin: The Price of the Ticket—cinéma vérité passé*. His presence was constant throughout, his contribution substantial. It continues to this day.

Notes

1 James Baldwin, "Autobiographical Notes," in *Notes of a Native Son* (1955) (New York, Beacon Press, 1990), pp. 7, 8.

2 David Leeming, "Introduction," in Baldwin, *Notes of a Native Son*, p. xix.

3 James Baldwin, *The Devil Finds Work* (New York, Dial Press, 1976), p. 8.

4 *Ibid.*, p. 10.

5 *Ibid.*, p. 13.

6 *Ibid.*, p. 6; Karen Thorsen (dir.), *James Baldwin: The Price of the Ticket* (Maysles Films & PBS/American Masters, 1990).

7 Baldwin, *The Devil Finds Work*, pp. 8, 7.

8 James Baldwin, *The Fire Next Time* (New York, Dial Press, 1963), pp. 29–30; Baldwin, *The Devil Finds Work*, p. 34.

9 Baldwin, *The Devil Finds Work*, pp. 45, 60; James Baldwin, *No Name in the Street* (New York, Dial Press, 1972), p. 97.

10 Baldwin, *No Name in the Street*, p. 120.

11 Baldwin, *The Fire Next Time*, pp. 23–4.

12 Baldwin, *No Name in the Street*, p. 193.

13 James Baldwin, "The Northern Protestant," in *Nobody Knows My Name* (1961) (New York, Dell, 1986), p. 138.

14 James Baldwin, "Fifth Avenue, Uptown," in *Nobody Knows My Name*, p. 59.

15 *Ibid.*

16 James Baldwin, "The Black Boy Looks at the White Boy," in *Nobody Knows My Name*, p. 183.

17 Jane Howard, "Doom and Glory of Knowing Who You Are," *LIFE Magazine*, 54:21, 24 May 1963, p. 89.

18 Baldwin, "The Black Boy Looks at the White Boy," p. 171.

19 Baldwin, "The Northern Protestant," pp. 134, 143.

20 Baldwin, *The Devil Finds Work*, p. 107.

21 Baldwin, "The Black Boy Looks at the White Boy," pp. 176, 177.

22 Baldwin, "The Northern Protestant," p. 143; Baldwin, "The Black Boy Looks at the White Boy," p. 176; Studs Terkel, "An Interview with James Baldwin," *Almanac*, WFMT, Chicago, 29 December 1961, in *James Baldwin: The Last Interview and Other Conversations* (New York, Melville House, 2014), p. 31.

23 Baldwin, "The Northern Protestant," p. 133; Baldwin, *The Devil Finds Work*, p. 96.

24 Baldwin, *The Devil Finds Work*, p. 99.

25 *Ibid.*, p. 112.

26 *Ibid.*, p. 109.

27 *Ibid.*, p. 100.

28 *Ibid.*, p. 55.

29 Thorsen (dir.), *James Baldwin: The Price of the Ticket*.

30 Leslie Bennetts, "James Baldwin Reflects On 'Go Tell It' PBS Film," *New York Times*, 10 January 1985, Section C, p. 17.

31 Baldwin, "Preface," 1984 edition, in *Notes of a Native Son*, p. xxix.

32 An account of this collaboration, by South African filmmaker Michael Raeburn, appears in *James Baldwin Review*, 5 (2019).

33 Grace Nagata, "Interview with James Baldwin, 'I Can't Blow This Gig,'" *Cinema*, 4:2 (1968), p. 3.

34 David Leeming, *James Baldwin: A Biography* (New York, Alfred A. Knopf, 1994), p. 298.

35 Baldwin, *The Devil Finds Work*, p. 96.

36 Leeming, *James Baldwin*, p. 297; Baldwin, *No Name in the Street*, p. 99; James Baldwin, "Carmen Jones," in *Notes of a Native Son*, p. 46.

37 Nagata, "Interview with James Baldwin," p. 3.

38 Baldwin, *The Devil Finds Work*, p. 97.

39 Leeming, *James Baldwin*, p. 300.

40 Baldwin, *The Devil Finds Work*, p. 99; Baldwin, *No Name in the Street*, p. 11.

41 Baldwin, *The Devil Finds Work*, p. 95.

42 Baldwin, "The Black Boy Looks at the White Boy," p. 177.

43 *Ibid.*, p. 178.
44 Baldwin, *The Devil Finds Work*, p. 56.
45 Albert Maysles, http://mayslesfilms.com/albert-maysles/ (accessed 15 June 2020).
46 Baldwin, "The Northern Protestant," pp. 135, 136.
47 *Ibid.*, p. 136.
48 Albert Maysles, http://mayslesfilms.com/albert-maysles/.
49 Baldwin, *No Name in the Street*, p. 63; Terkel, "An Interview with James Baldwin," p. 31; Baldwin, *The Devil Finds Work*, p. 121.

Works Cited

Baldwin, James, "Autobiographical Notes," in *Notes of a Native Son* (1955) (New York, Beacon Press, 1990), pp. 3–12.
_____ "The Black Boy Looks at the White Boy," in *Nobody Knows My Name* (1961) (New York, Dell, 1986), pp. 169–98.
_____ "Carmen Jones," in *Notes of a Native Son* (1955) (New York, Beacon Press, 1990), pp. 46–56.
_____ *The Devil Finds Work* (New York, Dial Press, 1976).
_____ "Fifth Avenue, Uptown," in *Nobody Knows My Name* (1961) (New York, Dell, 1986), pp. 53–64.
_____ *The Fire Next Time* (New York, Dial Press, 1963).
_____ *No Name in the Street* (New York, Dial Press, 1972).
_____ *Nobody Knows My Name* (1961) (New York, Dell, 1986).
_____ "The Northern Protestant," in *Nobody Knows My Name* (1961) (New York, Dell, 1986), pp. 131–43.
_____ *Notes of a Native Son* (1955) (New York, Beacon Press, 1990).
Bennetts, Leslie, "James Baldwin Reflects On 'Go Tell It' PBS Film," *New York Times*, 10 January 1985, Section C, p. 17.
Howard, Jane, "Doom and Glory of Knowing Who You Are," *LIFE Magazine*, 54:21, 24 May 1963, pp. 81–4.
Leeming, David, *James Baldwin: A Biography* (New York, Alfred A. Knopf, 1994).
Nagata, Grace, "Interview with James Baldwin, 'I Can't Blow This Gig,'" *Cinema*, 4:2 (1968), pp. 2–3.
Raeburn, Michael, "We can love one another in other ways": Collaborating with James Baldwin on a Screenplay of *Giovanni's Room*," *James Baldwin Review*, 5 (2019), pp. 129–42.
Terkel, Studs, "An Interview with James Baldwin," *Almanac*, WFMT, Chicago, 29 December 1961, in *James Baldwin: The Last Interview and Other Conversations* (New York, Melville House, 2014), pp. 2–34.
Thorsen, Karen (dir.), *James Baldwin: The Price of the Ticket* (Maysles Films & PBS/American Masters, 1990).

Contributor's Biography

Karen Thorsen is an award-winning writer/filmmaker who finds inspiration at the intersection of art and social justice. Her heroes are game-changers, the artist/activists who shape history; her films tell stories without narration, weaving first-person narratives with archival treasures. Thorsen began as a writer. After graduating from Vassar with a year at the Sorbonne, she was an editor for Simon and Schuster, journalist for *Life* and foreign correspondent for *Time*. Screenwriting followed, then directing. Her first feature-length documentary was *James Baldwin: The Price of the Ticket* (1990), produced with Maysles Films and PBS/ American Masters. Now considered a classic, it has been honored in twenty-five countries. Recently remastered in WideScreen 2KHD, the new 'Digital Baldwin' is a centerpiece of the *James Baldwin Project*'s nationwide series of community forums on racism, discrimination, and the meaning of brotherhood. Supported by the Ford Foundation, NEA, and others, these film screenings and 'talkbacks' have already reached tens of thousands. Beyond Baldwin, Thorsen's credits include broadcast productions, museum installations, documentary shorts, and interactive media—often in collaboration with DKDmedia's Douglas K. Dempsey. Their films have screened on six continents and in six museums on the National Mall; permanent installations include the Smithsonian Museum of American History, George Washington's Mount Vernon, Great Platte River Archway, and Pilgrim Hall Museum. Recognition ranges from multiple THEA and festival honors to Parents Choice and the Oscars short list. Thorsen's current projects include *Keep It Lit!*, a digital design-your-own James Baldwin curriculum (with the National Writing Project); *Inside the Glass House: Exploring Philip Johnson*, an interactive mix of long- and short-form documentaries with photogrammetry, point clouds, and 3D imagery (with the National Trust for Historic Preservation); *Thomas Paine: Voice of Revolution*, a feature-length documentary and museum app (an NEH "We The People" project); and *Joe Papp in Five Acts*, a feature-length documentary codirected with Tracie Holder that premiered at the Tribeca Film Festival and will be on PBS/American Masters.

BIBLIOGRAPHIC ESSAY

Trends in Baldwin Criticism, 2016–17

Joseph Vogel   Merrimack College

Abstract

This review article charts the general direction of scholarship in James Baldwin studies between the years 2016 and 2017, reflecting on important scholarly events and publications of the period and identifying notable trends in criticism. Surveying the field as a whole, the most notable features are the "political turn" that seeks to connect Baldwin's social insights from the past to the present, and the ongoing access to and interest in the Baldwin archive. In addition to these larger trends, there is continued interest in situating Baldwin in national, regional, and geographical contexts as well as interest with how he grapples with and illuminates issues of gender and sexuality.

Keywords: James Baldwin, African-American literature, literary criticism, political turn, archive, Raoul Peck, *I Am Not Your Negro*

The Baldwin renaissance reached perhaps its highest peak to date in the years 2016 and 2017—years that saw a major gathering of scholars, activists, and artists in Paris for the fifth International James Baldwin Conference; a major new acquisition of Baldwin's papers by the Schomburg Center for Research in Black Culture; and, most prominently, the premiere of Haitian filmmaker Raoul Peck's Oscar-nominated documentary, *I Am Not Your Negro*.

Released in the wake of former reality TV star and real estate mogul Donald Trump's shocking election as president of the United States, Peck's film hit a nerve. In America, the national mood was tense, coiled. Baldwin had already been absorbed by the Black Lives Matter movement in the Obama era, when police violence, regular mass shootings—including the Charleston massacre at the Emanuel African Methodist Episcopal Church by white supremacist Dylann Roof—and a festering backlash to the first Black president indicated troubling signs about the direction of the country. But by February 2017, when the film hit

James Baldwin Review, Volume 6, 2020, © The Authors. Published by Manchester University Press and
The University of Manchester Library
http://dx.doi.org/10.7227/JBR.6.10

theaters, the need for Baldwin's incisive moral clarity was greater than ever. Trump seemed to be the grotesque embodiment and culmination of everything Baldwin warned against, particularly in the post-civil rights era, when many wanted to believe the struggle for racial justice was over and the author's still-razor sharp indictments of America were perceived as bitter and passé. Decades later, those same words crackled with prescient fury.

For director Peck, the film was an opportunity to illuminate both past and present.

> We see why Baldwin is efficient, because he went to those fundamental issues. And what has really changed, fundamentally, in this country? Is there less inequality? Is the problem of poverty solved? Is the problem of racism solved? No. Thirty years is nothing in the life of a country and we can't just pretend as if everything is beautiful. That's why his voice is essential and I can understand that the shock is real. While working on this, although I knew all those things, I was seeing how the daily news was making this story even sharper.[1]

I Am Not Your Negro grossed $7.7 million at the box office, an unprecedented figure for a documentary about a literary figure. Described as Magnolia Pictures' "breakout hit," the film surpassed 2004's *Woman, Thou Art Loosed* as the independent distributor's top-grossing film of all time.[2] It earned a number of accolades, including a nomination for Best Documentary Feature from the Academy Awards, and winning Best Documentary from the British Academy of Film and Television Arts and at the NAACP Image Awards. It also received widespread critical and popular acclaim, generating an approval rating of 98 percent on review aggregation website *Rotten Tomatoes*. Most importantly, however, it offered a platform for James Baldwin, introducing the author to millions of people, many of whom had never been exposed to his voice and work.

The loosely structured, impressionistic film was based on Baldwin's unfinished manuscript, "Remember This House." That manuscript, acquired from the James Baldwin Estate, was a meditation not only on civil rights icons Medgar Evers, Malcolm X, and Martin Luther King, Jr., but also on the often overlooked cultural underpinnings of America—ideas and ideologies, representations and illusions. Narrated by Samuel L. Jackson, it allowed the author to bear witness to a new generation, deftly intersplicing visuals of the past and present accompanied by Baldwin's hauntingly prophetic words.

The film was not without its flaws. In *The Atlantic*, scholar Dagmawi Woubshet notes the documentary's near-silence on Baldwin's sexuality. Woubshet praises the film's "imperfect power," particularly for giving the viewer direct access to Baldwin, "[an] ingenious move [that] allows viewers to fully appreciate Baldwin's unmatched eloquence and form a portrait of the artist through his own words."[3] Yet for Woubshet, the decision to omit an exploration of Baldwin's sexuality, "especially the time in Baldwin's life when his sexuality became a liability to his public role, is a missed opportunity. And it forgoes the chance to have Baldwin's complex life reflect the complexity of our contemporary identities."[4]

Still, *I Am Not Your Negro* represented a watershed moment for the legacy of James Baldwin. As A. O. Scott observed in the *New York Times*, "you would be hard-pressed to find a movie that speaks to the present moment with greater clarity and force, insisting on uncomfortable truths and drawing stark lessons from the shadows of history."[5] Following its theatrical run, *I Am Not Your Negro* was released on DVD/Blu-ray and as a tie-in book, as well as on streaming platforms such as Amazon Prime, further expanding its audience. "James Baldwin died in 1987, but his moment is now," declared the *New York Times* in April 2017. "His books are flying off the shelves."[6] In the summer of 2017, CBS News reported a 110 percent increase in Baldwin's book sales, a remarkable figure given that the author's popularity had already surged in the previous years.[7]

The film also seemed to inspire a spike in scholarship, though its full effect may not be known for years, given the longer process of academic publishing. Three articles, published in 2017, began to explore the impact and meanings of Peck's film: Warren Critchlow's "Baldwin's Rendezvous with the Twenty-First Century: *I Am Not Your Negro*," published in *Film Quarterly*; Robert J. Corber's "Queering *I Am Not Your Negro*: Or, Why We Need James Baldwin More Than Ever," published in volume 3 of *James Baldwin Review*; and Thomas Chatterton Williams's "Going to Meet the Man," published in *Sight & Sound*. In his essay, Critchlow praises Peck's film for "reanimating the archive through bricolage," allowing Baldwin to realize his vision of speaking both within and beyond his time, thus interrogating and generating "new imaginaries for the future."[8] Corber, meanwhile, concurs with Dagmawi Woubshet that, while Peck's film represents a "remarkable achievement," it does so by privileging Baldwin's "blackness over his queerness," thus denying audiences the author's full complexity.[9] Finally, Thomas Chatterton Williams's review elaborates on this temptation to appropriate Baldwin to fill contemporary needs. Williams sees the film as an extension of the success of Ta-Nehisi Coates's bestselling book *Between the World and Me*, a book modeled both stylistically and tonally on Baldwin's 1963 masterpiece, *The Fire Next Time*. Coates's book was famously praised by Toni Morrison as filling the "intellectual void" left by Baldwin. For Williams, however, Coates's book and Peck's documentary represent a flattening of the real Baldwin.

> The distillation of such a multitudinous writer to a single register has been so effective and complete that today it can feel as though contemporary writers like Coates are less the new Baldwin than that audiences are embracing Baldwin as the original Coates—in the process missing a large amount of the complexity that made him so special and difficult to categorize in the first place.[10]

While the media consensus of *I Am Not Your Negro* was almost universally positive, then, the scholarly assessment was much more mixed.

I dwell on *I Am Not Your Negro* in this bibliographic essay not only because of its influence on Baldwin scholarship and sizable cultural impact, but also because of what it represents. In terms of "trends," the documentary was at the center of what might be termed a "political turn" in Baldwin studies. James Baldwin's work, of course, has always been political. Moreover, over the past few decades numerous critics and scholars have highlighted the political dimensions and resonance of his work. But if there is one overarching trend to the field in the years 2016 and 2017—the first years of the racially charged Trump era—it is how invested it is in Baldwin's relationship to the political realities of his home country, both during his life and now.

Beyond Peck's documentary, this turn also includes two important books—Susan J. McWilliams's *A Political Companion to James Baldwin* (University Press of Kentucky, 2017) and William Maxwell's *James Baldwin: The FBI File* (Arcadia, 2017). Featuring fourteen original essays and an introduction by McWilliams, *A Political Companion to James Baldwin* not only analyzes Baldwin's pointed views on racial injustice, but also how he envisioned race, gender, sexuality, class, and religion within a broader, intersectional survey of democratic life in America. "For Baldwin," writes McWilliams,

> understanding the surface dilemma of racial injustice in the United States was never enough. For him, it was necessary to go deeper, to tend to the cringing ambivalences, the terrors of belonging, the screaming and anxious clamour of the American soul. In Baldwin's telling, the machinery of our history has mangled us all; even if we could take apart the machinery, we could not repair all the damage it has done to our selves.[11]

Simply "raising awareness," that is, is not enough; nor is implementing legislation or changing political leaders. As Baldwin famously put it when told by Robert F. Kennedy that in forty years we might have a Black president, he was less interested in whether America had a Black president than in what the country looked like when there was a Black president.

For McWilliams, "experience" is central to Baldwin's sense of American failure. The country, quite simply, refuses to grow up. We refuse to give up our illusions. We refuse to give up our (perceived) safety. We refuse to confront the realities that, if looked at carefully and thoughtfully, might lead to genuine discovery and progress. "Horror," she writes, "is the fact, and safety is the illusion. For Baldwin, accepting the truth is 'the source of all our power,' not just in the generally human but in the democratic sense."[12] This, contends McWilliams, is Baldwin's central insight about social progress—"the lesson of the American political experience and the lesson that precedes any true democratic achievement: we must know and name the fear in order to know and name ourselves."[13]

McWilliams divides her collection into four sections: collective consciousness and community; prophecy, religion, and truth; the individual life, the interior life, the unexamined life; and violence and vision. While some of the essays in the collection have previously appeared elsewhere, many of them are new. Each explores Baldwin's unique and multifaceted contribution to political and democratic theory, some read within the historical context in which Baldwin was writing, and others applied to more contemporary developments, including the presidency of Barack Obama and the Black Lives Matter movement. We keep experiencing "Baldwinian moments," argues McWilliams, because

> America is still that "exceedingly monotonous minstrel show," running over and again "through the same dances, same music, same jokes," and in which Baldwin played participant, viewer, and critic. "One has done (or been) the show for so long one can do it in one's sleep"; he had the script down. Before and since Baldwin's death thirty years ago, the American political experience, and particularly the racial politics that lie in the bloody and battered heart of that experience, keeps us turning back and back to the importance of turning back to Baldwin.[14]

Also published in 2017, William Maxwell's *James Baldwin: The FBI File* offers a more specific window into the charged politics of the civil rights era with the first book-length account of the F.B.I.'s secret dossier on Baldwin. As Maxwell notes, no artist or literary figure was followed as closely as Baldwin was from 1958 to 1974. Overseen by the bureau's infamous director, J. Edgar Hoover—whom Baldwin once described as "history's most highly paid (and most utterly useless) *voyeur*"— Baldwin's file is 1,884 pages in length. By comparison, novelist Richard Wright's file was only 276 pages; Henry Miller's was only nine.[15] The file was first obtained by Baldwin biographer James Campbell after a successful 1998 court challenge. It now resides in the public domain and has been explored by a handful of journalists and scholars, most notably in Douglas Field's outstanding chapter "Radical Baldwin and the FBI: From the Civil Rights Movement to Black Power," from *All Those Strangers: The Art and Lives of James Baldwin* (2015).

Maxwell's book includes hundreds of reproduced images of the F.B.I.'s collected papers, notations, and evaluations. "Tedious repetitions in the file have not made the cut," writes Maxwell, "but the documents included were chosen to reflect the file's complete range, from plainly mistaken information on Baldwin's marital status to piercing insight into his social and artistic commitments."[16] What emerges from this file is an author at once feared and admired. For the bulk of the period he was surveilled, Baldwin was classified as a Category IV threat in the Administrative Index (ADEX) for his perceived ties to the Black Power movement and communism, as well as his sexuality and subversive views on America. J. Edgar Hoover infamously characterized him as a "well known pervert," while assigning agents to tap his phone, rummage through his trash, scour his novels and speeches, and evaluate the "revolutionary elements" of his life and work. Baldwin, Maxwell notes, was not oblivious to this surveillance. To the contrary, he saw it as a violent intrusion and countered the F.B.I.'s efforts by looking back, publicly touting an exposé in progress on the bureau entitled "The Blood Counters"—"supposedly titled after 'the negroes' nickname for the FBI in the South during … recent civil rights incidents."[17] That work was never written, but the F.B.I. took note.

For all its suspicion, Maxwell observes that the F.B.I.'s file also inadvertently reads as a recognition of Baldwin's influence and literary merit. Next to bland telegraphs and memoranda are reviews of *The Fire Next Time* and *Another*

Country. Maxwell describes "these strange documents" as a confluence of "literary criticism and secret police work."[18] The montage of files, surveyed as a whole, reveals a sense of "astonishment over black literary sophistication and influence, the enduring product of the national security state's apprehension that modern literacy had trumped modern black slavery."[19] Maxwell connects some of the qualities that singled Baldwin out as subversive to the F.B.I. as part of his enduring political resonance, particularly to the Black Lives Matter movement. In his introduction, Maxwell dedicates nearly half of the space to how Baldwin has been embraced and wielded by young revolutionaries for precisely the reasons Hoover and the F.B.I. saw him as a potential threat to "its ideal of the American order, racial, sexual, and cultural."[20]

In the 1960s, notes Maxwell, Baldwin was deemed suspicious by the F.B.I., civil rights leaders, and Black Power leaders alike, largely because of his sexual orientation. In one "Airtel" message intercepted by the F.B.I., Martin Luther King, Jr.'s close friend and advisor Stanley Levison asserted that figures like Baldwin and veteran gay organizer Bayard Rustin were "better qualified to lead a homo-sexual movement than a civil rights movement."[21] Ironically, however, it is Baldwin's progressive views on gender and sexuality, once viewed as embarrassing baggage at best, and vicious blackmail material at worst, that have endeared him to the sensibility of the present moment. Maxwell quotes Thomas Chatterton Williams's assessment that the very "same characteristics of the Baldwin brand that so 'estranged' him from the concerns of his generation and of black America writ large—his intersectionality before that was a thing—are what make him such an exemplar of the queer-inflected mood of the #BlackLivesMatter era now."[22] While Maxwell takes issue with Williams's claim about Baldwin's near-complete alienation from his own generation in the civil rights era, he agrees with the reasons for his contemporary acceptance. In today's fraught racial and political environment, writes Maxwell, Baldwin

> reigns as the movement's literary touchstone, conscience, and pinup, its go-to ideal of the writer in arms whose social witness only enhances his artfulness. It's Baldwin's good name and impassioned queer fatherhood that aspiring movement intellectuals invoke in Twitter handles such as #SonofBaldwin, #Flames_Baldwin, and #Baemes-Baldwin. It's Baldwin's distilled racial wisdom, often mined from his heated Black Power-era interviews, that fortifies these intellectuals' posts and tweets.[23]

The Black Lives Matter section of Maxwell's introduction is a distillation of his 2016 essay "Born-Again, Seen-Again James Baldwin: Post-Postracial Criticism and the Literary History of Black Lives Matter," published in *American Literary History*. In that essay, Maxwell offers a deeper investigation into Baldwin's connections to the Black Lives Matter movement, highlighting the author's emphasis on the "physical precarity of black American life" and the ways in which it both utilizes and more hopefully bends Afro-pessimism. "All of these analogies," writes Maxwell, spotted through the lens of Baldwin's once invisible prereckoning with the stuff of neoliberal racial formation, have joined to make him the most-tweeted literary authority of BLM. The blend of political prophecy and theatrical self-exposure in nearly all of his essays, regardless of their topic, indeed anticipates the very twenty-first-century job description of the freedom fighter/social media star.[24]

In this way, it is not simply that Baldwin is frequently quoted and referenced, notes Maxwell, it is also his voice, rhetorical style, and language which has provided a model for a new generation of activists and writers, including Ta-Nehisi Coates, DeRay McKesson, Shaun King, and Jesmyn Ward. Simon and Schuster published a collection of such voices in a Baldwin-influenced collection entitled *The Fire This Time: A New Generation Speaks About Race*, published in 2016. Edited by National Book Award Winner Jesmyn Ward, the collection features over a dozen contributions from young writers using Baldwin as inspiration to grapple with the events and struggles of the present.

This impulse to use Baldwin as both temporal link and oracle has been the hallmark of a wave of new scholarship. In his 2016 essay "Thinking Historically," published in *Theory and Event*, Jack Turner explores the political and philosophical underpinnings of such connections. Drawing on Baldwin and other African-American intellectuals such as W. E. B. Du Bois, his article investigates the implications of history on political thinking. "When does the past begin to be past?" he asks. "When does the past cease to be present? How do we forge a language fully adequate to past and present's complex relation?"[25] Turner contends that Baldwin's conceptualization of a past that is interlinked with the present disrupts traditional Western "Cambridge School" approaches that bifurcate time and offer simplistic resolution. In its place, authors like Baldwin "think with the past."[26] What this means, Turner explains, goes beyond recognizing parallels between eras.

> Thinking *with* Baldwin helps us overcome ideologically ingrained myths of racial progress—for it brings historical continuity into sharp relief in a present saturated with insistence that "Things have changed." Thinking *with* Baldwin upsets Whig histories designed to blind us to historical continuity and therefore prevent us from bringing our harsh judgments of bygone periods of white supremacy—slavery and Jim Crow—to bear on one of its main contemporary configurations—the modern American police state … The example of Baldwin on police power urges us to resist hard and fast distinctions between the history of political thought and contemporary political reflection. The history of political thought may productively inform contemporary political reflection by serving as a counterweight to prevailing "common sense," helping us see the present more clearly.[27]

With such essays, books, and films, it is clear that the political exigencies of our time have shaped our responses to, and repurposing of, Baldwin. This engagement makes sense given Baldwin's consistent claim that artists, writers, and scholars have a social responsibility to their country, community, and people—a belief than many of his literary peers found naive and old-fashioned. Indeed, the author went so far as to describe abdicating that responsibility as a moral failure. "I think that it is a spiritual disaster to pretend that one *doesn't* love one's country," he said in a 1984 interview with the *Paris Review*. "You may disapprove of it, you may be forced to leave it, you may live your whole life as a battle, yet I don't think you can escape it."[28]

In the introduction to volume 2 (2016) of *James Baldwin Review*, the editors echo these sentiments. "We have to say something," Justin A. Joyce, Dwight A. McBride, and Douglas Field write,

> The litany of violent spectacles … seems to demand that we say something … But what is there to say here about the atrocities we encounter each day? That Baldwin is still relevant? That, prophetically, he saw it all coming? … These discourses, however, are apt to short circuit, to dwell and dissolve within their own closed loops. For to speak about Baldwin's continuing relevance and prophetic voice invites not only endless comparisons between him and more current writers, but also an endless array of disavowals. The conversation quickly becomes a Nostradamus-like search into whether or not Baldwin "saw it coming" or "got it right."
>
> But again, we have to say something. To introduce this volume's collection of essays without invoking the current geopolitical climate of terror, police violence, astonishingly narcissistic politicians grandstanding on platforms of virulent nationalism winning the hearts and minds of too many people, and a union of Europeans on the cusp of collapsing, seems naive at best. Surely, in the face of all these atrocities we have to say something.[29]

The articles, reviews, and dispatches in the journal did just that, from David W. McIvor's "The Struggle of Integration: James Baldwin and Melanie Klein in the Context of Black Lives Matter" to Mikko Tuhkanen's "Watching Time: James Baldwin and Malcolm X." In McIvor's essay, he couples Klein's psychoanalytic insights and Baldwin's politically grounded "object relations theory" to make sense of ongoing failures of social integration. Tuhkanen, meanwhile, focuses on the concept of time to explore why both Baldwin and Malcolm X rejected the notion of gradualism to achieve social progress.

In a powerful reflection written for *JBR* volume 3 (2017), soon after Donald Trump's election as president of the United States, Justin A. Joyce acknowledges the shattering silence we often feel in the wake of tragic and demoralizing events. Words often don't seem adequate. What do parents tell their children when America has exalted as its leader a man who so gratuitously flaunts all of the country's worst impulses? Yet it is in precisely these moments, writes Joyce, that we must turn to our artists and writers—not merely for comfort. "James Baldwin," notes Joyce, "refuses such succor. Arguing instead for a search for the hardest truths, the deepest confessions, a systemic upheaval, Baldwin's clarion call rings loudest in those silent moments when our words fail us."[30] This is the impetus behind the "political turn" in Baldwin studies—the recognition that Baldwin has not simply become popular or fashionable as a object of study, but that we need him. Our present moment needs his voice, his clarity, his rejection of easy answers, his refusal to cede to despair, his call for individual, social, and political responsibility.

While the politics surrounding the author have been the most prominent strain in Baldwin studies in these years, this is by no means the only significant trend.

Indeed, William Maxwell's book on Baldwin and the F.B.I., based on documents obtained through the Freedom of Information Act, points to another ongoing development: increased access to Baldwin's archives. In her 2015–16 Bibliographic Essay, Jenny M. James highlighted a "burgeoning archival turn" in Baldwin scholarship.[31] That trend received a major boost in April 2017 when it was announced that the Schomburg Center for Research in Black Culture, a division of the New York Public Library in Harlem, had acquired a substantial new collection of Baldwin's papers. The acquisition included over seventy boxes of material, including a rich trove of manuscripts, drafts, notes, letters, and audio tapes, most of which had never been seen before. "We are more than excited to have James Baldwin return home to Harlem," said Kevin Young, director of the Schomburg Center.

> Baldwin's amazing collection adds to our ever-growing holdings of writers, political figures, artists, and cultural icons across the African diaspora. With the current resurgence of interest in Baldwin's works and words, and renovation of our own spaces from the main gallery to the Schomburg Shop, the timing couldn't be better for Baldwin to join us at the Schomburg Center.[32]

While there is no doubt that the acquisition represented a coup for the Schomburg Center, Baldwin scholars, and anyone interested in the author's life and work, the collection did come with restrictions, particularly concerning Baldwin's personal correspondence. His private letters, including those to his brother David and friend/lover Lucien Happersberger, remain under a twenty-year seal. Author and critic Hilton Als famously described that private correspondence as the "one great Baldwin masterpiece waiting to be published, one composed in an atmosphere of focused intimacy."[33] One of the few people granted access to these documents, scholar and poet Ed Pavlić, wrote eloquently about his encounter with them for the *Boston Review* in 2015. Pavlić visited Baldwin's sister and literary executor, Gloria Karefa-Smart, in the summer of 2010, and was entrusted with an estimated 120 letters, amounting to 70,000 words. Writes Pavlić of this private correspondence: "They give an unprecedented picture of his life and work, an epistolary autobiography: they bristle and crackle with the trials, dangers, errors, mistakes, and triumphs of one of the most important literary figures of the twentieth century."[34] For now, Pavlić's vivid account is the most detailed and enticing glimpse of the letters the public has. However, the Schomburg Center's acquisition remains an important moment in Baldwin studies, both for what it currently holds, and for what it will reveal in the years to come.

In addition to the political turn and the ongoing access to and interest in the Baldwin archive, there have been other important developments and contributions to the field. Baldwin studies continues to see strong interest in the transnational Baldwin, considering his complex relationship to his various "homes." Indeed, in 2016 the academic journal *CR: The New Centennial Review*, which is devoted to comparative studies of the Americas, dedicated an entire section to Baldwin, including standout essays that consider the author in the context of place. Grant Farred's "Baldwin in Britain" explores the ideological and nationalist contours of the author's 1965 debate with conservative William F. Buckley at the Cambridge University Union—one of the most circulated Baldwin videos, that debate now has over 1.5 million views on YouTube.[35] Farred also considers the Horace Ové film, *Baldwin's Nigger*, which features a speech Baldwin gave at London's West Indian Student Center in 1969. John E. Drabinski's "Baldwin's Three Africans," meanwhile, draws primarily on Baldwin's essay "Princes and Powers" to consider "the existential, metaphysical, and affective attachments of the midcentury moment, its fixation on Africa and how that fixation, for [Baldwin], says too much about the meaning of blackness."[36] Drabinski finds a paradox at the center of Baldwin's writings on Africa: on the one hand, it is written from the outside, with a certain ambivalence; yet on the other hand, it is intimate and profoundly central to the Black American imaginary.

Beyond the *CR: The New Centennial Review* issue, a number of other recent articles situate Baldwin in particular geographical contexts. In her 2016 article "Mapping Narratives of Reversal in 'Baldwin's Paris,'" published in *CLA Journal*, Tyechia Lynn Thompson broadens her scope beyond the time Baldwin lived in Paris (1948–57), surveying his entire canon to map the meaning of this space to his literary output. "Quantifying, visually displaying, and analyzing 'Baldwin's Paris,'" argues Thompson, "expands the perception of Baldwin's Paris period and assists in evaluating Baldwin's representations of Paris pre-and-post-1963."[37] In his article "James Baldwin on Vacation in *Another Country*," published in *ELH: English Literary History*, Spencer Morrison takes a more specific approach, using Baldwin's 1962 novel to "situate its renderings of urbanity and mobility within post-WWII geopolitical upheavals." Against the critical consensus of characters in exile, Morrison reads accounts of transnational mobility in *Another Country* as a self-reflexive meditation on both privilege and "affect rooted in compassion."[38]

Baldwin's complex grappling with sexuality also continues to be a major area of interest in Baldwin studies. In Cynthia Barounis's essay "'Not the Usual Pattern': James Baldwin, Homosexuality, and the DSM," published in *Criticism: A Quarterly for Literature and the Arts* in 2017, she explores Baldwin's relationship to the word "homosexuality," which was first used in the *Diagnostic and Statistical Manual of Mental Disorders* (*DSM*) in 1952, just four years before the publication of *Giovanni's Room*. Barounis argues that his novel is "crucially engaged with this queer moment in the history of medicine," but that Baldwin's approach to the subject differs dramatically from gay activism of the time.[39] Barounis reads *Giovanni's Room* as an "exploration of how these diagnostic criteria might function, for some gay subjects, as a counterintuitive site of racial and class privilege—one which cleansed same-sex desire of many of its previous associations with effeminacy, poverty, interracial intimacy, and prostitution."[40] In his essay "'A Brutal, Indecent Spectacle': Heterosexuality, Futurity, and *Go Tell It on the Mountain*," published in *MFS: Modern Fiction Studies*, Mason Stokes examines Baldwin's views on heterosexuality, using the author's first novel to explore Gabriel's competing drives: desire itself and the desire to meet expectations and extend his family line through procreation. Stokes reads the novel as a deconstruction of heteroxuality, which he argues "contains within itself the seeds of its own undoing."[41] Meanwhile, in his article "Oedipus Complex in the South: Castration Anxiety and Lynching Ritual in James Baldwin's 'Going to Meet the Man,'" published in *CLA Journal*, Kwangsoon Kim explores the relationship between sexuality and violence using Baldwin's short story "Going to Meet the Man." Kim's essay focuses on Baldwin's choice to give the narrative voice in the story to Jesse, a white sheriff and victimizer, rather than the Black man being lynched. This choice, Kim argues, allows Baldwin to investigate the psychosexual dysfunction of a white man, and by extension, the white American South. In his essay "I've Got a Testimony: James Baldwin and the Broken Silences of Queer Men," published in *James Baldwin Review*, McKinley Melton focuses on Baldwin's rhetorical resistance within the context of the Black Church, connecting the space the author creates for queer voices and identities in the testimonial tradition to contemporary poet Danez Smith.

Associated with these explorations are two essays published in the special section of the 2016 issue of *CR: The New Centennial Review* focused on Baldwin's experience as and relationship with children, especially young boys. The first, Michele Elam's essay "Baldwin's Boys," draws our attention to how often boys, whether children or teenagers, appear in Baldwin's work, from his 1963 essay "My Dungeon Shook: Letter to My Nephew on the One Hundredth Anniversary of Emancipation," to his final 1985 book, *The Evidence of Things Not Seen*. For Baldwin, observes Elam, they play a multifaceted role: they "are sometimes intended audience, sometimes protagonist and interlocutor, sometimes echoes of the author, and always the most vulnerable."[42] Ultimately, Elam reads Baldwin's boys as a kind of "connection that yokes history with experience, that refuses "innocence," that challenges the conventions that state who can belong to who."[43] In her essay "17, or, Tough, Dark, Vulnerable, Moody," Marisa Parham also explores Baldwin's relationship to children, focusing more on the role of parenting and caregiving, "thus highlighting the motivational and expressive power of care in Baldwin's oeuvre, the revolutionary possibilities of Black American life embedded in loving children who are already in the world, no matter how they have arrived, where they have been, and who they might choose to become."[44]

Other notable Baldwin scholarship in this period include comparative analyses as represented by essays such as Jessica Kent's excellent essay "Baldwin's Hemingway: *The Sun Also Rises* in *Giovanni's Room*, with a Twist," published in *Twentieth Century Literature*, and Margaret Sönser Breen's "Race, Dissent, and Literary Imagination in John Bunyan and James Baldwin," published in *Bunyan Studies: A Journal of Reformation and Nonconformist Culture*; examinations of education, as represented by John P. Fantuzzo's "Facing the Civic Love Gap: James Baldwin's Civic Education for Interpersonal Solidarity," published in *Educational Theory*; and investigations of image and celebrity, as represented in Caryl Phillips's "Nothing Personal: James Baldwin, Richard Avedon, and the Pursuit of Celebrity," published in *ARIEL: A Review of International English Literature*.

These, then, are some of the most significant contributions and trends in the years 2016 and 2017. Looking at the field as a whole, the most notable features are the political turn that seeks to connect Baldwin's social insights from the past to the present, and the ongoing access to and interest in the Baldwin archive. In addition to these larger trends, we continue to see interest in situating Baldwin in national, regional, and geographical contexts, as well as with how he grapples with and illuminates issues of gender and sexuality. I echo a caveat issued by Jenny James in volume 5's Bibliographic Essay that this review of the Baldwin landscape is not intended to be exhaustive or comprehensive. Rather, it is a survey of as much work as could fit into a 7,000-word review, highlighting notable shifts and trends in the field.

I conclude by looking at one final essay, Magdalena Zaborowska's "Being James Baldwin, or Everything is Personal," published in the 2016 issue of *CR: The New Centennial Review*. I do so because it brings together some of the significant strands mentioned in this review of the field but leaves us with some thought-provoking questions as we move forward. Zaborowska recognizes the Baldwin renaissance as a positive development, but not without potential pitfalls. Of Baldwin's rise in popularity, she writes: "As if in response to our twenty-first century yearning for charismatic spokespersons and leaders who could offer more than superficially engineered images accompanied by equally shallow sound bites, he has been brought back from exile as a black cultural superstar."[45] Yet this new, twenty-first-century Baldwin, Zaborowska submits, is often divided into two different personas: "one slated for public consumption usually claims the early works and overshadows the writer's sexuality and complex ideas on gender, whereas the one we encounter in scholarship, while certainly more faithful to available sources, is largely inaccessible to lay readers."[46] In this way, Zaborowska echoes concerns registered in response to the two major developments in this period: the political Baldwin represented in Peck's documentary *I Am Not Your Negro* and the archival Baldwin represented in the Schomburg Center's acquisition of the author's papers. Both cases were seen as triumphs for Baldwin's legacy—and in many ways they were. Yet for Zaborowska and other scholars, both also left us with important questions about the Baldwin made public, and the more private, intimate, personal Baldwin who, for various reasons, remains hidden, or at least more obscure. The fact that more and more people are being exposed to Baldwin, even with limitations, is exciting and well deserved. But Zaborowska also asks us to consider: "What kind of Baldwin are we reintroducing to the American public, celebrating, reading, and teaching at universities and colleges today?"[47]

There is no easy answer to this question. Perhaps different parts of Baldwin are needed in different contexts, and certainly no one essay or film or book can account for the full complexity of his life and work. Yet it is an important note of caution as we celebrate his resurgence of popularity. Baldwin, after all, would be the first to interrogate how and why he is being elevated for mass consumption. We might consider doing the same even as we celebrate his flourishing legacy.

Notes

1 Olga Segura, "'I Am Not Your Negro,' James Baldwin, & Black Lives Matter: A Conversation with Raoul Peck," *America: The Jesuit Review*, 2 February 2017, www.americamagazine.org/arts-culture/2017/02/02/i-am-not-your-negro-james-baldwin-black-lives-matter-conversation-raoul (accessed 15 June 2020).

2 Graham Winfrey, "'I Am Not Your Negro': How Magnolia Pictures Launched a Smash Hit at the Box Office," *IndieWire*, 7 April 2017, www.indiewire.com/2017/04/i-am-not-your-negro-magnolia-smash-hit-box-office-1201802797/ (accessed 15 June 2020).

3 Dagmawi Woubshet, "The Imperfect Power of *I Am Not Your Negro*," *The Atlantic*, 8 February 2017, www.theatlantic.com/entertainment/archive/2017/02/i-am-not-your-negro-review/515976/ (accessed 15 June 2020).

4 *Ibid.*

5 A. O. Scott, "Review: *I Am Not Your Negro* Will Make You Rethink Race," *New York Times*, 2 February 2017, www.nytimes.com/2017/02/02/movies/review-i-am-not-your-negro-review-james-baldwin.html (accessed 15 June 2020).

6 Jennifer Schuessler, "James Baldwin's Archive, Long Hidden, Comes (Mostly) Into View," *New York Times*, 12 April 2017, www.nytimes.com/2017/04/12/arts/james-baldwins-archive-long-hidden-comes-mostly-into-view.html (accessed 15 June 2020).

7 CBS News, "Why James Baldwin's Influential Work Still Resonates," 10 July 2017.

8 Warren Critchlow, "Baldwin's Rendezvous with the Twenty-First Century: *I Am Not Your Negro*," *Film Quarterly*, 70:4 (2017), p. 9.

9 Robert J. Corber, "Queering *I Am Not Your Negro*: Or, Why We Need James Baldwin More Than Ever," *James Baldwin Review*, 3 (2017), p. 160.

10 Thomas Chatterton Williams, "Going to Meet the Man," *Sight & Sound*, 27:5 (2017), pp. 48–50.

11 Susan J. McWilliams, *A Political Companion to James Baldwin* (Lexington, KY, University Press of Kentucky, 2017), p. 6.

12 *Ibid.* p. 8.

13 *Ibid.* pp. 8–9.

14 *Ibid.* p. 2.

15 Douglas Field, *All Those Strangers: The Art and Lives of James Baldwin* (Oxford, Oxford University Press, 2015), p. 51.

16 William Maxwell, *James Baldwin: The FBI File* (New York, Arcade, 2017), p. 14.

17 *Ibid.*, p. 10.

18 *Ibid.*, p. 13.

19 *Ibid.*, p. 14.

20 *Ibid.*, p. 15.

21 *Ibid.*, p. 80.

22 *Ibid.*, p. 4.

23 *Ibid.*, pp. 2–3.

24 William Maxwell, "Born-Again, Seen-Again James Baldwin: Post-Postracial Criticism and the Literary History of Black Lives Matter," *American Literary History*, 28:4 (2016), p. 816.

25 Jack Turner. "Thinking Historically," *Theory and Event*, 19:1 (2016), p. 1.

26 *Ibid.*

27 *Ibid.*

28 James Baldwin, "The Art of Fiction LXXVII: James Baldwin," *Paris Review*, 26 (1984), pp. 49–82, www.theparisreview.org/interviews/2994/the-art-of-fiction-no-78-james-baldwin (accessed 15 June 2020).

29 Justin A. Joyce, Dwight McBride, and Douglas Field, "Lorem Ipsum Paris," *James Baldwin Review*, 2 (2016), p. 1.

30 Justin A. Joyce, "In media res, A Moment of Silence," *James Baldwin Review*, 3 (2017), p. 5.

31 Jenny M. James, "Trends in Baldwin Criticism, 2015–16," *James Baldwin Review*, 5 (2019), p. 143.

32 Press Release, "The Schomburg Center for Research in Black Culture Acquires Papers of Renowned Literary Icon James Baldwin," New York Public Library, 12 April 2017.

33 Hilton Als, "Family Secrets," *Pen America*, 8 January 2007, https://pen.org/family-secrets/ (accessed 15 June 2020).

34 Ed Pavlić, "Come On Up, Sweetheart," *Boston Review*, 14 October 2015, http://bostonreview.net/books-ideas/ed-pavlic-james-baldwin-letters-brother (accessed 15 June 2020).

35 Grant Farred, "Baldwin in Britain," *CR: The New Centennial Review*, 16:2 (2016), pp. 1–15.

36 John E. Drabinski, "Baldwin's Three Africans," *CR: The New Centennial Review*, 16:2 (2016), p. 81.

37 Tyechia Lynn Thompson, "Mapping Narratives of Reversal in 'Baldwin's Paris,'" *CLA Journal*, 59:3 (2016), p. 281.

38 Spencer Morrison, "James Baldwin on Vacation in *Another Country*," *ELH: English Literary History*, 83:3 (2016), p. 899.

39 Cynthia Barounis, "'Not the Usual Pattern': James Baldwin, Homosexuality, and the DSM," *Criticism: A Quarterly for Literature and the Arts*, 59:3 (2017), p. 395.

40 *Ibid.*, p. 396.

41 Kwangsoon Kim, "Oedipus Complex in the South: Castration Anxiety and Lynching Ritual in James Baldwin's 'Going to Meet the Man,'" *CLA Journal*, 60:3 (2017), p. 319.

42 Michele Elam, "Baldwin's Boys," *CR: The New Centennial Review*, 16:2 (2016), p. 19.

43 *Ibid.*, p. 29.

44 Marisa Parham, "17, Or, Tough, Dark, Vulnerable, Moody," *CR: The New Centennial Review*, 16:2 (2016), p. 66.

45 Magdalena J. Zaborowska, "Being James Baldwin, or Everything Is Personal," *CR: The New Centennial Review*, 16:2 (2016), p. 60.

46 *Ibid.*

47 *Ibid.*

Works Cited

Als, Hilton, "Family Secrets," *Pen America*, 8 January 2007, https://pen.org/family-secrets/ (accessed 15 June 2020).

Baldwin, James, "The Art of Fiction LXXVII: James Baldwin," *Paris Review*, 26 (1984), pp. 49–82, www.theparisreview.org/interviews/2994/the-art-of-fiction-no-78-james-baldwin (accessed 15 June 2020).

Barounis, Cynthia, "'Not the Usual Pattern': James Baldwin, Homosexuality, and the DSM," *Criticism: A Quarterly for Literature and the Arts*, 59:3 (2017), pp. 395–415.

Breen, Margaret Sönser, "Race, Dissent, and Literary Imagination in John Bunyan and James Baldwin," *Bunyan Studies: A Journal of Reformation and Nonconformist Culture*, 21 (2017), pp. 9–32.

Corber, Robert J., "Queering *I Am Not Your Negro*: Or, Why We Need James Baldwin More Than Ever," *James Baldwin Review*, 3 (2017), pp. 160–72.

Critchlow, Warren, "Baldwin's Rendezvous with the Twenty-First Century: *I Am Not Your Negro*," *Film Quarterly*, 70:4 (2017), pp. 9–22.

Drabinski, John E., "Baldwin's Three Africans," *CR: The New Centennial Review*, 16:2 (2016), pp. 81–96.

Elam, Michele, "Baldwin's Boys," *CR: The New Centennial Review*, 16:2 (2016), pp. 17–30.

Fantuzzo, John P., "Facing the Civic Love Gap: James Baldwin's Civic Education for Interpersonal Solidarity," *Educational Theory*, 68:4–5 (2018), pp. 385–402.

Farred, Grant, "Baldwin in Britain," *CR: The New Centennial Review*, 16:2 (2016), pp. 1–15.

Field, Douglas, *All Those Strangers: The Art and Lives of James Baldwin* (Oxford, Oxford University Press, 2015).

James, Jenny M., "Trends in Baldwin Criticism, 2015–16," *James Baldwin Review*, 5 (2019), pp. 143–59.

Joyce, Justin A., "In media res, A Moment of Silence," *James Baldwin Review*, 3 (2017), pp. 1–8.

Joyce, Justin A., Dwight McBride, and Douglas Field, "Lorem Ipsum Paris," *James Baldwin Review*, 2 (2016), pp. 1–5.

Kent, Jessica, "Baldwin's Hemingway: *The Sun Also Rises* in *Giovanni's Room*, with a Twist," *Twentieth Century Literature*, 63:1 (2017), pp. 75–93.

Kim, Kwangsoon, "Oedipus Complex in the South: Castration Anxiety and Lynching Ritual in James Baldwin's 'Going to Meet the Man,'" *CLA Journal*, 60:3 (2017), pp. 319–33.

Maxwell, William, "Born-Again, Seen-Again James Baldwin: Post-Postracial Criticism and the Literary History of Black Lives Matter," *American Literary History*, 28:4 (2016), pp. 816–27.

———— *James Baldwin: The FBI File* (New York, Arcade, 2017).

McIvor, David W., "The Struggle of Integration: James Baldwin and Melanie Klein in the Context of Black Lives Matter," *James Baldwin Review*, 2 (2016), pp. 75–96.

McWilliams, Susan J., *A Political Companion to James Baldwin* (Lexington, KY, University Press of Kentucky, 2017).

Melton, McKinley, "I've Got a Testimony: James Baldwin and the Broken Silences of Queer Men," *James Baldwin Review*, 2 (2016), pp. 6–27.

Morrison, Spencer, "James Baldwin on Vacation in *Another Country*," *ELH: English Literary History*, 83:3 (2016), pp. 899–925.

Parham, Marisa, "17, Or, Tough, Dark, Vulnerable, Moody," *CR: The New Centennial Review*, 16:2 (2016), pp. 65–80.

Pavlić, Ed, "Come On Up, Sweetheart," *Boston Review*, 14 October 2015, http://bostonreview.net/books-ideas/ed-pavlic-james-baldwin-letters-brother (accessed 15 June 2020).

Phillips, Caryl, "Nothing Personal: James Baldwin, Richard Avedon, and the Pursuit of Celebrity," *ARIEL: A Review of International English Literature*, 48:3 (2017), pp. 13–28.

Schuessler, Jennifer, "James Baldwin's Archive, Long Hidden, Comes (Mostly) Into View," *New York Times*, 12 April 2017, www.nytimes.com/2017/04/12/arts/james-baldwins-archive-long-hidden-comes-mostly-into-view.html (accessed 15 June 2020).

Scott, A. O., "Review: *I Am Not Your Negro* Will Make You Rethink Race," *New York Times*, 2 February 2017, www.nytimes.com/2017/02/02/movies/review-i-am-not-your-negro-review-james-baldwin.html (accessed 15 June 2020).

Segura, Olga, "'I Am Not Your Negro,' James Baldwin, & Black Lives Matter: A Conversation with Raoul Peck," *America: The Jesuit Review*, 2 February 2017, www.americamagazine. org/arts-culture/2017/02/02/i-am-not-your-negro-james-baldwin-black-lives-matter-conversation-raoul (accessed 15 June 2020).

Stokes, Mason, "'A Brutal, Indecent Spectacle': Heterosexuality, Futurity, and *Go Tell It on the Mountain*," *MFS: Modern Fiction Studies*, 62:2 (2016), pp. 292–306.

Thompson, Tyechia Lynn, "Mapping Narratives of Reversal in 'Baldwin's Paris,'" *CLA Journal*, 59:3 (2016), pp. 279–94.

Tuhkanen, Mikko, "Watching Time: James Baldwin and Malcolm X," *James Baldwin Review*, 2 (2016), pp. 97–125.

Turner, Jack, "Thinking Historically," *Theory and Event*, 19:1 (2016), pp. 1–4.

Williams, Thomas Chatterton, "Going to Meet the Man," *Sight & Sound*, 27:5 (2017), pp. 48–50.

Winfrey, Graham, "'I Am Not Your Negro': How Magnolia Pictures Launched a Smash Hit at the Box Office," *IndieWire*, 7 April 2017, www.indiewire.com/2017/04/i-am-not-your-negro-magnolia-smash-hit-box-office-1201802797/ (accessed 15 June 2020).

Woubshet, Dagmawi, "The Imperfect Power of *I Am Not Your Negro*," *The Atlantic*, 8 February 2017, www.theatlantic.com/entertainment/archive/2017/02/i-am-not-your-negro-review/515976/ (accessed 15 June 2020).

Zaborowska, Magdalena J., "Being James Baldwin, or Everything Is Personal," *CR: The New Centennial Review*, 16:2 (2016), pp. 47–64.

Contributor's Biography

Joseph Vogel is the author of several books, including *This Thing Called Life: Prince, Race, Sex, Religion, and Music* (Bloomsbury, 2018) and *James Baldwin and the 1980s: Witnessing the Reagan Era* (University of Illinois Press, 2018). His work has appeared in popular media, including *The Atlantic*, *The Guardian*, *Forbes* and *The Boston Review*, as well as peer-reviewed journals, including *James Baldwin Review*, the *F. Scott Fitzgerald Review*, the *Journal of Popular Culture*, the *Journal of American Culture*, and the *Journal of Popular Music Studies*. He is Assistant Professor of English and co-director of Film Studies at Merrimack College in Massachusetts.

Symposium Review: "In a Speculative Light: The Arts of James Baldwin and Beauford Delaney," Knoxville, Tennessee, 19–21 February 2020

D. Quentin Miller   Suffolk University

Abstract

This article is a review of a symposium entitled, "In a Speculative Light: The Arts of James Baldwin and Beauford Delaney," held at the University of Tennessee on 19–21 February 2020.

Keywords: James Baldwin, Beauford Delaney, Hilton Als, Fred Moten, David Leeming, mentorship

I have attended somewhere in the neighborhood of fifty academic conferences since I entered this profession, and I can count on one hand the number of times a speaker has received a spontaneous standing ovation. Actually, I can count it on one finger. It happened on the second day of the symposium on James Baldwin and his "spiritual father"—Beauford Delaney—at the University of Tennessee Knoxville's Humanities Center. The speaker was David Leeming, the author of the magisterial authorized biography *James Baldwin* (1994) and of the only biography of Delaney, *Amazing Grace: A Life of Beauford Delaney* (2000). Leeming spoke about the subjects of these two biographies with characteristic eloquence, grace, and humility, connecting their stories through the metaphor of "the unusual door" that opened repeatedly between them. When he finished, the audience rose and applauded for a solid minute.

The ovation moved me not only because it was a fitting tribute to a pioneering expert, but because David introduced me to Baldwin's work when I was a graduate student. He is, in a word, my mentor, and the main theme of the symposium was mentorship. Although many topics were covered with great passion and intelligence over the course of three days, the unique relationship that is mentorship was the connecting thread.

James Baldwin Review, Volume 6, 2020, © The Authors. Published by Manchester University Press and The University of Manchester Library
http://dx.doi.org/10.7227/JBR.6.11

The symposium began on Wednesday night with a special viewing of the exhibit "Beauford Delaney and James Baldwin: Through the Unusual Door" at the Knoxville Museum of Art (7 February–10 May 2020) followed by the first keynote speech by essayist, critic, and frequent *New Yorker* contributor Hilton Als, entitled "The Mentor: James Baldwin, Beauford Delaney, and the Habit of Doing." Als presented his talk fairly informally, electing to share the stage with symposium director Amy Elias, who provided a dialogue to his commentary in the form of intermittent questions to spark and redirect the conversation. Attendance throughout the symposium was robust, and this event was the most populated, with between 250 and 300 in attendance.

Als spoke about how the writer and director Owen Dodson mentored him by introducing him to a world of art and ideas he would not have had access to otherwise. There was a clear Baldwin connection: Dodson directed the initial performance of *The Amen Corner* at Howard University in 1955. The conversation between Als and Elias was largely unscripted, though Als did pause to read occasionally from Baldwin's writings and from his own, including a piece he had been inspired to write that very day after viewing the Delaney exhibit. Mentorship, he argued, was a two-way street: mentors are sought out by young artists who have to find the person who will help them become themselves. Some striking quotations emerged and hung in the air as Als spoke about language as performance, about writing as a way of seeing, about "the extraordinary power of friendship," and about how both Baldwin and Delaney would accept no limits to their work. Their shared belief was in "limitlessness." During the Q&A an interesting conversation about fashion and style ensued. Als made a distinction between the two modes: "A fashionable person wants to be tribal, while a stylish person has no choice but to be an individual." He resisted the notion that style was superficial and pointed to Baldwin as an example of how a deeply rooted sense of style could shape and almost become one's identity.

Along with Leeming's moving, personal talk, Als's willingness to offer his own experiences set the tone for the symposium in ways that enhanced the more formal academic conversations. Conferences dedicated to individual artists sometimes shade into hagiography or hero-worship, but I wouldn't describe this symposium in those terms. There was certainly a willingness to honor the work of these two artists and to regard it favorably, but that was balanced by a critical distance that enabled objective analysis and fostered a stimulating exchange of ideas. On Thursday morning Leeming shared his plenary session with Magdalena Zaborowska, whose work has been a consistent and significant contribution to the revival of Baldwin studies in recent years. She spoke of the vital act of empathy and suggested that our future readings of Baldwin might make more use of what she called the "tender narrator." Leeming's talk began with the origin story of the meeting between Baldwin and Delaney in which Baldwin's act of opening the door to Delaney's apartment in 1940 created an unprecedented bond between them and enabled Baldwin to open countless other doors throughout his celebrated life.

The second keynote speech, by the prolific and iconoclastic performance studies scholar Fred Moten, also began with a nod to mentorship as he acknowledged his debt to the great literature and jazz critic Robert O'Meally, a participant in the symposium who was present in the room at that time. Moten's talk, based largely on an aesthetic of improvisation, ranged widely between many subjects, from etymology, to blues music past and present, to the color blue in Delaney's painting, to individuation, to synesthesia, to name a few. The personal content of the talks by Als and Leeming was not as prominent here, but Moten did express some angst over his relationship with art. He suggested that he had recently been confronting the terror of facing the thing that he loves. Analyzing art, he argued, can put you outside of it; facing a work of visual art makes the relationship more confrontational, or adversarial, than standing next to it, and trying to get inside it. He spoke of how he was "sent away," like other young Black men, to pursue a life outside his home, and that the unintended effect of this move toward conventional success was to sow the seeds of alienation. This theme became another important point of discussion with regard to Baldwin's life as the symposium progressed.

The symposium featured about thirty speakers, and since the compact schedule necessitated that some panels be held concurrently, it wasn't possible to hear all the presenters. That fact, as well as space constraints here, prevent me from writing an assessment of all the papers I heard, but I will highlight a few other currents of thought I was able to glean. It's also worth mentioning the less formal elements of the conference, the ones that may not be represented if proceedings from the conference are published (which is a desired goal of the organizers).

Beauford Delaney was born in Knoxville, and although he spent most of his life in Paris and New York the conference felt like a homecoming; it was described explicitly in those terms on occasion. Banners bearing Delaney's visage were displayed on lampposts throughout Knoxville and on the UTK campus: I heard participants say repeatedly that the banners made it feel like he was present and watching over us. These banners came about through the efforts of Sylvia Peters, an octogenarian community activist who is heavily involved with the Delaney Project. Peters was a consistent presence throughout the symposium, willing to speak toward the end of every event and happy to talk enthusiastically with everyone who attended. Along with Monique Wells (who spoke to us through a video connection from Paris) and Renée Kesler (of the Beck Cultural Exchange Center), Peters presented the symposium speakers with an overview of some exciting new projects commemorating Delaney, including the restoration of his childhood home as a museum and educational space and a play about Delaney scheduled to be performed the day after the symposium ended. Kesler encouraged symposium participants to miss our planes to attend that play.

Another unique feature of the symposium was a pop-up portrait studio. Honoring the legacy of Delaney as a portraitist, UTK art professors and their students encouraged speakers to sit for 1–2 hours to have their portraits drawn. The results were displayed spontaneously as they were finished. There was also a small gallery of Delaney's work exhibited in the student union (where most of the talks took place) that served as a counterpart to the main Delaney exhibit in the Knoxville Museum of Art.

As the symposium progressed, there was a great deal of common ground between the talks. Speakers on the third day were able to reference the talks from the first two days so that the threads stitching the critical work together were visible. What I found striking was that virtually all the speakers managed to talk about both artists even if one were emphasized. I have been wondering lately if all the recently published work on Baldwin has signaled that we are approaching a saturation point, but I found that the addition of Delaney into the mix made for original readings of Baldwin's life and work. What has struck me in recent work on Baldwin is how he was able to be both subject and object, whether the medium is film, his own writings (particularly the nonfiction), and, in this case, Delaney's portraits. We see in those portraits a seer with special emphasis on his extraordinary eyes, eyes which Amiri Baraka described as "righteous monitors of the soulful." Even as we're looking at one of Delaney's portraits of Baldwin, we feel he is watching us: not judging, but observing, and inviting deeper critical witnessing.

As scholars continued to explore the idea of mentorship through the three-day conversation, such as Ed Pavlić talking about the way Baldwin created a three-generation household in Istanbul when Delaney needed him, or Robert Reid-Pharr pointing to Delaney's mentorship of Baldwin's collaborator Yoran Cazac, there was also a sustained inquiry into the relationship between visuality and language. Shawn Christian spoke of how Delaney both "forces and forges sight" in Baldwin's work and argued for a nuanced understanding of the way Baldwin has mentored a current generation of African-American artists (such as Jesmyn Ward and Kiese Laymon). My own paper was on the way chiaroscuro, or the interplay of light and darkness, operates in "Sonny's Blues," a story usually praised for its ability to evoke the sounds of jazz in a printed work of fiction. In preparing for my talk I was struck by how visual the story actually is, and I never would have arrived at this reading if I weren't reading it through the lens of Delaney's work and his explicit lessons to Baldwin. In a personally touching moment, my mentor David Leeming listened to my talk and approached me afterward. He shook my hand and said, "Well, the teacher has learned something from his student." I'll never need a standing ovation: that moment was quite enough for me.

In all, this symposium marked yet another important milestone in the ongoing rejuvenation of Baldwin studies. As we move forward, we would do well to use it as a model. Baldwin's work is in conversation with so many other currents of thought, artistic schools, individual artists, and literary innovations, before his time, in his time, and in ours. If we think innovatively and deeply, as Amy Elias did when she put together this stimulating event, we will continue to have ways to look at Baldwin anew. And, in the famous words of his spiritual father, to "look again."

Contributor's Biography

D. Quentin Miller is Professor of English at Suffolk University in Boston. He is the author of *"A Criminal Power": James Baldwin and the Law* (Ohio State University Press, 2012), the editor of *Re-Viewing James Baldwin: Things Not Seen* (Temple

University Press, 2000), a member of the editorial board for *James Baldwin Review*, and the author of more than two dozen articles and reference volume entries on Baldwin. His recent books include *The Routledge Introduction to African American Literature* (Routledge, 2016), *American Literature in Transition: 1980–1990* (Cambridge University Press, 2018), *Understanding John Edgar Wideman* (University of South Carolina Press, 2018), and the edited collection *James Baldwin in Context* (Cambridge University Press, 2019).

MANCHESTER
1824
Manchester University Press

FROM THE FIELD

Baldwin's Transatlantic Reverberations: Between "Stranger in the Village" and *I Am Not Your Negro*

Jovita dos Santos Pinto   University of Bern
Noémi Michel   University of Geneva
Patricia Purtschert   University of Bern
Paola Bacchetta   University of California, Berkeley
Vanessa Naef   University of Bern

Abstract

James Baldwin's writing, his persona, as well as his public speeches, interviews, and discussions are undergoing a renewed reception in the arts, in queer and critical race studies, and in queer of color movements. Directed by Raoul Peck, the film *I Am Not Your Negro* decisively contributed to the rekindled circulation of Baldwin across the Atlantic. Since 2017, screenings and commentaries on the highly acclaimed film have prompted discussions about the persistent yet variously racialized temporospatial formations of Europe and the U.S. Stemming from a roundtable that followed a screening in Zurich in February 2018, this collective essay wanders between the audio-visual and textual matter of the film and Baldwin's essay "Stranger in the Village," which was also adapted into a film-essay directed by Pierre Koralnik, staging Baldwin in the Swiss village of Leukerbad. Privileging Black feminist, postcolonial, and queer of color perspectives, we identify three sites of Baldwin's transatlantic reverberations: situated knowledge, controlling images, and everyday sexual racism. In conclusion, we reflect on the implications of racialized, sexualized politics for today's Black feminist, queer, and trans of color movements located in continental Europe—especially in Switzerland and France.

Keywords: James Baldwin, sexualized racism, queer of color movements, white innocence, "Stranger in the Village," *I Am Not Your Negro*

James Baldwin's work is preeminent in discussions around race in the U.S. and has recently gained renewed attention among Black, feminist, and queer of color social

James Baldwin Review, Volume 6, 2020, © The Authors. Published by Manchester University Press and
The University of Manchester Library
http://dx.doi.org/10.7227/JBR.6.12

and intellectual movements.[1] Baldwin's "born again, seen again" phenomenon has also touched continental Europe, as testified by several translations of his writings, by the highly acclaimed film *I Am Not Your Negro* (2017), and the success of the Baldwin-inspired essayist Ta-Nehisi Coates.[2] In short, Baldwin's writing prompts fascinating reverberations across contemporary Europe and the U.S.

In this article, we expand upon a discussion that tracked Baldwin's transatlantic reverberations by starting from Switzerland—a location which, interestingly, constitutes an important site of the renewed interest in Baldwin.[3] Indeed, rising attention has been paid to Baldwin's essay on Leukerbad from 1953, "Stranger in the Village," as well as to the 1962 film-essay (directed by Pierre Koralnik), which stages Baldwin reciting his essay in French as he returns to the Swiss village where he had stayed.[4] In the essay and the film-essay, Baldwin not only offers an analysis of postcolonial Switzerland, but also utilizes this tiny Swiss village in the Alps in order to contrast the racial formations of the U.S.A. and Europe.

How can Baldwin's writings and his artistic vision in general, "formed and informed by a Black queer imaginative capacity," contribute to today's understanding of racial relations in Europe?[5] Where can we follow, but where must we also part with Baldwin's transatlantic reflections on race? Privileging Black feminist, postcolonial, and queer of color perspectives, we wander between the audio-visual and textual matter of *I Am Not Your Negro* and "Stranger in the Village" and identify three sites of Baldwin's transatlantic reverberations: situated knowledge, controlling images, and everyday sexual racism. In conclusion, we reflect on the implication of racialized, sexualized politics for today's Black feminist, queer, and trans of color movements located in continental Europe—especially in Switzerland and France.

"No one resembling my father": Baldwin's Situatedness and Black Feminist and Radical Traditions

In these days, no one resembling my father has yet made an appearance on the American cinema scene.[6]

In spite of the fabulous myths proliferating in this country concerning the sexuality of black people, black men are still used, in the popular culture, as though they had no sexual equipment at all. Sidney Poitier, as a black artist, and a man, is also up against the infantile, furtive sexuality of his country. Both he and Harry Belafonte, for example, are sex symbols, though no one dares admit that, still less to use them as any of the Hollywood he-men are used.[7]

Jovita Pinto (Pinto): I want to start by pondering on Baldwin's way of writing and thinking. The "father" mentioned in the above-cited passage not only refers to Baldwin's father, but also alludes to Black men more broadly, who are represented in 1930s U.S. films as lazy, stupid, and forever smiling stereotypical figures. Baldwin's analysis entails a personal account as well as a testimonial of affects. Such a mode of writing has been rendered possible and "permissible" for theorization in the texts of women of color and other feminist work. Linking personal narrative with sharp analysis, to me, this passage is a beautiful example of situated knowledge. Might this be a reason why Baldwin's writing finds so much resonance today? I am thinking specifically about his reception in the queer and intersectionally declared Black Lives Matter movement?

Paola Bacchetta (Bacchetta): Baldwin's work is situated, but I think that all writing is situated. We have a long history, in the U.S.A., of feminist and queer of color theorizations around situatedness. Examples are the Combahee River Collective and the group Dyketactics! in the 1970s, or *This Bridge Called My Back*, first published in 1981, a now classic anthology co-edited by Gloria Anzaldúa and Cherríe Moraga.[8]

Noémi Michel (Michel): Baldwin's situatedness resonates with two interconnected bodies of writings. First with Black feminism, with bell hooks and Audre Lorde, but also with non-U.S. Black women, such as Maryse Condé.[9] Among many others, these Black women powerfully narrate their situated experiences and by doing so, produce meaning about our world. Second, Baldwin resonates with the Black radical tradition, for instance with W. E. B. Du Bois's mode of deploying the first person in *The Souls of Black Folk*, or with Frantz Fanon's phenomenological accounts in *Black Skin, White Masks*.[10] It is also worth emphasizing a resonance with Cedric Robinson's *Black Marxism*—which is barely known in Europe.[11] Robinson contrasts the Black radical tradition with Western radical thought or Marxism. Western radicalism is concerned with finding the new "man," or reinventing the human, while the Black radical tradition is concerned with preserving "the collective being, the ontological totality."[12] Being Black means always having to struggle with having one's being repressed or suppressed. By amplifying experiences, lives, feelings, and liberatory modes of self-expression, Baldwin's work, I suggest, can be associated with the artistic and intellectual radical labor of preserving the collective being.

Bacchetta: I totally agree, and the struggle with having one's being violently oppressed has been very meaningfully engaged through the question of death in the Black radical tradition. Death, escaping from death, and especially emancipation from the context of deadly racism, constitute central themes in the Black radical tradition.[13] I was always struck with how death is a recurring theme for Baldwin. For him, as a child, identifying with life meant identifying with whiteness. In the context of the U.S.A., this speaks to apprehending death across subalternities, within and outside of Black life. Indeed, to grow up in the U.S.A. until the late 1960s meant to be exposed to the massacres of Native Americans every day on television; it constituted "entertainment." This constant re-representation of the massacre of indigenous bodies eternally repeats the logic of "native" genocide *and* operates alongside the massive erasure of present-day native life. U.S. society is founded on and perpetuated by the death of indigenous subjects, Black and other subjects of color. Baldwin reveals how he first identified with life and thus whiteness, but then reached the self-realization that since he was not white, he would actually be on the side of death.

"Fabulous myths": Controlling Images in Europe and the U.S.A.

Patricia Purtschert (Purtschert): I find it striking how Baldwin talks about the sexualization of Black men and Black masculinity; there is the link between rape and Black men, which for many decades had been a pretext for lynching in the U.S. context. Framing men of color as rapists has also been used as a pretext for anti-migrant politics, including its deadly effects in the Mediterranean Sea, as we can see with regard to the discussion around the so-called "Cologne incidents" in Germany.[14] Baldwin also evokes the "desexualization" of Black masculinity, which is intertwined with its hypersexualization. How would you describe the current hyper- and desexualizing of Black masculinity, as constitutive of racist gender regimes? Also, how would you assess the influence of Black self-representations developed within a culture of resistance in past decades?

Michel: I have conducted a critical study of the controversy regarding the so-called "sheep poster" by the extremist right Swiss People's Party (SVP).[15] This political poster staged white sheep expelling a single black sheep from their territory, which was symbolized by the Swiss flag, under the slogan "for more security." It became the object of a wide controversy about representations of foreigners and Blackness in Switzerland. I studied the counter-posters and other images that were circulating in the public sphere after 2007, supposedly protesting the racism of the initial poster. Strikingly, most of the representations of Blackness and Black people could fall under the category of "controlling images."[16] In its videos and leaflets, the SVP represented Black bodies as dangerous and criminal, thus following the image of supposed "Black hypersexuality." However, opponents to the SVP campaign would also reproduce sexualizing images. For instance, a right-wing party in Geneva, the Liberal Party, circulated two counter-posters: an image of a headless Black cis-male torso in front of a brown screen, and an image of Beyoncé—without any mention of her name—on the beach in a revealing swimsuit. The slogan accompanying these images was: "You want to chase the black sheep; we do not." These posters and counter-posters all exemplify the association of Blackness with sexualized fantasy within dominant Swiss and European public culture.

The Liberal Party proponents took pride in having produced supposedly funny visuals that were intelligently contributing to the struggle against extreme right politics of representation. They situated themselves in the tradition of the Enlightenment. In their "enlightened" visuals, Black masculinity and femininity are presented as objects of sexual consumption. Whether horrific or delightful, Black bodies emerge in these examples as disposable. Black Swiss citizens were the only parties who proposed non-controlling and self-staged humanizing images of Blackness. However, their resisting images are absent from the collective memory of that important controversy. As exemplified by this case study, despite the increasing visibility and circulation—thanks to digital culture—of Black self-representations that counter controlling images, Baldwin's analysis remains very relevant for understanding the sexual racialization of both Black masculinity and femininity.

Bacchetta: Such a disposability of Black and brown bodies played out along similar lines in the campaign led by the French neoliberal organization *SOS Racisme*, founded by the (non-)Socialist Party. The organization produced posters of young cisgender Black and Arab women, with the slogan: "At least I am prettier than Le Pen"—in reference to Marine Le Pen, the leader of the extreme right-wing National Front. They thereby framed young Black and Arab women as sex objects, and as potentially appropriable, presumably by white French men. This campaign—lacking an intersectional analytic and inscribed within neoliberalism—reproduced sexism in the name of antiracism.

I also want to point toward Baldwin's relevance for understanding the U.S.A. Within the Black radical tradition, one can connect his work with the long history of literature devoted to what Charles Stember, writing in the 1970s, called "sexual racism."[17] Stember unpacks controlling images of Black masculinity and Black femininity, and how they correlate with living Black bodies in dominant discourses. That early work does not discuss nonheterosexual, transgender, nonbinary, or other sexually and genderly a-normative subjects. More recent scholarly work considers racialized sexualization as a process of a-normativization, wherein racialized bodies are assigned to sexual excess or sexual lack. Baldwin contributed to and reinforces this insight when he remarks that the Black body was de-sexed. Some Black feminists have further theorized such a logic with the notion of "ungendering."[18] The dominant culture's binary representational regime of racialized sexualization, of attributing lack (here of gender and sex as Baldwin points out)—and alternatively *excess*—to subalternly racialized bodies is still very much alive.

Regarding your question on self-representation, Black feminists and nonfeminists have produced a plethora of self-representations. They circulate in alternative cinema, art, media, and literature throughout Black popular culture. However, the dominant culture remains white-centric and Blackphobic. When Barack Obama was president of the U.S.A., mainstream magazines published insulting articles and photoshopped pictures of his family. In short, someone can be in the U.S.A.'s highest political position and still be subjected to sexualized racism.

Michel: On the matter of self-representation and sexual a-normativation of Blackness, I want to mention one very interesting platform called *Afrosexology*, which claims that Black liberation also begins with the possibility for self-narrations of pleasure.[19] Its purpose, beyond representation, sheds lights on the constrained relations of Black people with their possibility and freedom to experience pleasure in all the ways they want to. This is a big issue, because Black women, or gender nonconforming people, especially tend to be deemed either as excessively sexual or excessively respectable. What is possible between these two sides? What is the narrative that people can reclaim for themselves?

"Trapped in history": Everyday Racism, Historicity, and the Politics of Space

Purtschert: We turn to a passage from the essay "Stranger in the Village" from 1953. Pierre Koralnik, a Swiss filmmaker, returned to the Swiss town, Leukerbad, with Baldwin. They made a film-essay, with Baldwin reciting the text, roughly ten years later, in 1962, and so we present stills from the film. In the essay itself, Baldwin remarks:

> Joyce is right about history being a nightmare—but it may be the nightmare from which no one can awaken. People are trapped in history and history is trapped in them [...]
>
> I thought of white men arriving for the first time in an African village, strangers there, as I am a stranger here, and tried to imagine the astounded populace touching their hair and marveling at the color of their skin. But there is a great difference between being the first white man to be seen by Africans and being the first black man to be seen by whites. The white man takes the astonishment as tribute, for he arrives to conquer and to convert the natives, whose inferiority in relation to himself is not even to be questioned; whereas I, without a thought of conquest, find myself among a people whose culture controls me, has even, in a sense, created me, people who have cost me more in anguish and rage than they will ever know, who yet do not even know of my existence. The astonishment with which I might have greeted them, should they have stumbled into my African village a few hundred years ago, might have rejoiced their hearts. But the astonishment with which they greet me today can only poison mine.[20]

Pinto: The film and the text depict episodes of everyday racism from about half a century ago in the Swiss village of Leukerbad: for example, the touching of hair, the rubbing of skin, the stares of horror and wonder, the refusal to call Baldwin by his name, blackface, and the Christian buying of Black souls (Figures 1–4). In Switzerland we are coming to the end of Carnival Season. My Facebook feed during the month of February is filled with outcries about blackface and brown-face. When I compare them to the images in the film, I wonder about their histo-ricity?[21] Are we trapped in a colonial time-loop? What has shifted in these images since the 1950s? Do these episodes of everyday racism play out differently today?

Michel: Blackface, hands in the hair, depersonalization, appropriation of the body, and Black servant figurines are familiar scenes of everyday racism in today's Swit-zerland. I am particularly struck by today's ongoing circulation of artefacts that echo the Black figurines that the white villagers were buying to save African souls. For instance, in French-speaking Switzerland, you will encounter the "Sambo"-type figure of "Y'a bon Banania" on cups, boxes, and other products in vintage bou-tiques, restaurants, and in your friends' spaces.[22] What is the historicity of the images in the film then? Baldwin writes that "we are trapped in history." His words speak to my first impression: the past has not passed, it is still with us.

However, I want to complicate this first diagnosis with the help of my attempt to conceptualize what I call the "politics of postcoloniality." This notion points toward the constant negotiation of the weight of the racist and colonial past in today's lives and social relations in Switzerland and Europe in general.[23] In the "politics of postcoloniality," postcoloniality is understood as an entanglement of spaces and times. I rely on postcolonial perspectives, as the latter help us to approach history as not just being in the past, but as still having an impact on us. The past still resonates within, with, and on our bodies. In other words, the ways

Figure 1 Girl being pushed by other girls to shake Baldwin's hand (still from Pierre Koralnik, "Un Étranger dans le Village", copyright RTS Radio Télévision Suisse, Switzerland, 1962, 5:00).

we are embodied are constituted by the long colonial history. With this I mean all of us, not just racialized minorities, as whiteness is also embodied; it is a project constituted by history. Postcolonial studies are not only helpful to think about the historicity of the images of the Leukerbad documentary, but also of *I Am Not Your Negro*. Even if he might not relate his filmmaking to a postcolonial approach, Raoul Peck juxtaposes archives from the 1930s and from the 1960s with images and media footage from today. He sees the continuities and the links between the past and the present, and how the past has an impact on Black lives and horizons.

Now it is the "politics" in "politics of postcoloniality" giving me hope beyond history's trap. History exerts a weight on us, but we can also put weight on history. We can be accountable for our history, we can act upon the past. Engaging in the politics of postcoloniality means asking which past we want. How do we acknowledge the past? What do we do with the incessant reiteration of blackface? Do we really want this tradition to persist? An important debate has recently taken place in French-speaking Switzerland. One radio show decided to invite young Black Swiss commentators to discuss the use of blackface by a famous French soccer player.[24] The unavoidability of Black and brown voices within such debates constitutes a turn in the politics of postcoloniality. Afro-Europeans, Black minorities, and people of color have come to occupy a space in Europe and work toward holding their

Figure 2   A crowd of children following James Baldwin through the village (still from Pierre Koralnik, "Un Étranger dans le Village", copyright RTS Radio Télévision Suisse, Switzerland, 1962, 16:32).

collectivities accountable for the ongoing unfolding of the history of racism, giving an unprecedented direction to the negotiation of history's bearing upon us.

Bacchetta: When Baldwin says that "people are trapped in history and history is trapped in them," it is a statement about relations of power and subject formation, although I want to emphasize the sarcasm in this passage as well. On the one hand, Baldwin points to and analyzes a reality: the disjuncture and difference of disparately situated subjects; the place of history; how white "arrival" is untainted by prior controlling images while Black "arrival" is determined by them. Baldwin invokes a painful irony about white self-perception and white subjective relationality to historicity and to history. In the racist contexts that Baldwin lives in, whites can imagine themselves as human origin and as neutral subjects of history, the present and futurity, while they imagine Black people as a-historical, specific, caught in the past and always behind. All of this takes place in a present context of the multidimensional dispossession, oppression, and exploitation of Black bodies. Baldwin makes clear that differential "arrivals" cannot be understood without understanding the context of relations of power.

On the other hand, Baldwin communicates a kind of a hope that Europe is better than the U.S.A. in continuity with many other African Americans, then and today. Without generalizing, many African Americans who leave the U.S.A. feel that Europe is better for a multitude of reasons, including because in Europe they

Figure 3   Baldwin inserting coins into a money box with a black servant figurine on top (still from Pierre Koralnik, "Un Étranger dans le Village", copyright RTS Radio Télévision Suisse, Switzerland, 1962, 6:59).

are not as exposed to relationships with the descendants of U.S. slave owners. Stephen Small, in a recent book on Black Europe, delineates several points of differentiation for Black life between Europe and the U.S.A.[25] One of the main differences is historical: European racism did not develop alongside the sizable presence of Black people on the continent; it began to develop before Black people had gotten to continental Europe in greater numbers. In contrast, in the U.S.A., anti-Black racism developed in a relationship that was massively intimate: present, face-to-face, but also body-to-body under conditions of enslavement. Small argues that in continental Europe, racism arrived with less proximity, largely via colonial discourse. European racism was elaborated in the work of major philosophers and scientists. If the racial relationship in continental Europe is initially less intimate, less widely face-to-face, body-to-body, then it makes sense that Baldwin can perceive it as being less intense—even if this is not the case for non-U.S. people of color who live here today.

Pinto: Baldwin's focus lies in an analysis of the U.S.A. So, as he is looking at Leukerbad or Europe, he does so to differentiate it from the U.S.A. Thereby this experience of intimate coexistence between Black and white people becomes central for the U.S.A. and is constructed in opposition to a Europe that for Baldwin has never known any critical mass of coexistence of Black and white. As a Black European, who has worked on rendering visible a historical Black presence in Switzerland, I would argue Baldwin's U.S.A./Europe comparison presents a risk. It might feed

Figure 4 Money box for missionary donations is carried by a child in blackface (still from Pierre Koralnik, "Un Étranger dans le Village", copyright RTS Radio Télévision Suisse, Switzerland, 1962, 7:06).

into the figure of the "stranger," of the person of color being "an eternal newcomer" to Europe, to quote Fatima El-Tayeb.[26] Baldwin seems to reinstate the narrative that people of color cannot really be from Europe because originally there were only white Europeans. I am wondering about the effects of such a narrative for antiracist, Black, and people of color movements in Europe? What happens if we take a little distance from Baldwin's perspective—Europe as a mediation to think the U.S.A.—and look at Europe per se?

Bacchetta: You are right. Baldwin's narrative only makes sense in a comparative sense centered on the U.S.A. It is a different matter altogether if we think centrally about Europe. From a continental European perspective, Baldwin does indeed come dangerously close to reproducing the constant externalization of people of color. Europeans of color have always existed in continental Europe, not only in the non-continental parts; there are examples of this within my own family. However, Baldwin's considerations are about scale, about different scales of relatively large direct spatial racial intimacy. Black presence refers here to Black avoidability or unavoidability for white people on a daily basis. White people in the continental U.S.A. encounter Black people everywhere in the country, whether they want to or not. Some major continental U.S. cities are majority Black, such as Detroit or Jackson, that are over 80 percent Black. Such proportions are not present in continental France, historically.

Michel: I have sought to understand why *I Am Not Your Negro* was so successful in Switzerland. I have been doing research and been active on questions of race and racism for more than a decade and now, suddenly, those objects of research seem more legitimate thanks to *I Am Not Your Negro*, or Ta-Nehisi Coates's writings. The success of those cultural productions is related to the fact that they are dealing primarily with the U.S.A.

In "Stranger in the Village", Baldwin uses the village as a scene from which he deploys critical thoughts about the logics of racism, race, and colonialism in the U.S.A. One could say that he slightly instrumentalizes Switzerland in order to be critical about his own society—I see no problem with such a process. However, should such a process be taken up by us living and working here, in the European context marked by a taboo of race? Is it not risky to rely on an African American to prove the existence of race and racism in Switzerland? I have purposefully chosen not to cite "Stranger in the Village" in discussions about the existence of race here, in order to avoid the risk of feeding the ongoing externalizing of race and racism from the history of Europe. I avoid reproducing the narrative that Europe is homogeneous and not entangled with and influenced by other spaces and histories. Certain places in Europe have Black populations of 80 percent. They are not on the continent, but in Guadeloupe, Martinique, Guiana, which are (postcolonial) overseas departments of France, thus parts of Europe. However, these territories and populations are disconnected from the imagination of Europe. In a similar vein, when people think of Europe, they cannot think about the Haitian Revolution as being part of world history or the history of Europe specifically. They cannot imagine that this revolutionary event inspired the people of France.[27]

By evoking potentially problematic receptions of Baldwin's essay or Peck's movie, I do not aim to say that we should not read one or watch the other. Indeed, those materials allow us—especially us Afro-Europeans—to connect with converging experiences and to translate these experiences from the U.S.A. to our own contexts. However, such connections and translations are absent from the mainstream critique. This is why I suggest that the success of Peck's movie must be partly associated with the ongoing politics of externalization of race and racism from Europe. The movie can receive an award in the U.K., and it can be produced by the Radio Télévision Suisse (the Swiss public broadcasting organization), because it is centered on the U.S.A. But do we have examples of documentaries or movies about race and racism in Switzerland that have been funded by Swiss television?

Purtschert: I truly think we have to read this essay critically, including Baldwin's idea of being the first Black person whom the villagers of Leukerbad have ever seen. Supposedly, this is the way in which the village inhabitants have staged the encounter with Baldwin, and thus his experience. However, it is most probably not true that he was the first Black person in Leukerbad. The long history of Black people in Switzerland has continuously been erased up to present day.[28] It is thus not surprising that Baldwin did not come across any traces of this history. In addition, Leukerbad was not just the small and remote village Baldwin described, it was also part of an international trade route across the Alps, and a famous tourist destination.[29] Following critical historians of Switzerland, it seems important to ask how much the image of the secluded Alpine village has been part of a nationalist imaginary that dates back to the late nineteenth century, and might have informed Baldwin's view of Leukerbad as well.

Nevertheless, Baldwin provides us with helpful tools to work on postcolonial Switzerland. For instance, his notion of "innocence" speaks to the complete amnesia of colonial history, a mental state "in which black men do not exist."[30] Gloria Wekker's coining of "white innocence" for the Netherlands also works very well in the Swiss context, where "neutrality" is constantly mobilized to claim that the country stood outside of the horrors of modern history, had seemingly nothing to do with the transatlantic slave trade, colonialism, the two world wars, or fascism.[31] Baldwin offers us a powerful analysis of the careful crafting of such an innocence. What he calls "naïveté" in his essay relates not only to political discourse, but also to the powerful foundations of everyday racism in Switzerland. Baldwin writes: "wherever I passed, the first summer I was here, among the native villagers or among the lame, a wind passed with me—of astonishment, curiosity, amusement, and outrage."[32] This captures powerfully how Baldwin was confronted by being made a "spectacle of the other," which had a very intense affective dimension, as the quote shows. From the white Swiss perspective, however, people asserted the belief that they followed an innocent and pure interest in the strange Other, which was void of any historical traces or colonial entanglements. As you, Michel and Pinto have both reminded us, if one takes into account the experience of Black people in Switzerland, who are constantly invoked as Others, reverting to Baldwin's analysis of whiteness as innocence seems meaningful.

Michel: Of course, the essay and a lot of mechanisms he describes are important resources for us to think about race in postcolonial Switzerland, especially about what you, Purtschert, alongside two colleagues have relevantly called "colonialism without colonies."[33] The "without" says a lot of things. It is not just that Switzerland was colonial without having colonies, it is also that it defines itself and thinks of itself as a place where colonialism, colonial relations of power, colonial imaginaries, and colonial narratives did not take place. Your concept points toward that possibility for Switzerland to always redefine itself as an innocent nation, as having nothing to do with the colonial past, nor with racism.

Baldwin's analysis of astonishment is fascinating in "Stranger in the Village." He says that there are some people who have the privilege of always discovering the stranger and being astonished, without having to take responsibility for history, in contrast to him. When he is the object of this astonishment, it poisons him. There is no possibility for a real encounter between himself and the residents of this village. Even if Black people were not hugely present in Switzerland at the time, they were the objects of a huge imaginary. The children evoked by Baldwin had already encountered him, because they had already heard many stories about people of African descent; there is no space for him to be encountered as a human.

But at the same time the people who encounter him, mock him, and touch him do so while pretending that those very modes of encounter are rooted in an innocent form of astonishment (see Figures 1–2). Baldwin leads us to understand how racializiation and self-exoneration go hand-in-hand.

Bacchetta: That part of the essay also reminds me of Frantz Fanon's chapter "The Fact of Blackness," where a white child says, "Look ma, a Negro."[34] It makes me reflect on the construction of children—especially white children—as innocent, whereas Baldwin is coming from a country where Black children are constructed as always already guilty, adultlike subjects and imagined as threatening. The recent publicity around the heinous killing of 12-year-old Tamir Rice by police, while playing alone in a park with a toy gun, visibilizes a racialized disparity in the societal construction of innocence and the figure of the child—a central concern for both Fanon and Baldwin.

"White no longer": The Challenges of European Queer, Feminist Movements of Color

This world is white no longer, and it will never be white again.[35]

Pinto: I would like to turn to think about Black and people of color movements in Europe. What are the challenges that these movements face today? What problems do they address? What is the role of feminist and queer perspectives within those movements?

Bacchetta: In France, the Black feminist movement is currently strong. It is autonomous, not separatist. It is also under attack. For example, after having publicized its Black-only showing and discussion of the film *Black Panther*, the Black feminist group Mwasi, founded in 2014 in Paris, was immediately targeted.[36] The white, left, human rights group LICRA (International League against Racism and Anti-semitism) accused Mwasi of "anti-white racism" and of being against the values of the French Republic. Continental France constitutes a multitude of spaces that are completely white. LICRA has never protested against them. The accusation of "anti-white racism" or "reverse racism" is only possible in the context of unexamined structural coloniality and racism.

Autonomous groups of queers of color have existed since 1999, when the Group du 6 novembre—the first autonomous lesbian of color group in France—was founded. Prior to that, there were feminist of color groups such as the Black feminist group Mouvement des Femmes Noires (MODEFEN). France has a long history of feminist and queer of color analytics, "artivisms," and activisms, but these have been erased from French feminist and LGBTQ history, as though they were not French, and their analytics, "artivisms," and activisms did not take place on French soil.[37]

Right now, there is an enormous uprising of Black feminist and Black queer and transgender mobilizations in France. There are autonomous Black feminist and Black queer groups as well as autonomous groups of feminists and queers of color with

Black members. Examples of the latter are LOCs (Lesbians of Color), the Decolonizing Sexualities Network, the groups Transnational QTPOC (Queer and Trans People of Color), LTQ Revolutionaries, and more. French Black feminists and queers are weaving transnational links with a broader pan-African movement and with the heterogeneous decolonial movement. French Black activists are also connected with specific groups such as Black Lives Matter, which is now an international movement, with different resonances in disparate places, because the contexts are not identical. In the U.S.A., Black Lives Matter was founded by three queer-identified Black feminists, and its political stances against racism are queer-sensitive. However, in France, Black Lives Matter is not close to its queer roots.

Michel: We should name local Black feminists, intersectional, and antiracist groups in Switzerland such as Bla*Sh, that Pinto co-founded.[38] It is an important group that does a lot to render certain Black Swiss and European figures visible, as well as talking differently about race and racism.[39] New groups, such as Outrage and A qui le tour, have formed especially in the canton of Vaud—in Lausanne—after extreme police violence led to the deaths of two Black men.[40] A commonality among most of these movements, and I am not naming all of them, is their anchorage at the local level given the linguistic barriers, but also the difficulty for nonwhites to identify with the Swiss nation.

Thus, the challenge pertains to the possibility for scattered local initiatives to connect and last in their varieties and their differences across contexts, across Europe, and across linguistic barriers. Baldwin's life offers perspectives regarding such a challenge. Baldwin was so mobile; we tend to forget that he not only stayed in France and Switzerland, but also in Turkey. In Peck's film, we see Baldwin in London, in Palm Springs, and in New York. He is always traveling, and he says, "I am witness and to be a witness of human experience and black experience I have to travel." Since racism seeks to separate and segregate, his mobility is a testimony of both antiracist resistance and racism's persistence. Baldwin's crossing of borders and spaces at that time is criminalized for most people of color today.

Bacchetta: To further reflect on the challenge of scattering, I want to address the question of coalition. Gathering queer trans people of color (QTPOC) together in one space in France has been a real struggle. The first time we were able to do it with significant numbers was in March 2017 at Queer Week in Paris, when we created a QTPOC Town Hall.[41] The problems of fragmentation that we experience today are caused by deep-seated colonial divide and rule tactics. Our difficulties with coming together are also an effect of how we are differentially co-constituted in relations of power—colonialism, race, gender, class, sexuality—and the differential kinds of capital—financial, social, cultural, corporeal privilege—we have. Nonetheless, we are coming together. Our next QTPOC Town Hall will tackle decoloniality, anticapitalism, and antiracism.[42]

Purtschert: Your description of movements that go beyond national borders draws me to the last sentence of Baldwin's essay "Stranger in the Village": "This world is white no longer, and it will never be white again." I would like to conclude the discussion by asking what it means to take this statement seriously? How does this crucial insight inform our postcolonial present, culturally, politically, and socially?

Bacchetta: My hope is that there will not be two worlds: one that remains the dominant white world and then the rest of us as the Other. I am hoping that we can get free, transform ourselves and the planet, and invent new modes of life. I do not know why I have such hope, but I think that otherwise one just drops dead. Those of us who have not yet dropped dead, or who have not become the living dead—who are alive—have to have hope.

Michel: We can also change the tense of this last sentence from Baldwin's essay, and say that the world was never white. The movie by Raoul Peck shows us how whiteness is a phantasmatic construction. This construction is real in its effects, but let us nonetheless think of a world that was never white. What happens if we think this way? What kind of space does such thought open for people who have multiple belongings, people who do not want to be defined merely in relation to one space and one national history, or one continental history? If we think with this sentence and bring it home, I think it gives us a lot of space for our identities and their complexity. It allows us to breathe, but also to act with these complexities and multiple identities, gendered, racialized, cultural, religious, and so forth.

Afterword

Since the above discussion took place in early 2018, the aforementioned feminist, queer, and trans* of color movement(s) have flourished, and intensified translocal connections across Europe in resistance to racist bordering. For instance, the French collective Mwasi initiated an "Afrofemtour" through major cities in Europe for 2019–20, co-organized with local and other Afro-feminist and Black queer collectives.[43] Online accessible media and platforms stemming from people of color movements have thrived. Among numerous examples are the podcasts *le Tchip* and *Kiffe ta race*, centered on racial relations in France and hosted by binge audio; the academic podcast *Decolonization in Action*, created at the Max-Planck Institute for the History of Science; and *Vocal About It*, a podcast initiated privately in Brussels.[44] We also wish to evoke the pan-African and multilingual website *Cases Rebelles*, the various online and translocal events organized by the European Race and Imagery Foundations (ERIF), as well as the now well-established U.K. feminist and queer of color media platform gal-dem.[45]

Through the efforts of Black and of color movements themselves, James Baldwin's presence in continental Europe, especially in Switzerland and France, has gained acknowledgment within dominant culture. However, his reflections on Europe as a racialized space remain widely unaddressed. Will future conferences on Baldwin, like the one originally slated to convene in Saint-Paul de Vence in 2020, also address his transatlantic reverberations, or will they run the risk of once again omitting nonwhite queer struggles in Europe, especially if none of the key presenters are scholars working on racialized Europe? At the time of this writing, this remains to be seen.[46]

Lastly, with regard to the increasing reception of James Baldwin in European universities, we want to ask what it means when we say "the world is white no longer, and will never be white again" in a neoliberal university, set within a European context of racial taboo? Critical race scholars, especially women and queer of color scholars, have shed light on depoliticized appropriations of terms and concepts associated with radical histories of resistance, such as "postcolonial," "intersectional," "decolonial," and "epistemologies of the global south(s)." Within academia, such terms have been invoked to demonstrate "marketable expertise" on "diversity," while the existing forms of knowledge production, personnel policy, curricula, and canon formation have largely persisted in maintaining Black and other people of color's bodies and voices in precarious positions within institutions of knowledge.[47]

Notes

1 For examples, see Matt Brim, *James Baldwin and the Queer Imagination* (Ann Arbor, MI, University of Michigan Press, 2014); Consuela Francis, *The Critical Reception of James Baldwin, 1963–2010: "An Honest Man and a Good Writer"* (Rochester, NY, Camden House, 2014); and the first five volumes of *James Baldwin Review*.

2 William J. Maxwell, "Born-Again, Seen-Again James Baldwin: Post-Postracial Criticism and the Literary History of Black Lives Matter," *American Literary History*, 28:4 (2016), pp. 812–27; Ta-Nehisi Coates, *Between the World and Me* (New York, Spiegel & Grau, 2017).

3 This article is an adapted transcript of a roundtable at the cultural center Kosmos in Zürich, after the screening of Raoul Peck's film on 9 February 2018. The screening and discussion were a prelude to the conference, "'The Evidence of Things not Seen.' Queering Europe with James Baldwin," in February 2018 at the Interdisciplinary Center of Gender Studies at the University of Bern, www.izfg.unibe.ch/forschung/emanzipatorische_bewegungen/the_evidence_of_things_not_seen/index_ger.html (accessed 18 November 2019). Invited guests were Noémi Michel and Paola Bacchetta, and the discussion was facilitated by Jovita dos Santos Pinto and Patricia Purtschert.

4 For the reception of "Stranger in the Village" in Switzerland, see Patricia Purtschert and H. Fischer-Tiné, "The End of Innocence: Debating Colonialism in Switzerland," in Patricia Purtschert and H. Fischer-Tiné (eds.), *Colonial Switzerland: Rethinking Switzerland from the Margins* (Basingstoke, Palgrave Macmillan, 2015), pp. 1–26; Patricia Purtschert, *Kolonialität und Geschlecht im 20. Jahrhundert. Eine Geschichte der weissen Schweiz* (Bielefeld, transcript, 2019), pp. 62–8; Ntando Cele, "Stranger," blog entry, 2 January 2014, www.ntandocl.blogspot.com (accessed 27 March 2019). On 4 March 2018 the Black artist Sasha Huber installed a portrait of James Baldwin made with a staple gun on the shutter of the house where Baldwin used to stay in the village discussed in this article; see S. Huber, "The firsts—James Baldwin," blog entry, 2018, www.sashahuber.com/?-cat=10075&lang=fi&mstr=10009 (accessed 27 March 2019). For additional perspectives on the essay, see also Teju Cole, "Black Body: Rereading James Baldwin's 'Stranger in the Village,'" *New Yorker*, 19 August 2014, www.newyorker.com/books/page-turner/black-body-re-reading-james-baldwins-stranger-village (accessed 15 June 2020); Teju Cole, "Schwarzer Körper," *Das Magazin*, 19 August 2014, pp. 8–17; James Baldwin, *Fremder im Dorf. Ein Schwarzer New Yorker in Leukerbad* (Zürich, Sacré, 2011); Christian Walther,

"*Fremd*". *Kurzfilm über James Baldwin* (Insertfilm/SRF, 2013); Michael Stauffer and R. Hermann, "*Wie ein Schaf in der Wüste*". *Passage Sendung* (SRF, 2012).

5 Brim, *James Baldwin and the Queer Imagination*, p. 175.

6 James Baldwin, *I Am Not Your Negro (Compiled and Edited by Raoul Peck)* (London, Penguin, 2017), p. 20.

7 *Ibid.*, p. 63.

8 Combahee River Collective, "A Black Feminist Statement," in Akasha (G. T.) Hull, Patricia Bell-Scott, Barbara Smith (eds.), *But Some of Us Are Brave: Black Women's Studies* (Old Westbury, NY, Feminist Press, 1982), pp. 13–22; Paola Bacchetta, "Dyketactics!," in Howard Chiang et al. (eds.), *Global Encyclopedia of Lesbian, Gay, Bisexual, Transgender, and Queer History* (New York, Macmillan, 2019), pp. 483–6; Gloria Anzaldúa and Cherríe Moraga (eds.), *This Bridge Called My Back: Writings by Radical Women of Color* (New York, Kitchen Table, 1983).

9 For an influential example of non-U.S. Black womanism, see Maryse Condé, *La Vie sans fard* (Paris, Latte, 2012).

10 W. E. B. Du Bois, *The Souls of Black Folk: Essays and Sketches* (New York, Magnavision, 1903); Frantz Fanon, *Black Skin, White Masks* (New York, Grove Press, 2008).

11 Cedric Robinson, *Black Marxism: The Making of a Black Radical Tradition* (Chapel Hill, NC, University of North Carolina Press, 2000).

12 *Ibid.*, p. 171.

13 See, for example, Abdul R. JanMohamed, *The Death-Bound-Subject: Richard Wright's Archaeology of Death* (Durham, NC, Duke University Press, 2005).

14 On the night of 31 December 2015, during New Year's Eve celebration, numerous thefts and sexual assaults took place in public places in Cologne and in other German cities. The mainstream media mainly ascribed these attacks to asylum seekers of Arab and/or North African descent, thereby drawing on racist images of men of color. This sparked a large and highly controversial debate about current (anti-)refugee politics and about the ways in which sexism and racism are interconnected in contemporary Germany. See Gabriele Dietze, *Sexueller Exzeptionalismus. Überlegenheitsnarrative in Migrationsabwehr und Rechtspopulismus* (Bielefeld, transcript, 2019), pp. 41–58; Stefanie C. Boulila and Christiane Carri, "On Cologne: Gender, Migration and Unacknowledged Racisms in Germany," *European Journal of Women's Studies*, 24:3 (2017), pp. 286–93.

15 Noémi Michel, "Sheepology: The Postcolonial Politics of Raceless Racism in Switzerland," *Postcolonial Studies*, 18:4 (2015), pp. 410–26.

16 "Controlling images" is a term that stresses that representations, ideas, and images have material effects on the lives of all people who are exposed to them, albeit differentially. See the chapter "Mammies, Matriarchs, and Other Controlling Images," in Patricia Hill Collins, *Black Feminist Thought* (New York, Routledge, 2000), pp. 79–96.

17 Charles Herbert Stember, *Sexual Racism: The Emotional Barrier to an Integrated Society* (New York, Elsevier, 1976).

18 Hortense Spillers proposes the notion of "ungendering" to describe how Black bodies were transformed into gender-undifferentiated Black flesh during the Middle Passage; see Hortense Spillers, *Black, White and in Color: Essays on American Literature and Culture* (Chicago, University of Chicago Press, 2003). In separate works, Samantha Pinto and Jennifer Nash point out that the idea of Black ungendering and the ungendered Black body has much resonance in Afro-pessimism scholarship, especially in the current context of theorizations of Black death and how Black life is lived alongside and with Black death; see Samantha Pinto, "Black Feminist Literacies: Ungendering, Flesh, and

Post-Spillers Epistemologies of Embodied and Emotional Justice," *Journal of Black Sexuality and Relationships*, 4:1 (2017), pp. 25–45; Jennifer C. Nash, *Black Feminism Reimagined after Intersectionality* (Durham, NC, Duke University Press, 2019), pp. 20–1.

19 Afrosexology, www.afrosexology.com (accessed 6 February 2019).

20 James Baldwin, "Stranger in the Village," in *Notes of a Native Son* (Boston, MA, Beacon Press, 1984), pp. 162–4.

21 Using the term *historicity*, we ask not simply about the history of these images, but about *how* these images are embedded in historical time and play out differently through time. This differentiation seems pertinent after a long critique of the colonial binary of historical time (and its subjects) as a linearly evolving process in opposition to things and subjects without history. For postcolonial discussions of history and historicity, see Johannes Fabian, *Time and the Other: How Anthropology makes its Subjects* (New York, Columbia University Press, 2014); Dipesh Chakrabarty, *Provincializing Europe: Postcolonial Thought and Historical Difference* (Princeton, NJ, Princeton University Press, 2008).

22 Banania is a French chocolate and banana flavored beverage brand that was first commercialized in the wake of World War I. The advertizing and customizing of this product shows a caricatured Senegalese trooper, smiling over the product while exclaiming "Y a bon!" in French pidgin. See Anne Donadey, "'Y'a Bon Banania': Ethics and Cultural Criticism in the Colonial Context," *French Cultural Studies*, 11:31 (2000), pp. 9–29.

23 Michel, "Sheepology", p. 411.

24 "'Blackfacing', Histoire d'un Racisme Ordinaire," *Radio Lac*, 20 December 2017, www.radio-lac.ch/podcasts/le-8220Blackfacing8221-histoire-d8217un-racisme-ordinaire-20122017-3/ (accessed 29 March 2019).

25 Stephen Small, *20 Questions and Answers on Black Europe* (Amsterdam, Amrit, 2018).

26 On the history of Black women in Switzerland, see Jovita dos Santos Pinto, "Spuren. Eine Geschichte Schwarzer Frauen in der Schweiz," in Shelley Berlowitz, Elisabeth Joris, and Zeedah Meierhofer-Mangeli (eds.), *Terra incognita? Der Treffpunkt Schwarzer Frauen in Zürich* (Zürich, Limmat, 2013), pp. 143–85. On the figure of the "eternal newcomer," see Fatima El-Tayeb, *European Others: Queering Ethnicity in Postnational Europe* (Minneapolis, MN, University of Minnesota Press, 2011), p. xx.

27 On the silencing of the Haitian Revolution, see Michel-Rolph Trouillot, *Silencing the Past: Power and the Production of History* (Boston, MA, Beacon Press, 1995).

28 On the erasure of Black history in Switzerland, see Pinto, "Spuren."

29 See Purtschert and Fischer-Tiné, "The End of Innocence," p. 3.

30 Baldwin, "Stranger in the Village," p. 174.

31 Gloria Wekker, *White Innocence. Paradoxes of Colonialism and Race* (Durham, NC, Duke University Press, 2016).

32 Baldwin, "Stranger in the Village," p. 161.

33 On the concept of "colonialism without colonies," see Patricia Purtschert, Francesca Falk, and Barbara Lüthi, "Switzerland and 'Colonialism without Colonies,'" *Interventions: International Journal of Postcolonial Studies*, 18:2 (2015), pp. 286–302.

34 Frantz Fanon, *Black Skin, White Masks* (1952) (London, Pluto Press, 2008), pp. 82–108.

35 Baldwin, "Stranger in the Village," p. 175.

36 Mwasi Collectif Afrofeministe, https://mwasicollectif.com/ (accessed 29 March 2019).

37 On the history of queer of color groups in France and continental Europe, see Paola Bacchetta, "QTPOC Critiques of 'Post-Raciality,' Segregationality, Coloniality and Capitalism in France," in Sandeep Bakshi, Suhraiya Jivraj, and Silvia Possado (eds.), *Decolonizing Sexuality: Transnational Perspectives, Critical Interventions* (London, Counterpress,

2016), pp. 264–81; Paola Bacchetta and Jin Haritaworn, "There Are Many Transatlantics: Homonationalism, Homotransnationalism and Feminist-Queer-Trans of Color Theories and Practices," in Kathy Davis and Mary Evans (eds.), *Transatlantic Conversations: Feminism as Travelling Theory* (Farnham, Ashgate, 2011), pp. 127–44; Paola Bacchetta, "Co-Formations: sur les spatialités de résistance de lesbiennes 'of Color' en France," *Genre, sexualité et société*, 1 (2009), http://gss.revues.org; Paola Bacchetta, Fatima El-Tayeb, and Jin Haritaworn, "Queers of Color and (De)Colonial Spaces in Europe," in Paola Bacchetta, Sunaina Maira, and Howard Winant (eds.), *Global Raciality: Empire, Postcoloniality, Decoloniality* (New York, Routledge, 2019), pp. 158–70.

38 Bla*Sh, https://facebook.com/NetzwerkBlackShe/ (accessed 27 March 2019).

39 In the (very small) French-speaking part of Switzerland, there are three intersectional feminist collectives: Faites des Vagues (https://fr-fr.facebook.com/faitesdesvagues/), the Collectif AfroSwiss (https://collectifafroswiss.wordpress.com/author/collectifafroswiss/), and the Collectif Amani (www.instagram.com/collectifamani/, all accessed 12 December 2019).

40 For a reflection on racial profiling in raceless Switzerland, see Noémi Michel, "Racial Profiling und die Tabuisierung von Rasse," in Mohamed Wa Baile et. al. (eds.), *Racial Profiling. Struktureller Rassismus und antirassistischer Widerstand* (Bielefeld, transcript, 2019), pp. 87–106. On the groups formed in the wake of the incidents in Vaud, see Outrage Collectif, https://outragecollectif.noblogs.org/ (accessed 27 March 2019), "À Qui le Tour? Un Nouveau Collectif Antiraciste," *solidaritéS*, 305 (2017), p. 15, www.solidarites.ch/journal/d/article/7998/A-qui-le-tour-Un-nouveau-collectif-antiraciste (accessed 27 March 2019).

41 Queer Week Edition 2017, "Trajectoires," www.queerweek.com/2017/programme-queer-week-2017.pdf (accessed 27 March 2019).

42 Queer Week Edition 2018, "Town Hall—Queer and Trans Politics of Color," www.queerweek.com/2018/inauguration-queer-and-trans-politics-of-color-town-hall/ (accessed 9 December 2019).

43 https://mwasicollectif.com/afrofemtour/ (accessed 10 December 2019).

44 On the podcasts mentioned, see https://soundcloud.com/le-tchip; https://soundcloud.com/kiffe-ta-race; https://vocalaboutit.podbean.com; https://decolonizationinaction.com (all accessed 10 December 2019).

45 On the platforms mentioned, see www.cases-rebelles.org/, http://gal-dem.com/ (both accessed 12 December 2019), and ERIF's latest campaign, Quotes of Resistance, which amplifies antiracist voices across Europe. See https://quotesofresistance.wordpress.com/ (accessed 12 December 2019).

46 www.lamaisonbaldwin.fr/conference2020 (accessed 10 December 2019). The conference, like so many other events, was postponed due to the COVID-19 pandemic. As of this writing in April of 2020, the conference is being planned instead for 2021.

47 See the contributions and testimonies by Black women and women of color in "Part IV Surviving the Academy" of the edited volume by Akwugo Emejulu and Francesca Sobande, *To Exist Is to Resist: Black Feminism in Europe* (London, Pluto Press, 2019). See Sirma Bilge, "Intersectionality Undone. Saving Intersectionality from Feminist Intersectionality Studies," *Du Bois Review*, 10:2 (2013), pp. 405–24; Vanessa Naef and Nora Trenkel, "Es darf nicht alles beim Alten bleiben in den Gender Studies!," *genderstudies. Zeitschrift des Interdisziplinären Zentrums für Geschlechterforschung IZFG*, 32 (2018), pp. 8–11; Patricia Purtschert, "Prolog: Mehr als ein Schlagwort. Dekolonisieren (in) der Postkolonialen Schweiz," *Tsantsa*, 24 (2019), pp. 14–23.

Works Cited

Anzaldúa, Gloria, and Cherríe Moraga, *This Bridge Called My Back: Writings by Radical Women of Color* (New York, Kitchen Table, 1983).

Bacchetta, Paola, "Co-formations: sur les spatialités de résistance de lesbiennes 'of color' en France," *Genre, sexualité et société*, 1 (2009), https://doi.org/10.4000/gss.810.

———— "Dyketactics!," in Howard Chiang et al. (eds.), *Global Encyclopedia of Lesbian, Gay, Bisexual, Transgender, and Queer History* (New York, Macmillan, 2019), pp. 483–6.

———— "QTPOC Critiques of 'Post-Raciality,' Segregationality, Coloniality and Capitalism in France," in Sandeep Bakshi, Suhraiya Jivraj, and Silvia Possado (eds.), *Decolonizing Sexuality: Transnational Perspectives, Critical Interventions* (London, Counterpress, 2016), pp. 264–81.

Bacchetta, Paola, Fatima El-Tayeb, and Jin Haritaworn, "Queers of Color and (De)Colonial Spaces in Europe," in Paola Bacchetta, Sunaina Maira, and Howard Winant (eds.), *Global Raciality: Empire, Postcoloniality, Decoloniality* (New York, Routledge, 2019), pp. 158–70.

Bacchetta, Paola, and Jin Haritaworn, "There Are Many Transatlantics: Homonationalism, Homotransnationalism and Feminist-Queer-Trans of Color Theories and Practices," in Kathy Davis and Mary Evans (eds.), *Transatlantic Conversations: Feminism as Travelling Theory* (Farnham, Ashgate, 2011), pp. 127–44.

Baldwin, James, *Fremder im Dorf: Ein Schwarzer New Yorker in Leukerbad* (Zürich, Sacré, 2011).

———— *I Am Not Your Negro (Compiled and Edited by Raoul Peck)* (London, Penguin, 2017).

———— *Later Novels*, ed. Darryl Pinckney (New York, Library of America, 2015).

———— "Stranger in the Village" (1955), in *Notes of a Native Son* (Boston, MA, Beacon Press, 1984), pp. 159–75.

Bilge, Sirma, "Intersectionality Undone: Saving Intersectionality from Feminist Intersectionality Studies," *Du Bois Review*, 10:2 (2013), pp. 405–24.

Boulila, Stefanie C., and Christiane Carri, "On Cologne: Gender, Migration and Unacknowledged Racisms in Germany," *European Journal of Women's Studies*, 24:3 (2017), pp. 286–93.

Brim, Matt, *James Baldwin and the Queer Imagination* (Ann Arbor, MI, University of Michigan Press, 2014).

Cele, Ntando, "Stranger," blog entry, 2 January 2014, www.ntandocl.blogspot.com (accessed 27 March 2019).

Chakrabarty, Dipesh, *Provincializing Europe: Postcolonial Thought and Historical Difference* (Princeton, NJ, Princeton University Press 2008).

Coates, Ta-Nehisi, *Between the World and Me* (New York, Spiegel & Grau, 2017).

Cole, Teju, "Black Body: Rereading James Baldwin's 'Stranger in the Village,'" *New Yorker*, 19 August 2014, www.newyorker.com/books/page-turner/black-body-re-reading-james-baldwins-stranger-village (accessed 15 June 2020).

———— "Schwarzer Körper," *Das Magazin*, 19 August 2014, pp. 8–17.

Combahee River Collective, "A Black Feminist Statement," in Gloria T. Hull, Patricia Bell Scott, and Barbara Smith (eds.), *But Some of Us Are Brave: Black Women's Studies* (Old Westbury, NY, Feminist Press, 1982), pp. 13–22.

Condé, Maryse, *La Vie sans fard* (Paris, Latte, 2012).

Dietze, Gabriele, *Sexueller Exzeptionalismus: Überlegenheitsnarrative in Migrationsabwehr und Rechtspopulismus* (Bielefeld, transcript, 2019).

Donadey, Anne, "'Y'a Bon Banania': Ethics and Cultural Criticism in the Colonial Context," *French Cultural Studies*, 11:31 (2000), pp. 9–29.

Du Bois, W. E. B., *The Souls of Black Folk: Essays and Sketches* (New York, Magnavision, 1903).

El-Tayeb, Fatima, *European Others: Queering Ethnicity in Postnational Europe* (Minneapolis, MN, University of Minnesota Press, 2011).

Emejulu, Akwugo, and Francesca Sobande, *To Exist is to Resist: Black Feminism in Europe* (London, Pluto Press, 2019).

Fabian, Johannes, *Time and the Other: How Anthropology Makes its Objects* (New York, Columbia University Press, 2014).

Fanon, Frantz, *Black Skin, White Masks* (1952) (New York, Grove Press, 2008).

_____ "The Fact of Blackness," in *Black Skin, White Masks* (1952) (London, Pluto Press, 2008), pp. 82–108.

Francis, Consuela, *The Critical Reception of James Baldwin, 1963–2010: 'An Honest Man and a Good Writer'* (Rochester, NY, Camden House, 2014).

Hill Collins, Patricia, *Black Feminist Thought* (1990) (New York, Routledge 2000).

Huber, Sasha, "The firsts—James Baldwin," www.sashahuber.com/?cat=10075&lang=fi&m-str=10009 (accessed 27 March 2019).

JanMohamed, Abdul R., *The Death-Bound-Subject: Richard Wright's Archaeology of Death* (Durham, NC, Duke University Press, 2005).

Maxwell, William J., "Born-Again, Seen-Again James Baldwin: Post-Postracial Criticism and the Literary History of Black Lives Matter," *American Literary History*, 28:4 (2016), pp. 812–27.

Michel, Noémi, "Racial Profiling und die Tabuisierung von Rasse," in Mohamed Wa Baile, Serena O. Dankwa, Tarek Naguib, Patricia Purtschert, and Sarah Schilliger (eds.), *Racial Profiling: Struktureller Rassismus und antirassistischer Widerstand* (Bielefeld, transcript, 2019), pp. 87–106.

_____ "Sheepology: The Postcolonial Politics of Raceless Racism in Switzerland," *Postcolonial Studies*, 18:4 (2015), pp. 410–26.

Naef, Vanessa, and Nora Trenkel, "Es darf nicht alles beim Alten bleiben in den Gender Studies!," *genderstudies. Zeitschrift des Interdisziplinären Zentrums für Geschlechterforschung IZFG*, 32 (2018), pp. 8–11.

Nash, Jennifer C., *Black Feminism Reimagined after Intersectionality* (Durham, NC, Duke University Press, 2019).

Patterson, Orlando, *Slavery and Social Death: A Comparative Study* (Cambridge, MA, Harvard University Press, 1982).

Pinto, Jovita dos Santos, "Spuren. Eine Geschichte Schwarzer Frauen in der Schweiz," in Shelley Berlowitz, Elisabeth Joris, and Zeedah Meierhofer-Mangeli (eds.), *Terra incognita? Der Treffpunkt Schwarzer Frauen in Zürich* (Zürich, Limmat, 2013), pp. 143–85.

Pinto, Samantha, "Black Feminist Literacies: Ungendering, Flesh, and Post-Spillers Epistemologies of Embodied and Emotional Justice," *Journal of Black Sexuality and Relationships*, 4:1 (2017), pp. 25–45.

Purtschert, Patricia, "Prolog: Mehr als ein Schlagwort. Dekolonisieren (in) der Postkolonialen Schweiz," *Tsantsa*, 24 (2019), pp. 14–23.

Purtschert, Patricia, Francesca Falk and Barbara Lüthi, "Switzerland and 'Colonialism without Colonies,'" *Interventions: International Journal of Postcolonial Studies*, 18:2 (2015), pp. 286–302.

Purtschert, Patricia, and Harald Fischer-Tiné, "The End of Innocence: Debating Colonialism in Switzerland," in Patricia Purtschert and Harald Fischer-Tiné (eds.), *Colonial Switzerland: Rethinking Switzerland from the Margins* (Basingstoke, Palgrave Macmillan, 2015), pp. 1–26.

Purtschert, Patricia, Barbara Lüthi, and Francesca Falk (eds.), *Postkoloniale Schweiz: Formen und Folgen eines Kolonialismus ohne Kolonien* (Bielefeld, transcript, 2012).

Rankine, Claudia, *Citizen: An American Lyric* (Minneapolis, MN, Graywolf Press, 2014).

Robinson, Cedric, *Black Marxism: The Making of a Black Radical Tradition* (Chapel Hill, NC, University of North Carolina Press, 2000).

Small, Stephen, *20 Questions and Answers on Black Europe* (Amsterdam, Amrit, 2018).

Spillers, Hortense, *Black, White and in Color: Essays on American Literature and Culture* (Chicago, University of Chicago Press, 2003).

Stauffer, Michael, and R. Hermann, *"Wie ein Schaf in der Wüste". Passage Sendung* (SRF, 2012).

Stember, Charles, *Sexual Racism: The Emotional Barrier to an Integrated Society* (New York, Elsevier, 1976).

Trouillot, Michel-Rolph, *Silencing the Past: Power and the Production of History* (Boston, MA, Beacon Press, 1995).

Walther, Christian, *"Fremd". Kurzfilm über James Baldwin* (Insertfilm/SRF, 2013).

Wekker, Gloria, *White Innocence: Paradoxes of Colonialism and Race* (Durham, NC, Duke University Press, 2016).

Contributors' Biographies

Jovita dos Santos Pinto is a cultural historian, doctoral student, and research assistant at the Interdisciplinary Center for Gender Studies at the University of Bern, Switzerland, with an emphasis on critical race studies, feminist and queer theory, and emancipatory movements. Her published articles include "Handwerksgeschichten. Schwarze Frauen im Gespräch" (co-authored by Rahel El-Maawi; transcript, 2019), "Zur Aktualität des postkolonialen Feminismus für die Schweiz" (co-authored by Patricia Purtschert; Widerspruch, 2018) and "Spuren. Eine Geschichte Schwarzer Frauen in der Schweiz" (Limmat Verlag, 2013). She is also a co-founder of Bla*Sh – Network of Black Womyn in Switzerland.

Noémi Michel is Senior Lecturer in Political Theory at the Department of Political Science of the University of Geneva, Switzerland. Her research and teaching interests are in postcolonial and critical race theory, with a focus on diasporic Black feminist thought. Her recent work has been published in *Darkmatter, Critical Horizons, Postcolonial Studies* and *Social Politics*. Her current research explores, on the one hand, conflicting grammars of antiracism in European public debates and institutions and, on the other, Black feminist theorization of political voice. She is member of the European Race and Imagery Foundation as well as of the feminist and intersectional *Collectif Faites des Vagues*.

Patricia Purtschert is a philosopher, professor of gender studies, and co-director of the Interdisciplinary Centre for Gender Studies at the University of Bern, Switzerland. Her publications include *Kolonialität und Geschlecht im 20. Jahrhundert. Eine Geschichte der weißen Schweiz* (transcript, 2019), *Racial Profiling. Struktureller*

Rassismus und antirassistischer Widerstand (co-edited with Mohamed Wa Baile, Serena O. Dankwa, Tarek Naguib, and Sarah Schilliger; transcript, 2019), *Colonial Switzerland: Rethinking Colonialism from the Margins* (co-edited with Harald Fischer-Tiné; Palgrave, 2015), *Postkoloniale Schweiz. Formen und Folgen eines Kolonialismus ohne Kolonien* (co-edited with Barbara Lüthi and Francesca Falk; transcript, 2012), and *Grenzfiguren. Kultur, Geschlecht und Subjekt bei Hegel und Nietzsche* (Campus, 2006).

Paola Bacchetta is Professor of Gender and Women's Studies at the University of California, Berkeley. She is former director of the Berkeley Gender Consortium, and current co-director of the Political Conflict, Gender and Peoples' Rights Project. She is an Advisory Board member of Berkeley's Center for Race and Gender, and Center for Right Wing Studies. Her books include *Co-Motion: On Feminist and Queer of Color Alliances* (Duke University Press, forthcoming), *Global Racialities: Empire, Postcoloniality, and Decoloniality* (co-edited with Sunaina Maira and Howard Winant, Routledge, 2019), *Femminismi Queer Postcoloniali: critiche transnazionali all'omofobia, all'islamofobia e all'omonazionalismo* (co-edited with Laura Fantone, Ombre Corte, 2015), *Gender in the Hindu Nation* (Women Unlimited, 2004), and *Right-Wing Women: From Conservatives to Extremists around the World* (co-edited with Margaret Power, Routledge, 2002). She is currently co-editing a book entitled *Fatima Mernissi for Our Times* (with Minoo Moallem) and another on lesbian of color writing in France (with Nawo Crawford). She has also published over sixty articles and book chapters on sexuality and racism, transnational and decolonial feminist theory, queer of color theory and practices, decolonizing sexualities, global southern theory, right-wing movements, political conflict, critical theory, and space. Her geographical areas of specialization are France, India, and the U.S.A. Her work has been published in multiple languages. In 2020, she has Fulbright for a current book project on sexuality and colonialism.

Vanessa Naef is pursuing a M.A. in Sociolinguistics and Gender Studies at the University of Bern, Switzerland, and holds a B.A. in German Language and Literature with a Minor in English Languages and Literature. She works at the Interdisciplinary Center for Gender Studies at the University of Bern, Switzerland, in the fields of postcolonialism, feminist and queer theory, and emancipatory movements.

FROM THE FIELD

Rebranding James Baldwin and His Queer Others: A Session at the 2019 American Studies Association Conference

Magdalena J. Zaborowska   University of Michigan
Nicholas F. Radel   Furman University
Nigel Hatton   University of California, Merced
Ernest L. Gibson III   Auburn University

Abstract

"Rebranding James Baldwin and His Queer Others" was a session held at the annual meeting of the American Studies Association in November 2019 in Honolulu, Hawaii. The papers gathered here show how Baldwin's writings and life story participate in dialogues with other authors and artists who probe issues of identity and identification, as well as with other types of texts and non-American stories, boldly addressing theoretical and political perspectives different from his own. Nick Radel's temporal challenge to reading novels on homoerotic male desire asks of us a leap of faith, one that makes it possible to read race as not necessarily a synonym for "Black," but as a powerful historical and sexual trope that resists "over-easy" binaries of Western masculinity. Ernest L. Gibson's engagement with Beauford Delaney's brilliant art and the ways in which it enabled the teenage Baldwin's "dark rapture" of self-discovery as a writer reminds us that "something [has been missing] in our discussions of male relationships." Finally, Nigel Hatton suggests "a relationship among Baldwin, Denmark, and *Giovanni's Room* that adds another thread to the important scholarship on his groundbreaking work of fiction that has impacted African-American literature, Cold War studies, transnational American studies, feminist thought, and queer theory." All three essays enlarge our assessment of Baldwin's contribution to understanding the ways gender and sexuality always inflect racialized Western masculinities. Thus, they help us work to better gauge the extent of Baldwin's influence right here and right now.

Keywords: Black queer, James Baldwin, *Giovanni's Room*, David Leavitt, Beauford Delaney, salvific manhood, gaze, publishing, Denmark

James Baldwin Review, Volume 6, 2020, © The Authors. Published by Manchester University Press and The University of Manchester Library
http://dx.doi.org/10.7227/JBR.6.13

James Baldwin's titanic presence as a revolutionary Black queer writer, whose reckoning with conundrums of intersectional identities in twentieth-century American
literature has yet to be matched, has often meant that his work is explored in nar-
rower contexts than warranted. His recent popularity on social media, and the
release of two films—an art-film/documentary by Raoul Peck (*I Am Not Your
Negro*, 2016) and Barry Jenkins's adaptation of Baldwin's sixth novel from 1974 (*If
Beale Street Could Talk*, 2018)—have branded him as a Black cultural icon, and
vaulted his words, often out of context, onto blogs, websites, even merchandize.
This "Baldwin brand," however, often elides, obscures, and at times erases the complexity and urgency of his message on racialized gender and sexuality, a message
that is particularly salient in our moment of divisive politics, alt-right white supremacy, and hate speech.[1]

A passionate critic of American imperialism, during his lifetime Baldwin was
recognized as an international public intellectual and was frequently appreciated
more abroad than at home, especially in the wake of his third essay volume, *The
Fire Next Time* (1963). First published in *The New Yorker*, Baldwin's passionate
indictment of U.S. Cold War politics and systemic oppression of its African-American citizens made him front-page news and a star, while his work was branded as
angry and incendiary by U.S. white liberal critics who wanted him to testify to,
rather than interpret, the so-called "Negro problem."[2] Baldwin's pro-integrationist
message that closes the "Letter from the Region in My Mind" also flew in the face
of Black nationalism, while his recounting of a meeting with Elijah Muhammad of
the Nation of Islam, whose sexism and exclusionary identity politics he rejected,
estranged him from Black Muslims and the Black Power generation. Distilled into
Eldridge Cleaver's homophobic vitriol in *Soul on Ice* (1968), Baldwin's unflinching
honesty and eloquence were seen as betrayals of both race and heteropatriarchal
national manhood. As the Penguin Random House web page still advertises its
edition of *Soul on Ice*, "What Cleaver shows us, on the pages of this now classic
autobiography, is how much he was a man."[3] It is precisely the topic of "being a
man," one who desires other men, that the essays introduced here take on. They do
so by bringing Baldwin's works into conversation with those of three other "queer"
artists: the Jewish American gay writer David Leavitt; Baldwin's father figure and
artistic mentor, the renowned Black American painter Beauford Delaney; and the
little-known Danish sculptor Yan Kai Nielsen, who created a beautiful sandstone
bust of the author during Baldwin's first years abroad.

The idea for this session originated with Professor Nicholas Radel, who proposed its theme and focus on Baldwin's little-known international and American
ethnic interlocutors. Aware that Baldwin, especially after the publication of his
second novel, *Giovanni's Room* (1956), had been enshrined as a father figure of the
mid-century male gay movement on the one hand, and that his mid-century novel
had become something of an ur-"white homosexual abroad" text on the other,
Radel was intrigued by the idea of exploring specific cases of Baldwin's cultural
and literary historical impact both in the United States and in Europe. Conse-
quently, Radel and I solicited these three essays for presentation at the annual

meeting of the American Studies Association in November 2019 in Honolulu, in a session entitled "Rebranding James Baldwin and His Queer Others." I served as chair and respondent to all three, and it is my honor and pleasure now to introduce them as examples of new scholarship on the writer to *James Baldwin Review*.

The papers gathered here show how Baldwin's writings and life story participate in dialogues with other authors and artists who probe issues of identity and identification, as well as with other types of texts and non-American stories, boldly addressing theoretical and political perspectives different from his own. All three essays enlarge our assessment of Baldwin's contribution to understanding the ways gender and sexuality always inflect racialized Western masculinities. Thus, they help us work to better gauge the extent of Baldwin's influence right here and right now.

Professor Radel's temporal challenge to reading novels on homoerotic male desire in "Tainted Love: The Absent Black Gay Man in David Leavitt and James Baldwin" asks of us a leap of faith, one that makes it possible to read race as not necessarily a synonym for "Black," but as a powerful historical and sexual trope that resists "over-easy" binaries of Western masculinity. Since the mid-twentieth century, such binaries have reinscribed not only love between men, but also how we see ourselves and others in the world, and how we tell stories about all that. Hence Leavitt's novel *The Indian Clerk* —a 2007 novel about science and desire in a postcolonial framework—can be understood, as Radel argues, "within a narrative of representational relations between African-American and white gay American men in Europe similar to that found in *Giovanni's Room*." Radel's reading emphasizes the agency of the reader within the novel's complex historical frame of reference. Like one of Shakespeare's historical plays, Leavitt's work creates in the reader, in the novelist's words, a contradictory yearning to "*want* to read *The Indian Clerk* as a novel written in the 21st century," and thus as being about us, but also as a novel about the early twentieth century, and thus alien to us. The novel's temporal dislocations leave us stranded alongside the "absent Black gay man" who haunts both Leavitt's and Baldwin's novels.

Professor Gibson's engagement with Beauford Delaney's brilliant art and the ways in which it enabled the teenage Baldwin's "dark rapture" of self-discovery as a writer reminds us that "something [has been missing] in our discussions of male relationships." Baldwin's stepfather, David, whose last name the writer inherited after his mother's marriage to him in early childhood, was a stern fundamentalist preacher who despised his stepson's sissy mannerisms and bookishness. In contrast, Delaney, a son of a preacher and gay like Baldwin, welcomed him with open arms. As an artistic father figure Delaney introduced the young author to the great cultural heritage of Black America, and mentored him to come into his own as a "painterly" writer.[4] While Delaney made many portraits of his protégé, the one referenced in Gibson's essay is the only nude vision of young Baldwin's body, created in 1941 and entitled *Dark Rapture*. Author of the groundbreaking *Salvific Manhood: James Baldwin's Novelization of Male Intimacy* (2019), Gibson argues for embracing "the powerful way Baldwin wrote intimacy and love and the possibility of salvation in love between men." In his deep reading, *any kind* of revolutionary

love challenges the reductives of gender binaries by asking for tenderness, for lay-
ing on of hands, for the closeness and honesty missing in normalized, competitive
male relationships. Gibson's twenty-first-century reading uncovers a clear narrative scripting tender Black masculinity that flies directly in the face of Cleaver's
dismissal of Baldwin and his gendered vision.

Professor Hatton's "The Novel and the Police: *Giovanni's Room* and the Sculpting of Queer Danish Life" suggests "a relationship among Baldwin, Denmark, and
Giovanni's Room that adds another thread to the important scholarship on his
groundbreaking work of fiction that has impacted African-American literature,
Cold War studies, transnational American studies, feminist thought, and queer
theory." This essay journeys to the space where Baldwin met and inspired the Danish sculptor Yan Kai Nielsen, who sculpted in sandstone a beautiful bust of a twen-
tysomething Baldwin in Paris in the early 1950s. Hatton shows how the meeting
of Baldwin and Nielsen in Paris can be attributed to "both the postwar trend of
African Americans finding community and freedom in the city and Danish artists
leaving the North to seek the latest training in the arts in Europe's cultural capital,"
thus reminding us how *worldly*, in Edward Said's elegant formulation, literary culture has always been. Indeed, while racism marred the scene of Baldwin's imagined homeland's democracy and liberty, Nielsen's homeland was "deep in
homosexual panic, arresting homosexuals for modeling in fear that homoeroticism could lead to prostitution and inevitably widespread crime." In the encounter
between Baldwin and Nielsen, Hatton sees narrative, and the genre of the novel
specifically, as the key that enables us to restore a humanizing gaze, or the precious
ability to "read people." As we have heard, the "Danish roots of *Giovanni's Room*"
is another proof that literature makes "things happen," that stories we tell about
others teach us what I tell my students every year: If you don't learn how to read
books, you will never learn how to read people.

Baldwin's writings on sexual minorities, communities of color, and immigrants
in New York, San Juan, Paris, London, or Ankara inspired, and continue to inspire,
numerous and varied artists across the world. Vitally and vibrantly, his works create
spaces for alternative, novel, and radical types of political and literary critiques and
cultural imaginaries, all within, and in solidarity with, communities of color and
non-normative sexualities in the U.S. and abroad. Baldwin's international, humanistic, wise-ancestor message reminds us that, while we cling to seeing mostly what
divides us, we often neglect to focus on what, however painfully, inextricably connects us all.

Magdalena J. Zaborowska

Tainted Love: The Absent Black Gay Man in David Leavitt and James Baldwin

I want to speak today about the work of two men widely—and I will argue
erroneously—imagined to inhabit different, indeed contradictory spaces: the

African-American, sometimes man-loving James Baldwin, a writer justly credited with being one of America's most subtle thinkers on the vexed inter-sections of race and sexuality, and the white gay American David Leavitt, an author frequently criticized for evading the pressures of race and his own Jewish heritage in exploring the lives of white, middle-class, gay men.[5] Rather than reinscribe that over-easy binary, however, I am going to argue, to the contrary, that Leavitt's work—exemplified by his 2007 novel *The Indian Clerk*—can be understood within a narrative of representational relations between Afri-can-American and white gay American men in Europe similar to that found in *Giovanni's Room*, Baldwin's groundbreaking 1956 novel about same-sex desire.

Giovanni's Room reveals some of the ways homosexual desires were linked his-torically in twentieth-century American cultural representation to dark-skinned and ethnic peoples. It provides an example of the ways American racialized sexu-ality associated same-sex desire with a moral depravity frequently represented in explicitly ethnic or racial terms. Baldwin, thus, peers into the paradoxes of an American homosexuality that cannot quite escape its morally murky past and tra-ditional identification with ethnic and Black Americans, as a result of which it can only denigrate dark-skinned, Black, and Black gay Americans. In making such connections, Baldwin anticipated the astute sociological analysis of critics such as Mason Stokes, Siobhan Somerville, and Roderick A. Ferguson. These scholars demonstrated conclusively that starting in the late nineteenth and early twentieth centuries, racial purity, including white racial purity, was measured against emerg-ing discourses of homosexuality linked not only with dark-skinned races and eth-nic peoples but with moral aberration.[6] Baldwin's is a prescient vision, then, in which questions of homosexual legitimation are inextricably linked to racial iden-tifications, and the paradoxes he identifies may account for some of the difficulties Baldwin discovered in trying to accommodate Black racial difference to same-sex sexuality—at least in his early writings.

My main point in this paper, however, is to suggest that *Giovanni's Room* narrativ-ized homosexuality in terms of a problematic racial binary that persisted within the cultural memory of post-Stonewall discourses in white gay America. I am not sug-gesting that Baldwin is Leavitt's explicit source, but, rather, that both *Giovanni's Room* and *The Indian Clerk* come at the issue of homosexual or gay ontology through questions of race and racialized sexuality that precede them both. There are, of course, differences between the two authors. But because cultural scripts that make race central to American—and perhaps Western—conceptions of homosexuality shape both men's apprehensions, I emphasize their similarities. Both authors are the subjects of, or are subjected by, discourses prior to them, discourses that have been formative of both gay white and African-American thought throughout the twenti-eth and twenty-first centuries. In reading them together we see better how racial cultural memories intersect with discourses of sexuality in the United States to render coherent, unitary conceptions of homosexuality—white or Black—nearly unimaginable. That is, we see that there are no homosexualities, even white ones, that fail to intersect with other vectors of power and identity, in particular race.[7]

I take as my point of departure a fantasy of Europe, which both Baldwin and Leavitt employ as a setting to examine male homosexuality and race. In *Giovanni's Room*, David, the gay white protagonist, imagines his expatriation to Europe as a flight that began in his youth, a flight from an erotic entanglement with a dark-skinned boy, Joey, in the U.S. Although as an adult in Europe he is involved with a white woman, Hella, he nevertheless becomes entangled again in a homosexual relationship with an ethnically marked Italian, Giovanni. Baldwin, thus, thema-tizes within his novel a turning away from American racial complication that, without question, reflects many of his own thoughts and feelings. In Leavitt's case, this authorial turning away from America toward Europe is not so much thematic or a matter of the individual character. It is, rather, to be discerned in Leavitt's decision to write primarily about English characters in post-Edwardian England. *The Indian Clerk* is a historical work about the chaste but eroticized relationship between the famous mathematicians G. H. (Godfrey Harold) Hardy and Srinivasa Ramanujan at Cambridge. In the only sustained exploration of race and sex in his growing body of work, Leavitt turns away from his present context in the United States to write about English history. And in doing so, he effects a double displace-ment of time and place that recalls Baldwin's narrative of white homosexuality in flight from a darker, unsettling African-American history.

Magdalena J. Zaborowska makes clear some of the ways Baldwin carefully parses the "underlying exclusionary politics" of American racial and sexual iden-tities in *Giovanni's Room*.[8] She shrewdly argues that when the novel's gay white protagonist leaves the U.S. and acts on his homosexual desire in 1950s Paris, he transgresses not only American sexual but also racial norms—for the hegemonic regime of American masculinity is performed both heteronormatively and as whiteness. In other words, David's gay European sojourn reflects the outside of American heteronormative whiteness. But that European sojourn signals as well David's desire to escape a homosexuality coded in the novel as a kind of darkness, even perhaps specifically as African-American. *Giovanni's Room*, thus, reveals the racial complications everywhere present in American same-sex imagining, even the author's own.

When the white—blonde, of course—protagonist recalls his first "act" of gay "love" as a teenager in Brooklyn, it is with a boy named Joey.[9] Perhaps not defini-tively marked African-American, Joey nevertheless has "curly" dark hair and brown skin, which suggests that he may be.[10] Indeed, Zaborowska suggests that "if we read the text closely, [Joey] might be both gay and black."[11] But the point is that when David reacts phobically to his desire for Joey, he images his horror in a dis-course that links moral abstractions of color to a racially evoked body. He speaks of the "taint" his love causes him to feel.[12] Joey's "body," he says, "suddenly seemed the black opening of a cavern in which I would be tortured till madness came, in which I would lose my manhood."[13] So, in the course of the novel, David flees to Paris, the city of light. Baldwin's white protagonist might be said to be in exile from a gay desire that references darkness in moral terms and may even be founded literally in an African-American body. David's turn to Europe is a journey away from the American heart of darkness, an attempt to flee both the African American in his bed and the racial/sexual taint of his embeddedness in homophobic America.

In Europe, David's paranoid efforts to perform heterosexuality lead him repeatedly to associate his intended wife Hella with family and reproduction in ways that necessarily reveal the link between heterosexuality and—in this case, white—racial purity.[14] To put it bluntly, he seeks not only to conform sexually but to regain the whiteness from which he fears he is excluded. But his attempted flight into white heteronormativity is forestalled by the re-emergence of homosexual feelings that in American thought are so often drawn in the moral language of darkness. So Baldwin portrays David as becoming irresistibly drawn into an affair with the dark-skinned, ethnically marked Giovanni. Europe offers David no easy escape from the "taint" of a sexual difference that marginalizes him in terms of its association with threatening racial and ethnic difference.[15] Indeed, Baldwin's novel reveals Europe complexly, as a location where gay American men flee to escape the pressures of heteronormative exclusion, American homophobia, and a racialized sexual morality. Yet Baldwin remains aware that this vision of Europe is only a fantasy of white and homosexual purity. David is trapped anew by the very sexual and racial forces he had sought to flee.

To be clear, Europe is not, of course, an exclusive home to white people; its history is not singularly white. As Richard Dyer argues, the racial notion of whiteness was a concept introduced in nineteenth-century America "as part of the process of establishing US identity."[16] It was then referred back to Europe, which even in the nineteenth century had a complex history of negotiating cultural life with peoples of varying skin colors, ethnic traditions, and cultural realities from both outside and within the present geographical boundaries of Europe—and which are, themselves, open to continuing contestation.[17] My identification of Europe with whiteness in this essay proceeds, then, largely on assumptions written into the texts I study. In Baldwin's case, Europe initially seemed to represent a space outside an American homosexuality tainted by racial identifications. But in fact, for Baldwin's self-loathing protagonist, Paris, like Giovanni's room itself, is redolent of the "taint" he finds in the body of his first lover, Joey. Indeed, David's operant imaginary seems primarily to be his fantasized idealization of a blonde, masculine self betrayed by his liaison with Giovanni, one, ironically, bound to America as an abstraction of home. We might discern this fantasy in a small moment in the novel when David notices a sailor, "dressed all in white," on the streets of Paris.[18] The young man's blonde masculinity evokes both desire and identification with David's younger self. And it makes him "think of home," not as a "place but simply an irrevocable condition."[19] In this case, home seems consonant with whiteness and the fantasy of white gay desire outside the contaminating taint of a racially inflected homosexuality from which neither Europe nor America offers respite. Such perspicuous revelations of the intersections of race and white gay sexuality point, then, toward ways we might see anew the tensions of race and whiteness in a writer like Leavitt.

In the whole of the white, Jewish Leavitt's work, Europe might seem to stand, as it initially did in Baldwin, as a non-place of the African-American diaspora, and we can read the representation of such a non-place as signifying something about its author's thoughts on American homosexuality and race. In *The Indian Clerk*, Leavitt specifically revisits the American dialectic between wanting and wasting the racial "other" that Baldwin discerns embryonically in *Giovanni's Room*.[20] And he does so—again as we saw in Baldwin—within a paranoid narrative framework that can only struggle to consolidate white with gay identifications. To be sure, Leavitt rejects the homosexual self-loathing that Baldwin's protagonist David expresses in valorizing a reproductive heterosexuality that reproduces whiteness as fetish. The younger writer is concerned, typically, with white gay characters seeking self-affirming gay identifications, especially in middle-class domestic contexts. Leavitt's early works are, without doubt, as Les Brookes suggests, among the first American fictions to utilize newer ethnic models of identity based on an essentialist sexuality rather than the pugilistic constructionist stance of earlier gay liberationists.[21] But these newer identifications fetishize whiteness, as we might see in the myriad ways they displace their connections with nonwhite races and the history of American racialized sexuality. If in Baldwin gay self-loathing is linked to its protagonist's racial misidentifications, so too is Leavitt's own struggle to legitimize gay desire linked to such misidentifications.

The Indian Clerk seems designed to appeal to a contemporary, white, gay American audience that has moved beyond the conundrums of homosexual desire we find in Baldwin. In this story about the erotics of the never consummated relationship between the white Hardy and the Indian mathematical genius Ramanujan, homosexuality is apparently a historical fact, and therefore a seeming point of over-easy knowing or identification for the contemporary reader. The novel's exposure of a homosocial world in post-Edwardian Cambridge perhaps encourages a sanguine understanding of homosexuality as a universal desire. And, to be sure, the novel also reveals the destabilizing aspect of such modern sexual knowledge as it explores queer, non-homosexually normative forms of desire that emerge between Hardy and his various academic collaborators.

So, for instance, in one intriguing comment, Hardy's colleague John Littlewood contrasts his working relationship with Hardy to his romantic affair with a married woman to suggest, surprisingly, that "Hardy is permanent. Spouse or collaborator, it comes to the same thing."[22] As for the homosocial bond between Hardy and Ramanujan, it is summed up in words spoken by the historical figure Hardy himself: "my association with [Ramanujan]," he said, "was the one romantic incident in my life."[23] In imagining the relationship between Hardy and the dark-skinned Ramanujan as a type of romantic relationship, Leavitt usefully explores a version of white, Western homoerotic desire that is not formulated as identity and is not in retreat from the alien, dark-skinned, and foreign. Indeed, the variegated textures of non-specifiable desire woven throughout *The Indian Clerk* seem queer in the sense that we can understand them in terms of that "opacity" of identification that the Antillean poet and theorist Édouard Glissant theorizes in contrast to the transparency of simple difference: "Opacities can coexist and converge, weaving fabrics," Glissant writes. "To understand these truly one must focus on the texture of the weave and not on the nature of its components."[24] On its surface, Leavitt's novel evokes eroticism across gendered, racial, and class boundaries through its multiple interweaving vantage points.

To be clear about it, however, this erotic exploration never quite gets Leavitt's characters into bed with anyone, much less dark-skinned and foreign peoples. So, any potentially queer reading of the novel does not close down the other ways it creates in the white, English Hardy a highly recognizable, post-Stonewall, white, gay, sexually essential identity.[25] Read more carefully, the novel adjudicates the boundaries separating legitimate homoerotic identifications and more ephemeral homosocial ones, such as those felt by Littlewood or Ramanujan. Throughout the novel, Ramanujan functions as the Eastern "other." He remains the person against whom Hardy judges himself and against whom, in some ways, Leavitt evaluates his protagonist. Ramanujan's is neither the controlling intellect nor the privileged sexuality of the novel—indeed, Ramanujan represents an ascetic denial of sexuality. So, homosexual agency is primarily imagined in the space of the white, English man, Hardy, whose self-possession fools even the blatantly homophobic character D. H. Lawrence into imagining he is straight. No matter how others might identify with the multiple queer identities of the novel, modern, white, gay-identified sensibilities are potentially privileged in their association with the rationalist, white Hardy, who is able to pass as that most essential of creatures, the straight man.

There is something of a paradox at the heart of the novel, then. Its sexualities straddle the boundary between a queer space outside the homosexual norm and the privileged space in which white male homosexuality speaks as a newly emergent voice of masculinity. To the extent that such paradox wrests power from dominant heterosexual structures and gives them to gay men, *The Indian Clerk* seems progressive. But in so far as it remains sanguine in its vision of the dark-skinned man as object rather than subject of desire, the novel is neither queer nor productive of salutary new formulations of power and privilege. Instead, it seems to replicate that discourse of white gayness in distinction to—and perhaps in flight from—dark-skinned people that we see more explicitly anatomized in Baldwin.

That, however, is not my main point. Rather, it is that when Leavitt moves into white, European history to explore seemingly gay characters, and in particular that famous collaboration at Cambridge in which race, sex, and intellect overlapped to queer English mathematical history in productively racialized ways, he effects a displacement of the figures troubling to his own American present: the religious Jew and the gay African American. These figures almost never appear in Leavitt's fictional world, and when they do, as in the author's earlier, 2001 novel, *Martin Bauman; or, A Sure Thing*, they appear as threats to trouble Bauman's ascendancy into middle-class gay respectability. In *The Indian Clerk*, Ramanujan, the tragic, dark-skinned "other" the white gay protagonist comes to love, can be seen, like Giovanni, as a surrogate for understanding American racial desire in relation to the African American. But that African American, in any case, never appears. And the conflict between Hinduism and atheism that Leavitt explores in the relations between Ramanujan and Hardy seems, as well, a displacement for the tensions between religious and secular Jewish lives specific to Leavitt's American experience. As surrogate, the religious, dark-skinned Ramanujan does not fully reconstitute these spectral presences in precise American terms. But the novel uses him to stage a series of psychic displacements that attempt—unsuccessfully I think—to distance the darker histories of American homoeroticism from white gay identity in *The Indian Clerk*.

In the first such displacement, the novel's most sexually explicit vision of love between light and dark-skinned people is displaced onto a woman, Alice Neville, who falls in love with Ramanujan. So, the homoerotic love for dark skin the novel teases us with never materializes in any bodily sense. Second, Ramanujan's own ascetic non-sexuality conspires with this dematerialization as it displaces the potential love between white and Black men that Hardy seems to desire. Third, religious irrationalities that arise in relation to Leavitt's explorations of Jewish American life are displaced onto Ramanujan, who, as a Hindu man, serves as a benign symbol of an irrational religion that might otherwise trouble the place of secular gay characters—whether Hardy or any of Leavitt's Jewish characters. Finally, and most troubling of all because of its implication in the tragic diasporic history of African Americans, the English setting displaces gay Black Americans entirely from a place in the history of same-sex relations imagined in the novel. The novel's setting in Europe and its interest in the dark-skinned, different but definitely not African-American Ramanujan remind us of what Leavitt has so insistently left unexplored. *The Indian Clerk* reveals another aspect of the African-American diaspora, then, for it moves the gay African American entirely out of the representational domain of same-sex relations in the white gay American novel.[26]

Leavitt and Baldwin come closer to one another than we might at first imagine. Both represent their homosexual protagonists within a fantasized but failed white space, Europe, in which they seem at first able to concentrate on questions of sexuality and race outside the compromised structures of racialized sexuality in the United States. And both create protagonists whose sexual agency is negotiated in relation to dark-skinned or seemingly exotic partners. But rather than providing either author a greater understanding of the ways race and sex might intersect productively within an American imaginary, this narrative in fact reveals what Baldwin evocatively suggested was "the black opening of [a] cavern," literally a black hole in American conceptions of homosexuality: the inability to locate—much less embrace—the African-American man in its midst. To be fair, this was one of the themes of Baldwin's next novel, *Another Country*, and by the time he came to write *Just Above My Head*, Baldwin was discovering increasingly complex ways to engage Black homosexuality.

Nevertheless, both *Giovanni's Room* and *The Indian Clerk* are significant for revealing some of the ways unitary, as opposed to intersectional, gay identities, white and Black, remain problematic and incoherent. They remain so for Baldwin because the moral taint of homosexuality threatens to subsume Black sexual identifications within a supremacist structure in which desire is pure only as whiteness; and they do so for Leavitt because he seems unable to embrace completely the dark otherness within American homosexuality that might begin to dismantle such supremacist sexual structures. Excluded from both novels is an untroubled image of Black homosexuality. But that exclusion is not simple racism on Leavitt's part or gay self-loathing on Baldwin's. It is the legacy of a cultural memory that makes that figure more difficult to assimilate to flawed modern conceptions of homosexuality than we have previously thought. If Marlon Riggs's famous pronouncement, "Black Men Loving Black Men is the Revolutionary Act," is correct, it may be because it imagines an act of undoing histories of racialist identifications from which Baldwin and Leavitt—and few to follow—have yet escaped.[27]

Nicholas F. Radel

Dark Rapture: James Baldwin, Beauford Delaney, and Black Queer Joy

If you walk into my office, your eyes will inevitably meet a large-framed print of James Baldwin. The photo offers a profile shot of Baldwin rendered in black and white. The light magnifies a certain intensity in his face, his forehead gently furrowed, his lips on the edge of a smile or a protest. Most striking are his eyes—big and piercing and full of wonder. This is one of the most beautiful shots of Baldwin; or, perhaps, to be more accurate, this is a photo that captures so much of Baldwin's beauty.

James Baldwin begins the introduction to his final and most robust collection of essays, *The Price of the Ticket*, by stating, "My soul looks back and wonders how I got over—indeed…"[28] Baldwin tells us how his life in Greenwich Village began at 15 when his friend, Emile Capouya, told him of "this wonderful man he had met" and how "[Baldwin] must meet him."[29] That man was Beauford Delaney, the African-American modernist painter who would become mentor, friend, and salvific figure to James.[30]

> I was terrified, once I had climbed those stairs and knocked on that door. A short, round, brown man came to the door and looked at me. He had the most extraordinary eyes I'd ever seen. When he had completed his instant X-ray of my brain, lungs, liver, heart, bowels, and spinal column … he smiled and said, "Come in," and opened the door. He opened the door alright.[31]

Perhaps it was Baldwin's nervousness that terrified him, perhaps it was the realization of how the dread at home has led him to this man's doorstep and he was uncertain of how he would be received, how he would be viewed.

The way Delaney's eyes capture Baldwin's attention, the way in which Baldwin understands them as "extraordinary," and Baldwin's focus on the artist's "X-raying" situates Delaney's gaze and sight as a necessary point of inquiry in the Baldwin–Delaney relationship. That day, in 1940, the 15-year-old Black boy from Harlem told us how:

I walked through that door into Beauford's colors—on the easel, on the palette, against the wall—sometimes turned to the wall—and sometimes (in limbo?) covered by white sheets … I walked into music. I had grown up with music, but, now, on Beauford's small black record player, I began to hear what I had never dared or been able to hear.[32]

This paper, which might be more meditation than criticism, is interested in the relationship between Beauford Delaney's artistic sight and James Baldwin's Black queer joy. I am curious how Baldwin's symbolic walking into "Beauford's colors" might be recognized as a departure from the dreariness of his home, how Delaney's Black queer and male artistry instituted a reconstitution of Baldwin's vision of himself. I am thinking of how the music of Delaney's studio undermined the silence of Baldwin's stepfather, how an ability to hear something new pushes against the absurd and violent sounds of home, of Harlem, of the United States. I am arguing that somewhere within Delaney's gentle gazing upon Baldwin, within Jimmy's vulnerable need to be seen, and within Beauford's door, we are able to critically examine the relationship between sight and "dark rapture," to identify the tethering of Black male friendship and Black queer joy.

Thirteen years after meeting the man who would recolor a young Baldwin's view of himself, the world received its first glimpse of the author in 1953 with the publication of *Go Tell It on the Mountain*—a semi-autobiographical novel. There are many ways to read this work; however, I argue that at the heart is Baldwin's novelistic catharsis—a wrestling with visibility, vulnerability, and joy. John Grimes's stepfather's inability to see him in the way in which sons wish to be seen by fathers hinders, if not precludes, the possibility of joy. By extension, we learn of Baldwin's personal struggle with joy's attainment, one that is compounded by his queer or non-heteronormative identity.

Go Tell It's metatextual strength presents itself at the precise moment where we can identify how the text mediates Baldwin's reflection of self. In a scene where John Grimes is gazing upon his photographed nakedness on the mantelpiece, the protagonist attempts to objectively see what others saw of him. John, to his own dismay, only sees the details:

Two eyes, and a broad, low forehead, and the triangle of his nose, and his enormous mouth, and the barely perceptible cleft in his chin, which was, his father said, the mark of the devil's little finger. These details did not help him, for the principle of their unity was undiscoverable, and he could not tell what he most passionately desired to know: whether his face was ugly or not.[33]

John's pursuit in this moment of self-gazing parallels Baldwin's in the act of writing. For Baldwin, *Go Tell It* allows a textual gazing upon the self, an opportunity to perhaps "discover" an answer to the question of his own perceived ugliness. That John was ugly according to Gabriel, and that he later attempts to verify this ugliness, suggests the inevitable personal confrontation happening at the site of the text for Baldwin. This particular feeling or wrestling is born out of a father–son relationship, one that is fraught with a heaviness Baldwin would eventually share with his friend Emile. In Baldwin's official biography, David Leeming reveals the conversation between Jimmy and Emile on a park bench. In that conversation, "Jimmy had burst into tears and revealed that he was illegitimate. He had learned this 'terrible truth' about himself in a conversation between his parents."[34] Leeming ends the chapter entitled "Awakenings" with this moment of familial discovery; a moment that foreshadows Baldwin's departure from the Church and one that points toward Beauford Delaney's role in his life. For Baldwin, love would become a question of how he was seen, and a source of his happiness would inevitably be connected to its answer.

If *Go Tell It* captures the complex and discordant relationship between Baldwin and his stepfather David, then it is also instructive in its move beyond it. For the young John Grimes, ugliness was not simply imposed from a father who likened him to Satan; rather, it was the result of New York and America's racial absurdity. Standing atop a hill in Central Park, John thinks:

> He remembered the people he had seen in that city, whose eyes held no love for him. And he thought of their feet so swift and brutal, and the dark gray clothes they wore, and how when they passed they did not see him, or, if they saw him, they smirked. And how their lights, unceasing, crashed on and off above him, and how he was a stranger there.[35]

Baldwin's choice to locate John's awareness of white people's lack of love in their eyes suggests that the racial absurdity and alienation he is to face is based largely in how they see him. While it is clear that Baldwin means to move beyond the limited scope of physicality or the visual, the other's sight or gaze is an important signifier of Baldwin's existential wonder. Whether in his fiction or his real world, what remains fixed in Baldwin's itinerary is his flight from his father's house. What is different in the itineracy is that John climbs a hill in Central Park only to realize how the white world before him cannot see him and will treat him as a stranger. Baldwin climbed the stairs at 181 Greene Street to be fully seen and invited in by Beauford Delaney.

Go Tell It on the Mountain must be recognized for the way in which it echoes Baldwin's struggle with visibility. Specifically, we must walk away knowing this struggle was located both in home and homeland, and how the feelings of being unseen translated into a sentiment of being unloved. More importantly, we ought to reckon with unlovability as a fulcrum of Black queer vulnerability, where the prospect and promise of joy are seemingly forever evasive. In this way, Black queer male friendships emerge as refuge, as sanctum, as salvific possibilities. And it is within the friendship between Jimmy and Beauford that we see those possibilities actualized, and where, in ways that betray the dark spaces he would inhabit, we see Baldwin bright-eyed, wide-smiled, and full of joy.

In the near forty years of knowing each other, Baldwin and Delaney would experience the best of friendship. A glimpse:

From the beginning the young Baldwin senses a natural connection with Beauford Delaney. He sensed that when he observed him he was really seeing himself as well. Here was a black man, an artist, an outsider, somehow a later version of himself. It was as if Jimmy had found his long-lost father … Beauford taught his protégé to react to life as an artist … The vocabulary of color and sounds learned in Beauford's presence was to become the basis of Baldwin's art. Delaney was to reconcile for his protégé the music of the Harlem streets with the music of the Harlem churches, and this helped Baldwin to reconcile his sexual awakening with his artistic awakening. Beauford taught his charge how to see beauty even in the metaphorical and literal gutter.[36]

Delaney's teaching reached the most vulnerable parts of Baldwin's Black manhood. Not only did he influence Baldwin's artistry, he influenced his self-perception. I would add to Leeming's declaration about Delaney and the teaching of beauty by stating how Delaney also taught Baldwin to see beauty within himself. Such teaching happened through their excursions, through their intimate dinners and gatherings, through their adventures and sojourns in the Village in New York and in the streets of France. This teaching happened through music and dancing, through heartbreak and tragedy. And, without surprise, we see this teaching, or a trace of this teaching, most pronounced in Delaney's art.

Over the course of their friendship, Delaney painted more than ten portraits of James Baldwin. In being painted, Baldwin was able to understand himself as art, as someone worthy of capture, as having something beautiful meant to be rendered in color. Delaney's portraits varied in their artistic depictions of Baldwin. They spoke to the various faces our beloved Jimmy would enjoy throughout his literary career. For instance, in a 1967 oil on canvas portrait,[37] the viewer or reader is first drawn to the dominant and slightly heavy red of the background. The combination of blue, yellow, and red creates a backdrop of fire easily reminiscent of Baldwin's acclaimed *The Fire Next Time*, published within the same decade. Baldwin's face is both hard and meshed with this fiery backing, which reflects the radical political voice witnessed in his more popular essays. His eyes remain a focal point, a synecdochic representation of Baldwin's potent Black vocality. The title, *The Sage Black*, exalts and appreciates Baldwin's voice, situates him as a valuable and wise member of the activist community, and reflects a "seeing" back to the author which Baldwin was beginning to question in the late 1960s and early 1970s.

If *The Sage Black* captures the strength of Baldwin's political voice or his position as one of America's fiercest critics, then Delaney's earlier 1963 portrait,[38] completed as pastel on paper, offers a counter-vision. This portrait, now housed in the National Portrait Gallery of the Smithsonian Institute, emanates the warmth of Delaney that many came to know, but also highlights the beauty and joy often found within Baldwin. Saturated in a yellow often likened to that used by Van Gogh, the portrait endures a split interpretation. Within the art world, this portrait is often read outside the language of affection or gentle sentimentality. Instead, some art critics suggest the color and its application are more about Delaney's anxieties than Baldwin's warm state of being.[39] Considered within the larger collection of Baldwin portraiture, it proves difficult to ignore the affective elisions and ruptures happening at the site of the canvas. Undoubtedly, this is a warm rendering of Baldwin. Those big eyes are joyful, wanderlusting, and seeing. The mouth is pleasant, unaffected by the bitter taste of the 1960s that is to come.

I imagine part of the mis-viewing of this portrait stems from the desire to map Van Gogh onto Delaney. If this yellow is meant to convey the angst so characteristic of the darker parts of the artist's world, then there are a couple of ways to read this in a modified context. The heaviness within the yellow might be read as a darkened sun promised to Black folk coming up in the South or Harlem or the United States or the mid-century. Delaney's placing an undeniably contented Baldwin against what some art critics have termed that "heated and confrontational" yellow can therefore represent the resilient capacity to conjure or embody joy in or against the backdrop of racial absurdity. Or folk can simply understand that color application brings about new meaning when mediated by a racialized painting subject. Ultimately, when we view the different iterations of Baldwin throughout Delaney's collection, we find the many ways the latter was able to see Baldwin. And, I argue, Delaney's polyfocality,[40] or the manifold ways in which he focused his artistic eye upon Baldwin, allowed one of his greatest subjects to gaze upon himself and all of his beauty in new and unmolested ways.

One of the greatest gifts bestowed upon Baldwin in his relationship with Delaney was the latter's teaching him how to see and how to appreciate light. In a musing simply entitled "On the Painter Beauford Delaney," Baldwin states the following: "I learned about light from Beauford Delaney, the light contained in every thing, in every surface, in every face."[41] Baldwin is literally talking about light in this moment—how objects, or our perceptions of objects, particularly their color, are perceptively changed by light. But he is also more abstractly talking about a new way of seeing. Through his friendship with Delaney, he was able to see light in spite of the darkness surrounding him, and he was also able finally to see the light within himself. As he relays, "He was then, and is now, working all the time, or perhaps it would be more accurate to say that he is seeing all the time; and the reality of his seeing caused me to begin to see."[42] The gift of vision extended to Baldwin from Delaney would dramatically shift his way of seeing and envisioning the world. Even more, it would reorient how he came to see himself. In that new view we see a Jimmy more joyful in his self-gazing, freer in his artistry, and more loving in his sight.

I want to end with one of my favorite portraits of James Baldwin, painted by those brilliant hands and eyes of Beauford Delaney very early in their friendship; in fact, it was the first he ever completed (1941). It is entitled *Dark Rapture*.[43] I will not write much about this, except how the title captures the complex raciality of Baldwin as a darker complexioned Black man caught within the darkness of racial absurdity, and how that is coupled with this idea of rapture, an intense experience or expression of joy. The innocence of Baldwin's young male beauty explodes through this oil on canvas. What else I have to say, I forfeit lest I betray the affecting power to a language unable to hold it. But I will leave us with Baldwin on Delaney, as we gaze upon this meeting of love and joy:

Well, that life, that light, that miracle are what I began to see in Beauford's paintings, and this light began to stretch back for me over all the time we had known each other, and over much more time than that, and this light held the power to illuminate, even to redeem and reconcile and heal. For Beauford's work leads the inner and the outer eye, directly and inexorably, to a new confrontation with reality. At this moment, one begins to apprehend the nature of his triumph. And the beauty of his triumph, and the proof that it is a real one, is that he makes it ours. Perhaps I should not say, flatly, what I believe—that he is a great painter, among the very greatest; but I do know that great art can only be created out of love, and that no greater lover has ever held a brush.[44]

Indeed, Baldwin's manhood was painted out of Delaney's love, and Beauford's sight captured Jimmy's joy—a *dark*, and I'll add, beautiful, *rapture*.

Ernest L. Gibson III

Sculpting a Human Being: James Baldwin, *Giovanni's Room*, and the Police in Denmark

Writers as distinct as the Nigerian playwright Wole Soyinka and the U.S. American novelist William Styron have acknowledged James Baldwin as a transnational and "cosmopolite" thinker with a complex moral ethics, a writer who understood love as "the First Principle of the meaning of human existence."[45] Their claims can be explained through an analysis of Baldwin's essays, but the assertions are more substantive and true to Baldwin's moral vision when examined through his novels, stories, plays, and poetry, sites of epistemological play, prophecy, and correction. This essay demonstrates how that first principle, cultivated in Baldwin's autobiographical existential crucible, imported from New York to Paris, and bound everywhere in Baldwin from his likeness to his pen, found its way north to Denmark and fictively intervened in one of that country's mid-twentieth-century moral dilemmas—homosexuality, or the moral right of two people from the same sex to have a life together. Whereas Denmark recognized same-sex civil partnerships in 1989 and same-sex marriage in 2012, the cultural, social, and political realities were less welcoming in the 1950s when Baldwin's fiction first appeared, resulting in an encounter between Baldwin's prose, homosexuality, and the Danish authorities. The clash represents what Baldwin's novels have done for decades now: elegantly place discarded lives back into their rightful cultural and social spheres.

When he wrote *Go Tell it on the Mountain* (1953), Baldwin began a moral philosophy of his own, enabling a discourse that would extend to a universal being who differed from the universal being of ancient Athens, "the rights of man," or "we the people." *Giovanni's Room* (1956) enriched Baldwin's metaphysics, showing the importance of what Soyinka has referred to as the First Principle of love. *Another Country* (1962), the third novel in Baldwin's oeuvre, envisioned just that—a place where the disjointed lives of New Yorkers would reveal an America antithetical to the master narrative of privileged prosperity and progress. For Baldwin, one of the most neglected and important aspects of his novel was that "a lot of people in that book had never appeared in fiction before. People overlook this fact. And there's an awful lot of my experience which has never been seen in the English language before."[46] Lives formerly on the periphery also find recognition in his later novels—*Tell Me How Long the Train's Been Gone* (1968), *If Beale Street Could Talk* (1974), and *Just Above My Head* (1979). By the end of his fictional journey, Baldwin would have shown his definition of a human being to mean any individual, without reservation, wherever they might fall on the continuums of race, gender, sexuality, and possibility.

Like the canonical thinkers of the Western intellectual tradition who continue to dominate modern political theory and humanist thought, from Plato to Kant, Baldwin's work offers compelling ideas about how we should situate and define important concepts such as justice, humanity, fraternity, representation, difference, love, pleasure, citizenship, and companionship. *"Negroes want to be treated like men,"* he reasoned, yet "people who have mastered Kant, Hegel, Shakespeare, Marx, Freud, and the Bible find this statement utterly impenetrable. A kind of panic paralyzes their features, as though they found themselves on the edge of a steep place."[47] Baldwin, who spent a career attacking this paradox, encountered no such paralysis, and his work restores to humanist and political thought a diverse, dialectical universalism. The writer Toni Morrison suggests that he made the American English language "genuinely international," "modern dialogic, representative, humane."[48] What is clear is that Baldwin is interrogating the Western intellectual tradition, inserting life where the tradition has assumed lifelessness for particular populations.

Understanding Baldwin's fiction as moral and political thought, I trace a relationship between Denmark, a nation-state, and *Giovanni's Room*, a novel, that adds another thread to the important scholarship on his fiction as a site of deliberation, anxiousness, and disavowal in modern societies. The relationship is also connected to a striking sculpture made of Baldwin by a Danish artist in Paris in 1950, and two translations of *Giovanni's Room* that appeared in Denmark, the first in 1957 (and in a pocket paperback edition in 1966) and again (re-translated) in 2019. Whereas the Baldwin renaissance that opened the twenty-first century resulted in multiple new translations of several of Baldwin's novels and essay collections into European languages (French, German, Swedish, Norwegian), the only new Danish translation to appear was of *Giovanni's Room*. In 2020 a new German translation of *Giovanni's Room* appeared, but alongside several other new German translations of Baldwin's work, and with a different appearance than that of its Scandinavian counterpart to the north. I am suggesting that *Giovanni's Room* has a special place in Denmark, that its "transcendent appeal" has a certain history.[49] The twenty-first-century Danish and German translations of *Giovanni's Room*, products of the renaissance of interest in Baldwin's work, and their differing entrances into literary public space stem from Baldwin's 1950s Danish encounter. Their shelf lives perform the interplay between novels and nation-states, and embody the extension and limits of how European moral agency simultaneously welcomes and abandons global citizenship as seen in the ghost of a figure, the universal citizen, fictitiously alluded to in international treaties, declarations and covenants, or the unnamed yet European human in human rights discourses.

Baldwin revises the image of this ghost of a human being, a revision I am suggesting comes through a Danish artist's 1950 sculpture of Baldwin as he experienced the milieu that would become his signature Paris novel. *Giovanni's Room* is Baldwin's Enlightenment revision, human rights corrective, and modernity amendment, a rejoinder to the Universal Declaration of Human Rights that traveled the same 1948 New York-to-Paris route to fame and global presence as Baldwin himself.

The sculptor and painter Yan Kai Nielsen was born on 21 December 1919, in Copenhagen, Denmark, to artist parents. His father was the well-known national sculptor Kai Nielsen, whose art can be seen in museums and public spaces across Denmark, and his mother Janna Lange was also a painter. Yan Kai Nielsen followed in the artistic footsteps of both his parents, sculpting in a variety of media, with a noted emphasis on welded steel and iron pieces that express abstract meaning. The range of his work differs greatly from the small number of sandstone busts he produced early in his artistic career. He trained at the Norwegian National Academy of Craft and Art Industry from 1938 to 1940, and studied abroad at the Académie de la Grande Chaumière in Paris in 1949–50, where he most likely encountered Baldwin for the first time. Founded in 1905, the school was an important space for African-American artists and writers, among them Baldwin and artists like Beauford Delaney, Augusta Savage, Aaron Douglas, and others. Nielsen trained with the Russian-French sculptor Ossip Zadkine, whose son, Nicolas Hasle, was the result of Zadkine's affair with a Danish woman, Annelise Hasle. Thus, the meeting of Baldwin and Nielsen in Paris can be attributed to both the postwar trend of African Americans finding community and freedom in Paris and Danish artists leaving the North to seek the latest training in the arts in Europe's cultural capital.[50]

The intimacy of artist and subject represented in the creation of the sculpture anticipated what would be *leitfmotifs* of both Baldwin's and Nielsen's careers: their common ability to recognize the humanity in others. Nielsen's rare portrait bust of Baldwin joins at least one other he made in 1950, that of a woman named Carolyn Stewart from Washington, U.S.A. Baldwin and Stewart are rendered in their separate likenesses, but the style, form, and gaze of the sculptures are similar, making them both unique and the same, a recognition and merging of selves in the hands of the artist. After a 1951 exhibition of Nielsen's work in Denmark, a critic wrote a review asking, "Quo Vadis, Yan?—How is it going?"[51] The review featured a photo of "Yan's bust of the Negro writer Jimmy Baldwin." With the adjacent Baldwin bust staring intently, the critic, Ole Vinding, proceeded to link Nielsen's exhibition with his life struggles at the time, a long and lonely artist's struggle with his form. The critic suggested that despite the struggle, Nielsen's bust of Baldwin demonstrated that he had inherited a gift from his sculptor father, the gift "to see people."

The gift was both a blessing and a curse. The good of the gift is likely what drew Baldwin and Nielsen together in Paris. The curse similarly linked Nielsen to Baldwin, as the former was in great conflict over the struggle to establish his own artistic identity in the shadow of his famous sculptor father whose name was known all over Denmark. Indeed, Nielsen's effort to differentiate the artistic reputation of "Yan Kai Nielsen" from that of "Kai Nielsen" succeeded no more than his

Figure 1   A sculpture (1950) of James Baldwin by the Danish
artist Yan Kai Nielsen (1919–2001) (photo by the author, 2020).

sister Nina Kai Nielsen's efforts to break free from the prominence of their artist
father. In a 1946 article, Nina Kai Nielsen expressed her and her brother's desire to
make names for themselves even as they carried the familiar name of their father.
"We will have the right to our *own* adult chance in life," she wrote.[52] It is likely that
the young Baldwin, having fled the United States while also experiencing challenges in his relationship with his stepfather, bonded over this struggle with Nielsen, who faced challenges regarding his family, artistry, and postwar conditions.
As artists, sons, brothers, new Parisians, and creators gifted with the vision to "see
people," Baldwin and Nielsen joined together in the glaring sandstone bust depict-
ing young Baldwin with his masterful gaze.

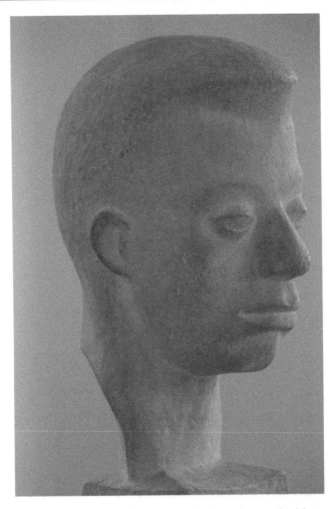

Figure 2   Critics called Yan Kai Nielsen's sculpture of Baldwin
an example of Nielsen's ability "to see people" (photo by the
author, 2020).

A Danish translation of Baldwin's *Giovanni's Room* (*Giovanni's Værelse*) appeared
in Denmark in 1957, priced at 14.50 Danish crowns. It was published by Steen
Hasselbalchs Forlag, a Copenhagen publisher that also produced the first Danish
edition of *The Fire Next Time* (*Næste Gang*) in 1963 and a translation of *Go Tell it
on the Mountain* (*Råb det fra Bjergene*) in 1965. Interestingly and conversely, the
publisher had earlier produced the first edition of Margaret Mitchell's *Gone with
the Wind* in Danish. It sold out its first edition in under two weeks. The publisher,
known for his aggressive marketing, reflected the nation's varying relationship to
the idea of America: on the one hand, readers were taken with the fascination of

Gone with the Wind; on the other, they were also riveted by Baldwin's searing syntax and prose.

The Danish translation of *Giovanni's Room* appeared shortly after a scandal in Denmark, during a time when the "antihomosexual climate of the 1950s made it virtually impossible for the Forbundet af 1948," one of the country's first LGBTQ+ organizations, "to pursue actively a homosexual political agenda."[53] The decade was marked by "harassment by the police, legal discrimination, and societal oppression of homosexuals."[54] In 1955,

> Axel Lundahl-Madsen, and his partner Eigil Eskilden [founders of Forbundet af 1948], with whom he had lived since 1950, were convicted on pornography charges and sentenced to short prison terms for running a gay modeling agency that sold pictures of naked men. While in prison, they melded their first names into the shared surname Axgil as a public show of defiance.[55]

After this scandal, the Danish press reported that as many as seventy Danes committed suicide out of fear of being outed by the authorities. Accordingly, the afterword to the 1957 Danish translation of *Giovanni's Room* was written by a police commissioner (*politiadvokat*) with the Copenhagen police force. Commissioner Aage Maurizio Lotinga, who wrote a 1948 book entitled *The Sexual Deviant and Society* (*De sexuelt afsporede og Samfundet*), spent part of his career advocating that society should not look at homosexuality as a moral issue, but as a matter of concomitant crime, like the theft and public indecency associated with male prostitution. According to historian Peter Edelberg, "The moral discourse achieved hegemony, or, if you will, consensus in the press in the second half of the 1950s."[56]

In the afterword to *Giovanni's Room*, Lotinga acknowledges Baldwin's art for seeing people, and his writing a novel that expressed not only the physical drive of homosexuality, but also what Lotinga refers to as the "soulful and complicated drives in which homosexuality has its origination." Lotinga writes that he recognizes the tragedy unfolding in the novel from his many years working with sex crimes. For him, "Giovanni is drawn with a rare artistic accuracy and a delicate, yes almost tender understanding. Here we face the unrelenting human tragedy, a shaky drama of fate."[57] It is interesting to note that Lotinga sympathizes with Giovanni while at the same time he condemns homosexuality as a public nuisance which he mostly associates with male prostitution. Male prostitution is far worse than female prostitution, Lotinga suggests, because it is almost always accompanied by theft and violence. *Giovanni's Room* is primarily a crime novel for Lotinga, but Baldwin's triumph is that he managed to make the police official acknowledge the moral questions that emerge in the work. While Baldwin and Nielsen were sharing their ways of seeing people in the bohemian Paris of 1949–50, Lotinga was in Denmark constructing the criminalization of homosexuality that would breathe fear into Danish gay life for the length of the decade.

Lotinga's criminal reading of *Giovanni's Room* crept into the translation of the novel not only in the character of Giovanni, but also in the meeting of David and

Joey. After David's encounter with Joey, he confesses, "I was ashamed. The very bed, in its sweet disorder, testified to vileness."[58] The 1957 translation renders the moment as "Jeg skammede mig. Selv sengen med dens søde uorden vidnede om lastefuldhed."[59] The key term here is *lastefuldhed* for "vileness." *Lastefuld*, a form of carelessness, echoes the story of Sodom and Gomorrah, and links "vileness" to criminality. Lotinga, after all, urged the public to remove the issue from any discussion of morality. In one of many instances of restoring the Danish text to match Baldwin's moral cosmos, Pial Juul, translator of the 2019 Danish edition of *Giovanni's Room*, changed the word for "vileness" from *lastefuld* to *unmoralsk*, or "immoral." The new translation eschews criminality in favor of Baldwin's moral difficulty, a form of social upheaval and reckoning that transfers from the decision to live in Henry James's *The Ambassadors* to the choice of love in *Giovanni's Room*. As the critic and astute Baldwin reader Hilton Als points out, "For Baldwin, the first principle of love was love withheld; it was all he had ever known."[60]

James Baldwin and Yan Kai Nielsen met in the environment of the artists' colonies in Paris in 1949 or 1950, shortly after Baldwin arrived from the United States to escape American racism and pursue his career as a writer and poet, and after Nielsen arrived from Denmark to hone his craft as a sculptor and to establish a name for himself separate from his famous father. A remarkable sandstone bust of Baldwin commemorates their union. If racism marred Baldwin's imagined democracy- and liberty-loving homeland, Nielsen's homeland was deep in homosexual panic, arresting homosexuals for modeling for fear that homoeroticism would lead to prostitution and widespread crime.

The Danish publication of *Giovanni's Room* changed state attitudes toward homosexuality, leading the primary author of the "gay sex as crime spree" narrative to admit the humanity of Giovanni's predicament. Perhaps Nielsen, married three times and enduring the artist's struggle, witnessed the arrival of the novel in Denmark and the rise of Baldwin's international career. Baldwin did make a trip to Copenhagen in the mid-1960s at the same time that he visited Sweden for his well-known exchange with Ingmar Bergman, but it is unclear if he reunited with Nielsen. While, as we know, Nielsen sculpted Baldwin, is it possible that Baldwin sculpted Nielsen? The first-person portrayal of David that appears at the start of *Giovanni's Room*—was it inspired by Yan Kai Nielsen? Does the figure of Nielsen appear in Baldwin's fiction? Is he related to the artist Fonny in *If Beale Street Could Talk*? Did Baldwin have Denmark in mind when he began chapter 5 of *Giovanni's Room* with "It was a terrific scandal."[61] Was Yan Kai-Nielsen the inspiration for the "Danish-looking" hipsters standing near the jukebox talking about Frank Sinatra in *Another Country*? Is he related to the Minnesotan Hella in *Giovanni's Room*? Or to David's Seattle-born mother? Both cities experienced migration from Scandinavia that required the conquering of already inhabited spaces, much as the introduction to the first-person narrative of *Giovanni's Room* begins. There is a particular scene where Danishness arises via Americanness in Paris:

The trees grew green those mornings, the river dropped, and the brown winter smoke dropped downward out of it, and fishermen appeared. Giovanni was right about the fishermen, they certainly never seemed to catch anything, but it gave them something to do. *Along the quais the bookstalls seemed to become almost festive, awaiting the weather which would allow the passerby to leaf idly through the dog-eared books, and which would inform the tourist with a passionate desire to carry off to the United States, or Denmark, more colored prints than he could afford, or, when he got home, know what to do with.* Also, the girls appeared on their bicycles, along with boys similarly equipped, and we sometimes saw them along the river as the light began to fade, their bicycles put away until the morrow. This was after Giovanni had lost his job and we walked around in the evenings. (emphasis mine)[62]

Already in the novel, Baldwin's narrator David has described the tour buses "from Holland, from Denmark, from Germany" that "stood in the square before the cathedral." The Parisian experience represents the cultural ("tourist"), intellectual ("dog-eared books"), and sexual ("passionate desire") capital that Danes and Americans wish to carry in excessive amounts ("more colored prints than he could afford") back to their respective homelands, spaces complicated with possibilities and problems, vision and violence, social welfare and capital gain. If Nielsen started the artistic relationship with Baldwin via his commanding sculpture of the writer, Baldwin returned the favor with a Parisian portrait of the human being facing state power in societies as varied as Denmark and the United States. To the list of ways in which we must describe *Giovanni's Room*, we must add that is also a Danish novel, responsible for a turn in the politics of homosexuality in the nation, and a symbol of the ways of seeing people in artistic life.

I close with a final thought on Baldwin's interventions and the cost of denying them. Danish publisher Gyldendal acknowledged Baldwin's artistic humanism with cover art for the 2019 Danish translation that embraces men and women of all backgrounds.[63] The multi-color image of blues, reds, oranges, pinks, whites, and grays forms a medley of sculptures that depend on one another to reveal the presence of a human profile. The art represents not just Giovanni or David in the novel, but all of the characters, minor, major, silent, speaking. *Giovanni's Room* is Hella's novel just as much as it is David's or Giovanni's or Joey's. The colorful cover contrasts with the dark gray of the earlier edition, representative of its taboo subject matter and the need to be hidden in the 1950s. Baldwin's legacy in Denmark, vis-à-vis *Giovanni's Room*, is tied up with the nation's progress in advancing the rights of all human beings and the change in attitudes toward homosexual life. Conversely, in Germany, publisher Deutscher Taschenbuch Verlag opted to set aside the potentialities of allegorical hybridity and transcendence for the cover of its 2020 German translation.[64] The cover art represents Giovanni as a chiseled and handsome European man in a provocative white tank top, reminiscent of earlier representations of the novel and claims about Baldwin that scholars have carefully problematized.[65] The publisher presents a singular narrative in opposition to Baldwin's multiple worlds, a stark contrast to the colorful, ambiguous yet recognizable human on the Danish *Giovanni's Room*.

On its own, the German cover might be understood as a missed opportunity, but its relationship to the erasure evident in other German publishing decisions related to Baldwin and Blackness suggests a troubling trend. In 2019 the German publisher Männerschwarm Verlag produced a translation of the novel *Since I Laid My Burden Down* by the African-American writer and Baldwin protégé Brontez Purnell.[66] The semi-autobiographical novel draws on the life of Purnell, a brown-skinned man who grew up in the American South. Männerschwarm Verlag opted to entitle the German edition of the novel *Alabama*.[67] This is understandable, as the literal translation of *Since I Laid My Burden Down* into German might lose or alter its meaning. The problem concerns the cover, which features the image of a man whose skin is much lighter than that of the protagonist in the novel. Brontez Purnell expressed excitement at the prospect of a German translation of his novel, but he was disappointed by the message conveyed by the image on the cover. To be sure, the image is not wrong—rather, it raises the question, "Why did the publisher make the change from dark skin to light?" Why do German publishers of Baldwin's classic novel and the novels it inspired fear Blackness or indeterminacy?

A review of the new German translation appeared in a February 2020 edition of the German newspaper *Süddeutsche Zeitung*, one of the most widely read newspapers in the country. Literary critic Gustav Siebt noted the novel's classic status alongside Thomas Mann's *Death in Venice* and argued that *Giovanni's Room*, both its metaphysical meaning and its physical materiality as a book, represented a defense of minorities, a safeguard against their appropriation.[68] Baldwin's object, the book *Giovanni's Room*, sculpted human beings.

Nigel Hatton

Notes

1 https://www.goodreads.com/author/quotes/10427.James_Baldwin; https://scalar.usc.edu/works/under-the-watchful-fbeye/media/baldwin4_p44; https://shop.thenation.com/products/james-baldwin-t-shirt (all accessed 15 June 2020).

2 https://www.newyorker.com/magazine/1962/11/17/letter-from-a-region-in-my-mind (accessed 15 June 2020).

3 Published in 1999: https://www.penguinrandomhouse.com/books/28698/soul-on-ice-by-eldridge-cleaver/ (accessed 15 June 2020).

4 Quentin Miller used this term in his presentation at "In the Speculative Light: The Arts of James Baldwin and Beauford Delaney" symposium at the University of Tennessee, 20–21 February 2019, https://calendar.utk.edu/event/in_a_speculative_light_the_arts_of_james_baldwin_and_beauford_delaney (accessed 15 June 2020).

5 For instance, in his book *The Queer Renaissance: Contemporary American Literature and the Reinvention of Gay and Lesbian Identity* (New York, NYU Press, 1997), Robert McRuer identifies Leavitt as a "mainstream gay writer" in contrast to other authors who "share a commitment to interrogating sexual and social identities that are made marginal by contemporary society" (p. 29). As regards the author's Jewish identity, Susanne Klingstein suggests that "[t]he fiction of the most prominent Jewish writer of gay fiction, David Leavitt, has no Jewish content." See "Jewish American Fiction, Act III: Eccentric Sources of Inspiration," *Studies in American Jewish Literature*, 18 (1999), p. 84.

6 The issues are too complex to be handled fully in a conference presentation. For sociolog-
ically inflected arguments, see Siobhan B. Somerville (ed.), *Queering the Color Line: Race
and the Invention of Homosexuality in American Culture* (Durham, NC, Duke University
Press, 2000); Mason Stokes, *The Color of Sex: Whiteness, Heterosexuality, and the Fictions
of White Supremacy* (Durham, NC, Duke University Press, 2001); and Roderick A. Ferguson, *Aberrations in Black: Toward a Queer of Color Critique* (Minneapolis, MN, University
of Minnesota Press, 2004). For a theoretical deconstruction of the ways queer theorists
have conceived homosexuality as being "raceless," see Marlon B. Ross, "Beyond the Closet
as Raceless Paradigm," in E. Patrick Johnson and Mae G. Henderson (eds.), *Black Queer
Studies: A Critical Anthology* (Durham, NC, Duke University Press, 2005), pp. 161–89.

7 The question of why Baldwin uses a white gay protagonist in *Giovanni's Room* has been
considered carefully by a number of critics. In particular, Marlon B. Ross, "White Fantasies of Desire: Baldwin and the Racial Identities of Sexuality," in Dwight A. McBride
(ed.), *James Baldwin Now* (New York, NYU Press, 1999), makes a comment that allows
me to define my own argument more carefully. He writes that "[i]f the characters [in
Giovanni's Room] had been black, the novel would have been read as being 'about' blackness, whatever else it happened actually to be about. The whiteness of the characters
seems to make invisible the question of how race or color has, in fact, shaped the characters—at least as far as most readers have dealt with the novel" (p. 25). My argument is
slightly different in suggesting that neither Baldwin's nor Leavitt's novel makes whiteness
invisible as race if we read it within the long history of racialized sexuality in America.

In a wide-ranging essay on the place of Baldwin's homosexuality within Black Studies,
Dwight A. McBride makes what I take to be a valid point when he writes that *Giovanni's
Room* "may be among the possible progenitors of the area of whiteness studies." See "On
Straight Black Studies: African American Studies, James Baldwin, and Black Queer Studies,"
in E. Patrick Johnson and Mae G. Henderson (eds.), *Black Queer Studies: A Critical Anthology* (Durham, NC, Duke University Press, 2005), pp. 78–9. And to be sure, in making my
argument, I hope to contribute to, in bell hooks's words, "a discourse on race that interro-
gates whiteness." See "Critical Interrogation: Talking Race, Resisting Racism," in *Yearning:
Race, Gender, and Cultural Politics* (Boston, MA, South End Press, 1990), p. 54. But again,
my point is that whiteness reveals itself as a racial construction even outside the consciousness of the individual author. My emphasis, I hope, points to the ways in which racialized
sexuality in America distorts both Black and white gay narratives—albeit never equally.

8 Magdalena J. Zaborowska, "Mapping American Masculinities: James Baldwin's Inno-
cents Abroad, or *Giovanni's Room* Revisited," in Magdalena J. Zaborowska (ed.), *Other
Americans, Other Americas: The Politics and Poetics of Multiculturalism* (Aarhus, Aarhus
University Press, 1998), p. 122.

9 James Baldwin, *Giovanni's Room* (New York: Dell, 1956), p. 14.

10 My reading is suggestive rather than definitive, appealing as it does to physical markers
not specific to any race.

11 Zaborowska, "Mapping," p. 128.

12 Baldwin, *Giovanni's Room*, p. 11.

13 *Ibid.*, p. 15.

14 Again, this dynamic is noted by Zaborowska, "Mapping," p. 125.

15 Race is not, of course, ethnicity, and in a longer version of this essay I draw out the kinds
of displacements through which Baldwin himself substitutes ethnic difference for racial
difference in his evocation of white homosexuality.

16 Richard Dyer, *White* (New York, Routledge, 1997), p. 19.

17 Place, as Doreen Massey argues, is not essential but rather a construction at the intersection of social and historical forces, one that subjects, who are themselves constructed
   within such interstices, help, in turn, to construct, so that "the identity of place is a
   double articulation." See Doreen Massey, "Double Articulation: A Place in the World,"
   in Angelika Bammer (ed.), *Displacements: Cultural Identities in Question* (Bloomington,
   IN, Indiana University Press, 1994), p. 118.
18 Baldwin, *Giovanni's Room*, p. 121.
19 *Ibid.*
20 Although I try to avoid the problematic term *other* in this essay, I use it in quotation
   marks when it seems necessary to signal a construction of the problematic racial dynamic
   that is my subject.
21 See Les Brookes, *Gay Male Fiction Since Stonewall: Ideology, Conflict, and Aesthetics*
   (New York, Routledge, 2009), esp. p. 13.
22 David Leavitt, *The Indian Clerk* (London, Bloomsbury, 2007), p. 299.
23 Quotation from G. H. Hardy, *A Mathematician's Apology* (1940), quoted in Leavitt, *The
   Indian Clerk*, p. 5.
24 Édouard Glissant, *Poetics of Relation* (1990), trans. Betsy Wing (Ann Arbor, MI, University of Michigan Press, 1997), p. 190.
25 Like one of Shakespeare's historical plays, *The Indian Clerk* represents not simply the
   past but the present of its writing. Leavitt spoke to this precise concern in his appearance at the John Adams Institute in Amsterdam, 16 June 2009. In response to moderator
   Tim Overdiek's questions about point of view, Leavitt said, "I didn't want to write a
   period piece ... I didn't want to create the illusion that the novel had been written at the
   time that it takes place ... The novel I want to read as a novel written in the 21st century,
   but a novel about the 20th century. That was a very conscious decision." https://www.
   youtube.com/watch?v=v5188OVTfoA&t=3055s. (accessed 24 February 2020).
26 It is immensely troubling that Ramanujan is the object of multiple desires (white and
   other) whose own sexual agency remains uncharacterized, so that his body seems, in
   some ways, to replicate those captive bodies of African-American slaves that Hortense
   Spillers describes as being "sever[ed] ... from [their] motive will." See "Mama's Baby,
   Papa's Maybe: An American Grammar Book," *diacritics*, 17 (1987), p. 67. Spillers argues
   that this condition represents part of the diasporic plight of Africans transported to the
   New World, and it helps ground my assertion that gay, African-American men are also
   severed not only from their bodies but from representation itself in their disappearance
   from the European fiction of an American novelist such as Leavitt.
27 Marlon Riggs, *Tongues Untied* (California Newsreel, 1991); Riggs tropes Joseph Beam's
   prefacing quotation, "Black men loving black men is a call to action, an acknowledge-
   ment of responsibility," in Essex Hemphill (ed.), *Brother to Brother: New Writings by
   Black Gay Men* (Washington, D.C., Redbone Press, 1991), p. v.
28 Karen Thorsen (dir.), *James Baldwin: The Price of the Ticket* (Maysles Films & PBS/
   American Masters, 1990).
29 David Leeming, *James Baldwin: A Biography* (New York, Alfred A. Knopf, 1994), p. x.
30 By salvific figure, I am drawing from my theory of salvific manhood, where those agents
   defined as salvific are "entities or institutions endowed with the power to offer salvation"
   (*Salvific Manhood: James Baldwin's Novelization of Male Intimacy* [Lincoln, NE, University of Nebraska Press, 2019], p. 3) and where intimacy becomes both a necessity and
   means for achieving such possibility. Here, then, I am alluding to the ways in which
   Delaney's intimate mentorship and friendship served as a sanctum for Baldwin.

31 Leeming, *James Baldwin*, p. x.
32 *Ibid.*
33 James Baldwin, *Go Tell It on the Mountain* (New York, Dell, 1985), p. 23.
34 Leeming, *James Baldwin*, p. 31.
35 *Ibid.*
36 *Ibid.*, pp. 33–4.
37 The portrait can be viewed via artnet.com, http://www.artnet.com/magazine/news/ntm5/ntm8-1-1.asp (accessed 15 June 2020).
38 Portrait available for viewing through National Portrait Gallery, https://npg.si.edu/object/npg_NPG.98.25?destination=edan-search/default_search%3Fedan_q%3D-James%2520baldwin%26edan_fq%255B0%255D%3Donline_visual_material%253A-true (accessed 15 June 2020).
39 The description accompanying this portrait of James Baldwin in the National Portrait Gallery mentions Delaney's "inner anxieties" and his stays in psychiatric hospitals in order to make a claim for the "heated and confrontational" color application. I am pushing against such a reading, in favor of a warmer reading of Baldwin.
40 Here, I mean to introduce Black polyfocality as a method or process of seeing that goes beyond its use within the realms of science, technology, and medicine. Indeed, polyfocalism, as a theory, allows us to better understand the myriad ways in which African-American writers and artists petitioned for or ushered in new ways of seeing. I am thinking of Ralph Ellison's coupling of the visual and auditory when he speaks of seeing and hearing "around corners" as a method of navigating Blackness in America.
41 James Baldwin, "On the Painter Beauford Delaney," *Transition*, 75/76, (1997), p. 88.
42 *Ibid.*
43 Portrait is viewable through the Wells International Foundation, https://wellsinternationalfoundation.org/dark-rapture-1941/ (accessed 15 June 2020).
44 Baldwin, "On the Painter Beauford Delaney," p. 89.
45 In his *Reclaiming the Enlightenment: Toward A Politics of Radical Engagement*, Stephen Eric Bronner argues that Baldwin "gave a profound insight into the existential moment of cosmopolitanism" that was a part of Enlightenment thinking. Stephen Eric Bronner, *Reclaiming the Enlightenment: Toward a Politics of Radical Engagement* (New York, Columbia University Press, 2004), p. 148. See Wole Soyinka, "Foreword: James Baldwin at the Welcome Table," in Quincy Troupe (ed.), *James Baldwin: The Legacy* (New York: Simon and Schuster, 1989), p. 11.
46 John Hall and James Baldwin, "James Baldwin, A Transition Interview," *Transition*, 41 (1972), p. 23.
47 James Baldwin, "Fifth Avenue, Uptown: A Letter from Harlem," in *Nobody Knows My Name*, in *Collected Essays*, ed. Toni Morrison (New York, Library of America, 1998), p. 177.
48 Toni Morrison, "Life in His Language," in Troupe (ed.), *James Baldwin: The Legacy*, p. 76. Morrison made the remarks as part of her eulogy for Baldwin.
49 As Arnold Rampersad points out, "Time takes its toll on the appeal of every literary text. Only the concerted efforts of educators—teachers, critics, and scholars, with their syllabuses and lectures and articles and new editions—keep alive our respect for even the finest writers, including Shakespeare. But no amount of scholarly glossing or canonical reverence can save a book or a text if does not contain the burning core of transcendent appeal that makes a text survive from generation to generation," See Arnold Rampersad, "Introduction," in W. E. B. Du Bois, *The Souls of Black Folk* (1903) (Oxford, Oxford University Press, 2007), p. xxvi.

50 See, for example, Kerry Greaves, *The Danish Avant-Garde and Word War II: The Helhesten Collective* (New York, Routledge, 2019), and Tyler Stovall, *Paris Noir: African Americans in the City of Light* (Boston, MA, Houghton Mifflin, 1996).

51 Ib Paulsen, *Fynske kunstnerportrætter X. Robert Lund-Jensen Yan* (Odense, Denmark, Andelsbogtrykkeriet, 1959) p. 47.

52 *Ibid.*, p.49.

53 Bonnie Zimmerman, *Encyclopedia of Lesbian and Gay Histories and Cultures* (New York, Garland, 2000), p. 394.

54 *Ibid.*, p. 395.

55 Associated Press, "Axel Axgil, 96, Danish Advocate for Gay Rights," *The New York Times*, 31 October 2011, Section B, p. 8.

56 Peter Edelberg, "Den grimme lovs genealogi. Et kapitel af homoseksualitetens historie i Danmark," *Historisk Tidsskrift*, 110:1 (2013), p. 69, https://tidsskrift.dk/historisktidsskrift/article/view/56454 (accessed 9 June 2020).

57 James Baldwin, *Giovannis værelse* (Copenhagen, Hasselbalchs Forlag, 1957).

58 James Baldwin, *Giovanni's Room* (1956) (New York, Vintage, 2013), p. 9.

59 Baldwin, *Giovannis værelse*, p. 16.

60 Hilton Als, "The Enemy Within: The Making and Unmaking of James Baldwin," *New Yorker*, 16 February 1998, pp. 72–80, www.newyorker.com/magazine/1998/02/16/the-enemy-within-hilton-als (accessed 15 June 2020).

61 Baldwin, *Giovanni's Room*, p. 149.

62 Baldwin, *Giovanni's Room*, pp. 76–7.

63 The cover image can be found on the publisher's website, www.gyldendal.dk/produkter/james-baldwin/giovannis-v%C3%A6relse-47105/indbundet-9788702256499 (accessed 15 June 2020).

64 The cover image can be found on the publisher's website, www.dtv.de/special-james-baldwin/giovannis-zimmer/c-2070 (accessed 15 June 2020).

65 See, for example, Dwight McBride's reading of *Giovanni's Room* in *Why I Hate Abercrombie & Fitch: Essays on Race and Sexuality in America* (New York, NYU Press, 2005), pp. 40–8.

66 Brontez Purnell, *Since I Laid My Burden Down* (New York, Feminist Press, 2017). The cover image can be found on the publisher's website, www.feministpress.org/books-n-z/since-i-laid-my-burden-down (accessed 15 June 2020).

67 Brontez Purnell, *Alabama* (Berlin, Albino, 2019). The cover image can be found on the publisher's website, www.maennerschwarm.de/index.php/12-titel/746-alabama (accessed 15 June 2020).

68 Gustav Seibt, "James Baldwins 'Giovannis Zimmer': Vom seelischen Erfrieren," *Süddeutsche Zeitung*, 27 February 2020, www.sueddeutsche.de/kultur/roman-james-baldwin-giovannis-1.4823880 (accessed 15 June 2020).

Works Cited

Als, Hilton, "The Enemy Within: the Making and Unmaking of James Baldwin," *New Yorker*, 16 February 1998, pp. 72–80, www.newyorker.com/magazine/1998/02/16/the-enemy-within-hilton-als (accessed 15 June 2020).

Associated Press, "Axel Axgil, 96, Danish Advocate for Gay Rights," *The New York Times*, 31 October 2011, Section B, p. 8.

Avedon, Richard, and James Baldwin, *Nothing Personal* (New York, Atheneum, 1964).

Baldwin, James, *Giovanni's Room* (New York, Dell, 1956).

———— *Giovanni's Room* (1956) (New York, Vintage 2013).

———— *Giovannis værelse* (Copenhagen, Hasselbalchs Forlag, 1957).

———— *Go Tell It on the Mountain* (New York, Dell, 1985).

———— *Nästa Gång Elden* (Stockholm, Norstedts, 2019).

———— *Nobody Knows My Name* (1961), in *Collected Essays*, ed. Toni Morrison (New York, Library of America, 1998), pp. 131–285.

———— "On the Painter Beauford Delaney," *Transition*, 75/76 (1997), pp. 88–9.

Bronner, Stephen Eric, *Reclaiming the Enlightenment: Toward a Politics of Radical Engagement* (New York, Columbia University Press, 2004).

Brookes, Les, *Gay Male Fiction Since Stonewall: Ideology, Conflict, and Aesthetics* (New York, Routledge, 2009).

Du Bois, W. E. B., *The Souls of Black Folk* (1903) (Oxford, Oxford University Press, 2007).

Dyer, Richard, *White* (New York, Routledge, 1997).

Edelberg, Peter, "Den grimme lovs genealogi. Et kapitel af homoseksualitetens historie i Danmark," *Historisk Tidsskrift*, 110:1 (2013), pp. 166–209, https://tidsskrift.dk/historisk-tidsskrift/article/view/56454 (accessed 9 June 2020).

Ferguson, Roderick A., *Aberrations in Black: Toward a Queer of Color Critique* (Minneapolis, MN, University of Minnesota Press, 2004).

Gether, Christian, *Billedhuggeren Kai Nielsen 1882–1924* (Odder, Denmark, Narayana Press, 1986).

Gibson, Ernest, *Salvific Manhood: James Baldwin's Novelization of Male Intimacy* (Lincoln, NE, University of Nebraska Press, 2019).

Glissant, Édouard, *Poetics of Relation* (1990), trans. Betsy Wing (Ann Arbor, MI, University of Michigan Press, 1997).

Greaves, Kerry, *The Danish Avant-Garde and World War II: The Helhesten Collective* (New York, Routledge, 2019).

Hall, John, and James Baldwin, "James Baldwin, A Transition Interview," *Transition*, 41 (1972), pp. 20–4.

Hemphill, Essex (ed.), *Brother to Brother: New Writings by Black Gay Men* (Washington, DC, Redbone Press, 1991).

hooks, bell, "Critical Interrogations: Talking Race, Resisting Racism," in *Yearning: Race, Gender, and Cultural Politics* (Boston, South End Press, 1990), pp. 51–6.

Klingstein, Susanne, "Jewish American Fiction, Act III: Eccentric Sources of Inspiration," *Studies in American Jewish Literature*, 18 (1999), pp. 83–92.

Leavitt, David, *The Indian Clerk* (London, Bloomsbury, 2007).

Leeming, David, *James Baldwin: A Biography* (New York, Alfred A. Knopf, 1994).

Massey, Doreen, "Double Articulation: A Place in the World," in Angelika Bammer (ed.), *Displacements: Cultural Identities in Question* (Bloomington, IN, Indiana University Press, 1994), pp. 110–21.

McBride, Dwight A., *James Baldwin Now* (New York, NYU Press, 1999).

———— "On Straight Black Studies: African American Studies, James Baldwin, and Black Queer Studies," in E. Patrick Johnson and Mae G. Henderson (eds.), *Black Queer Studies: A Critical Anthology* (Durham, NC, Duke University Press, 2005), pp. 68–89.

———— *Why I Hate Abercrombie & Fitch: Essays on Race and Sexuality* (New York, NYU Press, 2005).

McRuer, Robert, *The Queer Renaissance: Contemporary American Literature and the Reinvention of Gay and Lesbian Identity* (New York, NYU Press, 1997).

Morrison, Toni, "Life in His Language," in Quincy Troupe (ed.), *James Baldwin: The Legacy* (New York: Simon and Schuster, 1989), pp. 75–8.

Nielsen, Nina Kai, *Børn og Billeder* (Copenhagen, Forlaget Spectator, 1969).

Overdiek, Tim, Interview with David Leavitt at John Adams Institute, Amsterdam, 16 June 2009, https://www.youtube.com/watch?v=v5188OVTfoA&t=3055s (accessed 24 February 2020).

Paulsen, Ib, *Fynske kunstnerportrætter X. Robert Lund-Jensen Yan* (Odense, Denmark, Andelsbogtrykkeriet, 1959).

Purnell, Brontez, *Alabama* (Berlin, Albino, 2019).

_____ *Since I Laid My Burden Down* (New York, Feminist Press at the City University of New York, 2017).

Riggs, Marlon, *Tongues Untied* (California Newsreel, 1991).

Ross, Marlon B., "Beyond the Closet as Raceless Paradigm," in E. Patrick Johnson and Mae G. Henderson (eds.), *Black Queer Studies: A Critical Anthology* (Durham, NC, Duke University Press, 2005), pp. 161–89.

_____ "White Fantasies of Desire: Baldwin and the Racial Identities of Sexuality," in Dwight A. McBride (ed.), *James Baldwin Now* (New York, NYU Press, 1999), pp. 13–55.

Seibt, Gustav, "James Baldwins 'Giovannis Zimmer': Vom seelischen Erfrieren," *Süddeutsche Zeitung*, 27 February 2020, www.sueddeutsche.de/kultur/roman-james-baldwin-giovannis-1.4823880 (accessed 15 June 2020).

Somerville, Siobhan B. (ed.), *Queering the Color Line: Race and the Invention of Homosexuality in American Culture* (Durham, NC, Duke University Press, 2000).

Soyinka, Wole, "Foreword: James Baldwin at the Welcome Table," in Quincy Troupe (ed.), *James Baldwin: The Legacy* (New York: Simon and Schuster, 1989), p. 11.

Spillers, Hortense, "Mama's Baby, Papa's Maybe: An American Grammar Book," *diacritics*, 17 (1987), pp. 65–81.

Stokes, Mason, *The Color of Sex: Whiteness, Heterosexuality, and the Fictions of White Supremacy* (Durham, NC, Duke University Press, 2001).

Stovall, Tyler Edward, *Paris Noir: African Americans in the City of Light* (Boston, MA, Houghton Mifflin, 1996).

Thorsen, Karen (dir.), *James Baldwin: The Price of the Ticket* (Maysles Films & PBS/American Masters, 1990).

Troupe, Quincy (ed.), *James Baldwin: The Legacy* (New York, Simon and Schuster, 1989).

Zaborowska, Magdalena J., "Mapping American Masculinities: James Baldwin's Innocents Abroad, or *Giovanni's Room* Revisited," in Magdalena J. Zaborowska (ed.), *Other Americans, Other Americas: The Politics and Poetics of Multiculturalism* (Aarhus, Aarhus University Press, 1998), pp. 119–31.

Zimmerman, Bonnie, *Lesbian Histories and Cultures: An Encyclopedia* (New York, Garland, 2000).

Contributors' Biographies

Magdalena J. Zaborowska is Professor in the departments of American Culture and Afroamerican and African Studies at the University of Michigan. She is the author of the MLA award-winning *James Baldwin's Turkish Decade: Erotics of Exile* (Duke University Press, 2009), and *How We Found America: Reading Gender through East European Immigrant Narratives* (University of North Carolina Press,

1995) along with numerous articles and essays. Her most recent book, *Me and My House: James Baldwin's Last Decade in France* was published in 2018 by Duke University Press. She has taught and been a Distinguished Visiting Professor at the University of Oregon, Furman University, Tulane University, Aarhus University in Denmark, University of Italy in Cagliari (Sardinia) and Université Paul-Valéry in Montpellier, France. Her current projects include a digital humanities-based writer's house-museum exhibit for James Baldwin at the University of Michigan and the NMAAHC/Smithsonian in Washington D.C., as well as two books currently in progress: a digitally published volume, *Archiving James Baldwin's House*, and a monograph on the transcultural proliferation of U.S. notions of race, gender and sexuality in post-Cold War Eastern Europe, *Racing Borderlands*.

Nicholas F. Radel is Professor of English at Furman University. He is the author of *Understanding Edmund White* (University of South Carolina Press, 2013) and co-editor along with Tracey Fessenden and Magdalena Zaborowska of *The Puritan Origins of American Sex* (Routledge, 2000). He has published numerous essays on the history of sexuality, queer theory, and the intersections of race and sexuality in early modern and modern literature. He is currently at work on a biography of Edmund White.

Nigel Hatton is Associate Professor of Literature and Philosophy at the University of California, Merced, contributing editor for *James Baldwin Review*, founding member of the Critical Refugee Studies Collective, and a member of the Faculty Committee for the Prison University Project at San Quentin State Prison in San Rafael, California. His publications engaging the intersections of international human rights discourses and global imaginative literature have appeared in *Literatur in Wissenschaft und Unterricht*, *Globalization in Literature*, *Peace Review*, *James Baldwin Review*, *Kierkegaard Research*, and *A-Line: A Journal of Progressive Thought*.

Ernest L. Gibson III is Associate Professor of English and co-director of Africana Studies at Auburn University. He is the author of *Salvific Manhood: James Baldwin's Novelization of Male Intimacy* (University of Nebraska Press, 2019). An interdisciplinary scholar by training, his research lies at the intersections of literary, cultural, and queer theories, and often pivots on questions of manhood, masculinity, and vulnerability. He is currently at work on his second book project, *Between Ritual and Rebellion: Black Male Joy and Vulnerable Masculinities*.